MARIO VARGAS LLOSA

Touchstones

Essays on Literature, Art and Politics

Selected, translated and edited
by John King

faber and faber

First published in 2007
by Faber and Faber Limited
3 Queen Square London WC1N 3AU

Photoset by Faber and Faber
Printed in England by Mackays of Chatham

A CIP record for this book
is available from the British Library

ISBN 978-0-571-21499-0

2 4 6 8 10 9 7 5 3 1

For Efraín Kristal,
wise and generous friend

Contents

CONTENTS

Editor's Preface

Paradise is not of this world and those who set out to look for it
or to construct it here are irremediably condemned to failure
(*'Traces of Gauguin'*, p. 194)

Some ten years after the publication of an anthology of essays by
Mario Vargas Llosa entitled *Making Waves*, this new volume, *Touchstones*, includes essays written, in the main, over this intervening
decade. 'Touchstone' is the title of Vargas Llosa's regular column –
'Piedra de toque' – in the Spanish newspaper *El País*. The two contrasting titles naturally imply a shift in the writer's outlook, between
'making waves' and using a touchstone, between being immersed in
every debate – as epitomised by his running for the presidency of
Peru in the late 1980s – and having a more detached, perhaps less
optimistic view of the possibility of taming or overcoming the
demons that haunt our own lives or inhabit wider society.

The critic Efraín Kristal has usefully divided the development of
Mario Vargas Llosa's work into three distinct periods from the early
1960s to the late 1990s – his socialist beginnings, in which his novels
diagnosed the corruption of capitalist society in Latin America; the
liberal period which followed his break with the Latin American left
in the 1970s, during which he explored the dangers of fanaticism and
utopian thinking; and the period since losing the Peruvian elections
of 1990, in which he seems to have lost his optimism regarding the
effectiveness of political action. His contempt for authoritarianism
remains as strong as ever, but is tempered by a recognition of the
frailties of those with whom he disagrees.*

* Efraín Kristal, *Temptation of the Word. The Novels of Mario Vargas Llosa*, Vanderbilt University Press, Nashville, 1998, pp. 185–6.

Making Waves consisted principally of essays from the first two of these stages. *Touchstones* covers those written in the post-1990 period, together with several essays on literature written at the time of his direct involvement in politics in the preceding years.

The view that Vargas Llosa has become more pessimistic – others might say more realistic – or conciliatory with the years, does not suggest that he has become any less outspoken about certain political developments, in Peru and in the wider world, as we will discuss below: just read the essays dedicated to the fall of President Fujimori in Peru and the imprisonment of his sinister right-hand man, Montesinos, or the more recent essays on the rise of the left in Latin America where he contrasts the 'boring' (in a good way) Chilean model of gradual social development of a Ricardo Lagos or a Michelle Bachelet with 'Third World' Latin American elections 'where countries going to the ballot box are staking their political model, their social organisation and often even their simple survival' (p. 335), and where we find the increasing influence of the populist president Hugo Chávez in Venezuela.

Nor does this view suggest any slackening in an extraordinary pace and breadth of production. If we take the decade from 1996 to 2006, not only has he published four novels, but also, in terms of non-fictional writing, a book-length study of the Peruvian writer José María Arguedas; a collection of essays taken from his 'Piedra de toque' articles published in *El País*; a short book, *Cartas a un joven novelista* (*Letters to a Young Novelist*, 1997); a 2002 re-edition of his book of essays on twentieth-century fiction, *La verdad de las mentiras* (*The Truth of Lies*); an *Iraq Diary* (2003); a book-length study of Victor Hugo, based on lectures given in Oxford in 2004; a short book on Israel and Palestine that came out early in 2006 – all in addition to writing a regular column for *El País* and giving lectures all over the world, in a number of different languages, most of which have been published in some form.

Essays on contemporary politics in Latin America and across the world, essays on art – which has taken an increasingly prominent place in his fictional and non-fictional worlds – and essays on literature. These are the three broad categories I have used in selecting material for this book from the vast range of Vargas Llosa's writings in Spanish.

The epigraph to this introduction was written in January 2001, on the island of Atuona. Vargas Llosa is a meticulous researcher and an inveterate traveller. For his novel based on the early nineteenth-century political activist Flora Tristán and her grandson, Paul Gauguin – *The Way to Paradise* – he retraced the itineraries of his central characters. This involved, in the case of Gauguin, a trip to the South Seas, where Gauguin had sought an ever-elusive utopian space for his art and his life. The journey to the Marquesas Islands in search of Gauguin's final resting place had involved many hours on increasingly small and bumpy planes. In an essay written in 1999, he had confessed to a fear of flying: 'Fear of flying wells up suddenly, when people not lacking in imagination and sensitivity realise that they are thirty thousand feet in the air, travelling through clouds at eight hundred thousand miles an hour, and ask, "What the hell am I doing here?" And begin to tremble' (p. 131). He eventually discovered that this fear could not be overcome by sleeping pills or alcohol, or fasting and just drinking copious amounts of water – 'these forced diets made me very miserable, and added to my fear the demoralising torture of hunger and constant peeing' (p. 132) – but by reading a good book that would last precisely the duration of the journey. His literary pharmacy in this article includes stories and short novels by Carpentier, Melville, Henry James, Stevenson, Rulfo, Monterroso, Faulkner, Virginia Woolf and Isak Dinesen, especially Dinesen's delirious tale 'The Monkey'.

He also discovered that literature could be a source of comfort and repose during his immersion in politics between July 1987, when he first spoke out against the privatisation of banks in Peru, under the government of Alan García, and June 1990, when he narrowly lost the presidency of the country to a then obscure politician, Alberto Fujimori. On the campaign trail, his life threatened by the Shining Path guerrilla group, every moment taken up in political debate, in meetings and campaign rallies, he found himself at the beginning and end of the day rereading his favourite works of twentieth-century fiction and, in hastily snatched moments, writing articles on them. He was unable at this time to write fiction – 'it was as if my beloved demons had fled from my study, resentful at my lack of solitude during the rest of the day'* – but reading fiction offered a private, personal space of ideas and dreams. He is explicit about this in his essay on *The Tin Drum*. He read the novel for the first time in English in the 1960s, living in a tedious London suburb, where everything shut down at ten at night. In this mind-numbing environment, the Günter Grass novel was an exciting adventure. More than twenty years later, on the campaign trail, he returns to *The Tin Drum*:

> I have reread it now in very different conditions, at a time when, in an unpremeditated and accidental way, I have found myself caught up in a whirlwind of political activities, at a particularly difficult moment in my country's history. In between a debate and a street rally, after a demoralising meeting where the world was changed by words, and nothing happened, or at the end of dangerous days, when stones were hurled and shots were fired. In these circumstances as well, the Rabelaisian odyssey of Oskar Matzerath with his drum and glass-shattering voice was a compensation and a refuge. Life was also this: fantasy, words, animated dreams, literature. (p. 113)

These essays would be collected in *La verdad de las mentiras*. The section on literature draws extensively from this volume, first published in 1990 with twenty-six essays, and reissued, in an expanded version with thirty-seven essays, in 2002. In his prologue to the 2002 edition, Vargas Llosa writes:

> I would like to think that in the arbitrary selection included in this book – which responds to no other criteria than my preferences as a reader – we can see the variety and richness of novelistic creation in the century that has just passed, both in the range and originality of the topics explored and in the subtlety of the forms employed. Although it is true that the nineteenth century – the century of Tolstoy and Dostoyevsky, Melville, Dickens, Balzac and

---

* *A Fish in the Water. A Memoir*, Faber and Faber, London, 1994, p. 209.

Flaubert – can justifiably be called the century of the novel, it is no less true that the twentieth century deserves the same title, thanks to the ambition and visionary daring of a few narrators from different traditions and languages, who could emulate the remarkable achievements of nineteenth-century writers. The handful of fictions analysed in this book prove that, despite the pessimistic prophecies about the future of literature, the deicides are still wandering the cities, dreaming up stories to make up for the shortcomings of History.*

Limitations of space allow us to choose only a dozen or so titles from this book. We can add to these the essays on Dos Passos, Faulkner, Hemingway, Joyce and Lessing from the same collection included in *Making Waves*; however, essays on the work of Bellow, Böll, Canetti, Carpentier, Frisch, Greene, Hesse, Huxley, Kawabata, Koestler, Lampedusa, Moravia, Pasternak, Scott Fitzgerald, Steinbeck and Solzhenitsyn still await translation and publication.

What do these essays on literature tell us about the recurrent concerns of Vargas Llosa the writer? In 'Seed of Dreams', he points out that every writer is first of all a reader, and that being a writer is a different way of continuing to read. His first childhood attempts at literature were rewritings of stories that he had heard or read. As a writer, therefore, he is a 'flagrant literary parasite', rewriting, amending or correcting other works of literature. In addition, everything he has invented as a writer, he argues, has its roots in lived experience: 'It was something that I saw, heard, but also *read*, that my memory retained with a singular and mysterious stubbornness, that formed certain images which, sooner or later, and for reasons that I also find very difficult to fathom, became a stimulus for fantasy, a starting point for a complete imaginary construction' (p. 12–13). While literary influence is seen as a largely unconscious process, Vargas Llosa is clear that the greatest influence on his work was William Faulkner: 'It was thanks to the Yoknapatawpha saga that I discovered the prime importance of form in fiction and the infinite possibilities offered by point of view and the construction of time in a story' (p. 14).

* *La verdad de las mentiras*, Alfaguara, Madrid, 2002, pp. 13–14.

His analysis of the 'twenty-first-century novel' *Don Quixote* points out the skill with which Cervantes deals with the two main problems all writers have to solve: the construction of the narrative point of view and the question of time in fiction. *Don Quixote* also explores an area of constant interest to Vargas Llosa, the *truth* of the *lies* of fiction: the ways in which reality is contaminated by fiction, the ways in which great writers create such a persuasive alternative fictional world that the fictions become more powerful and truthful than reality itself. The Cervantes novel is also used to illustrate Vargas Llosa's views on liberty and of the nation, which we will examine below.

Other essays are also concerned with the craft of fiction. Virginia Woolf offers a model of writing, in particular the effortless complexity of the narrative point of view – the melding of the *style indirect libre* and the interior monologue – which was to be a hallmark of Vargas Llosa's own writings from the 1960s. In Woolf, also, the demarcation between the real world and the world of fiction is made very clear: 'What gives a novel its originality – marks its difference from the real world – is the added element that the fantasy and art of the writer provides when he or she transforms objective and historical experience into fiction . . . Only failed fictions reproduce reality: successful fictions abolish and transfigure reality' (p. 51–52). This interest in Virginia Woolf as a stylistic revolutionary was shared by Vargas Llosa's contemporary Gabriel García Márquez, who signed his early journalistic writings from the late 1940s as Septimus, in homage to the tormented character in *Mrs Dalloway*.

Literature can also explore mankind's desires, the demons that have to be banished in order to live in society. This is a theme that runs through the essays on Conrad and Thomas Mann. Writing about *The Heart of Darkness* in 2001, he argues that it is 'an exploration of the roots of humankind, those inner recesses of our being which harbour a desire for destructive irrationality that progress and civilisation might manage to assuage but never eradicate completely. Few stories have managed to express in such a synthetic and captivating manner this *evil*, that resides in the individual and in society' (p. 37). In his analysis of *Death in Venice*, he argues that 'the quest for the integral sovereignty of the individual . . . predates the conventions and rules that every society . . . imposes' (p. 43–44). Even ascetic intellectuals like the protagonist Gustav von Aschenbach can succumb at any moment to 'the temptation of the abyss'.

Terms like 'evil' and 'sovereignty' refer us to the writings of Georges Bataille, one of Vargas Llosa's most quoted influences. Bataille argued that the desire to transgress (evil) is inherent in all of us, for it is through transgression of different prohibitions that we can assert our own individual sovereignty. Yet there must be a way of expressing these desires without undermining society. Literature, especially erotic literature, offers a site where such Dionysian trans- gressions can be envisaged: 'Sex is the privileged domain where these transgressive demons lurk . . . to exile them completely would impoverish life, depriving it of euphoria and elation – fiesta and adventure – which are also integral to life' (pp. 44).

The essays on Henry Miller and Nabokov pick up on the ways in which literature explores restraint and excess. The essay on Breton also explores the link between surrealism, transgression and the erotic, an abiding interest in Vargas Llosa's work. It was from his early readings of the Peruvian surrealist César Moro, whose own work stressed the exploration of irrational drives as a way of achiev- ing freedom, that Vargas Llosa would start out on a route that would take him to Breton and, in particular, to Bataille, and to his abiding interest in the *maudit* writers of contemporary fiction.

While Vargas Llosa is drawn to both the adventurous practitioners of technical innovation and the demonic explorers of desire, he is also attracted by well-crafted, exemplary, moral stories, as illustrat- ed by the novels of André Malraux. He is fascinated by the life and work of Malraux, a writer now much maligned. As a 'literary fetishist', in his own words, Vargas Llosa's criticism always gives a sense of a writer's life and milieu – and nothing could be more excit- ing and glamorous than the biography of the writer and man of action, Malraux. When Vargas Llosa first read about Malraux's involvement in many of the great events of the twentieth century,

> I knew that his was the life that I would have liked to have led . . .
> I feel the same every time I read his autobiographical accounts, or
> the biographies that, following the work of Jean Lacouture, have

appeared in recent years with new facts about his life, that was as abundant and dramatic as those of the great adventurers of his novels. (p. 66)

Here is a man of action, but also a writer who did not allow politics to weigh down his writing, who was instead lucid and inventive enough to transform lived experience into successful fiction, moral stories that represent 'the human condition' in its most exemplary form. When he writes about Malraux, Vargas Llosa could in many ways be writing about himself.

Karen Blixen, the writer Isak Dinesen, also led a life of adventure – in her case in Africa – before turning to fictions which did not attempt to 'reflect' the world around her, but instead to express an unbridled fantasy. True to the creed of the 'truth of lies', Dinesen is a writer whose re-creation of history and life itself can express a more profound, a more coherent, truth than those writers who look merely to reflect society. Dinesen's protagonists, like their author, are inveterate storytellers, characters akin to those of the *Arabian Nights*: 'The truth of fiction was the lie, an explicit lie, so well constructed, so exotic and precious, so excessive and attractive, that it was preferable to truth' (p. 85). Another great adventurer, Ernest Hemingway, offers a similar moral outlook to that of Malraux: the idea that life is always challenging, and that ordinary men and women can achieve moral greatness, a justification for existence, even though they might be defeated.

Vargas Llosa's study of Günter Grass reveals another crucial aspect of his conception of the novel. *The Tin Drum* reveals a 'colossal appetite to tell everything, to embrace the whole of life in a fiction . . . which, above all, defined the writing of literature in the century of the novel, the nineteenth century' (p. 114). The novel is a 'deicide', offering 'such a minute and vast reconstruction of reality that it seems to compete with the Creator, breaking up and re-forming – correcting – what He created' (p. 114). For Vargas Llosa, great novels (and here Victor Hugo's *Les Misérables* comes to mind) are often big novels. He also believes that the novel tends to find sustenance in its depiction of the city, although he acknowledges that the landscape of the country and its inhabitants often has a crucial role to play, especially in Latin American writing.

XVI

Günter Grass is the subject of Vargas Llosa's most recent article, which I am reading while putting the finishing touches to this introduction. It is a response to journalists' repeated questions about Grass's declaration that he had served in the Waffen-SS for a few months when he was seventeen years old. For Vargas Llosa, this disclosure, which Grass had been hiding for some sixty years, was a sign of his humanity; the revelation did not jeopardise in any way Grass's own radical novels or his frequent statements in favour of progressive democracy. Vargas Llosa had maintained a sometimes heated polemic with Grass in the 1980s regarding the nature of political development in Latin America, in which he accused Grass of double standards, of preaching social democracy for Europe and revolution for Latin America. In this 2006 article, however, he sides once more with his erstwhile opponent. In a revealing comment, he argues that the reason that Grass is currently being 'pilloried' is because he was really too much for the society he lived in, the last of a line of figures such as Victor Hugo, Thomas Mann, Albert Camus and Jean-Paul Sartre who believed that writers could also be guides or polemicists with respect to the great social, political, cultural and moral issues of our age. Nobody today, according to Vargas Llosa, believes that writers should be the 'conscience of society', and so figures such as Grass are debunked for maintaining these aspirations. The condemnation of Grass, then, is not a personal attack, it is rather an attack

> on the idea of the writer that he had tried to embody, desperately, throughout his life: the idea of a writer who had opinions on and debated everything, who wished that that life could be moulded to dreams and ideas, in the same way as fictions, the idea that the writer's function was most important of all because writers do not just entertain, they also educate, teach, offer guidance, give directions and offer lessons.*

Shifting to apostrophe, Vargas Llosa concludes: 'This was another fiction that captivated us for a long time, Günter Grass, my friend. But it is over.' This blend of pessimism, conciliation and a very clear

* 'Günter Grass en la picota', El País, 27 August 2006.

wistfulness, an elegiac tone, can be found in several articles in this book concerning the role of writers and intellectuals and the social function of literature. It is also very clear in his most recent novel, *Las travesuras de la niña mala* (*The Bad Girl*).

With Arguedas and Neruda we look at two literary figures from Latin America. Vargas Llosa has long been fascinated by his compatriot Arguedas: he was the subject of one of Vargas Llosa's first published articles, in 1955, and a book-length study in 1996 entitled *La utopía arcaica: José María Arguedas y las ficciones del indigenismo* (*The Archaic Utopia: José María Arguedas and the Fictions of Indigenismo*). In the opening chapter, Vargas Llosa argues that Arguedas was one of a generation of writers and intellectuals for whom social issues were more important than purely artistic or literary concerns: 'This idea of literature, that Arguedas embraced, often at the expense of his talent, did not allow a writer to be responsible just to him or herself . . . it demanded of a writer ideological commitment and political involvement. Writers had to become, through their writings and their words, actively involved in finding solutions to the problems of their country.'* In the case of Arguedas this meant exploring the genre of *indigenismo*, which sought to represent the indigenous community of Peru in literature and art and, following the teachings of the Marxist intellectual José Carlos Mariátegui and others, concentrate on the political rights and revolutionary potential of the Indian population. The young Vargas Llosa sympathised with the radical aspects of this creed, although he was never convinced that the main responsibility of a Peruvian writer was to concentrate on Andean, Indian culture. He always rejected *indigenismo* as a genre, while pointing out Arguedas's successes as a writer, almost despite the burden of social and political responsibility placed on him. But over the years, especially following his disenchantment with Marxism from the early 1970s, Vargas Llosa came to feel that the 'archaic utopia' of Indian life was just that, both utopian and increasingly out of step with the modernisation of society, and that socialist solutions, based on pre-Columbian social organisation as advocated by Mariátegui, were

* *La utopía arcaica: José María Arguedas y las ficciones del indigenismo*, Fondo de Cultura Económica, Mexico, 1996, p. 17.

equally utopian. These views, intricately conveyed in *Utopía*, have consistently been attacked by Vargas Llosa's critics, who continue to support a Mariátegui-style analysis of indigenous communities. These debates have become more acute in recent times, when left-wing governments in Latin America often espouse the cause of indigenous rights, as in the case of Evo Morales in Bolivia.

In the late 1970s, Vargas Llosa criticised the Chilean poet Pablo Neruda's support for Communist regimes, accusing him of being Manichean and dogmatic in his politics. In a recent essay, however, he offers a most sympathetic portrait of Neruda. He stresses the sensual man behind the symbol of Latin American social poetry, as well as expressing his own preference for Neruda's early surreal poetry, written in the late 1920s and early 1930s. He remembers that, despite Neruda's constant embrace of socialist causes and his long commitment to the Communist party of Chile, he was often caught in ideological disputes, attacked by the dogmatic left. One example of this was at the famous PEN Club meeting in New York in 1966, which attracted many writers from Latin America, but which was vilified by the Cubans, who sought out Neruda for their specific opprobrium at having accepted an invitation to appear in the imperial north. Despite constant attacks from critics, Vargas Llosa's Neruda is a man who at the end of his life – he died of cancer a few days after the Chilean coup of 11 September 1973 – was looking to forget ideological differences and accept erstwhile enemies. Students of Vargas Llosa might also remember the remarkable tendency in his earliest novels, written in the 1960s, to imagine unlikely reconciliations (for example, between Alberto and Jaguar in *La ciudad y los perros* (*Time of the Hero*, 1963), and the doctor and the priest in *Conversación en la catedral* (*Conversation in the Cathedral*, 1969)). It is as if, in some Borgesian way, the early writer has already imagined this, his later self.

While Vargas Llosa writes in the main about literary figures and works, in recent years art has played a more central role in his work. He has been writing about painting since the mid-1970s. The first of a series of essays on the Peruvian painter Fernando de Szyszlo, for example, was published in Octavio Paz's magazine *Plural* in 1976. In a blend of art and politics, it was in Szyszlo's studio in Lima that

Vargas Llosa helped launch a new political party, the Freedom Movement, in September 1987. References to art have become increasingly prominent in his novels since his publication of the erotic novel *Elogio de la madrastra* (*In Praise of the Stepmother*) in 1988, which is structured around a fantasy gloss on different paintings. The sequel to *Stepmother*, *Los cuadernos de Don Rigoberto* (*The Notebooks of Don Rigoberto*, 1997), is in part a meditation on the work of the Viennese painter Egon Schiele. And, of course, his most sustained fiction about art and artistic inspiration is *El Paraíso en la otra esquina* (*The Way to Paradise*, 2003), which also contains a number of close readings and reinterpretations of the most famous late works of Gauguin – the painter who would often refer to himself as a 'savage Peruvian'. This volume contains several essays written at the time the novel was being researched: they explore Gauguin's bisexual interests, his relationship with van Gogh and his utopian search for artistic and personal fulfilment in the South Seas. The erotic charge of art – the artist's quest for sovereignty in Bataille's terms – is explored in the essay on Picasso. And for Vargas Llosa the transgressive artist of the twentieth century par excellence is George Grosz:

Grosz was not a 'social artist'. He was a *maudit* . . . What I mean is that Grosz's work is absolutely authentic, and expresses an unrestrained freedom. His fantasies stirred the bilge of society and the human heart, and his invention of reality has, over time, become more powerful and truthful than reality itself. When we talk of the 'Berlin years' today, we are not thinking of the years that Germany suffered and enjoyed, but rather the years that Grosz invented. (p. 183)

The bullfight has been a lifelong fascination for Vargas Llosa ever since his uncle first took him as a boy to the bullring in Cochabamba. It is another transgressive spectacle, a moment that appeals to the 'appetite that, deep within us, links us to our remote ancestors and their savage rites, in which they could unleash their worst instincts, the instincts that need destruction and blood to be sated' (p. 214). This spectacle would also appeal to the Colombian painter Fernando

Botero, who, at one point in his remarkable career produced an extensive series of works based on the bullfight (see Vargas Llosa's essay on Botero's artistic development in *Making Waves*). However, unlike Grosz, and unlike Goya's depiction of the bullfight, Botero is a painter who can remake the world in his art as a serene space, who can cleanse the bullfight of all its frightening cruelty and present it as a serene spectacle: 'Botero's bullfight is a civilised celebration of the senses, in which a discrete intelligence and a flawless technique have skilfully remade the world of the bullfight, purifying it, stripping it of all that burden of barbarism and cruelty that links the real bull-fight to the most irresponsible and terrifying aspects of human experience' (p. 214–215).

The link between art and transgression is not the only recurrent concern in Vargas's Llosa's writings on art and literature. Describing the Prado Museum in Madrid, he writes: 'We go to a museum . . . to step out of real, pedestrian life and live a sumptuous unreality, to have our fantasies embodied in other people's fantasies' (p. 154). Describing the effect of reading literature, he argues:

> Literature can only pacify momentarily this dissatisfaction with life, but, in this miraculous interval, in this provisional suspension of life afforded by literary illusion – which seems to transport us out of chronology and history and turn us into citizens of a time-less, immortal country – we do become these others. We become more intense, richer, more complex, happier, more lucid, than in the constrained routine of our real life . . . Even more, perhaps, than the need to maintain the continuity of culture and to enrich language, the main contribution of literature to human progress is to remind us (without intending to in the main) that the world is badly made, that those who argue the contrary – for example the powers that be – are lying, and that the world could be better, clos-er to the worlds that our imagination and our language are able to create. (p. 143)

For Vargas Llosa, art and literature can offer moments of respite, of imagined intensity, but they also bring the realisation that the world of art is not the real world, and that our reality can never

achieve the perfection of art or literature. On a further visit retracing
the steps of Gauguin, he finds himself in the Place Lamartine in
Arles, where Gauguin and Van Gogh had lived together for a time in
the famous Yellow House, a stormy cohabitation that ended, as we
know, with Van Gogh's self-laceration. Inspired by his recollections
of the two friends, Vargas Llosa decides to drink an absinthe, that literary, *maudit* tipple:

> I had imagined it as an exotic, aristocratic spirit, a green viscous
> colour, that would have a dramatic effect on me, but I was brought
> instead a rather plebeian pastis. The horrible drink smelt of phar-
> maceutically prepared mint and sugar and, when I rather unwise-
> ly forced it down, I started retching. Yet one further proof that dull
> reality will never live up to our dreams and fantasies. (p. 189)

Absinthe will always taste better in the poetry of Verlaine or Baudelaire or Rubén Darío, or in paintings.

While Vargas Llosa generally acknowledges that he no longer
believes in the view he held in the 1960s – that art and literature can
help change the world – he still clings, at least in his essays, to some
vestiges of optimism about the social function of fiction. If it cannot
radically change the world, it can make it more bearable and, mod-
erately, better; at the very least, it can attenuate the world's ills. He
now argues that what he calls the 'lies' of fiction contains certain fundamental truths. In the final paragraph of his book-length study *La
tentación de lo imposible. Victor Hugo y Les Misérables* (*The Temptation of
the Impossible. Victor Hugo and Les Misérables*, 2004) he states:

> There is no doubt – that in the history of literature, *Les Misérables* is
> one of the works that has been most influential in making so many
> men and women of all languages and cultures desire a more just,
> rational and beautiful world than the one they live in. The most
> minimal conclusion we can make is that if human history is
> advancing, and the word progress has a meaning, and that civili-
> sation is not a mere rhetorical fabrication but a reality that is mak-
> ing barbarism retreat, then something of the impetus that makes
> all this possible must have come – and must still come – from the
> nostalgia and enthusiasm that we readers feel for the actions of

Jean Valjean and Monseigneur Bienvenu, Fantine and Cosette, Marius and Javert, and all who join them on their journey in search of the impossible.*

This optimism is contained in his view of globalisation, which leads us to his essays on politics. In his essay 'Culture and the New International Order', he argues that good literature traverses and breaks down borders and barriers between nations and classes. He gives an example from the 1960s when, as a young journalist in Paris, he heard a group of writers giving readings from literature and explaining their choices to very diverse audiences. He remembers the writer Michel Butor talking about Borges to a group of French workers, hypnotising them with Borges's world of fantasy. Interestingly, Vargas Llosa has recently started his own equivalent of this programme, giving a series of readings from his selection of different works of literature, a performance to which he once again gives the title 'The Truth of Lies'.

Culture creates a sense of community, by recognising the humanity of others, beyond the differences between ethnicities, creeds and languages. Vargas Llosa does not support the neo-imperial argument that globalisation equates with Americanisation, and he uses this essay to focus his attack on nationalism in whatever form. Collective identity, the breeding ground of nationalism, is, for him, an ideological fiction:

> When we explore the cultural, ethnic and social mix that is Latin America, we find that we are linked to almost all the regions and cultures of the world. And this, which prevents us from having a unique identity – we have so many that we have none – is, contrary to what nationalists believe, our greatest wealth. It also gives us excellent credentials for us to feel fully-fledged citizens in the global world of today. (p. 253)

Cervantes had intuited such a world when he talks about Don Quixote and Sancho Panza moving in a world of 'homelands', where, before the barriers of the nation state are erected, the charac-

* *The Temptation of the Impossible*, Princeton University Press, 2007, pp. 176–77

ters carry their sense of place with them, in a landscape where boundaries are porous.

In contrast to this image of fluidity, Vargas Llosa sees nationalism as an abiding ill. In an essay written just after losing the presidential election in 1990, he states:

> Nationalism is the culture of the uncultured, the religion of the demagogue, and a smokescreen behind which prejudice, violence and often racism can be found lurking . . . It is the easiest thing in the world to play the nationalist card to whip up a crowd, especially if that crowd is made up of poor and ignorant people who are looking to vent their bitterness and frustration on something or someone. (p. 223).

This essay is structured around an appreciation of the work of Isaiah Berlin, who became increasingly influential on Vargas Llosa's thought as he moved away from his socialist convictions of the 1960s. Berlin's essays began to appear, thanks to the dedicated editorial work of his former student Henry Hardy, from 1978 with the volume *Russian Thinkers*. The collection *Against the Current* came out in 1979. The title of Vargas Llosa's volumes of collected essays, *Contra viento y marea* (*Against the Wind and the Tide*), which first appeared in 1986, alludes to Berlin's title.

Berlin provides Vargas Llosa with certain ways of expressing a liberal credo, such as the term 'negative' liberty, which allows individuals to do what they want as long as this does not impinge on other people's freedom, as opposed to 'positive' liberty (the basis of socialism and communism), which seeks to use politics to liberate people from either inner or outer barriers or repressions. Democratic government in the main offers a better guarantee of negative freedom than other regimes. Vargas Llosa often quotes Berlin's insight that the values underlying democracy – equality, freedom and justice – usually contradict each other, leading to possible conflict and loss. It was because of these contradictory values that Berlin came to reject any notion of an ideal society or ideal human behaviour, an insight that would inform Vargas Llosa's criticism of utopias, in particular the utopia of socialism.

Berlin also offered a reading of historical thinkers that pointed out the roots and the dangers of cultural nationalism – for example, in the German Romantic movement, with its insistence on a distinctive German *Kultur*. Ultimately, Berlin was perhaps too much the rationalist for Vargas Llosa, in need of a dose of Georges Bataille, although Michael Ignatieff's biography of Berlin – reviewed in this volume – conveys to Vargas Llosa a much more complex character than the *belle lettriste* essayist might reveal, a man riven by torment and self-doubt.

Berlin was less interested in commenting on contemporary politics, and when he did so he lacked the subtlety of his philosophical and historical essays. The intellectual Jean-François Revel, by contrast, was very much immersed both in the everyday (as the editor of *L'Express*) and in current political upheavals. He began his career as a philosopher; according to Vargas Llosa, he never stopped writing about philosophy, basing his discussions around a current problem or event. Revel was a man who showed him that 'journalism can be highly creative, a genre that can combine intellectual originality with stylistic elegance' (p. 237–38). Revel's own intellectual trajectory was not dissimilar to that of Vargas Llosa: he had started out on the left, critical of De Gaulle and a candidate in the 1960s for Mitterrand's Parti Socialiste, but he came to reject the authoritarianism of socialist parties and governments in such works as *La Tentation totalitaire* (1976) and *Le Terrorisme contre la démocratie* (1987). In his obituary to Revel, published on 7 May 2006 in *El País*, Vargas Llosa states that they became friends in the 1970s, 'comrades on the barricades' because neither of them were ashamed at being called liberals. Perhaps they also shared a sense of being caught up in continual polemic, as he points out when reviewing Revel's memoirs: 'These memoirs show Revel on top form: ardent, troublesome and dynamic, passionate about ideas and pleasure, insatiably curious and condemned, because of his unhealthy intellectual integrity and his polemical stance, to live in perpetual conflict with almost everyone around him.' (p. 240–41)

Karl Popper is the third political theorist whom Vargas Llosa quotes extensively (see the essay on Arguedas in this volume). In his essay 'Karl Popper Today' ('Karl Popper al día'), Vargas Llosa talks about Popper's theses, in particular the idea of relative rather than absolute truths, truths that must always be submitted to a process in which conjectures are refuted by more plausible conjectures. This means that all dominant truths must be constantly subject to questioning and revision. Criticism – the exercise of freedom – thus becomes the basis of progress. Critical intelligence dispels dogma and mythical or magic thinking. There is a progression from 'closed' societies, dominated by the tribe and magical thinking, to 'open' societies – from the 'first world' of things or material issues to the 'third world' of art, science and culture in general. This definition of tribal thought is premised on the belief that there are certain truths that cannot be doubted: in such thinking the roots of religious or political fanaticism can grow. The danger of closed societies is that they tend to embrace utopian ideas. In such 'historicism' lies the road to fascism and communism.* Vargas Llosa talks of his immersion in Popper's work at the time he was campaigning for the Peruvian presidency. In his treasured hour or two of reading each day he would read novels or testing works such as those of Popper: 'Ever since *The Open Society and Its Enemies* fell into my hands in 1980, I had promised myself to study Karl Popper. I did so in these three years, every day, early in the morning, before going out for my daily run, when it was just barely daylight and the quiet of the house reminded me of the prepolitical period of my life.'†

While on occasion Vargas Llosa does talk about theoretical ideas in the abstract, in the main he is a consummate storyteller, and his ideas usually emerge with greatest clarity when he describes a scene or responds to a concrete situation. The dangers of 'closed' thinking can be seen in the horrors of the 9/11 bombings. The terrorists needed to bomb New York, he argues, since that city represents everything that is open and plural:

I have always felt in New York that I was in the centre of the world, in modern Babylon, a sort of Borgesian aleph, containing

* 'Karl Popper al día', *El País* 27 April 1989 and 5 June 1989.
† *A Fish in the Water*, p. 210.

all the languages, races, religions and cultures of the planet, a place that, like a giant heart, sends out to the furthest corners of the globe fashions, vices, values, trivia, ways of behaving, music and images that have been formed by the incredible mixture of people in the city. The feeling of being a tiny grain of sand in an *Arabian Nights* cosmopolis might be somewhat depressing; but, paradoxically, it is at the same time very energising, as Julio Cortázar once remarked about Paris: 'It is infinitely preferable to be nothing in a city that is everything than to be everything in a city that is nothing'. I never felt what he felt about the capital of France; but in New York, yes, every time. (p. 264)

Cosmopolitanism is diametrically opposed to fanaticism, and he has commented on the terrorist atrocities in New York, Madrid and London, contrasting his own memories of living in these vibrant cities with the outrages committed by fanaticism.

If such outrages bring to attention the difference between 'closed' and 'open' mentalities and societies, they also illustrate Vargas Llosa's continued interest in the means that are used to effect social change, in particular the utopia of revolutionary change. In his article on the London bombings, he draws a comparison with the anarchist bombers in London of the late nineteenth and early twentieth century – immortalised in Conrad's depiction of political fanatics, *The Secret Agent* – who targeted specific, 'class' enemies, with the indiscriminate killing of dozens of people on London underground trains and buses. His essay on Malraux's *La Condition humaine* in this book (written in 1999) also explores the issue of the moral justification for violence.

Vargas Llosa's own novel *Historia de Mayta* (*The Real Life of Alejandro Mayta*, 1984) depicts a deluded revolutionary activist in the early 1960s, and several of his novels of the 1980s and early 1990s explore the utopia of revolutionary violence, with increasing criticism of fanaticism in whatever form. For Vargas Llosa, the explanation for the bombings of the last years seems to be the creation of a world purged of sacrilegious and corrupt elements of whatever race or background, in which 'only the community of the true believers will reign. This is the craziest utopia yet amongst all the utopias that have littered the history of humanity with corpses'.* Yet in his latest work he does not paint all utopian thinking with the same brush of fanaticism, as his analysis of *La Condition humaine* reveals. *Travesuras de la niña mala* (2006) contains a fictionalised account of a friend who joined the guerrilla movement in Peru in the 1960s and was killed. This character is treated with much greater sympathy and understanding than the deluded Mayta of the mid-1980s; there is an understanding of what might be seen as wrongdoings in others.

In recent years Mario Vargas Llosa has worked with his daughter Morgana, who is a photographer, on several projects, including two illustrated books, one on Iraq – *Diario de Iraq* (*Iraq Diary*, 2003) – and the other on the Israel–Palestine conflict – *Israel/Palestina: paz o guerra santa* (*Israel/Palestine: Peace or Holy War*, 2006). Both of these are based on a core group of eight articles, initially published in *El País*, describing visits to Iraq in the immediate aftermath of the invasion, and the West Bank/Gaza Strip at a moment when several Jewish settlements were being removed.

This volume includes the eight central articles from the *Iraq Diary*. When interviewed about the threatened invasion of Iraq in February and early March 2003, he declared himself to be against the invasion without the proper UN mandates. Two and a half months after the symbolic toppling of the statue of Saddam Hussein in Baghdad, he visited Iraq to see for himself the aftermath of the regime. In the course of a packed twelve-day visit, from 25 June to 6 July, he gained access to some of the most important political figures involved, from US Ambassador Paul Bremer to the principal Shia ayatollah, Mohammed Bakr al Hakim, as well as a range of other interlocutors: students, businessmen, teachers, army officials, religious clerics, people in the street surveying the effects of the widespread looting, chance encounters in cafés and restaurants. Three of his main sources, the imam al Hakim, the UN special envoy Sergio Vieira de Mello and (Spanish) navy captain Manuel Martín-Oar, were assassinated between his departure from Iraq on 6 July and his writing a prologue to the book on 6 September. In the course of this visit, he changed his mind about the invasion and argued that in very exceptional circumstances it could be

---

* 'King's Cross', *El País*, 24 July 2005.

justified as a lesser of two evils, since it rid the world of an abominable dictator. The invasion should have had a UN mandate, but Jacques Chirac – one of his pet hates, along with other self-serving French politicians – had vetoed this option. His observations about Iraq and the people he interviewed, his depiction of a devastated but still optimistic society (certain political commentators see the six months following the invasion as a time of relative optimism, before the situation became increasingly violent) rank amongst his best journalistic writings. The book operates in part as a non-fictional sequel to *La fiesta del chivo* (*The Feast of the Goat*, 2000), his novel about the dictatorship of Trujillo in the Dominican Republic and its aftermath: many of the actions of Saddam Hussein and his brutal son Uday – torture, massacre and overwhelming cruelty – remind Vargas Llosa of what he heard about the Dominican dictator. I say non-fictional, but Vargas Llosa also adds a fictional gloss to the photographs taken by Morgana, imagining the daily lives of the Iraqi people in the pictures – images that, in general, show some degree of optimism, of people in the immediate aftermath of the invasion hoping for a better future.

The book on Israel–Palestine has appeared recently, too recently to be included in this selection of essays. It is based on a two-week visit to the region between 30 August and 15 September 2005, and once again it shows an independent line with respect to international relations. A long-time defender of Israel and recipient of the 1995 Jerusalem Prize, Vargas Llosa is not afraid to point out his opposition to what he sees as a mistaken policy towards the Palestinian population. In this analysis, he supports a number of Israeli critics working inside Israel. He makes what might at first appear a surprising observation, declaring that the only place he can ever feel left-wing now is in Israel, amongst the Israeli left that he sees as undogmatic, open, heroic and ethical: *les justes*, in Camus's terms.

It is this community of *les justes* that he finds in the main lacking among the left in Latin America. He speaks of a moment in the mid-1970s when he visited Israel for the first time, a moment when he was reconsidering his attachment to the 'hemiplegic' left – a phrase borrowed from Revel to describe moral double standards – in Latin America which, at that time, 'would condemn dictators if they were right-wing, whilst praising them and bathing them in incense if they declared themselves communist, like Fidel Castro', defending populism and turning a blind eye to corruption, intellectual censorship and outmoded state-led, *dirigiste* economies.*

His conversion in the 1970s to what he calls 'bourgeois democracy, individual sovereignty, a reduced State and an expanded civil society, and the market politics of liberal philosophy'† also marks his current writing on the nature of Latin American societies. I have included four examples, two on the break-up of the Fujimori regime in 2001, and two that chart the advances of Chile, a country forging, after the dictatorship of Pinochet, a strong social democracy. Fujimori, who defeated Vargas Llosa in the presidential election campaign of 1990, is seen in these two articles as a corrupt dictator, abetted by a sinister henchman, Vladimiro Montesinos, who kept a video record of all the politicians, businessmen, judges, bankers and media personnel he bribed over the decade. Chile is now seen as a model for Latin American development, turning its back on the seventeen-year dictatorship of Pinochet – who should be subject to the processes of international law for systematic violations of human rights – embracing liberal reforms and conducting itself in accordance with the rules of democratic processes.

The failure of this desired liberal model has been shown in recent months in Peru when, after one presidential term, post-Fujimori, of Alejandro Toledo, the surprise front-runner for the presidency was an army officer, Ollanta Humala, running on both a populist and indigenous ticket. It was only through an alliance of all parties opposing Ollanta Humala that Alan García was elected president in June 2006. García was the president in the late 1980s whose economic policies so incensed Vargas Llosa that he stood as the leader of a new political party that went on to contest the elections. The story of García is told in great detail in Vargas Llosa's autobiography, *El pez en el agua. Memorias* (*A Fish in the Water. A Memoir*, 1993). Vargas Llosa justifies his subsequent vote for García in 2006 in the following terms:

* *Israel/Palestina: Paz o Guerra Santa*, Aguilar, Madrid, 2006, pp. 107–8.
† Ibid.

The victory of Alan García in the Peruvian presidential elections has been a serious setback for Hugo Chávez, the Venezuelan quasi-dictator, and his megalomaniac ambitions to create a group of loyal client states the length and breadth of Latin America that would follow the populist, nationalist and state-led model that is rapidly turning Venezuela into a typical little Third World republic. And it has probably saved Peruvian democracy from falling once again into another military authoritarian regime, led by Comandante Ollanta Humala, a confessed admirer of the dictator Juan Velasco Alvarado, the general who ended constitutional government in Peru in 1968 (democracy would only be restored some twelve years later).*

García, then, rather than being a cause for optimism, is very much the lesser of two evils. Vargas Llosa's dystopian vision, narrowly averted for now in Peru, sees the rise of the left in Latin America as being controlled by a Castro–Chávez axis, with willing amanuenses such as Evo Morales in Bolivia. For Vargas Llosa, the model of political democracy, economic growth and increased income distribution is represented by Spain or Chile.

While he is an outspoken advocate of liberal democracy and the market, and is scathing in his opposition to autarkic populism, Vargas Llosa today seems more conciliatory towards those that try to bring certain utopian ideas to this world. He has always been drawn to heroism, courage in the face of abuse, and idealism, and sees all these attributes in the early nineteenth-century French-Peruvian political activist, Flora Tristán, the grandmother of Paul Gauguin, and the subject of Vargas Llosa's penultimate novel, *The Way to Paradise*. Hers was in many ways an exemplary life, full of incident and dedicated to a cause – the formation of a great international workers' movement, a Workers' Union, that would secure the rights of women – that Tristán believed in and campaigned for until her early death. Of Tristán Vargas Llosa says:

She was a bold and romantic campaigner for justice who, first in her difficult life, plagued by adversity, then in her writings and

* 'La segunda oportunidad', *El País*, 18 June 2006.

finally in the passionate militancy of the last two years of her life, offered an example of rebelliousness, daring, idealism, naivety, truculence and adventurousness which fully justifies the praise that she received from the father of surrealism, André Breton. (p. 340)

Tristán is without doubt one of *les justes*. Society may have little place for such figures, as Vargas Llosa argued in the case of Grass, and indeed, as he wrote of Gauguin, paradise may not be of this world. Nevertheless, for Vargas Llosa the world today needs *les justes* more than ever.

John King
Warwick University

31 August 2006

LITERATURE

Seed of Dreams

The house in Ladislao Cabrera Street in Cochabamba, where I spent my earliest years, had three patios. It was single-storey and very big, at least in my recollection of that period, which my memory preserves as an innocent and happy time. What for many people is a stereotype – the paradise of childhood – was for me a reality, although doubtless since that time this reality has been embellished by distance and nostalgia.

In this Eden, the main focus is the house with the solid front door that opened onto a hallway with a concave roof which sent back an echo of people's voices. This led to the first, square patio, with its tall trees that were good for rerunning Tarzan movies, around which the bedrooms were laid out. The last year that we lived there, one of those rooms housed the Peruvian Consulate, which, for economic reasons, my grandfather moved from a building close to the Plaza de Armas to the family home. At the end of that patio there was a pillared terrace, protected from the sun by an awning, where my grandfather would nod off in a rocking chair. To hear him snoring, his mouth an open invitation to flies, made my cousins and me fall about laughing. From there, one entered the dining room that was always busy and noisy on a Sunday when the vast family tribe all appeared to savour the spicy dishes and that dessert prepared by grandmother Carmen and Mamaé that was everyone's favourite: pumpkin fritters.

Then there was a small corridor, with the bathroom on the right,

3

that linked the first to the second patio, where the kitchen, a pantry and the servants' rooms were located. At the far end were wooden railings with a squeaky little door through which one could glimpse the third patio, which must have once been a garden with vegetables and fruit. But then it was just open ground: it was used as a corral and sometimes as a zoo, because on one occasion it housed a goat and at another time a monkey, both species brought by my grandfather from the country estate in Saipina, around Santa Cruz, where he had been sent from Arequipa by the Saíd family to start up cotton cultivation. And there was also a talkative parrot which imitated me and screamed 'granmaaaaaa' all day long. The laundry room was there, and lines with sheets and tablecloths and clothes billowing in the breeze that the washerwoman came to wash and iron every week. The gardener, Saturnino, was a very old Indian who carried me on his shoulders; the day the Llosa family returned to Peru, he came to the train station to see us off. I remember him, holding on to my grandmother Carmen, sobbing.

There were many people living there: grandfather Pedro and grandmother Carmen, Mamaé, my mother and I, uncle Juan and aunt Laura and their two daughters, my cousins Nancy and Gladys, uncle Lucho and aunt Olga. Their first daughter, Wanda, was born in the house one memorable afternoon when, caught up in the general excitement, I climbed a tree in the first patio to spy on what was happening. I could not have understood much because it was only later, in Piura and in 1946, that I learned how babies came into the world and how their fathers made them. Uncle Jorge also lived there until he married aunt Gaby, as did uncle Pedro, who turned up in Cochabamba to spend the holidays, because he was studying medicine in Chile. There were at least three employees in the second patio, together with two intermediate figures of uncertain status: Joaquín, an orphan boy that grandpa had found in Saipina, and Orlando, a boy who had been abandoned by a cook in the house who had disappeared without trace. Grandma Carmen ended up grafting them onto the family.

My cousin Nancy was a year younger than me, and cousin Gladys was two years younger. They were magnificent playmates, involved in all the adventures that I invented, which were usually inspired by the films that we saw in the Roxy Cinema and the Acha Theatre on Saturday matinées or Sunday morning screenings. The serials were wonderful – three chapters per performance, with the serials lasting for several weeks – but the film that touched us, and made us cry, laugh and, above all, dream, and that we went back to see several times (it convinced me that I should become a bullfighter), was *Blood and Sand* with Tyrone Power, Linda Darnell and Rita Hayworth.

There were infinite sources of fun in Cochabamba. There were outings to Cala-Cala and to Tupuraya where aunt Gaby's family had a country house, and open-air concerts in the Plaza on Sundays at midday, after eleven o'clock mass, and the reddish meat pasties served up in a restaurant in the arcades. There were circuses that came around the time of the independence anniversary celebrations, the tightrope walkers, trapeze artists and animal tamers who made our pulses race and the wonderful clowns who made us roar with laughter. (My first platonic love was a trapeze artist in a pink leotard.) There were the exciting and very wet Carnivals – my cousins and I threw balloons full of water from the rooftops at the passers-by below – in which during the day we saw our aunts and uncles and their friends involved in intense water fights with shells, balloons, big buckets and hosepipes, and, at night, we saw them set off for the celebrations in fancy dress and wearing masks. There was Holy Week, with its mysterious processions and the visit to different churches, to pray at the Stations of the Cross. And, above all, there was Christmas, the coming of Baby Jesus (Father Christmas did not yet exist), with the presents, on the night of 24 December. The preparations for the New Year's Eve party were long and very detailed, and these rituals stirred our imagination. With us under their feet, grandma and Mamaé sowed wheat seeds in little containers that decorated the crib. The crib figures, the shepherds, wise men, Roman soldiers, apostles, sheep, donkeys, Virgin Mary, Joseph and Baby Jesus, were kept in a trunk inlaid with metal that was only opened once a year. The most important thing for me and for my cousins was to write the letter to the Son of God, asking him for the presents that he placed at the foot of our beds on Christmas Eve. Before we

5

learned how to write, we dictated our letter to uncle Pedro and signed it with a cross. As the date approached, our nervousness, curiosity and anticipation reached indescribable extremes. On the night of 24 December, no one, not our grandparents or my mother, or uncles Juan and Lala had to encourage us to jump into bed straight after dinner. Would he come? Had he got our cards? Would he bring everything we had asked for?

I remember having asked for some pilot's glasses, like the ones worn by Bill Barnes, some boots identical to those of the hero of a serial about explorers, skittles, Meccano pieces, but, as soon as I learned to read, I always asked for books, long lists of books that I would first select when I came out of school in a bookshop in General Acha Street, where every week we bought the magazines for the whole family: *Para Tí* and *Leoplán* for grandma, Mamaé, my mother and my aunts, and, for me and my cousins, *El Peneca* and *Billiken* (the first was Chilean and the second was Argentine).

I learned to read when I was five – in 1941 it would have been – in my first year at primary school in the Colegio de La Salle. My classmates were a year older than me, but my mother was anxious to get me into school since my pranks were driving her mad. Our teacher was Brother Justiniano, a slim, angelic little man, with white, closely cropped hair. He made us sing the letters, one after another, and then, holding hands in circles, we had to identify and spell out the syllables of each word, copy them and memorise them. From coloured spelling books with little animal illustrations, we moved to a little book of sacred history and finally onto cartoons, poems and stories. I am sure that on that Christmas in 1941, Baby Jesus placed on my bed a pile of adventure stories, from Pinocchio to Little Red Riding Hood, from the Wizard of Oz to Snow White, from Sleeping Beauty to Mandrake the Magician.

Although I cried in my first days at school – my mother had to take me to the door, holding my hand – I soon got used to La Salle and made many friends. Grandma and Mamaé so indulged me (I was a fatherless child and that made me the most spoiled grandchild and nephew in the family) that I once invited twenty classmates – Cuéllar, Tejada, Román, Orozco, Ballivián, Gumucio, Zapata – for tea at home so that we could act out some epic films in the three patios. And grandma and Mamaé prepared coffee with milk and toast and butter for everyone.

It was exactly ten blocks from the house in Ladislao Cabrera to La Salle, and I think that from my second year at primary school my mother let me go to school on my own, although I usually made the walk with a schoolmate from the neighbourhood. We went through the arcade in the Plaza, past the photographic studio of Mr Zapata, the father of my great friend Mario Zapata, whom I shared a desk with, a journalist who was murdered twenty or thirty years later in Cala-Cala. This ten-block trip, four times a day – schoolchildren had lunch at home in those days – was an expedition full of discoveries. It was, of course, obligatory to look at the bookshop windows and the posters outside the cinemas on the way. The most amazing thing that could happen to us was to come across the imposing figure of the Bishop in the middle of the street. He seemed an Olympian, semi-divine figure to us, wrapped in his purple habit, with his white beard and a big gleaming ring. With religious earnestness and a touch of fear, we would kneel to kiss his hand and to receive the few kind words that his strong Italian accent bestowed on us.

That bishop gave me and a number of my classmates our first communion when we were in the third or fourth year of primary school. It was a memorable day, preceded by many weeks of preparation that we received every afternoon in the school chapel, extra classes on religion given by the headmaster, the bald, square-jawed Brother Agustín. They were splendid classes, with stories taken from the Gospels and from the lives of the saints, miraculous, heroic, exotic and surprising stories, in which purity and faith always overcame the most terrible odds, with happy endings, when the heavens opened to receive with a choir of angels the martyred Christians who had been ripped apart in pagan coliseums by wild beasts, or who had been executed for refusing to betray the Lord, or the repentant sinners, so desperate to atone for their infamous deeds that, like the Duke of Normandy, also called Robert the Devil, they would live on all fours, like dogs, to seek the Virgin's forgiveness. Brother Agustín told them with eloquence and passion, accompanied by

7

large gestures, like a consummate narrator, and they stayed in our memory, sparking like fireworks. As the day approached, there were various rituals to perform: go and try on the suit, buy the white shoes, have a photograph taken in Mr Zapata's studios, under arc lights. We took communion in a chapel adorned with fresh flowers, overflowing with the families of the communicants, and then there was a breakfast of hot chocolate and cakes served to the throng in the school patio. And then another party, this time a family one, in Ladislao Cabrera, with lots of presents for the hero of the day.

The great adventure of that period was the trip I made with my mother, my grandma and Mamaé in 1940 to attend the Eucharistic Congress in Arequipa, the homeland that remained alive in the innumerable stories and nostalgic memories of the family. We stayed at the house of uncle Eduardo, a kindly bachelor, who was a judge. His cook Inocencia prepared red-hot soups brimming with monstrous crustaceans, whose red shells and moving claws fascinated me. I remember that journey as a great expedition: the train from Cochabamba to La Paz, the steep streets of the Bolivian capital, the small boat that crossed Lake Titicaca in the night, arriving in Puno at dawn. And then on the train again until we reached the White City. There were so many things that I knew about, but only by hearsay: the square-hewn stone houses; the Misti and the volcanoes; the house where I was born, that was pointed out to me, on the Boulevard Parra; the frozen cheese and the pastries from the Ibérica. The prayers and chants of the crowds at the Eucharistic Congress frightened me, but what terrified me most was the voice of the orator, a very important man with a bow-tie who stabbed the air with his finger: Víctor Andrés Belaunde. By the time we returned to Cochabamba, I already felt grown-up.

These first ten years of my life were intense, full of many exciting events, very dear friends and kindly adults who were easy to win over through jokes and sweet-talking. My greatest desire was, of course, that my oldest and favourite uncle – uncle Lucho, who looked like a film actor and who had all the women swooning over him – would take me to one of the two swimming pools in Cocabamba – the Beverley and the Urioste – where I learned to swim (almost at the same time as learning to read). It was the sport that I enjoyed most as a child, and the one I was least bad at. To be as good a swimmer as Tarzan sometimes competed with my desire to be a bullfighter (although, after some Bill Barnes adventures, I shifted allegiance and wanted to become a pilot). The first bullfight I saw in my life was around that time, when I went with my uncle one Sunday afternoon to the small bullring in the upper part of the city. I also went to my first play in Cochabamba: not a school production, but a drama with grown-up people that my grandparents and my mother took me to see one evening, from a box in the Acha Theatre. My only memory of the work is that, at a certain moment, to everyone's consternation, a man gave a woman a loud slap.

However, even though I had a good time in the real world during those years in Bolivia, I had an even better time in the other, the invented world, the one I read about in the stories in *El Peneca* and *Billiken* and in the adventure stories that I devoured with gluttony. At that time, we children read fictions rather than seeing them: the drawings in the comics had not yet taken over from the written stories. Donald Duck and Mickey Mouse and their friends were not as popular as they would later become, or, at least, they were not for me or, I think, for my friends in Cochabamba. *El Peneca* and *Billiken* had stories that we had to co-invent, using our imagination to the limit, from the information given in the words. These stories and mini-novels were turning us into *readers*, while the cartoons, with their few words suspended in white clouds above the heads of the characters like skinny Olive and muscle-bound Popeye, or Puss in Boots, where the cartoonist had already visualised the fiction for us, exonerated us of a great deal of mental effort, and, instead of readers, they were forming spectators, more passive consumers of the imaginary world. Mine was probably the last generation of child readers for whom the need for a fictive life would be assuaged primarily through reading; those that came later would satisfy this thirst not so much with words as with images, firstly the images of cartoons, then the images of cinema and lastly the images of television. I do not deplore this; I am merely pointing it out, and registering my joy at having been born at the right time, so that I would acquire the vice

9

of reading. This is a vice that does not go unpunished, as Valéry pointed out: we pay dearly for it, in fact, through feeling dissatisfied with and mistrustful of life as it is, for it can never scale the heights and plummet to the depths that we invent, spurred on by our desires.

In any event, the fictions of my Bolivian childhood are more vivid in my memory than flesh-and-blood people. Memory is decisive proof. Although the recollections of my friends and adventures are very much alive, the landscapes and characters of the literary illusion are even more alive, they still sparkle in my memory. The woods of Genevieve of Brabant and those of Ivanhoe, full of knights with lances and armour, mounted on graceful white horses with flowing manes. The African jungle where Tarzan meets Jane (who talks to him in every imaginable language, without him understanding her), presents her to Chita and swings her on lianas through the undergrowth, saving her from crocodiles and cannibals. The burning mountains of the Mission of San Juan de Capistrano, where the crack of the avenging whip of Zorro resounds. The seas of Sandokan and his partner Yanes, and of the terrible pirates who fought with scimitars and daggers with complicated shapes, like the wavy-bladed kris, into whose depths the *Nautilus* of Captain Nemo slides silently and fantastically. The currents of air that propel the balloon of Phileas Fogg on his journey round the world, just in time to win the bet. And the icy and violent steppes, with the brave and blinded courier of the Tsar galloping on his horse.

It was not in Bolivia, however, but later, in Piura, that I experienced my first literary passion: Alexandre Dumas. The immortal three musketeers, who were four – D'Artagnan, Athos, Porthos and Aramis – dazzled me for ever. My final years of primary school and my first years of secondary school were lived in the shadow of Dumas, whose series of novels – *The Count of Monte Cristo*, *The Queen's Necklace*, *Memories of a Doctor*, the musketeers book, *Twenty Years After* and the *Vicomte Bragelonne* and so many others – filled those years with heroic gestures and romantic tenderness, bathed in bright and spectacular colour. But in Cochabamba I had a taste of what was in store for me in two books by Miguel de Zevaco, *Nos-*

tradamus and *The Son of Nostradamus*, which I managed to borrow from a young friend of my mother called Julia Urquidid who – such are life's surprises – I would end up marrying ten years later. Although, if I had to mention just one of these fictional heroes that stands out from the rest in my memory of my earliest readings, it would be William, the boy invented by Richmal Crompton. The *Just William* books had red covers, and each told a different story of a boy who was about my age, who, like me, had an unquenchable thirst for adventures and also a grandpa who was both an accomplice and a friend, despite the age difference.

Grandfather Pablo wrote poems that he sometimes recited to family gatherings, and he had a number of poetry books in an old glass-fronted bookcase. He was very proud of his father, my great grandfather, Don Belisario Llosa Rivera, a poet and a writer, and he kept a novel of his (*Sor María*, that had won a prize in a competition organised in 1886 by the Ateneo in Lima), which he gave me. It disappeared in all the moves and journeys that my maternal family (in effect, the only family I had) made after 1945, when a relative of ours, José Luis de Bustamante, was elected President of Peru, and he nominated my grandfather Prefect of Piura. My mother and grandparents were delighted that I was such a keen reader, and they encouraged me to learn poems by heart and recite them in front of the family. Grandma and Mamaé read poems by José Santos Chocano and Juan de Dios Peza and novels by Xavier de Montépin – *The Mad Women's Doctor* and *Paris-Lyon-Mediterranean* – and a novel by Vargas Vila ('the only presentable novel by him', they said), *Aura or the Violets*, that had many ellipses and that I flicked through. My mother had on her bedside table an edition with a blue cover dotted with little golden stars of *Twenty Love Poems and a Song of Despair* by Pablo Neruda that she had forbidden me to read. This was the first *maudit* book that I read in my life, nervously, in hiding, with that particular delight that danger brings. Two lines from the first poem ('My rough labourer's body tunnels into you / And makes the child leap up from the depths of the earth') really intrigued me, but I intuited that it would be imprudent to ask the grown-ups to decipher them for me.

11

There is no doubt that my vocation as a writer began to gestate there, in that house on Ladislao Cabrera, in the shade of these readings and as a natural derivation of the hypnotic happiness that I felt as I lived all those adventures through the miracle of reading. That life was not the same life of school, my friends, the family and Cochabamba but, although it was intangible, it was no less real, that is, no less felt, enjoyed or suffered than the other life. And it was also much more diverse and intense than the life of daily routines. To be able to travel, by simply concentrating on the letters in a book, to the depths of the ocean, to the stratosphere, to Africa, England, Belgium or the seas of Malaysia, and to travel back from the twentieth century to the France of Richelieu and Mazarin, and, with each character of fiction, to be able to change skin, face, name, love, fate, to become in this way so many different people while staying myself, was a miracle that revolutionised my life and put me from that time on completely under the spell of fiction. I would never tire of repeating this magic, with the fascination and enthusiasm of my early years, until it became the central concern of my existence.

Every writer is firstly a reader and to be a writer is also a different way of continuing to read. I discovered the intimate relationship between reading and writing in those years because – and I'm also sure of this – the first things that I wrote, or, better, I scribbled, were changes to, or extensions of, the adventures I was reading, either because I was sad that they had come to an end or because I would have liked them to have turned out differently to the ways decided by their authors. These corrections and additions were, as I understand them, precocious manifestations of the vocation that would produce, years later, all the stories, novels, essays and plays that I have written. And I do not feel in the least uncomfortable, quite the reverse, to recognise that in my vocation and in my fictions, I am a flagrant literary parasite.

Everything I have invented as a writer has its roots in lived experience. It was something that I saw, heard, but also *read*, that my memory retained with a singular and mysterious stubbornness, that formed certain images which, sooner or later, and for reasons that I also find very difficult to fathom, became a stimulus for fantasy, a starting point for a complete imaginary construction. I would not have written *Time of the Hero* if I had not spent two years as a cadet at the Leoncio Prado Military Academy, where the action of the novel takes place, nor would I have invented the stories about Fushía and Aquilino, Lalita and the Jungle Woman, the missionary nuns of Santa María de Nieva and the unfortunate Aguaruna head man Jum, without the trip to the Upper Marañón that I went on in 1958 with the Mexican anthropologist Juan Comas, organised by the University of San Marcos and the Summer Linguistic Institute. That journey gave me material for *The Green House*, as did the solitary brothel, in the middle of the sands of Piura, that was the focus of my school-mates' fantasy and desires in the Salesian college where I was enrolled as soon as we settled in that northern city in Peru after leaving Cochabamba.

In Piura I also lived or experienced in some way the events that, turned into memories, became the raw material for most of the stories in my first book, *The Cubs*: the attempt at a school strike, the fist-fights in the dry river bed, the abuses of the estate owners on their lands, where they still ruled as tyrants. The world of nostalgia and youthful memories that my grandparents and Mamaé retreated into as their long lives neared the century gave me the theme and characters of *The Young Lady from Tacna*. I found the story of Pichulita Cuéllar, by contrast, in a newspaper I was reading in Lima, on the bus from Miraflores to the city centre. The hired scribe I invented in *Kathie and the Hippopotamus*, who exaggerates and sugar-coats the travel journal through 'the yellow Orient and black Africa' written by a woman from Lima who had discovered her literary vocation somewhat late in life, was based on my life, in the first instance, when I was doing piecework in a Paris garret for a woman with an inventive imagination and deficient syntax.

But just as much as my lived experience, what I have read – which is another, sometimes more noble and sumptuous, way of living – has also had a decisive influence on the gestation of all my stories, although, in this case, I hesitate when it comes to giving specific authors and titles. I am sure that Sartre's ideas on committed writing, which in the fifties and early sixties I believed in blindly, had a

13

great deal of influence on the critical intentions and ethical preoccupations of my first novels, and that the epic style and romantic mythology of André Malraux, whom I read with great passion during my university years, left its traces in my first stories along with my idols of those years, the US novelists Hemingway, Dos Passos, Caldwell, Steinbeck, Scott Fitzgerald and younger writers like Truman Capote and Paul Bowles. But the greatest influence was, had to be, that of the supreme teacher of so many novelists of my generation (and also of the generations that immediately preceded and followed mine) throughout the world: William Faulkner. Without the wonderment that I felt when I discovered the richness of shades, allusions, perspectives, harmonies and ambiguities of his prose, and the absolutely original way in which he organised his stories, I would never have dared to rearrange 'real' narrative chronology in my own work, or to present an episode from different points of view and levels of reality, as I did in *Time of the Hero*, *Conversation in the Cathedral* and in the rest of my novels, nor would I have written a book like *The Green House*, in which the words are as visible, and sometimes more visible, a presence as the characters themselves – a landscape for the story – and in which the construction – the perspectives, the flow of time and the changing narrators – is all of labyrinthine complexity. For it was thanks to the Yoknapatawpha saga that I discovered the prime importance of form in fiction and the infinite possibilities offered by point of view and the construction of time in a story.

'Influence' is a dangerous word, and, when applied to the writing of literature, it is also a contradictory term. There are influences that stifle originality and others that allow writers to discover their own voices. In any event, it is very likely that the most fertile literary influences are those that are not very evident to us, that we are not very conscious of. For that reason, although I know which authors captivated me and opened up to me the world of dreams, and which writers taught me about writing and the structure of fiction, I would not venture to say that these are the writers – and I would add to that list, of course, Flaubert, Melville, Dickens, Balzac, Tolstoy, Martorell's *Tirant lo Blanc*, Thomas Mann and many others – to whom I owe the greatest debt, let alone specifying exactly what this debt might be.

The only thing that I am absolutely certain about is that it was in these early childhood years, spent in that large house on Ladislao Cabrera Street in Cochabamba, in the heart of my extensive, almost biblical, family presided over by my grandparents, when I started reading my first stories, in books and children's magazines that Baby Jesus brought me for Christmas or which I bought with my pocket money, that I first became interested in writing fiction, something that has shaped my life from then on. And in some discreet and distant way, these early stories still kindle my dreams.

London, 24 June 1997

A Twenty-First-Century Novel

In the first place, *Don Quixote de la Mancha*, the immortal novel by Cervantes, offers us an image: the image of an hidalgo in his fifties, crammed into anachronistic armour, as scrawny as his horse, accompanied by a coarse, podgy, peasant riding on a donkey, who acts as his squire, travelling the plains of La Mancha, frozen in winter and baking hot in summer, in search of adventures. He is spurred on by a mad plan: to revive the time long since past (and which, furthermore, never existed) of the knights errant, who travelled the world helping the weak, righting wrongs, and offering justice to ordinary men and women that they would not otherwise receive. He draws inspiration for all this from his readings of romances of chivalry, which he takes as true stories, as truthful as the most meticulous history book. This ideal is impossible to achieve because everything in the reality that Don Quixote lives in gives the lie to it: there are no longer knights errant, and no one professes the ideas or respects the values that they adhered to. Similarly, war is no longer a matter of individual challenges, in which two knights resolve disputes in a precise ritual. Now, as Don Quixote himself sadly laments in his speech on arms and letters, war is not decided by swords and lances, that is by the courage and skills of an individual, but by the thunder of cannons and gunpowder, an artillery that, through its noisy slaughter, has blown apart the codes of individual honour and the deeds of heroes like the mythic figures of Amadis of Gaul, Tirant Lo Blanc and Tristan de Leonis.

Does this mean that *Don Quixote de la Mancha* is an old-fashioned book, and that Alonso Quijano's madness stems from a desperate nostalgia for a world now lost, from a visceral rejection of modernity and progress? This would be the case if the world that Don Quixote longs for and tries to revive had ever been part of history. For in truth, this world only ever existed in the imagination, in the legends and utopias fashioned by human beings in order to escape, to some extent, from the insecurity and brutality of their lives, and to find refuge in a society of order, honour and principles, of men who would seek justice and redemption for them, and offer redress for the violence and sufferings that made up the true lives of men and women in the Middle Ages.

The chivalric literature that makes Don Quixote lose his mind – this is an expression that must be taken metaphorically rather than literally – is not 'realist', because the delirious exploits of its champions do not reflect a lived reality. But it is a genuine, imaginative response to this reality, full of hopes and desires, which above all else rejects a very real world which was totally opposite to this ceremonious and elegant order of things, to this representation in which justice always triumphed and crime and wickedness was punished. It was in the real world, full of anxieties and despair, that people avidly read the romances of chivalry (or listened to them being read aloud in taverns and town squares).

So the dream that turns Alonso Quijano into Don Quixote de La Mancha is not an attempt to revive a past, but something much more ambitious: it is an attempt to make the myth a reality, to transform fiction into living history. In the course of the novel this endeavour, that seems purely and simply absurd to everyone around Alonso Quijano, especially to his friends and acquaintances in his unnamed village – Nicolás the barber, the housekeeper and his niece, Bachelor Sansón Carrasco – gradually begins to infiltrate reality, one might say because of the fanatical conviction with which the Knight of the Sorry Face imposes it on his surroundings, without being in the slightest bit daunted by the kicks and blows and misfortunes that rain on him from all sides because of it. In his splendid analysis of the novel, Martín de Riquer insists that from the beginning to the

17

end of his long journey, Don Quixote does not change – he repeats himself time and again, without ever wavering in his certainty that it is the sorcerers who change reality so that he seems to be mistaken when he attacks windmills, skins of red wine, goats or pilgrims, thinking them to be giants or enemies.* That analysis is doubtless correct. But although Don Quixote does not change, bound up as he is in his rigid, chivalric view of the world, what does change are his surroundings, the people around him, and reality itself which, as if contaminated by his powerful logic, becomes gradually less and less realistic until – as in a Borges story – it becomes a fiction. This is one of the subtlest, and also one of the most modern, aspects of Cervantes's great novel.

Fiction and Life

The major theme of *Don Quixote de La Mancha* is fiction, its *raison d'être*, and the ways in which, as it seeps into life, it shapes and transforms this life. Thus what seems to many modern readers to be the quintessential 'Borgesian' theme – one that we find in 'Tlön, Uqbar, Orbis Tertius' – is, in fact, a Cervantes theme that, several centuries later, Borges would take up, giving it his own personal seal.

Fiction is a central issue in the novel because the hidalgo from La Mancha who is the main protagonist has been 'driven crazy' – and we must also see his madness as an allegory or a symbol rather than as a clinical diagnosis – by the fantasies in the romances of chivalry. And, since he believes that the world is as it is described in the romances of Amadis and Palmerin, he goes out into the world in search of adventures, which become parodies, suffering and causing minor catastrophes along the way. He does not learn any lessons in reality from these bad experiences. With the unshakeable faith of the fanatic, he blames evil sorcerers for the fact that his deeds always unravel and become farcical. In the end, he gets his way. Fiction contaminates life and reality gradually bends to the eccentricities and fantasies of Don Quixote. Even Sancho Panza, who in the opening chapters is presented as a supremely earthy, materialistic and prag-

---

* Martín de Riquer, *Para leer a Cervantes*, Barcelona, 2003.

matic being, has in the second part also succumbed to the enchant-ments of fantasy and, when he is made governor of the island of Barataria, he cheerfully adapts to a world of deceit and illusion. His language, which is direct and popular at the beginning of the story, becomes refined in the second part, and there are passages where he sounds as mannered in speech as his own master.

Is it not through fiction that poor Basilio attempts to win back the beautiful Quiteria, preventing her marriage to rich Camacho, and having her marry him instead (I, 19–21)? Basilio 'commits suicide' as the wedding is about to take place, driving a sword into his body and bathing himself in blood. And, in his death throes, he asks Qui-teria whether, before he dies, she will give him her hand because, if not, he will die without making his confession. As soon as she does so, Basilio revives, revealing that his suicide was a piece of theatre and that the blood spilled had been hidden in a hollow tube. The fic-tion is effective, however, and, with the help of Don Quixote, it becomes a reality, because Basilio and Quiteria marry.

Don Quixote's friends in the village, who are so hostile to literary romances that they make an Inquisition bonfire of his library, resort to fiction with the pretext of curing Don Quixote of his madness: they devise and enact scenes to return the Knight of the Sorry Face to sanity and the real world. But, in fact, they achieve the opposite: the fiction begins to devour reality. Bachelor Sansón Carrasco disguises himself twice as a knight errant, the first time with the pseudonym of the Knight of the Mirrors, the second, three months later in Barcelona, when he appears as the Knight of the White Moon. On the first occasion, the deception is counterproductive because it is Don Quixote who gets his way; the second time, however, he achieves his goal, defeats Don Quixote and makes him promise to give up arms for a year and return to his village. With this, the story moves towards its end.

This ending is a rather depressing and forced anticlimax, and per-haps for that reason Cervantes finished it off so quickly, in a few pages. For there is something untoward, even unreal, in the fact that Don Alonso Quijano relinquishes his 'madness' and returns to reali-ty when that reality around him has been so largely transformed into fiction. The grieving Sancho Panza (the reality man) reveals as much when he pleads with his master, on his deathbed, not to die, exhorting him to get up so that they can go into the countryside dressed as shepherds and act out, in real life, the pastoral fiction that is Don Quixote's final fantasy (II, 74).

This process of fictionalisation of reality reaches its climax with the appearance of the mysterious, unnamed Duke and Duchess who, from chapter 31 of the second part, accelerate and multiply the transformation of daily life into theatrical and fictional fantasies. Like so many other characters, the Duke and Duchess have read the first part of the novel, and when they come across Don Quixote and Sancho Panza, they are as bewitched by the novel as Don Quixote is by romances of chivalry. And then they arrange things in such a way that in their castle life becomes fiction, and everything in it reproduces the unreality that Don Quixote is living in. For many chapters, fiction takes over from life, turning it into fantasy, a dream become reality, literature lived as life itself. The Duke and Duchess do this for their own egotistical, even despotic reasons, so that they can amuse themselves at the expense of the madman and his squire; at least, that is what they think. What happens is that the game begins to take them over and absorb them to such an extent that, later on, when Don Quixote and Sancho Panza leave for Zaragoza, they do not accept this and send out their servants and soldiers to scour the vicinity until they find them and bring them back to the castle where they have staged the fabulous funeral ceremony and purported resurrection of Altisidora. In the world of the Duke and Duchess, Don Quixote is no longer an eccentric: he is quite at home because everything around him is a fiction, from the island of Barataria where Sancho Panza finally lives out his dream of becoming a governor, to the airborne flight on the back on the artificial horse, Clavileño, the air from large bellows creating the winds through which the great man of La Mancha gallops amid clouds of illusion.

Like the Duke and Duchess, another powerful figure in the novel, Don Antonio Moreno, who offers Don Quixote lodging in Barcelona and entertains him, also puts on shows that make reality unreal. For example, he has in his house an enchanted bronze head that replies to questions, since it knows people's pasts and their futures. The narrator explains that this is an 'artifice' because the so-called fortune teller is a hollow machine with enough room inside to fit a student, who answers the questions. Is this not living a fiction, turning life into a theatrical performance, just as Don Quixote does, although here done with malice, and not with his naïveté?

During his stay in Barcelona, when his host Don Antonio Moreno is taking Don Quixote around the city (with his name in large letters on a sign stuck to his back), a Castilian comes up to the Ingenious Hidalgo and says: 'You're a madman . . . but you have the ability to turn everyone who has anything to do with you mad and stupid just like you' (II, 62).* Don Quixote's madness – his hunger for unreality – is contagious, and he has given those around him his appetite for fiction.

This explains the blossoming tales, the dense thicket of stories and novels that comprise *Don Quixote de La Mancha*. It is not just the evasive Cide Hamete Benengeli, the other narrator of the novel, who boasts that he is the mere transcriber and translator of the novel (although he is also, in fact, the editor, and takes notes and offers commentary), who reveals this passion for the fantasy life of literature, incorporating into the main story of Don Quixote and Sancho adventitious stories such as 'The man who was recklessly curious' and the tale of Cardenio and Dorotea. The characters also share this narrative propensity or vice which leads them, like the beautiful Morisca, or the Knight of the Green Coat, or Princess Micomicona, to tell true or invented stories, which create, through the course of the novel, a landscape of words and imagination that becomes superimposed over, and at time blots out completely, the other world, that natural landscape that seems so unreal, so bound up in commonplace forms and conventional rhetoric. *Don Quixote de La Mancha* is a novel about fiction in which the life of the imagination is everywhere, in the character's actions, in the words they utter and in the very air that they breathe.

* All quotations are taken from Miguel de Cervantes, *The Ingenious Hidalgo Don Quixote de La Mancha*, translated by John Rutherford, Penguin, London, 2000.

A Novel of Free Men

Just as it is a novel about fiction, so *Don Quixote* is a song of freedom. We should pause a minute to reflect on that very famous statement that Don Quixote makes to Sancho Panza: 'Freedom, Sancho, is one of the most precious gifts bestowed by heaven on man; no treasures that the earth contains and the sea conceals can compare with it; for freedom, as for honour, men can and should risk their lives and, in contrast, captivity is the worst evil that can befall them' (II, 58).

Behind this sentence, and the fictional character that utters it, we find the shadow of Miguel de Cervantes himself, who knew very well what he was talking about. The five years that he spent in captivity by the Moors in Algeria and the three times that he was imprisoned in Spain for debts and for being found guilty of discrepancies in tax accounts when he was a tax inspector in Andalucía for the Navy, must have intensified his desire for freedom and his horror at any restrictions on freedom. This background lends authenticity and power to Don Quixote's statement and gives a particular libertarian bias to the story of the Ingenious Hidalgo.

What idea of freedom is this? The same idea that, from the eighteenth century, the so-called liberals would formulate in Europe: that freedom is the sovereignty of the individual to decide his or her life without pressure or conditions, in accordance solely with their intelligence and their wishes. That is what, several centuries later, Isaiah Berlin would term 'negative freedom', to be free from interference and coercion when thinking, expressing oneself and acting. What is at the heart of this idea of freedom is a profound mistrust of authority, of the excesses that power, all power, can perpetrate.

Let us not forget that Don Quixote delivers this passionate eulogy to freedom just as he has left the estate of the anonymous Duke and Duchess, where he has been regally treated by the exuberant lord of the castle, the very incarnation of power. But in the midst of all the flattery and attention that he received, the Ingenious Hidalgo felt that his freedom was imperceptibly being threatened and constrained: 'I could not enjoy such luxuries [the gifts and attention lavished on him] with the same freedom as if they had been my own'

(II, 58). This declaration implies that the foundation of freedom is private property, and that true pleasure is only complete when the people experiencing the pleasure do not feel that they cannot take any initiative, that their freedom to think and act are being curtailed. Because, 'the obligation to repay the benefits and favours received is a bond that prevents the spirit from campaigning freely. Happy is he to whom heaven has given a crust of bread and who is under no obligation to thank anyone for it except heaven itself.' What could be clearer? Freedom is individual and requires a minimum level of prosperity to be real. Because people who are poor and depend on gifts or charity to survive, can never be totally free. It is true that there was a time long since past, as Don Quixote recalls to the terrified goatherds in his speech on the Golden Age (I, 11), in which virtue and goodness held sway in the world, and that in this age of paradise, before private property, 'men living in such times did not know those words, "yours" and "mine"', and 'all things were held in common'. But then history changed, and 'our detestable times' arrived in which, for security and justice to prevail, 'the order of knights errant was founded to defend maidens, protect widows and succour orphans and the needy'.

Don Quixote does not believe that justice, social order and progress emanate from authority, but rather that they are the work of individuals who, like his models, the knights errant, and he himself, shoulder the task of making the world they live in less unjust, freer and more prosperous. That is the knight errant: an individual who, dedicated to a life of generosity, heads out on the highways to seek redress for all the evils on the planet. Authority, when it appears, hinders rather than aids this task.

Where is the authority in the Spain that Don Quixote travels around on his three sallies? We have to step out of the novel to know that the King of Spain who is alluded to on several occasions is Philip III, because within the fiction, except for a very few, fleeting appearances, such as the appearance of the governor of Barcelona when Don Quixote visits that city, the authorities are conspicuous by their absence. And the institutions that embody authority, like the Holy Brotherhood, which enforces law in the countryside, and which is alluded to on Don Quixote's and Sancho's journeys, are mentioned as something distant, dark and threatening.

Don Quixote has not the slightest qualm in standing up to authority and defying the laws when they go against his own conception of justice and freedom. On his first sally he confronts a rich man, Juan Haldudo, from Quintanar, who is whipping one of his servants for losing some sheep, something that, in keeping with the barbarous customs of the time, he was quite entitled to do. But the man from La Mancha considers this entitlement intolerable and he rescues the boy, thus righting what he considers to be a wrong (although, as soon as he leaves, Juan Haldudo, despite his promises to the contrary, starts beating Andrés again, leaving him half dead) (I, 4). The novel is full of episodes like this, where his individualistic and freedom-based view of justice leads the bold hidalgo to defy the established powers, laws and customs in the name of what for him is a superior moral imperative.

The adventure where Don Quixote takes his libertarian principles to almost suicidal lengths – demonstrating that his idea of freedom anticipates by some two centuries certain aspects of anarchist thinking – is one of the most famous in the novel. It is when he frees twelve criminals, including the sinister Ginés de Pasamonte, the future Master Pedro, despite the fact that the Ingenious Hidalgo is perfectly aware, from their own words, that they are all criminals, condemned to the king's galleys (I, 22). The reasons he gives for his open defiance of authority – that it is not right that honourable men should be the executioners of other men – scarcely masks, in its vagueness, the real motivation for his behaviour which, in this regard, is utterly coherent throughout the novel. This motivation is his overwhelming love of freedom which, if he has to choose, he even places above the law, and his profound scepticism towards authority that, for him, offers no guarantee of what he calls, rather ambiguously, 'distributive justice', an expression that seems to imply a desire for equality, that sometimes counterbalances his libertarian ideals.

In this episode, as if to dispel even the slightest doubt as to how unbridled and free his thinking really is, he praises the office of the pimp: it is seen as an office for intelligent people, one that is very necessary in a well-ordered society. He is angry to hear that an old man has been sent to the galleys for this because, in his opinion, a pimp should have been sent there, not to row but to lead and to command. Anyone daring to rebel in such an open fashion against the political and moral correctness of the time was a unique kind of madman who, and not just when he spoke about romances of chivalry, said and did things that questioned the very roots of the society that he lived in.

The Homelands of Don Quixote

What image of Spain emerges from the pages of Cervantes's novel? That of a vast and diverse world, without geographical borders, made up of an archipelago of communities, villages and towns, which the characters call their 'homelands'. This is very similar to the way in which empires and kingdoms are described in romances of chivalry, even though Cervantes was supposedly ridiculing the genre in *Don Quixote*. (Instead, he paid them a magnificent homage, and one of his great literary achievements was to bring them up to date, preserving, through playfulness and humour, everything that could survive from the chivalric romances, and incorporating all of this into the social and artistic values of the seventeenth century, a very different period to the time when the romances had first appeared.)

On his three sallies, Don Quixote travels round La Mancha and parts of Aragon and Catalonia, but, since there are so many diverse characters and references to places and things throughout the novel, Spain appears to be much larger, united in its geographical and cultural diversity, with vague borders that seem to be defined not in terms of territories and administrative districts, but rather in terms of religious boundaries. Spain ends in those vague, specifically marine, boundaries where the dominions of the Moors, the religious enemies, begin. But while Spain provides the context, the varied and inescapable limits that encompass the relatively small area that Don Quixote and Sancho Panza move around in, what is described, with great vividness and warmth, is the 'homeland', that concrete, human space, bounded by memory, a landscape, certain people, certain habits and customs that men and women retain in their memory as their patrimony, as the thing that best defines them. The characters of the novel travel the world, we might say, with their towns and villages on their backs. They turn up with these credentials, their 'homelands', and everyone can remember, with irrepressible nostalgia, these small communities where they have left loved ones, friends, family, houses and animals. When at the end of the third journey, after so many adventures, Sancho Panza catches sight of his village, he falls to his knees, visibly moved, and exclaims, 'open your eyes, my longed-for village, and see your son Sancho Panza returning' (II, 72).

Because, with the passage of time, this idea of the homeland would gradually disintegrate and begin to meld instead with the concept of the nation (which does not appear until the nineteenth century), we should point out that the 'homelands' in *Don Quixote* have nothing to do with, indeed they sit uncomfortably with, this abstract, general, schematic and essentially political concept of the nation. This nation is at the root of all nationalisms, a collectivist ideology that purports to define individuals through their belonging to a human conglomerate marked out as different to others by certain characteristics such as race, language and religion. This concept is poles apart from the impassioned individualism shown by Don Quixote and those who accompany him in Cervantes's novel, a world in which 'patriotism' is a generous and positive feeling, of love of the land and one's own people, an adherence to memory and the family past, and not a way of setting oneself apart, becoming exclusive and erecting barriers against 'others'. Don Quixote's Spain does not have borders, and it is a diverse, multicoloured world, made up of innumerable homelands, which opens up to the outside world and merges with it, and opens its doors to people who come from other parts, so long as they come in peace and can overcome the hurdle (which was insurmountable in the Counter-Reformation mentality of the period) of religion (that is, by converting to Christianity).

A Modern Book

Don Quixote's modernity can be found in the rebellious quest for justice that leads the main character to take on, as his personal responsibility, the task of changing the world for the better even when, as he attempts to put this into practice, he makes mistakes, comes up against insuperable obstacles and is beaten, ill-treated and turned into an object of derision. But it is also a contemporary novel because, in his account of Don Quixote's exploits, Cervantes revolutionised the narrative forms of his time and laid the foundations for the modern novel. Even if they do not know it, contemporary novelists who play with form, distort time, mix up different points of view and experiment with language, are all indebted to Cervantes.

The revolution in form that is *Don Quixote* has been studied and analysed from every possible standpoint, and yet, as happens with these exemplary masterpieces, it is an inexhaustible source because, like *Hamlet* or *The Divine Comedy* or the *Iliad* and *Odyssey*, it evolves with the passage of time and recreates itself in accordance with the aesthetic values of each different culture, becoming in this way a real Ali Baba's cave, whose treasures are never-ending.

Perhaps the most innovative aspect of the narrative form of *Don Quixote* is the way in which Cervantes dealt with the problem of the narrator, the basic problem that any novelist must first resolve: who is going to tell the story? The answer that Cervantes gave to this question brought a subtlety and complexity to the genre which modern novelists still benefit from, and which was the equivalent in its day to the impact in our times of Joyce's *Ulysses*, Proust's *Remembrance of Things Past*, or, in the Latin American field, of García Márquez's *One Hundred Years of Solitude* or Cortázar's *Hopscotch*.

Who is telling the story of Don Quixote and Sancho Panza? Two narrators: the mysterious Cide Hamete Benengeli, whom we never read directly because his original manuscript is in Arabic, and an anonymous narrator, who sometimes speaks in the first person but most frequently in the third person of omniscient narrators, who, supposedly, translates Cide Hamete Benengeli's manuscript into Spanish and, at the same time, adapts, edits and comments on it. This is a Chinese box structure; the story that we are reading is contained in another, earlier and much larger structure that we can only guess at. The existence of these two narrators introduces into the story an ambiguity and a sense of uncertainty about this 'other story', Cide Hamete Benengeli's account, which lends a subtle relativism to the adventures of Don Quixote and Sancho Panza, a subjective aura that is a key component of the autonomy, sovereignty and originality of the work.

But these two narrators, and the delicate dialectic between them, are not the only ones in this novel of compulsive storytellers and narrators: many characters take over from them, as we have seen, recounting their own misfortunes, or the misfortunes of others, in episodes that comprise a number of smaller Chinese boxes nestling within this vast world of fiction full of individual fictions that we call *Don Quixote de La Mancha*.

Using what was a commonplace in romances of chivalry (many of them were supposedly manuscripts discovered in exotic and strange places), Cervantes used Cide Hamete Benengeli as a device to introduce ambiguity and playfulness as central elements of the narrative structure. And he also introduced important innovations into another fundamental aspect of narrative form: narrative time.

Time in *Don Quixote*

Like the narrator, time is also in every novel an artifice, an invention, something constructed to meet the needs of the plot, and never a mere reproduction or reflection of 'real' time.

In *Don Quixote*, various times are masterfully woven together, giving the novel its sense of being an independent, self-sufficient world, which makes it so persuasive a narrative. On the one hand there is the time in which the characters of the story move around, which comprises roughly six months since the three sallies that Don Quixote makes last firstly for three days, then a couple of months and lastly four months. We must then add the intervals between the journeys (the second is one month) which Don Quixote spends in his village, and the final days leading up to his death, a total of seven or eight months.

But there are also episodes that greatly extend the time-frame of the novel, back into the past and forward into the future. Many of the events that we hear about throughout the story have already happened before the story began, and we learn about them through the accounts of people who took part in or witnessed these events, and see the final outcome of many of them in the 'present time' of the novel.

The most notable and surprising aspect of narrative time, however, is that many characters in the second part of *Don Quixote*, like the Duke and Duchess, have read the first part. Thus we are made aware that another reality exists, other times, outside the novel, the fiction, in which Don Quixote and Sancho Panza exist as characters in a book, and where some readers are inside and others 'outside' the story, as is our case as present-day readers. This little ploy, which must be seen as something much more daring than a simple literary conjuring trick, has far-reaching effects with regard to the structure of the novel. It expands and multiplies the time of the fiction, which is now enclosed – another Chinese box – in a wider world in which Don Quixote, Sancho and other characters have already lived, been turned into heroes of a book and affected the readers of this 'other' reality, which is not exactly the reality that we are reading, and which contains this reality; just as with Chinese boxes, the larger contains the smaller, and the smaller contains another box, in a process that could, in theory, be infinite.

It is an amusing and also an unsettling game, which allows the story to be enriched by events such as those planned by the Duke and Duchess (who know, through the book they have read, of Don Quixote's obsessions and odd behaviour). And it also illustrates the complex relationship between fiction and life, the way in which life produces fictions and how they, in turn, affect life, enlivening it, changing it, adding to it colour, adventure, emotions, passions and surprises.

The relationship between fiction and life, a recurrent theme in classical and modern literature, is explored in Cervantes's novel in a way that anticipated the great literary adventures of the twentieth century, in which the best novelists would be tempted to investigate the enchantments of narrative form: language, time, characters, point of view and the function of the narrator.

In addition to these and many other reasons, the lasting appeal of *Don Quixote* is also due to the elegance and power of its style, one of the pinnacles of writing in the Spanish language. We need to speak perhaps not of one but of many styles in which the novel is written. There are two that are clearly distinguishable, corresponding to the two sides of reality that the story develops: the 'real' and the 'fictitious'. In the intercalated stories, the language is much more pompous and rhetorical than in the main story, in which Don Quixote, Sancho, the priest, the barber and the other people in the village talk in a much more natural and simple way. In the added stories the narrator uses a more affected – a more literary – language, through which he achieves a distancing effect, one of unreality. Similar differences can be detected in the language used by the characters, according to the social status, level of education and occupation of the speakers. Even the popular sectors speak very differently: simple villagers are very clear, while galley slaves or city thugs use slang, like the galley slaves whose criminal slang is completely incomprehensible to Don Quixote. He himself does not use just one form of expression. Since Don Quixote, according to the narrator, only exaggerated or began raving when he talked about issues of chivalric romance, he can talk about other issues quite precisely, objectively, sensibly and intelligently. But when the topic of chivalric romance arises, he becomes an unstoppable fount of literary matters, erudite allusions, literary references and delirious fantasies. Sancho Panza's language is equally variable. As we have seen, he changes his way of speaking during the course of the novel, starting out with a spicy, lively turn of phrase, punctuated by refrains and sayings that express a whole heritage of popular wisdom, and ending with a convoluted, elaborate style that he has picked up from his master, which can be seen as a humorous parody of the parody that is Don Quixote's language. Cervantes rather than Sansón Carrasco should have been dubbed the Knight of the Mirrors, because *Don Quixote de la Mancha* is a veritable labyrinth of mirrors where everything, the characters, the artistic form, the plot, the styles, split in two and multiply, in images that express all the infinite subtlety and diversity of human life.

That is why the two of them are immortal, and why four hundred years after they were first brought into the world by Cervantes, they continue to ride on, relentlessly, without losing heart. Through La Mancha, Aragon, Catalonia, Europe, America and the whole world. And there they are still, in the rain, the roaring thunder, the burning sun, where the stars shine in the great silence of the polar night, or in the desert, or in the jungle thickets, arguing, observing and having different interpretations of everything that they encounter or hear, but, despite this disagreement, needing each other more and more, indissolubly linked in that strange alliance that is between dreaming and waking, reality and the ideal, life and death, spirit and flesh, fiction and life. They are two unmistakable figures in literary history, the one long and lofty like a Gothic arch, the other stout and short, two attitudes, two ambitions, two ways of seeing. But in the distance, in our memories as readers of their fictional epic journeys, they join together and meld with each other and become 'a single shadow', like the couple in the poem by José Asunción Silva, that depicts our human existence in all its contradictory and fascinating truth.

Madrid, September 2004

Heart of Darkness

The Roots of Humankind

I. The Congo of Leopold II

On a plane journey, the historian Adam Hochschild found a quotation from Mark Twain in which the author of *The Adventures of Huckleberry Finn* asserted that the regime imposed in the Free State of the Congo between 1885 and 1906 by Leopold II, the King of the Belgians who died in 1909, had exterminated between five and eight million of the native inhabitants. Disconcerted, and with his curiosity aroused, he began an investigation that, many years later, would culminate in *King Leopold's Ghost*, an outstanding document on the cruelty and greed that drove the European colonial adventure in Africa. The information contained in the book and the conclusions that it reaches greatly enrich our reading of Joseph Conrad's masterpiece, *Heart of Darkness*, which was set in that country just at the time when the Belgian Company of Leopold II – who must rate alongside Hitler and Stalin as one of the bloodiest political criminals of the twentieth century – was perpetrating the worst of its insanities.

Leopold II was an obscenity of a human being; but he was also cultured, intelligent and creative. He planned his Congolese operation as a great economic and political enterprise designed to make him both a monarch and a very powerful businessman, with a fortune and an industrial and commercial network so vast that he would be in a position to influence political life and development in the rest of the world. His Central African colony, the Congo, which was the size of half of western Europe, was his personal property until 1906, when pressure from various governments, and from public opinion

32

that had been alerted to his monstrous crimes, forced him to cede the territory to the Belgian state. It was also an astute public relations exercise. He invested considerable sums in bribing journalists, politicians, bureaucrats, military men, lobbyists and church officials across three continents to put in place a massive smokescreen that would make the world believe that his Congolese adventure had the humanitarian and Christian aim of saving the Congolese from the Arab slave traders who raided their villages. With his sponsorship, lectures and congresses were organised that attracted intellectuals – mercenaries without scruples, both naive and stupid – and many priests to discuss the most practical means of taking civilisation and the Gospels to the cannibals in Africa. For a number of years, this Goebbels-style propaganda was effective. Leopold II was decorated, praised by religious groups and the press, and was considered a redeemer of black Africans.

Behind this imposture the reality was different. Millions of Congolese were subjected to iniquitous exploitation in order to fulfil the quotas on rubber, ivory and resin extraction that the Company imposed on villages, families and individuals. The Company had a military organisation and abused the workers to such an extent that, in comparison, the former Arab slave traders must have seemed like angels. They worked with no fixed hours and without payment, terrified at the constant threat of mutilation and death. The physical and mental punishments became sadistically refined: anyone not reaching their quota had a hand or a foot cut off. Dilatory villages were sacked and burned in punitive expeditions that kept the population cowed and thus curbed runaways and attempts at rebellion. To keep families completely submissive, the Company (it was just one company, hidden behind a dense thicket of different enterprises) kept in their custody either the mother or one of the children. As it had few overheads – it did not pay wages and its only real expense was arming uniformed bandits to keep order – its profits were fabulous. As he had set out to be, Leopold II became one of the richest men in the world.

Adam Hochschild calculates, persuasively, that the Congolese population was reduced by half in the twenty-one years that the outrages of Leopold II continued. When the Free State of the Congo passed to the Belgian state in 1906, even though many crimes were still being committed and the merciless exploitation of the native population was maintained, conditions did improve quite considerably. Had that system continued, it is in the realms of possibility that these people might have been completely wiped out.

Hochschild's study demonstrates that, while the crimes and tortures inflicted on the native population were grotesquely horrendous, the greatest damage done to them was the destruction of their institutions, their kinship systems, their customs and their most fundamental dignity. It is not surprising that when, some sixty years later, Belgium gave independence to the Congo in 1960, the ex-colony, in which no local professional infrastructure had been created by the colonising power in almost a century of exploitation, plunged into chaos and civil war. And finally it fell into the hands of General Mobutu, an insane satrap, a worthy successor of Leopold II in his voracity for wealth.

There are not only criminals and victims in *King Leopold's Ghost*. There are also, fortunately for humankind, people who offer some redemption, like the black American pastors George Washington Williams and William Sheppard who, when they discovered the true nature of the farcical regime, took immediate steps to denounce to the world the terrible reality of Central Africa. But the two people who, showing extraordinary bravery and perseverance, were mainly responsible for mobilising international public opinion against Leopold II's butchery in the Congo, were an Irishman, Roger Casement, and a Belgian, Morel. Both deserve the honours of a great novel. The former (who in later years would first be knighted and later executed in Great Britain for participating in a rebellion for the independence of Ireland) was, for a period, the British vice-consul in the Congo. He inundated the Foreign Office with lapidary reports on what was happening there. At the same time, in the customs house in Antwerp, an enquiring and fair-minded official, Morel, began studying, with increasing suspicion, the shipments that were leaving for the Congo and those that were returning from there. What a strange trade it was. What was sent to the Congo was in the main rifles, munitions, whips, machetes and trinkets of no commercial value. From there, by contrast, came valuable cargoes of rubber, ivory and resin. Could one take seriously the propaganda that, thanks to Leopold II, a free trade zone had been created in the heart of Africa that would bring progress and freedom to all Africans?

Morel was not only a fair-minded and perceptive man. He was also an extraordinary communicator. When he discovered the sinister truth, he made it known to his compatriots, skilfully circumventing the barriers erected to keep out the truth of what was happening in the Congo, which were kept in place by intimidation, bribes and censorship. His analyses and articles on the exploitation suffered by the Congolese, and the resulting social and economic depredation, gradually gained an audience and helped to form an association that Hochschild considers to be the first important movement for human rights in the twentieth century. Thanks to the Association for the Reform of the Congo that Morel and Casement founded, Leopold was no longer seen as some mythic civilising force, but rather in his true colours as a genocidal leader. However, by one of those mysteries that should be deciphered one day, what every reasonably well-informed person knew about Leopold II and his grim Congolese adventure when he died in 1909 has now disappeared from public memory. Now no one remembers him as he really was. In his own country he has become an anodyne, inoffensive mummy, who appears in history books, has a number of statues and his own museum, but there is nothing to remind us that he alone caused more suffering in Africa than all the natural tragedies and the wars and revolutions of that unfortunate continent.

II. Konrad Korzeniowski in the Congo

In 1890, the merchant captain Konrad Korzeniowski, Polish by birth and a British national since 1888, could not find a post senior enough for his qualifications in England, and signed a contract in Brussels with one of the branches of the Company of Leopold II, the Société Anonyme Belge that traded in the upper Congo, to serve as a captain on one of the company's steamboats which navigated the great

African river between Kinshasa and Stanley Falls. He was employed by Captain Albert Thys, an executive director of the firm and a close associate of Leopold II, to take command of the *Florida*, whose previous captain, Freisleben, had been killed by local people.

The future Joseph Conrad took the train to Bordeaux and embarked for Africa on the *Ville de Maceio*, with the idea of remaining in his new post for three years. He disembarked in Boma at the mouth of the river Congo and from there he travelled the forty miles to Matadi on a small boat, arriving on 13 June 1890. Here he met the open-minded Irishman Roger Casement, with whom he lived for a couple of weeks. He would later write in his diary that of all the people he met in the Congo, Casement was the person he most admired. Through Casement he would doubtless have received detailed information about other horrors taking place there, alongside those that were immediately apparent. From Matadi he left on foot for Kinshasa, accompanied by thirty native bearers with whom he shared adventures and setbacks very similar to those experienced by Charlie Marlow in *Heart of Darkness*, as he covered the two hundred miles that separated the camp from the Central Station.

In Kinshasa, Conrad was informed by the directors of the Company that instead of boarding the *Florida*, the boat that he had been asked to captain, but which was being repaired, he would serve as second-in-command on another steamer, the *Roi des Belges*, under the command of its Swedish captain, Ludwig Koch. The boat's mission was to go upriver to the camp at Stanley Falls, to pick up an agent of the Company, Georges Antoine Klein, who was seriously ill. Like Kurtz in the novel, Klein died on the return journey to Kinshasa, and Captain Ludwig Koch also fell ill on the journey, so Conrad ended up in charge of the *Roi des Belges*. Troubled by diarrhoea, disgusted and disillusioned by his Congolese experience, Conrad did not stay the three years in Africa that he had intended, but instead returned to Europe on 4 December 1890. His journey through the hell created by Leopold II therefore lasted just over six months.

He wrote *Heart of Darkness* nine years later, describing quite faithfully through the character of Marlow, whom it would not be unjust to call his alter ego in the novel, the different stages and developments in his own Congolese adventure. In the original manuscript, there is a sardonic reference to Leopold II ('a third-rate king'), some geographical references, as well as the authentic names of the Company's factories and stations along the banks of the river Congo that were later taken out or changed in the novel. *Heart of Darkness* was published in instalments in February, March and April 1899, in the London review *Blackwood's Magazine*, and three years later in a book – *Youth: A Narrative; And Two Other Stories* – that included two further stories.

III. Heart of Darkness

Conrad would not have been able to write this story without the six months that he spent in the Congo that was being devastated by the Company of Leopold II. But although this experience was the primary material for the novel, which can be read, among many possible readings, as an exorcism of colonialism and racism, *Heart of Darkness* transcends these historical and social circumstances and becomes an exploration of the roots of humankind, those inner recesses of our being which harbour a desire for destructive irrationality that progress and civilisation might manage to assuage but never eradicate completely. Few stories have managed to express in such a synthetic and captivating manner this *evil* that resides in the individual and in society. Because the tragedy that Kurtz personifies has to do with both historical and economic institutions corrupted by greed, and also that deep-seated attraction to the 'fall', the moral corruption of the human spirit, which Christian religion calls original sin and psychoanalysis calls the death wish.

The novel is much more subtle and hard to pin down than the contradictory interpretations that have been made of it: the struggle between civilisation and barbarism, the return to the magic world of the rituals and sacrifices of primitive man, the fragile layer that separates modernity from savagery. In the first place, it is without doubt, and despite the strong criticism launched against it by the African writer Chinua Achebe who condemned it for being preju-

37

diced and 'bloody racist',* a trenchant critique of Western civilisation's inability to transcend cruel and uncivilised human nature, like that shown by the white men that the Company has installed in the heart of Africa to exploit the native peoples, to strip bare their forests and their land, and to exterminate the elephant population in search of precious ivory. These individuals represent a worse form of barbarism (since it is deliberate and self-interested) than that shown by the barbarians, the cannibals and pagans, who have made Kurtz a mini-god.

Kurtz, who is in theory the central character in this story, is a pure mystery, a hidden piece of information, an absence rather than a presence, a myth that his fleeting appearance at the end of the novel does not manage to replace with a concrete being. At one point he was intellectually and morally far superior to the bunch of greedy mediocrities that were his colleagues in the Company, according to the stories that Marlow hears as he travels up the river towards the remote station where Kurtz is based, or after his death. Superior because he was then a man of ideas – a journalist, a musician, a politician – convinced, judging by the report that he prepared for the 'International Society for the Suppression of Savage Customs', that, in doing what it was doing – collecting ivory for export to Europe – European capitalism was undertaking a civilising mission, a kind of commercial and moral crusade of such importance that it justified the worst excesses committed in its name. But this is the myth. When we see Kurtz in the flesh, he is a shadow of himself, a mad, delirious, dying man with no trace remaining of the ambitious project that had seemingly captivated him at the beginning of his African adventure, a human ruin in which Marlow cannot glimpse a single one of those supposedly extraordinary ideas that had previously engrossed him. The only definite things we manage to learn about him are that he has plundered more ivory than any other company employee and that – in this he is different and superior to other white men – he has managed to communicate with the native inhabitants, to seduce them, to bewitch those savages that his colleagues are content merely to exploit, and, in a way, to become one of them: a little king to

* 'An Image of Africa', *Massachusetts Review*, 18:4 (Winter 1977), pp. 782–94.

whom they express complete devotion and who rules over them as a primitive despot.

This dialectic between civilisation and barbarism is a central theme in *Heart of Darkness*. For any except the most blinkered reader it is clear that the novel does not argue that barbarism is equated with Africa and civilisation with Europe. There is an explicit, cynical barbarism that the Company embodies. The only reason for the Company's presence in jungles and rivers is to pillage them, exploiting to this end, with limitless cruelty, the labour of cannibals who are enslaved, repressed and killed without any scruples, in the same way that herds of elephants are butchered for the white gold, the coveted ivory. Kurtz's madness is the most extreme form of this barbarism that the Company (presented as a demonic abstraction) took with it to the African heart of darkness.

Madness, moreover, is not the exclusive domain of Kurtz, but rather a state of mind or illness that seems to take hold of Europeans as soon as they set foot on African soil, as the Company doctor hints to Marlow when he examines him, measures his head and speaks to him about 'the mental changes' that take place in people out there. Marlow confirms this as soon as he reaches the mouth of the great river and sees a French warship absurdly bombarding, not a concrete military target, but rather the jungle, the African continent, as if the soldiers had taken leave of their senses. Many of the whites that he meets on his journey show signs of imbalance, from the impassive, manic accountant and the elated pilgrims to the nomadic, garrulous Russian dressed as a harlequin. The boundary between lucidity and madness is shattered in the savage, feverish note that appears at the bottom of Kurtz's report to the Society for the Suppression of Savage Customs. How much time has passed between the report and this exhortation – 'Exterminate all the brutes' – we do not know. What we do know is that between these texts came the reality of Africa, and that this was enough for Kurtz's mind (or his soul) to swing from reason to madness (or from Good to Evil). When he scribbled this command to exterminate, Kurtz was doubtless already putting it into practice, and around his cabin were heads swaying on stakes.

This tale offers, to say the least, a very pessimistic vision of the European civilisation represented by the 'spectral city' or the 'white sepulchre' where the Company has its main office, at whose doors visitors are greeted by women knitting. These women, as the critics have pointed out, bear a suspicious likeness to the Fates in Virgil or Dante, who guard the gates of the underworld. If this civilisation exists then it has, like the god Janus, two faces: one for Europe and the other for Africa, where there is a resurgence of all the violence and cruelty in human relationships that we thought had been abolished in the old continent. In the best of cases, civilisation appears as a very thin film below which the old demons are crouched, waiting for the opportune moment to reappear and suffocate precariously civilised men in ceremonies of pure instinct and irrationality, like the ones presided over by Kurtz in his absurd kingdom.

The extreme complexity of the story is very well emphasised by the intricate structure of the narration, by the overlaid narrators, scenes and times that alternate in the tale. Communicating vessels and Chinese boxes are the techniques used to build this highly functional, subtle narrative. The river Thames and the great African river (the Congo, although it is never given a name) are the two locations woven by the story. Two rivers, two continents, two cultures, two historical times, between which the main character-narrator, Captain Charlie Marlow, moves as he recounts his old African adventure to four friends one night in London by the river. But, in this binary reality, in which there are two women associated with Kurtz – the 'barbarous and proud' black woman and his delicate white fiancée – there are also two narrators, since Marlow tells his story within the narration of another narrator-character (who speaks of a 'we' as if he were one of the friends listening to Marlow), this anonymous and furtive presence whose function is to blur the story, dissolving it in a mist of subjectivity. Or better, in a mist of subjectivities, which intersect and draw apart, to create the rarefied atmosphere in which the story takes place. An atmosphere that is at times confused and at times nightmarish, in which time thickens, seems to stop and then jumps, in syncopated fashion, to another moment, leaving intervening gaps, silences and inferences. This atmosphere, which is one of the book's greatest triumphs, is achieved through the powerful presence of a dense prose, which is at times grandiloquent and torrential, full of mysterious images and magical-religious resonance. One might say that it is impregnated with the abundance of vegetation and the steam of the jungle. The English critic F. R. Leavis deplored what he called the 'adjectival insistence' in the prose,* something that for me is one of the essential attributes of this style as it seeks to de-rationalise and dissolve the story into a climate of complete ambiguity, into the rhythm and flow of dream-like reality. This atmosphere reproduces Marlow's state of mind, for what he sees in his African journey to the posts and factories of the Company leaves him perplexed, confused, horrified, in a crescendo of excess that makes Kurtz's story, the absolute horror, quite believable. If it were told in a more measured and circumspect style, then that inordinate story would seem simply incredible.

This African experience changed the personality of Marlow as it changed Conrad's personality. It also changed his vision of the world, or at least of Europe. When he returns to the 'spectral city' with Kurtz's packet of letters and the portrait, he contemplates at a distance and with contempt these people who are 'hurrying through the streets to filch a little money from each other, to devour their infamous cookery, to gulp their unwholesome beer, to dream their insignificant and silly dreams.'† Why this aversion to these people, 'that trespassed on my thoughts', these 'intruders whose knowledge of life was to me an irritating pretence, because I felt so sure they could not possibly know the things I knew'? What, through his journey, he has learned about life and humankind has left him without innocence and without spontaneity, deeply critical and mistrustful of his fellow men. ('Before the Congo, I was merely an animal', Conrad confessed.‡)

Marlow, who had hated lying before his journey to Africa, does not think twice about lying on his return, when he tells Kurtz's betrothed that the last words he uttered were her name, when in

* F. R. Leavis, *The Great Tradition*, Stewart, New York, 1950, p. 179.
† Joseph Conrad, *Heart of Darkness*, Penguin, Harmondsworth, 1983, p. 112.
‡ See *Heart of Darkness*, Icon Critical Guides, edited by Nicholas Tredell, Icon Books, Cambridge, 1998, p. 50.

Death in Venice

The Call to the Abyss

Despite its brevity, *Death in Venice* tells a story that is as complex and deep as any that Thomas Mann would develop more extensively in his vast novels. And he achieves this so economically and with such stylistic perfection that this short novel deserves to figure alongside masterworks of the genre like Kafka's *Metamorphosis* or Tolstoy's *The Death of Ivan Ilyich*. All three are beautifully crafted, tell a fascinating story and, above all, set up an almost infinite number of associations, symbols and echoes in the mind of the reader.

After reading and rereading it on numerous occasions, we are left with the unsettling feeling that the text is still withholding a mystery even from the most attentive reader. Something murky and violent, almost abject, which can be found in the protagonist and which is also a common experience of humankind: a secret yearning that suddenly reappears, frightening us, because we thought that it had been banished once and for all from our midst through the work of culture, faith and public morals, or simply as a result of our need to live together in society.

How can we define this subterranean presence which works of art usually reveal involuntarily, indirectly, a will-o'-the-wisp that suddenly appears without the author's permission? Freud called it the death wish, Sade desire in freedom and Bataille, evil. It is the quest for the integral sovereignty of the individual that predates the conventions and rules that every society – some more, some less – imposes in order to make coexistence possible and prevent society

from falling apart and reverting to barbarism. The core of any definition of civilisation is that individual desires and passion must be
reined in so that private desires, stimulated by imagination, do not
endanger social organisation. This is a clear and healthy idea whose
benefit for the human race cannot be denied rationally because it has
enhanced life and kept at a distance, usually at a great distance, the
precarious and harsh primordial lives that preceded the horde and
the cannibal clan. But life is not formed just by reason but also by
passions. The angel that lives within men and women has never
been able entirely to defeat the devil that also lives within, even
when it seems that advanced societies have managed to do so. The
story of Gustav von Aschenbach shows us that even these fine examples of healthy citizens, whose intelligence and moral discipline
seem to have tamed all the destructive forces of personality, can succumb at any moment to the temptation of the abyss.

Reason, order and virtue ensure the progress of human society but
they rarely suffice to make individuals happy, for instincts, that are
kept in check in the name of social good, are always on the lookout,
waiting for an opportunity to come out and demand of life both
intensity and excess that, as a last resort, lead to destruction and
death. Sex is the privileged domain where these transgressive
demons lurk, in the recesses of our personality, and in some circumstances it is impossible to keep them at bay because they are also part
of human reality. What is more, even though their presence always
implies a risk for the individual and a threat of dissolution and violence for society, to exile them completely would impoverish life,
depriving it of euphoria and elation – fiesta and adventure – which
are also integral to life. These are the thorny issues that *Death in
Venice* illuminates with its twilight tones.

Gustav von Aschenbach has reached the threshold of old age as an
admirable citizen. His books have made him a celebrity but he
accepts this fame without vanity, concentrating on his intellectual
work, almost completely immersed in the world of ideas and principles, shorn of all material temptation. Since he lost his wife, he has
become an austere and solitary man. He does not have a social life
and rarely travels. In the holidays he retreats into his books in a

44

small house in the country outside Munich. The text states that 'he did not like pleasure'. This all seems to imply that this famous artist is confined within the world of the spirit, having quelled, through culture and reason, his passions, which are the agents of vice and chaos that lurk in the dark recesses of the human mind. He is a 'virtuoso' in the two meanings of the word: he is a creator of beautiful and original forms and he has purified his life through a strict ritual of discipline and continence.

But one day, suddenly, this organised existence begins to crumble thanks to his imagination, this corrosive force that the French very accurately call 'the mad woman of the house'. A furtive glimpse of a stranger in the Munich cemetery awakens in Von Aschenbach a desire to travel, and peoples his imagination with exotic images. He dreams of a ferocious, primitive, barbarous world, one completely opposed to his world of a super civilised man, imbued with a 'classic' spirit. Without really understanding why, he gives in to impulse and goes first to an Adriatic island and later to Venice. There, on the night of his arrival, he sees the Polish boy Tadzio who will turn his life upside down, destroying in a few days the rational and ethical order that has sustained it. He does not touch him or even speak to him; it is also quite possible that the faint smiles that Von Aschenbach thinks he detects are fantasies of his imagination. The whole drama develops away from prying eyes, in the heart of the writer and, of course, in those murky instincts that he thought he had tamed, and which, in the sticky and foul-smelling Venetian summer, are revived by the tender beauty of the adolescent. He comes to realise that his body is not merely the receptacle of refined and generous ideas so admired by his readers, but also harbours a beast on heat, greedy and egotistical.

To say that the writer falls in love with or is engulfed by desire for the beautiful boy would not be enough. Something happens to him that is much deeper: it changes his view on life and on men and women, on culture and on art. Suddenly ideas are relegated, displaced by sensations and feelings, and the body takes on an overwhelming reality that the spirit must serve rather than restrain. Sensuality and instincts take on a new moral significance, not as aspects of animality that human beings must repress to ensure civilisation, but as sources of a 'divine madness' that transforms the individual into a god. Life is no longer 'form', and spills out in passionate disorder.

Gustav von Aschenbach experiences the delights and the sufferings of a love-passion, albeit alone, without sharing it with the person who is the cause of these emotions. At first, realising the danger that he is running, he tries to run away. But then he changes and plunges into the adventure that will bring him first to a state of abjection and then to death. The former sober intellectual, now disgusted by his old age and ugliness, goes to the pitiful lengths of putting on make-up and dyeing his hair like a fop. Instead of his former Apollonian dreams, his nights are full of savage visions, where barbarous men indulge in orgies in which violence, concupiscence and idolatry triumph over 'the profound resistance of his spirit'. Gustav von Aschenbach then experiences 'the bestial degradation of his fall'.* Who is corrupting who? Tadzio leaves Venice at the end of the story, as innocent and immaculate as at the beginning, while von Aschenbach has been reduced to a moral and physical wreck. The beauty of the boy is the mere stimulus that starts up the destructive mechanism, the desire that von Aschenbach's imagination so inflames that it ends up consuming him.

The plague that kills him is symbolic in more than one sense. On the one hand it represents the irrational forces of sex and fantasy, the libertinage that the writer succumbs to. Freed from all restraint, these forces would make social life impossible because they would turn it into a jungle of hungry beasts. On the other hand, the plague represents the primitive world, an exotic reality in which, unlike the narrator's world of the spirit and civilised Europe, life is instinctual rather than based on ideas, where man can still live in a state of nature. The 'Asian cholera' that comes to ravage the jewel of culture and the intellect that is Venice comes from the remote parts of the planet 'among whose bamboo thickets the tiger crouches',[†] and to

* Thomas Mann, *Death in Venice together with Two Other Stories: Tristan, Tonio Kroger.* Penguin, Harmondsworth, 1955, p. 76.
† *Death in Venice*, p. 71.

some degree the havoc that it wreaks prefigures the defeat of civilisation by the forces of barbarism.

This part of the story is open to different readings. The plague represents, for some, the political and social decomposition of Europe that was emerging from the joyful excesses of the *belle époque* and was about to self-destruct. This is the 'social' interpretation of the epidemic that infiltrates the lakeside city in an imperceptible manner and engulfs it, like the poison of lust in the immaculate spirit of the moralist. In this reading, the epidemic represents the price of degeneration, madness and ruin that must be paid by those who give in to the call of pleasure and submit their intelligence to the irrational dictates of passion.

The man writing this is, without a doubt, another moralist, like von Aschenbach before his fall. Like his character – and it is well known that both Gustav Mahler and the author of *Death in Venice* himself acted as models for von Aschenbach – Thomas Mann also had an instinctual fear of pleasure, that region of experience that blots out rationality, where all ideas are shipwrecked. Here are two romantics disguised as classical writers, two men for whom the passion of the senses, the euphoria of sex, is a supreme moment of pleasure that men and women must experience, albeit conscious of the fact that it will plunge them into decline and death. These licentious puritans do not have a trace of the joyful, ludic eighteenth-century view of sex as a world of play and entertainment, in perfect harmony with life's other demands. The demands of the body and the spirit were two realms that the eighteenth century merged and which, in the nineteenth century, the century of romanticism, would become incompatible.

A symbol is, of itself, ambiguous and contradictory; it is always open to interpretations that vary according to the reader and the time of reading. Despite the fact that it is less than eighty years since *Death in Venice* was written, many of its allegories and symbols are now unclear to us because our age has emptied them of any content or made them irreconcilable. The rigid bourgeois morality that pervades the world of Thomas Mann and gives the fate of von Aschenbach a tragic air appears today, in our permissive society, a

47

picturesque anomaly, just like the Asian plague, with its medieval resonance, which modern-day chemistry would soon defeat. Why is it necessary to punish so cruelly the poor artist whose only sin is to discover late in the day – and, what is more, only in the imagination – the pleasure of the flesh?

And yet, even from our perspective of readers living in a time when our tolerance in sexual matters has made excess appear conventional and boring, the drama of this solitary fifty-year-old, so timid and so wise, who has fallen desperately in love with the Polish boy and who sacrifices himself in the flames of this passion, affects us and moves us deeply. Because, in the interstices of this story there is an abyss that can be glimpsed and which we immediately identify in ourselves and in the society in which we live. An abyss teeming with violence, desires and horrific, fevered ghosts, which we normally are not aware of except through privileged experiences which occasionally reveal it, reminding us that, however much we might try to consign it to the shadows and wipe it from our memory, it is an integral part of human nature and remains, with its monsters and seductive sirens, as a permanent challenge to the habits and customs of civilisation.

At a certain point in his internal drama, von Aschenbach attempts to sublimate his passion through myth. He moves it to the world of culture and transforms himself into Socrates, talking to Phaedrus about beauty and love on the banks of the Ilisos. This is a clever move by the author to cleanse to some extent the noxious vapours emanating from the pleasurable hell in which von Aschenbach finds himself, giving them a philosophical dimension, making them less carnal, broadening the scope of the story by providing a cultural context. Also, it is not gratuitous. Von Aschenbach was a living 'classic', and it is quite natural for his consciousness to search within the world of culture for precedents and references to what is happening to him. But the abyss that has opened up beneath his feet, and which the writer plunges into without any sense of remorse, is not a site of pure ideas or the spirit. It is the site of the body, which he had regulated and disdained and which now is reclaiming its rights, freeing itself and vanquishing the spirit that had held it captive.

This demand has a beginning but no end: awoken by any stimulus – the beauty of Tadzio, for example – free to grow and become immersed in daily life in search of a satisfaction that the fantasy that fuels it makes ever more unattainable, sexual desire, that source of pleasure, can also be a deadly plague for the city. For that reason, life in the city imposes limits and morality on sexual desire, religion and culture looks to tame it and confine it. In the final weeks of his life, Gustav von Aschenbach – and with him the readers of this beautiful parable – discovers that these attempts at control are always relative because, as happens to him, the desire to recover a total sovereignty, which has been stifled by individuals for the benefit of social existence, re-emerges from time to time, demanding that life should not just be reason, peace and discipline but also madness, violence and chaos. In the depths of this exemplary citizen, von Aschenbach, there lurked a painted savage, looking for the right moment to come into the light and take revenge.

Lima, September 1988

Mrs Dalloway

The Intense and Sumptuous Life of Banality

Mrs Dalloway recounts a normal day in the London life of Clarissa Dalloway, a dull upper-middle-class lady married to a Conservative MP, and the mother of an adolescent daughter. The story begins one sunny morning in June 1923, as Clarissa is walking through the centre of the city and ends that same evening when the guests at a party given at the Dalloways' house are beginning to leave. Although during the day one tragic event occurs – the suicide of a young man who had returned from the war with his mind unbalanced – what is significant about the story is not this episode, or the myriad small events and memories that make up the story as a whole, but the fact that all this is narrated from inside the mind of one of the characters, that subtle and impalpable reality where life becomes impression, enjoyment, suffering, memory. The novel appeared in 1925 and was the first of the three great novels – the others are *To the Lighthouse* and *The Waves* – in which Virginia Woolf would revolutionise the narrative art of her time, creating a language capable of persuasively imitating human subjectivity, the meanderings and elusive rhythms of consciousness. Her achievement is no less than that of Proust and Joyce: she complements and enriches their work through her particular feminine sensibility. I know how debatable it is to apply the adjective feminine to a work of literature, and I accept that in innumerable cases the use of such a term is somewhat arbitrary. But for books like *La Princesse de Clèves* or for authors like Colette or Virginia Woolf, it seems absolutely appropriate. In *Mrs Dalloway*, reality has been reinvented from a perspective that mainly, but not completely, expresses the point of view and condition of a woman. And for that reason, it is the feminine experiences of the story that are most vivid in the reader's memory, that seem to us essentially true, like the example of the formidable old woman, Clarissa's aunt Miss Helen Parry, who at eightysomething years old, in the hubbub of the party, only remembers the wild and splendid orchids of her youth in Burma, which she picked and reproduced in watercolours.

On some occasions, in masterpieces that mark a new development in narrative form, the form overshadows the characters and the plot to such an extent that life seems to become frozen and disappear from the novel, consumed by the technique, by the words and order or disorder of the narration. This is what occurs, at times, in Joyce's *Ulysses*, and what takes *Finnegans Wake* to the bounds of illegibility. None of this happens in *Mrs Dalloway* (although in *To the Lighthouse* and, above all, *The Waves* it is on the brink of happening). The balance between the form and content of the tale is perfect, and readers never feel that they are witnessing what this book is *as well*, a daring experiment; only that they are witnessing the delicate and uncertain network of events that happen to a handful of human beings on a hot summer's day in the streets, parks and houses of central London. Life is always there, on each line, in each syllable of the book, brimming with grace and refinement, prodigious and incommensurable, rich and diverse in all its aspects. 'Beauty was everywhere' is a sentence that springs to the befuddled mind of Septimus Warren Smith, who was to be driven by fear and grief to kill himself. And it is true; in *Mrs Dalloway* the real world has been remade and perfected to such a degree by the deicidal genius of its creator, that everything in it is beautiful, including what in our unstable objective reality we hold to be dirty and ugly.

To reach this sovereign state, a novel must free itself from real reality, convince the reader that it is a different reality, with its own laws, time, myths and other characteristics that are proper to it and to it alone. What gives a novel its originality – marks its difference from the real world – is the added element that the fantasy and art of the writer provide when he or she transforms objective and historical experience into fiction. The added element is never just a plot, a style, a temporal order, a point of view; it is always a complex combination of factors that affects the form and content and the characters of a story, and which gives it its autonomous existence. Only failed fictions reproduce reality: successful fictions abolish and transfigure reality.

The miraculous originality of *Mrs Dalloway* lies in the ways in which life is embellished, the secret beauty of every object and every circumstance being thrown into relief. Just as old Miss Parry has abolished from her memory everything except the orchids and some images of gorges and coolies, so the world of fiction has segregated from the real world sex, misery and ugliness and has metamorphosed everything that is in any way a reminder of them into conventional feelings, unimportant allusions or aesthetic pleasure. At the same time it has intensified the presence of ordinary, banal or intangible things, arraying them in unexpected sumptuousness and imbuing them with a hitherto unheard-of prominence, life and dignity. This 'poetic' transformation of the world – for once this epithet is justified – is radical and yet is not immediately perceptible, for, if it were so, it would give the impression of being a fake book, a forced distortion of real life, and *Mrs Dalloway*, by contrast, as with all persuasive fictions – these lies so well made that they pass as truths – seems to submerge us fully in the most authentic of human experience. But it is clear that the fraudulent reconstruction of reality in the novel, reducing it to the most refined, pure aesthetic sensibility, could not be more radical or complete. Why is this sleight of hand not immediately apparent? Because of the rigorous coherence with which the unreality of the novel is described – or, rather, invented – that world in which all the characters without exception have a marvellous ability to detect what is extraordinary in the mundane, what is eternal in the ephemeral and what is glorious in mediocrity, the way Virginia Woolf herself could do. For the characters of this fiction – of every fiction – have been fashioned in the image and likeness of their creator.

But is it the characters of the novel that have these exceptional attributes, or rather just the character who narrates and dictates them, and often speaks through their mouths? I am referring to the narrator – and here we should talk about a female narrator – of the story. The narrator is always the central character in a fiction. Invisible or present, singular or multiple, embodied in the first or second or third person, omniscient god or implied witness in the novel, the narrator is the first and most important character that a novelist must invent in order to make the tale convincing. This elusive, ubiquitous narrator of *Mrs Dalloway* is Virginia Woolf's great achievement in this book, the reason for the story's magic and irresistible power of persuasion.

The narrator of the novel is always located in the private world of the characters, never in the outside world. What is narrated to us comes through filters, diluted and refined by the sensibility of those people. The fluid consciousnesses of Mrs Dalloway, Richard, her husband, Peter Walsh, Elizabeth, Doris Kilman, the tormented Septimus and Rezia, his Italian wife, offer the perspectives from which that hot summer's morning is constructed, in the streets of London, with the din of horns and engines, and its green and scented parks. The objective world dissolves into these consciousnesses before it reaches the reader and is deformed and reformed according to the state of mind of each character; memories and impressions are added, which become blended with dreams and fantasies. In this way, the reader of *Mrs Dalloway* is never provided with an objective reality, but only with the different subjective versions that the characters weave out of this reality. This immaterial substance, as slippery as quicksilver, and yet, essentially human – life transformed into memory, feeling, sensation, desire, impulse – is the prism through which the narrator of *Mrs Dalloway* reveals the world and tells the story. This is what creates, from the opening lines, the extraordinary atmosphere of the novel: that of a suspended, subtle reality, suffused with the same evasive quality as light, scents and the tender and furtive images of memory.

This immaterial, evanescent climate that the characters inhabit gives the reader of *Mrs Dalloway* the impression of being faced with a totally strange world, despite the fact that what happens in the novel could not be more trivial or anodyne. Many years after the book was published, a French writer, Nathalie Sarraute, attempted to describe in a series of fictions what she called human 'tropisms', those pulses or instinctive movements that precede action and thought itself and establish a slender umbilical cord between rational beings, animals and plants. Her novels, which were interesting, but which were never more than audacious experiments, had the virtue, for me, of enriching retrospectively my reading of this novel of Virginia Woolf. Now that I have reread it, I am quite clear that in *Mrs Dalloway* she managed to describe this mysterious and recondite first stirring of life, the 'tropisms' that Nathalie Sarraute, with less success, would seek to explore some decades later.

This withdrawal into the subjective is one characteristic of the narrator; another is the ability to disappear into the consciousnesses of the characters, to become one with them. This is an exceptionally discreet and figurative narrator, who avoids being noticed and who often jumps – but always taking the utmost care not to reveal herself – from one interior consciousness to another. When it exists, the distance between the narrator and the character is minimal, and constantly disappears as the narrator disappears and is replaced by the character: the narration then becomes a monologue. These changes occur constantly, sometimes on several occasions in one page, and despite this, we hardly notice them, such is the skill with which the narrator carries out these transformations, disappearances and reappearances.

The beautifully fashioned narrative employs both an *indirect libre* style and interior monologue. The *indirect libre* style, invented by Flaubert, consists of narrating through an impersonal and omniscient narrator – from a grammatical third person – who is placed very close to the character, so close that on occasion the narrator seems to become confused with the character, abolished by the character. The interior monologue, perfected by Joyce, is the narration through a narrator-character – who narrates from the first person. The person who tells the story of *Mrs Dalloway* is at times an impersonal narrator, very close to the characters, who recounts to us their thoughts, actions and perceptions, imitating their voice, their accent, their reserve, taking on their sympathies and phobias, and at times it is the characters themselves, whose monologues cast out the omniscient narrator from the narration.

These 'changes' of narrator occur innumerable times in the novel, but are only noticeable on a few occasions. On many other occasions it is impossible to determine whether the narrator is the omniscient narrator or the characters themselves, since the narration seems to take place in a liminal space between the two, or seems to be both at once, an impossible point of view in which the first and third persons would not be contradictory but would form a single grammatical person. This formal flourish is particularly effective in the episodes relating to young Septimus Warren Smith, whose mental disintegration we witness from very close up, or we share from within the unfathomable depths of his insecurity and panic.

Septimus Warren Smith is a dramatic person in a novel where all the other characters have conventional and predictable lives, so decrepit and boring that only the revitalising, transforming power of the prose of Virginia Woolf can fill them with enchantment and mystery. The presence of this poor boy who went as a volunteer to the war and returned decorated and apparently unharmed, though wounded in spirit, is disquieting as well as piteous. Because it allows us to glimpse the fact that, despite the many pages that seek to bedeck it in beauty and loftiness, not everything is attractive, agreeable, easy or civilised in the world of Clarissa Dalloway and her friends. There also exists, albeit far from them, cruelty, grief, incomprehension and stupidity, without which the madness and suicide of Septimus would be inconceivable. All this is kept at a distance through rituals and good breeding, through money and good fortune, but at times it tracks them, on the other side of the walls they have erected to remain blind and happy, with its keen sense of smell. Clarissa has premonitions of it. For that reason she shudders in the presence of the imposing figure of Sir William Bradshaw, the psychiatrist, for she sees him, she does not know why, as a danger. She is not wrong: the story makes it very clear that if young Warren Smith was unhinged by war, it is the science of psychiatrists that makes him hurl himself into the abyss.

I read somewhere that a celebrated Japanese calligrapher was in

the habit of staining his writing with a blob of ink. 'Without this contrast, the perfection of my work would not be given its due,' he
explained. Without this small trace of raw reality that is the story of
Septimus Warren Smith, the world into which Clarissa Dalloway
was born, and which she helped so much to create, would not seem
so unpolluted and spiritual, so golden and so artistic.

Fuengirola, 13 July 1989

Nadja

Nadja as Fiction

Surrealism, and André Breton in particular, had a very low opinion of the novel: it was a pedestrian, bourgeois genre, too subordinate to the real world, society, history, rationality and common sense for it be able to express, like poetry – the preferred genre of the movement – the everyday-marvellous, to laugh at logical order or to delve into the mysterious recesses of dream and the world of the subconscious. In the *Surrealist Manifesto*, description – which is inseparable from narrative – is ridiculed as an impossible aspiration and a vulgar pursuit. No Surrealist worthy of the name could have written a text beginning, as novels are wont to begin, with sentences as banal as the one detested by Valéry: '*La marquise sortit à cinq heures'*.*

The novels that Breton tolerated and even praised were those hermaphrodite books which fell between story and poetry, between real reality and a visionary, fantastic order, like Gérard de Nerval's *Aurélia*, Aragon's *Le Paysan de Paris*, or the novels of Julien Gracq. His sympathy for the English Gothic novel or for Henry Miller's *Tropics* always underlined the eccentric, unconsciously rebellious or unruly nature of these works, and their marginality with respect to the form and content of what is usually considered to be the terrain of the novel.

However, the passage of time has altered the strict ideas that still separated the different genres when the Surrealists exploded on to

* On surrealism and literature, see Jacqueline Chénieux-Gendron, *Le Surréalisme et le roman (1922–1950)*, Paris, 1983.

the scene in the 1920s, and today, more than a century after Breton's birth, anyone trying to establish a border between poetry and the novel would find themselves in some difficulty. After Roland Barthes has proclaimed the death of the author, Foucault has discovered that man does not exist and Derrida and the deconstructionists have established that not even life exists, at least in literature, for literature, this dizzying torrent of words, is an autonomous and formal reality, in which texts refer to other texts and overlap with, replace, modify and clarify or obscure each other without any relation to life as lived and to flesh-and-blood bipeds – who, in these circumstances, would dare to keep poetry and the novel as two sovereign entities as André Breton and his friends once did?

With all the respect in the world for a poet and a movement that I discovered as an adolescent – thanks to a surrealist poet, César Moro – that I read with fervour and which has surely been an influence on my formation as a writer (although at first glance it would not appear so), I would have to say that I think that the passage of time has deconstructed surrealism both historically and culturally in the sense that would have upset André Breton the most. That is to say that it has become a quintessentially literary movement whose verbal stridency, provocative spectacles, word play, defence of magic and unreason, pursuit of verbal automatism and contempt for the 'literary', now appear undramatic, domesticated and non-belligerent, without the slightest power to transform customs, morality or history, quaint displays by a group of artists and poets whose chief merit lay in their ability to stir up trouble in the intellectual field, shaking it out of its academic inertia and introducing new forms, new techniques and new themes – a different use of word and image – in the visual arts and in literature.

Today Breton's ideas seem closer to poetry than to philosophy, and what we admire in them, apart from their casuistic intricacy and luxuriant verbosity, is the moral attitude that underpins them, that coherence between speech, writing and action that Breton demanded in his followers with the same severity and fanaticism that he applied to himself. This coherence is doubtless admirable; the same cannot be said of the intransigence shown to those who did not subscribe to the changing orthodoxy of the movement and were excommunicated as traitors or as sacrilegious or were struck down as Pharisees.

All this agitation and violence, the dictates and the cutting remarks, have remained in the past. What is there left? For me, apart from a rich collection of anecdotes, a storm in a glass of water, a beautiful utopia, never achieved and unachievable – to change life and to enthrone total human freedom through the subtle weapons of poetry – there are some beautiful poems – the best of them the 'Ode à Charles Fourier' – an anthology of black humour, a very partisan but absorbing essay dedicated to *Le Surréalisme et la Peinture*, and, above all, a delicate, highly original novel about love: *Nadja*.

Although definitions often confuse more than they illuminate, I will define the novel provisionally as that branch of fiction that sets out to construct, with imagination and words, a fictitious reality, a world apart that, although taking inspiration from reality and the real world, does not reflect them, but rather supplants and denies them. The originality of every fiction lies – although this might seem a tautology – in its being fictive, that is to say, in not resembling the world in which we live, but rather in freeing itself from this world and showing us a world that does not exist and, precisely because it does not exist, it is something we dream about and desire.

If that is a fiction, then *Nadja* is the best illustration there can be. The story that it tells is not of this world, even though it pretends to be so, as happens in all good novels whose powers of persuasion always have us taking as objective truth what is mere illusion, and even though the world that it describes – yes, that it *describes*, although in every novel description is synonymous with invention – seems, through a number of very precise references, to be Paris in the twenties, with a handful of streets, squares, statues, parks, woods and cafés recreated as a backdrop to the action and even illustrated with beautiful photographs.

The story could not be simpler. The narrator, who tells the story as a protagonist within it, casually meets in a café the female character Nadja, a strange, dreamy woman who seems to inhabit a private world of fantasy and dread, on the border between reason and madness, who from the first moment captivates him completely. An intimate relationship grows up between them that we might describe as sentimental rather than erotic or sexual, on the basis of planned or casual (the narrator would like us to call them magical) meetings which, in the few months that they last – from October to December 1926 – open for the narrator the doors to a mysterious and unpredictable world of great spiritual richness, not governed by physical laws or rational schema, but rather by those obscure, fascinating and indefinable forces that we allude to – that the narrator alludes to frequently – when we speak of the marvellous, of magic, or of poetry. The relationship ends as strangely as it began, and the last we hear about Nadja is that she is in a mental asylum, because she is considered mad, something that embitters and exasperates the narrator who hates psychiatry and asylums and who sees what society calls madness – at least in the case of Nadja – as an extreme form of rebellion, a heroic way of exercising freedom.

This is, of course, a profoundly romantic story due to its poetic nature, its extreme antisocial individualism and its tragic ending, and one could also consider the mention of Victor Hugo and Juliette Drouet in the first pages of the novel as an auspicious, premonitory indication of what will happen later. What distinguishes *Nadja* from those extreme stories of impossible love and couples torn apart by an implacable Fate that the romantic sensibility favoured, is not the plot but rather Breton's elegant, coruscating prose, with its labyrinthine pace and its unusual metaphors, and still more the originality of his structure, the daring way in which he organises his chronology and the different planes of reality from which the story is narrated.

Of course it is important to point out that that the main character in the story – the hero, in romantic terminology – is not the eponymous Nadja but the person who evokes her and tells her story, that overwhelming presence who is never away from the reader's eyes or mind for one second: the narrator. Visible or invisible, a witness or a protagonist who narrates from inside the narrative, or an all-powerful God the Father at whose commands the action develops, the narrator is always the most important character in any fiction and is always an invention, a fiction, even in those mendacious cases like

Nadja, where the author of the novel declares that he is hiding under the skin of the narrator. This is never possible. Between the author and narrator of a novel there is always the unbridgeable gap that separates objective reality from fantasy, words from deeds and the mortal being of flesh and blood from the verbal simulacrum.

Whether they know it or not, whether they do it deliberately or through simple intuition, authors of novels always invent the narrator, even though they might add their own name or include episodes of their biography. The narrator invented by Breton to tell the story of Nadja, whom he passed off as himself, has clear romantic affiliations in his monumental self-worship, that narcissism that drives him all the time that he is narrating to display himself in the centre of the action, to refract himself through the action, and the action through himself, so that the story of Nadja is, in truth, the story of Nadja filtered through the narrator, reflected in the distorting mirror of his exquisite personality. The narrator of *Nadja*, like the narrator of *Les Misérables* or *The Three Musketeers*, reveals himself as he reveals the story. It is not, therefore, surprising that from these first pages, he confesses his scant interest in Flaubert who, we remember, was opposed to narrative subjectivity and demanded that the novel had the semblance of impersonality, that is to say that it pretended to be a self-sufficient story (in reality told by invisible narrators).

Nadja is the complete opposite: an almost invisible story told by an overpowering subjectivity, which is shamelessly visible. In the story many things happen, of course, but what is really important is not what can be summarised concretely: the actions of the heroine, the rare coincidences that bring the couple together or separate them, their cryptic conversations, of which we are only given snippets, or the references to places, books, paintings, writers or painters that the astute narrator uses to frame the action. What is important is an *other* reality, different to the reality that offers a setting for what takes place in the novel, which begins to emerge in a subtle manner, somewhat awry, in certain allusions in the conversations, in Nadja's drawings that are full of symbols and allegories that are difficult to interpret, and in the sudden premonitions or intuitions of the narrator who, in this way, manages to make us share his certainty that real life, genuine reality is hidden beneath the reality that we live consciously, hidden from us by routine, stupidity, conformity and everything that he undervalues or despises – rationality, social order, public institutions – and that only certain free people, who are outside what Rubén Darío called the 'thick, municipal common herd' can have access to. The fascination that Nadja exerts over him, and that he transmits to us, is due precisely to the fact that she appears to be a *visitor* in our world, someone who comes from (and has not entirely left) another reality, unknown and invisible, that can only be glimpsed in premonitions by people of exceptional sensibility like the narrator, and can only be described through association or metaphor, approximating to notions like the Marvellous and the Fantastic.

This invisible reality, this life of pure poetry, without prose, where is it to be found? What is it like? Does it exist outside the mind or is it pure fantasy? In the prosaic reality of us common mortals (the phrase is from Montaigne), which Surrealism desperately wanted to transform through the magic wand of poetry, Freud had discovered the world of the unconscious and had described the subtle ways in which the phantoms sheltering there influenced behaviour, caused or resolved conflicts and meddled in people's lives. The discovery of this other dimension of human life influenced, as is well known, in a decisive (but not pious) way the theories and practices of Surrealism, and there is no doubt that without this precedent *Nadja* (which contains an ambiguous sentence that criticises but also shows respect for psychoanalysis) could not have been written, at least in the way that it was written. But a Freudian reading would give us a truncated, caricaturist version of the novel. For it is not the traumas that brought the heroine to the edge of madness – which a psychiatric reading of *Nadja* would focus on – that are of interest in her story, but rather the elated justification that the narrator makes for this borderline space, a domain that he considers a superior form of life, an existential realm where human life is more full and more free.

It is, of course, a fiction. A beautiful and seductive fiction that exists only – but this *only* must be understood as a universe of riches to beguile our sensitivity and fantasy – within the bewitching life of dreams and illusions that are the reality of fiction, that lie that we fashion and in which we believe in order better to endure our real lives.

Borges often said, 'I am eaten up by literature'. There is nothing pejorative in this remark when Borges makes it. Because what he most loved in life – and perhaps one could say that the only thing that he loved and knew deeply – was literature. But Breton would have considered it an insult if someone had said of *Nadja* what is now very obvious to us, that it is 'a book eaten up by literature'. Literature for Breton meant artifice, pose, empty gestures of content, frivolous vanity, conformity to the established order. But what is certain is that while literature can be all those things, it can also be, in outstanding cases like his, daring, novelty, rebellion, an exploration of the most remote recesses of the spirit and an enrichment of real life through fantasy and writing.

This is the operation that *Nadja* carries out on the real world that it purports to narrate: it transforms it into another world, by bathing it in beautiful poetry. The Paris of its pages is not the boisterous and carefree European city, the capital of artistic avant-gardes, of literary quarrels and inter-war political violence. In the book, thanks to its bewitching rhetoric and its theatrical trappings, its narrative strategy of silences and temporal leaps, of veiled allusions, puzzles, false trails and sudden poetic flourishes, its striking incidents – the terrible spectacle of *Les Détraquées*, the wonderful story about the amnesiac man – and its constant references to books and paintings that suffuse the story with its own special radiance, Paris has become a fantastic city, where the marvellous is an almost tangible reality and where everything seems to comply in docile fashion to those secret magic laws that only the diviners detect and the poets intuit, and which the narrator superimposes like a cartographer over the real city.

At the end of the story the Hôtel des Grands Hommes, the statue of Etienne Dolet, the coal-yards, the Port de Saint-Denis, the Boulevard theatres, the flea market, the bookshops, the cafés, the shops and the parks have become transformed into landmarks and monuments of a precious, buried world that is eminently subjective, and has mysterious correlations and assonances with people's lives, a perfect frame within which there can emerge a character so detached from everyday life, so removed from what is called common sense, like Nadja, the woman who enchants the narrator and who orders him at one point in the story: *'Tu écriras un roman sur moi'* ('You will write a novel about me').

The spell was so strong that Breton obeyed and did not limit himself to describing the Nadja that existed, the fleeting Nadja of flesh and blood. In order to tell the story persuasively, he used his fantasy more than his memory, he invented more than he recorded and, like all good novelists, he took every liberty with time, space and words, writing, *'sans ordre préétabli, et selon le caprice de l'heure qui laisse surnager ce qui surnage'* ('without any pre-established order, following the whim of the moment which allows things to float on the surface as they will').*

London, November 1996

---

* André Breton, *Nadja*, Gallimard, Paris, 1963, p. 22.

La Condition humaine

The Hero, the Buffoon and History

When in November 1996 the French government decided to move the remains of André Malraux to the Pantheon, there was a very harsh critical reaction against his work in the United States and Europe, in contrast to the many events organised in his honour by President Jacques Chirac and his supporters. A critical revision that, in some cases, amounted to a literary lynching. See, for example, the ferocious article in the *New York Times* – that barometer of political correctness in the Anglo-Saxon world – by a critic as respectable as Simon Leys. If we were to believe him and other critics, then Malraux was an overrated writer, a mediocre novelist and a wordy and boastful essayist with a declamatory style, whose delirious historical and philosophical declarations in his essays were mere verbal fireworks, the conjuring tricks of a charlatan.

I do not agree with this unjust and prejudiced view of Malraux's work. It is true, he did have a certain propensity to excessive wordiness – a congenital vice of the French literary tradition – and at times, in his essays on art, he could strain after rhetorical effect and fall into tricky obscurity (like many of his colleagues). But there are charlatans and charlatans. Malraux was one to the highest possible degree of rhetorical splendour, brimming over with such intelligence and culture that in his case the vice of wordiness often became a virtue. Even when the tumultuous prose that he wrote said nothing, as is the case in some pages of *Les Voix du silence* (*The Voices of Silence*), there was so much beauty in that tangled emptiness of words that it was enchanting. But if as a critic he was sometimes rhetorical, as a novelist he was a model of efficiency and precision. Among his novels is one of the most admirable works of the twentieth century, *La Condition humaine* (*Man's Fate*, 1933).

As soon as I had read it, charging through it in one night, and then got to know something about the author through a book by Pierre de Boisdeffre, I knew that his was the life that I would have liked to have led. I continued to think this in the sixties in France, when as a journalist I covered the actions, polemics and speeches of the Minister of Culture of the Fifth Republic. I feel the same every time I read his autobiographical accounts, or the biographies that, following the work of Jean Lacouture, have appeared in recent years with new facts about his life, that was as abundant and dramatic as those of the great adventurers of his novels.

I am also a literary fetishist, and I really like to find out everything there is to know about the writers I admire: what they did and did not do, what friends and enemies attributed to them and what they themselves invented for posterity. I am, therefore, overwhelmed by the extraordinary number of public revelations, betrayals, accusations and scandals that are now adding to the already very rich mythology surrounding André Malraux. For here was a man that was not only a great writer, but someone who managed, in his seventy-five years (1901–76), to be present, often in a starring role, at the great events of his century – the Chinese revolution, the anti-colonial struggles in Asia, the antifascist movement in Europe, the war in Spain, the resistance against the Nazis, decolonisation and the reform of France under De Gaulle – and to leave a distinct mark on his time.

He was a Communist travelling companion and a fervent nationalist; a publisher of clandestine pornography; a speculator on the Stock Exchange, where he became rich and later bankrupt in a few months (squandering all his wife's money); a raider of the statues of the temple of Banteai-Srei, in Cambodia, for which he was sentenced to three years in prison (his precocious literary fame gained him a reprieve); an anti-colonialist conspirator in Saigon; a driving force behind avant-garde literary magazines and a promoter of German

Expressionism, Cubism and all the artistic and poetic experiments of the twenties and thirties; one of the first critics and theoreticians of cinema; a participant in and witness to the revolutionary strikes in Canton in 1925; an organiser and member of an expedition (on a toy motorbike) to Arabia in search of the treasure of the Queen of Saba; a committed intellectual and a towering figure in all the congresses and organisations of European antifascist artists and writers; the organiser of the Spain Squadron (that would later be called the André Malraux Squadron) for the defence of the Republic during the Spanish Civil War; a hero of the French resistance and colonel of the Alsace-Lorraine Brigade; a political supporter and minister in all the governments of General De Gaulle who, from the time of their first meeting in August 1945, inspired an almost religious devotion in him.

This life is as intense and diverse as it is contradictory, and can be interpreted in many conflicting ways. What there is no doubt about is that his life offers that very rare alliance of thought and action, and at the highest level, because while he participated with such brio in the great events and disasters of his age, he was a man endowed with an exceptional lucidity and creative drive that allowed him to keep an intelligent distance from lived experience and transform it into critical reflection and vigorous fictions. A handful of writers who were his contemporaries were, like Malraux, completely involved in living history: Orwell, Koestler, T. E. Lawrence. These three writers wrote admirable essays on the tragic reality that they were living; but none of them captured it in fiction with the talent of Malraux. All his novels are excellent, although *L'Espoir* (*Days of Hope*) is too long and *Les Conquérants* (*The Conquerors*), *La Voie royale* (*The Royal Way*) and *Le Temps du mépris* (*An Age of Oppression*) are too short. *Man's Fate* is a masterpiece, worthy to be quoted alongside the work of Joyce, Proust, Faulkner, Thomas Mann or Kafka, as one of the most dazzling creations of our time. I say this with the certainty of one who has read it at least a half a dozen times, feeling, each time, the agonised shudder of the terrorist Chen before he plunges his knife into his sleeping victim, and moved to tears by Katow's magnificent gesture, when he gives his cyanide pill to two young

Chinese, condemned, like him, by the torturers of Kuomintang, to be burned alive. Everything in this novel is perfect: the epic story, spiced with romantic interludes; the contrast between personal adventure and ideological debates; the opposing psychologies and cultures of the characters and the foolish actions of Baron Clappique that give a touch of excess and absurdity – or, we might say, unpredictability and freedom – to a life that otherwise could have seemed excessively logical; but above all, the effectiveness of the syncopated, pared-down prose, which forces readers to use their imagination at all times to fill the spaces that are scarcely outlined in the dialogues and the descriptions.

Man's Fate is based on a real revolution that took place in 1927 in Shanghai, led by the Chinese Communist Party and its allies, the Kuomintang, against the Men of War, as the military autocrats who governed deeply divided China were called, a China in which the Western powers had managed to establish colonial enclaves, by force or corruption. An envoy of Mao, Chou-En-Lai, on whom the character of Kyo is partly based, led this revolution. But, unlike Kyo, Chou-En-Lai was not killed when, after defeating the military government, the Kuomintang of Chiang Kai-Chek turned against their Communist allies and, as the novel describes, savagely repressed them; he managed to escape and rejoin Mao, accompanying him on the Long March and remaining his deputy for the rest of his life.

Malraux was not in Shanghai during the time of the events that he narrates (or rather, invents); but he was in Canton during the insurrectionary strikes of 1925, and was a friend and collaborator (it has never been established to what degree), of Borodin, the envoy sent by the Comintern (in other words, by Stalin) to advise the Communist movement in China. This doubtless helped him to convey that sense of a 'lived' experience in the novel when he memorably describes the attacks and the street fighting. From an ideological point of view, *Man's Fate* is unambiguously pro-Communist. It is not Stalinist, however, but rather Trotskyist, since the story explicitly condemns the orders from Moscow, imposed on the Chinese Communists by the Comintern bureaucrats, to hand over their arms to Chiang Kai-Chek instead of hiding them and defending themselves when their Kuomintang allies turn against them. Let us not forget that these episodes take place in China, while in the Soviet Union the great debate between Stalinists and Trotskyists about permanent revolution or Communism in one country was intensifying (even though the extermination of Trotskyists had already begun).

But an ideological or merely political reading would miss the main point: that the world which the novel creates in such detail owes more to the imagination and the convulsive force of the tale than to the historical episodes that it uses as its raw material.

It is not so much a novel as a classical tragedy grafted onto modern life. A group of men (and a single woman, May, who in the essentially misogynist world of Malraux is barely a sketch, only slightly more clearly defined than Valérie and the courtesans who form part of the background) from different parts of the world face up to a superior enemy in order to, in Kyo's words, 'give back dignity' to those that they are fighting for: the wretched, the defeated, the exploited, the rural and industrial slaves. In this struggle, in which they are defeated and perish, Kyo, Chen and Katow reach a higher moral plane, achieve a greatness that expresses 'the human condition' in its most exemplary form.

Life is not like this, and, of course, revolutions are not made up of noble and despicable actions distributed in rectilinear fashion between the combatants of each side. To find such schematic political and ethical concerns in any of the fictions produced by socialist realism would be profoundly tedious. The fact that *Man's Fate* convinces us of its truth means that Malraux was capable, like all great creators, of pulling the wool over our eyes, masking his views with the irresistible appearance of reality.

The truth is that flesh-and-blood revolutions are not so clear cut in our own world of greys and shifting tones, nor do revolutionaries shine forth so pure, coherent, brave and self-sacrificing as in the turbulent pages of the novel. Why, then, do we find them so hypnotic? Why are we surprised and why do we suffer when Katow, that silent adventurer, accepts a terrible death as the price of his generous action, or why are we blown apart, with Chen, beneath the car that Chiang Kai-Chek was not travelling in? Why, if these characters are fabrications? Because they embody a universal ideal, the supreme aspiration to perfection and the absolute that resides in every human heart. But, more than this, because the skill of the narrator is so consummate that he manages to persuade us of the intimate truth of these secular angels, of these saints that he has brought down from heaven and turned into common mortals, heroes who appear to be just like any one of us.

The novel is superbly concise. The bare descriptions often emerge from the dialogues and reflections of the characters, rapid sketches that are sufficient to create the depressing urban landscape: teeming Shanghai, bristling with wire fences, swept by the smoke of the factories and the rain, where hunger, promiscuity and the worst cruelties coexist with generosity, fraternity and heroism. Concise, sharp, the style never says too much, always too little. Every episode is like the tip of an iceberg; but they radiate such intensity that the reader's imagination can reconstruct the totality of the action from this sparse description without difficulty, the place where it occurs as well as the state of mind and secret motivations of the protagonists. This synthetic method gives the novel a great density and an epic breadth. The street action sequences, like the capture of the police post by Chen and his men at the beginning, and the fall of the trench where Katow and the Communists have taken refuge at the end, are small, tense, masterly descriptions that keep the reader in suspense. These and other episodes in *Man's Fate* are visually cinematographic, something which Dos Passos also managed to achieve in his best tales in those same years.

An excess of intelligence is often fatal in a novel because it can work against the persuasive power of the fiction. But in Malraux's novels, intelligence is an atmosphere, it is everywhere, in the narrator and all the characters: the wise Gisors is no less lucid than the policeman Konig, and even the Belgian Hemmelrich, who is presented as a fundamentally mediocre person, reflects on his failures and frustrations with a dazzling mental clarity. Intelligence does not get in the way of verisimilitude in *Man's Fate* (by contrast it undermines realism in all Sartre's novels) because in the novel intelligence is a universal attribute of the living. This is one of the main characteristics of the 'added element' in the novel, which gives it sovereignty, its own life that is different to real life.

The great character of the book is not Kyo, as the narrator would have it, as he carefully stresses the discipline, team spirit and submission to leadership of this perfect militant. It is Chen, the anarchist, the individualist, who changes from being an activist to being a terrorist, a superior state, in his view, because by killing and dying he can accelerate history which, for the party revolutionary, is made up of slow collective movements in which the individual counts for little or nothing. In the character of Chen we find a sketch of what over the years would become Malraux's ideology: the hero who, thanks to his lucidity, force of will and daring, can prevail over the 'laws' of history. The fact that he fails – Malraux's characters are always defeated – is the price that he pays for the eventual triumph of the cause.

As well as being brave, tragic and intelligent, Malraux's characters are usually cultured: appreciative of beauty, well versed in art and philosophy, enthusiastic about exotic cultures. In *Man's Fate*, the emblematic figure in this respect is old Gisors; but Clappique is made of the same stuff, for behind his bragging exhibitionism, there is a subtle man with an exquisite taste for aesthetic objects. Baron Clappique is an irruption of fantasy, absurdity, freedom and humour in this grave, logical, lugubrious and violent world of revolutionaries and counter-revolutionaries. He is there to lighten, with a blast of irresponsibility and madness, that rarefied hell of suffering and cruelty. He also reminds us, contrary to what Kyo, Chen and Katow think, that life is made up not just of reason and collective values, but also of madness, instinct and individual passions that contradict and sometimes destroy these values.

Malraux's creative impetus was not confined to his novels. It also suffuses his essays and autobiographical works, some of which – like the *Anti-Mémoires* or *Les Chênes qu'on abat* (*Felled Oaks: Conversations with De Gaulle*) – have such an overwhelming persuasive force, due to the bewitching nature of the prose, the fascination of his stories and rounded way in which the characters are described, that they do not seem to be accounts of events and people from real life

71

but rather the fantasies of a conjurer, adept at the art of persuasion. I set out to read the last of these books, which narrates a conversation with De Gaulle at Colombey-les-deux-Églises on 11 December 1969, feeling rather hostile: it was political hagiography, a genre I detest, and I was sure that it would mythify and embellish nationalism, which is just as obtuse in France as it is in any other country. However, despite my firm decision, taken in advance, to detest the book completely, this dialogue between two monuments, who speak as only people in great books speak, with unremitting coherence and brilliance, broke down my defences, engrossed me in its delirious egotism and made me believe, as I read, the prophetic nonsense with which these two brilliant interlocutors consoled themselves: that, without De Gaulle, Europe would break up and that France, in the hands of the mediocre politicians that had come after him, would also go into decline. It seduced me, not convinced me, and now I try to explain it by saying that *Felled Oaks* is a magnificent, detestable book.

There is no one like a great writer to make us see mirages. Malraux could do this not only when he wrote, but also when he talked. This was another of his original gifts, one which, I believe, had no precursors or successors. Oratory is a minor art, superficial, full of mere sonorous and visual effects, usually devoid of thought, performed by and for garrulous people. But Malraux was an outstanding orator, as one can see from his *Oraisons funèbres* (*Funerary Orations*), capable of endowing a speech with a host of fresh and stimulating ideas, and clothing it with images of great rhetorical beauty. Some of these texts, like those that he read in the Pantheon over the coffin of the French resistance hero, Jean Moulin, and over the coffin of Le Corbusier, in the courtyard of the Louvre, are beautiful literary pieces, and those of us who heard him declaim them, with his thunderous voice, the necessary dramatic pauses and his visionary gaze, will never forget the spectacle (I heard them at a great distance, in the press pack, but I still went into a cold sweat and was very moved).

Malraux was like that throughout his life: a spectacle, that he himself prepared, directed and performed, with great skill and with due attention to the smallest detail. He knew that he was intelligent and brilliant and, despite this, he did not become an idiot. He was also very courageous; he did not fear death, and, because of that, even though death stalked him on many occasions, he was able to embark on all those risky undertakings that marked his existence. But he was also, thankfully, rather histrionic and narcissistic, a high-flying exhibitionist (a Baron Clappique), and that made him human, brought him down from those heights that his intelligence – that had so amazed Gide – had taken him to, down to our level, the level of simple mortals. Most of the writers I admire would have failed the Pantheon test; or their presence there, in that monument to official memory, would have seemed intolerable, an insult to their memory. How could a Flaubert, a Baudelaire, a Rimbaud have entered the Pantheon? But Malraux is not out of place there, nor do his works or his image become impoverished among those marbles. Because one of the innumerable facets of this symphonic man was that he loved showiness and theatricality, triumphal arches, flags, hymns, those symbols invented to cover over the existential void and feed our human vanity.

London, March 1999

Tropic of Cancer

The Happy Nihilist

I remember very clearly how I read *Tropic of Cancer* for the first time, thirty years ago: very quickly, overexcited, in the course of just one night. A Spanish friend had got hold of a French version of this *maudit* book about which so many stories were circulating in Lima, and when he saw how anxious I was to read it, he lent it to me for a few hours. It was a strange experience, completely different to what I had imagined, because the book was not scandalous, as was being said, because of its erotic scenes, but rather because of its vulgarity and its cheerful nihilism. It reminded me of Céline, in whose novels swearwords and filth also become poetry, and Breton's *Nadja*, because, in *Nadja* and in *Tropic of Cancer*, the most everyday reality suddenly becomes transformed into dream-like images and unsettling nightmares.

The book impressed me, but I don't think that I liked it. I had then – and I still have – a prejudice that novels should tell stories that begin and end, that they had an obligation to oppose the chaos of life with an artificial, tidy and persuasive order. *Tropic of Cancer* – like all Miller's subsequent books – is chaos in pure form, effervescent anarchy, a great, romantic, coarse, firework display, from which the reader emerges somewhat nauseous, disturbed and rather more pessimistic about human existence than before the show. The risk with this type of loose, formless literature is that it can become just clever showmanship, and Henry Miller, like another of his *maudit* contemporaries, Jean Genet, often fell into this trap. But *Tropic of*

Cancer, his first novel, fortunately avoided this danger. It is, without doubt, the best book that he wrote, one of the great literary creations of the inter-war period, and within the œuvre of Miller, the work that is closest to being a masterpiece.

I have reread it now with real pleasure. Time and the bad habits of our era have diminished its violence and what seemed to be its rhetorical daring; we now know that farts and gonorrhoea can also be aesthetic. But time has not impoverished the sorcery of his prose or lessened its impact. On the contrary, it has added to it both serenity and a sort of maturity. When it appeared in 1934, in a semi-clandestine edition, in linguistic exile, a victim of prohibitions and edifying attacks, what was praised or disparaged in the book was its iconoclasm, the insolence with which, in its sentences, the worst, most offensive, words displaced those considered as being in good taste, as well as its obsession with eschatology. Today this aspect of the novel shocks very few readers, since modern literature has adopted these elements that Miller introduced with *Tropic of Cancer*, to such an extent that in many ways they have become a platitude, like talking about the geometry of passions in the eighteenth century, or reviling the bourgeoisie in the Romantic era, or becoming historically committed at the time of existentialism. Rude words lost their rudeness some time ago, and sex and its ceremonies have been popularised to the point of tedium. All this has its downside, of course, but one of the clear advantages is that now we can finally judge if Henry Miller, as well as being an explosive writer and an erotic novelist, was also a genuine artist.

He was, without any doubt. He was a genuine creator, with his own world and vision of humanity and literature that clearly singled him out from other writers of his generation. He represented, in our time, like Céline or Genet, that satanic tradition of iconoclasts, of very different temperaments, for whom writing has throughout history signified defying the conventions of the age, spoiling the party of social harmony, bringing out into the light all the brutishness and filth that society – sometimes with good reason, at other times for no good reason – insists on repressing. This is one of the important functions of literature: to remind men and women that however firm the ground that they walk on appears to be, and however brightly the city that they live in shines, there are demons lurking everywhere that, at any moment, can cause a violent upheaval.

Cataclysm, apocalypse, are words that come immediately to mind when talking about *Tropic of Cancer*, despite the fact that in its pages the only blood spilled is in a few drunken brawls and the only war is the (always belligerent) fornication of its characters. But a premonition of imminent catastrophe haunts its pages, the intuition that everything that is being narrated is about to disappear in a holocaust. This intuition causes the novel's picturesque and promiscuous characters to live in such a dissolute frenzy. Theirs is a world that is ending, that is disintegrating morally and socially in a hysterical spree, waiting for the arrival of the plague and death, as in the terrifying fantasies of Hieronymus Bosch. In historical terms, all this is rigorously accurate. Miller wrote the novel in Paris between 1931 and 1933, at a time leading up to the great conflagration that would sweep through Europe some years later. These were years of bonanza and partying, of happy thoughtlessness and splendid creativity. All the aesthetic vanguard movements flourished, and the Surrealists enchanted modern-minded people with their poetic imagination and their 'provocation spectacles'. Paris was the capital of the artistic world and of human happiness.

In *Tropic of Cancer* we see the flip side of this story. Its world is Parisian, but it is light years away from that society of winners and prosperous optimists: it is made up of pariahs, pseudo-painters, pseudo-writers, drop-outs and parasites who live on the margins of the city, not participating in the feast, fighting over the scraps. Expatriates who have lost the intimate link with their country of origin – the United States, Russia – who have not taken root in Paris and live in a kind of cultural limbo. Its geographical reference points are brothels, bars, run-down hotels, sordid rooms, dreadful restaurants, and the parks, squares and streets that attract tramps. In order to survive in this difficult country, everything goes: from a mind-numbing job – correcting proofs in a newspaper – to scrounging, pimping or conning. Many use vague ideas about art to justify themselves – I have to write the important novel, to paint redemptive pictures, etc. – but in fact the only seriousness the group displays is their lack of seriousness, their promiscuity, their passive indifference and their slow disintegration.

This is a world – or rather an underworld – that I got to know at the end of the fifties, and I am sure that it was not very different to the one Miller frequented – and which inspired *Tropic of Cancer* – twenty years earlier. I was horrified by the slow, useless death of that bohemian Paris and I only got in touch with it out of necessity, when there was no other alternative. For that reason, I really can appreciate the feat of transforming this milieu into literature, of transforming these people, these rituals and all this asphyxiating mediocrity, into the dramatic and heroic characters that appear in the novel. But what is perhaps most noteworthy is that in this milieu, that was eaten away by inertia and defeatism, it was possible to conceive and complete a creative project as ambitious as *Tropic of Cancer*. (The book was rewritten three times and reduced by a third in its final version.)

Because the book is a creation rather than a testimony, its documentary value is indisputable, but what has been added by Miller's fantasy and obsessions is more important than the historical material, and it is what gives *Tropic of Cancer* its literary status. What is autobiographical in the book is a semblance rather than a reality, a narrative strategy to give an appearance of trustworthiness to what is a fiction. This inevitably happens in a novel, whatever the intention of the author. Perhaps Miller wanted to put himself into his story, to offer himself as a spectacle, in a great exhibitionist display of total nakedness. But the result was identical to that of a novelist who carefully retreats from his or her narrative world and tries to depersonalise it as much as possible. The 'Henry' of *Tropic of Cancer* is an invention who gains our sympathy or dislike through actions and attitudes that unfold in an autonomous way, from within the confines of the fiction: in order to believe in him – to see him, feel him and, above all, hear him – it is not necessary to compare him to the living model that supposedly inspired the creation. Between the author and the narrator of a novel there is always a distance; the author always creates a narrator, be it an invisible narrator, or one who is involved in the story, be it an all-powerful god who is not open to appeal and who knows everything, or someone who lives as a character among the other characters and has as limited and subjective a vision as that of any of his fictitious fellow humans. The narrator is, in every case, the first person that is imagined by that distiller of fantasies that we call a novelist.

The narrator-character of *Tropic of Cancer* is the great creation of the novel, the supreme achievement of Miller as a novelist. This obscene narcissist 'Henry', who despises the world, caring only for his phallus and his guts, has, above all, an unmistakable tone, a Rabelaisian vitality for changing crudeness and dirt into art, for spiritualising, with his great poetic voice, physiological functions, pettiness and squalor, for giving aesthetic dignity to vulgarity. What is most remarkable is not the freedom and naturalness with which he describes sex or fantasises about it, reaching extremes of explicitness that have no precedent in modern literature, but rather his moral attitude. Or would it be more precise, perhaps, to talk about his amorality? I don't think so. Because, although the behaviour of the narrator and his opinions defy established morality – or rather, established moralities – it would be unjust to argue that he is indifferent to this issue. His way of acting and thinking is coherent: his contempt for conventions is a response to a deep conviction, a certain vision of man, society and culture which, albeit in a somewhat confused way, is clearly shown throughout the novel.

One could define it as the morality of a romantic anarchist rebelling against modern, industrialised society, which he sees as a threat to individual sovereignty. The imprecations against 'progress' and the automatisation of humanity – what, in a subsequent book, Miller would call the 'air-conditioned nightmare' – are not very different to those hurled by Louis-Ferdinand Céline in those same years, in books similarly full of insults against the inhumanity of modern life, or Ezra Pound, for whom 'mercantile' society meant the end of civilisation. Céline and Pound – like Drieu la Rochelle and Robert Brasillach – believed that industrial society was synonymous with decadence, a deviation from certain exemplary standards that the West had achieved at certain moments in the past (Rome, the

Middle Ages, the Renaissance). This reactionary glorification of the past would throw them into the arms of fascism. This did not happen to Miller because he does not make his frontal assault on modern society in the name of an ideal, extinct or invented civilisation, but rather in the name of the individual, whose rights, whims, dreams and instincts are, for Miller, inalienable and precious values. These values, for him, are close to extinction, and they must be celebrated as loudly as possible before they are flattened by the implacable steam-rolling force of modernity.

His posture is no less utopian than that of other *maudit* writers who waged war against much-hated progress, but it is more sympathetic and, in the end, more defensible than that of those who became Nazis thinking that they were defending civilisation or tradition. Miller's furious individualism kept him safe from that danger. No form of social organisation and, above all, of collective life is tolerable to this rebel who has left his job, his family, and all types of responsibility because they represented for him different forms of slavery. He has chosen to be a pariah and a drop-out because, leading this kind of existence – despite the inconveniences and the hunger he suffers – is the best way of preserving his freedom.

It is this conviction – that living the life almost of a beggar, with no obligations and with no respect for any of the established social conventions, is freer and more authentic than being caught up in the horrid swarm of alienated citizens – that makes 'Henry', the incurable pessimist about human destiny, a humorous person who enjoys life and is, in a certain way, happy. This unusual mixture is one of the character's most original and attractive features, and the greatest delight in the novel, since it makes the atmosphere of frustration, amorality, abandon and filth in which the story takes place seem tolerable, pleasant and even seductive.

Although to talk of 'story' in relation to *Tropic of Cancer* is not quite exact. It would be better to talk of scenes, pictures, episodes, disconnected and without a precise chronology, brought together only by the presence of the narrator, who is such an overwhelming egotistical force that the other characters are reduced to blurred extras. But this disconnected form is not gratuitous: it corresponds to the narrator's character, it reflects his incorrigible anarchy, his allergic reaction to any type of organisation or order, the supreme arbitrariness that he confuses with freedom. In *Tropic of Cancer*, Miller achieved the difficult balance between the disorder of spontaneity and pure intuition and the minimal rational and ordered control that any fiction requires for it to be persuasive (because although fiction deals more with instincts and passions than with ideas, it must always appeal first to the intelligence of its readers before appealing to their emotions). In later books this was not the case, and for that reason many of them, despite containing memorable episodes and flashes of brilliant writing, are tedious, too amorphous to engage the reader. In this novel, however, the reader is captivated from the first sentence, and the spell does not break until the end, with the blissful scene by the Seine.

It is a fine book, and its somewhat naïve philosophy touches us. Of course no civilisation can sustain such intransigent and extreme individualism, unless it is prepared to go back to the days when men held clubs and grunted. But, even so, we still feel nostalgia as we read this summons to total irresponsibility, to the great disorder of life and sex that preceded society, rules, prohibitions, the law . . .

Lima, August 1988

Seven Gothic Tales

The Tales of the Baroness

Baroness Karen Blixen de Rungstedlund, who signed her books with the pseudonym Isak Dinesen, must have been an extraordinary woman. There is a photo of her, in New York, alongside Marilyn Monroe, when she was just a scrap of a person, consumed by syphilis, and it is not the beautiful actress but the wide, ironic and troubled eyes and the skeletal face of the writer that steals the photo.

She was born in Denmark, in a house on the seashore between Copenhagen and Elsinore, which is today very like her imaginative and surprising personality: an enclave of plants and exotic birds. She is buried there, in the middle of the countryside, under the trees that witnessed her first steps. She was born in 1885, but gave the impression of having been educated a century earlier, the century that began in 1781 and ended with the Second Empire in 1871, that she called the 'last great age of aristocratic culture'. Almost all her stories take place between those years. She was spiritually a woman of the eighteenth and nineteenth centuries, although, as she confessed in a radio interview towards the end of her life, her friends suspected that she was 'three thousand years old'. She never set foot in a school; she was educated by astonishing governesses who, at twelve, had her writing essays on Racine's tragedies and translating Walter Scott into Danish. Her upbringing was polyglot and cosmopolitan; although she was Danish, she wrote most of her work in English.

She began writing stories and tales as a child, but her literary vocation came late; her vocation as an adventurer came precociously early. She inherited both from her father, the very engaging captain Wilhelm Dinesen, who, after a perilous military career, fell in love with the native peoples of North America and went to live among them. The Indians accepted him and baptised him with the name of Boganis, which he put on the cover of his memoirs. He ended up hanging himself when Karen was ten years old. As befitted a baroness, she was married very young to a lazy and sickly cousin, Bror Blixen, and they both went to Africa to plant coffee in Kenya. The marriage did not go well (the *mal français* that devoured the life of Isak Dinesen was caught from her husband) and ended in divorce. When Bror returned to Europe, she decided to stay in Africa and manage the seven-hundred-acre estate on her own. She did this for a quarter of a century, in a stubborn fight against adversity. Her life on the African continent, which became an integral part of her, and whose people and landscapes were transformed by her irrepressible imagination into a unique vision, is beautifully captured in *Out of Africa* (first published in 1937 in Europe and 1938 in the United States).

While she was an agricultural pioneer, fighting against plagues and floods and administering her coffee estate, in the first decades of the century, Baroness Rungstedlund had no urgency to write. She merely scribbled in notebooks sketches of what would become some of her future stories. She was more attracted by safaris, expeditions to remote areas, getting to know the tribal peoples, having contact with Nature and with wild animals. The primitive surroundings, however, did not prevent her having a refined cultural life, which she organised herself, through her reading and through her contact with some curious representatives of the culture of Europe who appeared in those parts, like the mythical Englishman Denys Finch-Hatton, an Oxford aesthete and adventurer, with whom Karen Blixen maintained an intense emotional relationship. One can imagine them discussing Euripides or Shakespeare after having spent the day hunting lions. (It is not surprising, for that reason, that the only writer that Hemingway always spoke of with unreserved imagination was Isak Dinesen.) The isolation of that African plantation and the narrow circle of European expatriates that she frequented in Kenya explains to a large degree the kind of culture that so surprises the reader of Isak Dinesen. It is not a culture that reflects its age, but rather ignores it, a deliberate anachronism, something strictly personal and extraneous, a culture dissociated from the great movements and intellectual preoccupations of its time and from the dominant aesthetic values, a very singular re-elaboration of ideas, images, sights, forms and symbols that come from the Nordic past, from family tradition and an eccentric education, full of references to Scandinavian history, English poetry, Mediterranean folklore, African oral literature and the stories and way of narrating of the Arab *jongleurs*. A formative book in her life was the *Arabian Nights*, a forest of stories linked by the narrative cunning of Scheherazade, who was the model for Isak Dinesen. Africa allowed her to live, in an almost uncontaminated way, within a capricious culture, outside tradition, created for her own personal use. This culture shapes her world, and helps to explain the originality of the themes, the style, the construction and the philosophy of her stories.

Her vocation as a writer came about after the bankruptcy of her coffee estates. Despite the fact that the price of coffee kept going down, she, with characteristic temerity, carried on with the crop until she was ruined. She did not just lose her estate, but also her Danish inheritance. It was, she recalls, at that time of crisis, when she realised that her African experience was coming inevitably to an end, that she began to write. She wrote at night, fleeing from the anguish and business of the day. In this way, she finished the *Seven Gothic Tales*, which appeared in New York and in London after being rejected by several publishing houses. She would later publish other collections of stories, some of very high quality like the *Winter's Tales*, but her name would always be associated with her first stories published in that collection, which remains one of the most dazzling literary achievements of the twentieth century.

Although she also wrote a novel (the forgettable *The Angelic Avengers*), Isak Dinesen was, like Maupassant, Poe, Kipling or Borges, essentially a short-story writer. The world she created was the world of the story, with all the resonance of unbridled fantasy and childlike enchantment that this word implies. When one reads her it is impossible not to think of the book of stories par excellence, the *Arabian Nights*. In her stories – as in the *Arabian Nights* – the passion most commonly shared by all the characters is, alongside putting on disguises and changing identity, that of listening to and telling stories, evading reality in a mirage of fictions. This tendency reaches its apogee in 'The Roads Round Pisa', when the young Agnese della Gherardesca (dressed as a man) interrupts the duel between the old prince and Giovanni to tell the prince a story. This vice for fantasy gives the *Seven Gothic Tales*, like Scheherazade's stories, a Chinese box structure, stories that burst out of stories or dissolve into stories, among which the main story, hiding and revealing itself an ambiguous and elusive masked ball, is told.

Whether they take place in Polish abbeys in the eighteenth century, in nineteenth-century Tuscan inns, on a hayloft in Norderney about to be submerged by a deluge or in a burning night on the African coast between Lamu and Zanzibar, among cardinals with sybaritic tastes, opera singers who have lost their voice or storytellers like Mira Jama in 'The Dreamers', who had had his nose and ears cut off, Isak Dinesen's stories are always deceptive, full of secret and elusive elements. Of course it is difficult to know where they begin, and what the real story is – among all the entwined stories that the enthralled reader meanders through – that the author wishes to tell. This main story gradually emerges, obliquely, as if by chance, against the backcloth of a profusion of adventures that sometimes remain disparate or on other occasions, as in the disconcerting ending of 'The Dreamers', become fused into a single, coherent narration.

Artificial, brilliant, unexpected, bewitching, almost always beginning better than they end, the stories of Isak Dinesen are, above all else, extravagant. Nonsense, absurdity, grotesque or improbable details always break into the narrative, on occasion destroying the dramatic intensity or the delicacy of a scene. This tendency was much stronger than she was, an untameable habit, in much the same way that others might be drawn to laughter or to melodrama. One must always expect the unexpected in the tales of Isak Dinesen. She saw the essence of fiction as being its lack of verisimilitude. In 'The Deluge at Nordeney', the perverse and delicious Miss Malin Nat-og-Dag says as much to the Cardinal as they are speaking surrounded by the waters that will doubtless swallow them up, when she expounds her theory that God prefers masks to the truth since he knows that 'truth is for tailors and shoemakers'.* For Isak Dinesen, the truth of fiction was the lie, an explicit lie, so well constructed, so exotic and precious, so excessive and attractive, that it was preferable to truth. What the prince of the Church argues in this story – 'be not afraid of absurdity; do not shrink from the fantastic'† – could well be the definition of the art of Isak Dinesen. In this definition, however, we would need to specify our notion of the fantastic, a concept that, because of its excess and extravagance, cannot neatly be included in our conception of reality. We would need to exclude the supernatural variant of the fantastic because, in these stories, although a dead person – the privateer Morten de Coninck in 'The Supper at Elsinore' – comes from hell in order to dine with his two sisters, the fantastic, despite its excesses, always has its roots in the real world, as in the theatre or in the circus.

The past attracted Isak Dinesen because of the memory of her childhood, the education she received and her aristocratic sensibility, but also because the past is unverifiable; by situating her stories one or two centuries in the past, she could give free rein to the anti-realist passion that drove her, to her love of the grotesque and of arbitrariness, without feeling coerced by the present. What is curious is that the work of this author, who had such a free and eccentric imagination, who just before her death boasted to Daniel Gilles that she had not the 'slightest interest in social questions or in Freudian psychology' and whose only ambition was to 'invent beautiful stories', should appear in the thirties, when narrative in the West revolved maniacally around realist descriptions: political problems, social issues, psychological studies, local sketches. For that reason André Breton considered that the novel suffered from a kind of realist curse and expelled it from literature. There were exceptions to

* Isak Dinesen, *Seven Gothic Tales*, Putnam, London, 1934, p. 202.
† *Ibid*, p. 202.

this narrative realism, writers who barred themselves from this dominant tendency. One of these writers was Valle Inclán; another, Isak Dinesen. In both, the tale becomes a dream, madness, delirium, mystery, a game, poetry.

The seven Gothic tales of the book are all admirable; but 'The Monkey' is the one that best expresses her playful, refined, exquisitely wrought world, with its twisted sensuousness and unbridled fantasy. It is difficult to sum up this delightful jewel of a story in a few words. In a few pages, very different stories are told that are subtly interrelated. One of these is the intense struggle between two formidable women, the elegant Prioress of Closter Seven and the young, wild Athena, whom the Prioress wants her nephew to marry, employing to this end both licit and illicit methods, such as love philtres, deceit and rape. But the indomitable Prioress meets a will as inflexible as her own in the young giant Athena, who has been brought up wild in the woods of Hopballehus, who does not have the slightest qualm in knocking out two of the gallant Boris's teeth with a punch and wrestling with him, almost to the death, when the young man, encouraged by his aunt, tries to seduce her.

We will never know which of the two women wins in this contest because this story is abruptly interrupted just at the point where the reader is about to find out, by another story that, until then, had been stealthily sliding along, like a snake, underneath the earlier tale: the relationship between the Prioress of Closter Seven and a monkey, which had been given to her by her cousin, Admiral von Schreckenstein, on his return from Zanzibar, to which she was very attached. The violent appearance of the monkey – it comes into the Prioress's room by breaking her window, gripped by a fever that can only be sexual – when the Superior of the convent is about to spring her trap by forcing Athena to accept Boris as her husband, is one of the greatest moments of storytelling in the whole of literature. It is a hiatus, a sleight of hand, as brilliant as the carriage journey through the streets of Rouen that Emma and Léon take in *Madame Bovary*. We guess at what happens inside that carriage, but the narrator never tells us: he insinuates it, lets us guess, fuelling the imagination of the reader with his loquacious silence. A similar hidden fact structures this intense moment in 'The Monkey'. The clever description of the episode is full of superfluous detail and is silent about the essential point – the guilty relationship between the monkey and the Prioress – and, for that reason, this unspeakable relationship resonates and takes shape in the silence with as much or more force as the incredible scene witnessed by the terrified gaze of Athena and Boris. At the end of the tale, the sated monkey jumps onto a pedestal supporting the marble bust of the philosopher Immanuel Kant: this is quintessential Isak Dinesen, an example of her delirious craft.

Entertainment, amusement, diversion: many modern writers would be annoyed if they were reminded that these are also the responsibility of literature. When the *Seven Gothic Tales* appeared, fashion demanded that a writer should be the critical conscience of society or explore the possibilities of language. Commitment and experimentation are very respectable, of course, but when a fiction is boring, nothing can save it. Isak Dinesen's stories are sometimes flawed, sometimes too precious, but never boring. In this she was also an anachronism: for her, telling a tale was a form of enchantment, and boredom had to be avoided by any means – suspense, terrifying revelations, extraordinary events, sensationalist details, unlikely apparitions. Fantasy can suddenly submerge a story in a sea of other stories or else causes it to take a more unlikely direction. The reason for all these juggling acts is to surprise the reader, and this she never fails to do. Her tales take place in an imprecise realm, which is not the objective world, but nor is it the world of the fantastic. As happens also in Julio Cortázar's best stories, her reality draws from both these worlds and is different to each of them.

One of the constants features of her world is the changing identity of characters, who hide behind different names or sexes, and who often lead simultaneously two or more parallel lives. In this world of ontological instability, only objects and the natural world remain the same. Thus, for example, the Renaissance Cardinal in 'The Deluge at Nordeney' turns out at the end of the story to be the valet Kasparson, who killed his master and took his place. But the apotheosis of this switching of identities is Pellegrina Leoni, nicknamed Lucifera or Donna Quixotta de La Mancha, whose story appears among myriad of other stories in 'The Dreamers'. An opera singer who lost her voice through shock in a fire at La Scala in Milan during a performance of *Don Giovanni*, she has her admirers believe that she is dead. She is helped in her plan by her admirer and her shadow, the fabulously rich Jew Marcus Coroza, who follows her throughout the world, forbidden to speak to her or be seen by her, but always on hand to help her escape should an emergency arise. Pellegrina changes name, personality, lovers, countries – Switzerland, Rome, France – and profession – prostitute, artisan, revolutionary, aristocrat guarding the memory of General Zumalacárregui – and dies, finally, in an Alpine monastery, in a snowstorm, surrounded by four abandoned lovers who knew her at different times and in different guises, and only now discover her peripatetic identity thanks to Marcus Coroza. The Chinese box – stories within stories – is a technique used with admirable skill in this tale to piece together, like a jigsaw puzzle, through accounts that at first seem to have nothing in common, the fragmented and multiple existence of Pellegrina Leoni, will-o'-the-wisp, perpetual actress, made – like all Isak Dinesen's characters – not of flesh and blood but of dream, fantasy, grace and humour.

Isak Dinesen's language, like her culture and the topics she deals with, does not correspond to the models of the time; it is also a case apart, an inspired anomaly. When *Seven Gothic Tales* was published, its language disconcerted Anglo-Saxon critics with its slightly old-fashioned elegance, its exquisite, irreverent nature, its word play and sudden displays of erudition and its divorce from the English language spoken on the streets. But it was also disconcerting because of its humour, the delicate, cheerful, irony with which these tales refer to indescribable cruelty, vileness and savagery as if they were trivial, everyday occurrences. Isak Dinesen's humour is the great shock absorber of all the excesses of her world – be they human or spiritual – the ingredient that humanises the inhuman and gives a kindly appearance to what, without it, would cause repugnance or panic. There is nothing like reading her to prove the adage that anything can be told as long as one knows how to tell it.

Literature, as she conceived it, was something that writers of her time found horrifying: an escape from real life, an entertaining game. Today things have changed, and readers understand her better. By making literature a journey into the imaginary, the fragile Baroness de Rungstedlund was not evading any moral responsibility. On the contrary, she helped – by being distracting, bewitching and amusing – to placate that need that in human beings is as old as eating and clothing themselves: the hunger for unreality.

Paris, April 1999

L'Étranger

The Outsider Must Die

Along with *L'Homme révolté* (*The Rebel*), *L'Étranger* (*The Outsider*) is Camus's best book. It seems that the project was born in August 1937, albeit in a very vague way, when Camus was convalescing in a clinic in the Alps from one of the many relapses that he suffered following his attack of tuberculosis in 1930. In his *Cahiers* (*Notebooks*) he points out that he finished the novel in 1940. (But it was only published in 1942, by Gallimard, thanks to the support of André Malraux, who had been one of the literary models of the young Camus.)

The time and circumstances in which *The Outsider* was conceived are significant. The icy pessimism that pervades the references to society and the human condition in the story clearly stems in great part from the illness that weakened his fragile body over decades, and the anguished climate in Europe at the end of the inter-war years and at the outbreak of the Second World War.

The book was interpreted as a metaphor of the injustice of the world and of life, a literary illustration of that 'absurd sensibility' that Camus had described in *Le Mythe de Sisyphe* (*The Myth of Sisyphus*), an essay that appeared shortly after the novel. It was Sartre who best linked both texts, in a brilliant commentary on *The Outsider*. Meursault was seen as the incarnation of a man hurled into a senseless existence, the victim of social mechanisms that beneath the disguise of big words – The Law, Justice – were simply unjustifiable and irrational. Like the anonymous heroes of Kafka, Meursault personified the pathetic situation of the individual whose fate depends on forces that are uncontrollable as well as unintelligible and arbitrary.

But soon after there emerged a 'positive' interpretation of the novel: Meursault was seen as the prototype of authentic man, free from conventions, incapable of deception or self-deception, whom society condemns because he cannot tell lies or fake what he does not feel. Camus himself supported this reading of the character, writing in a prologue to a US edition of the novel:

> The hero of the book is condemned because he doesn't play the game . . . he refuses to lie. Lying is not only saying what isn't true. It is also, in fact especially, saying more than is true and, in the case of the human heart, saying more than one feels. We all do it, every day, to make life simpler. But, contrary to appearance, Meursault doesn't want to make life simpler. He says what he is, he refuses to hide his feelings and society immediately feels threatened . . . So one wouldn't be wrong in seeing *The Outsider* as the story of a man who, without any heroic pretensions, agrees to die for the truth.*

This is a perfectly valid interpretation – although, as we shall see, it is incomplete – and it has come to occupy almost canonical status in studies on Camus. *The Outsider* thus becomes a denunciation of the tyranny of conventions and of the lies on which social life is based. A martyr to the truth, Meursault goes to prison, is sentenced and presumably guillotined for his ontological inability to disguise his feelings and do what other men do: play a part. It is impossible for Meursault, for example, to pretend to feel more grief than he actually feels and to say the things that, in these circumstances, one expects a son to say. Nor can he – despite the fact that his life depends on it – pretend in court to feel remorse for the death that he has caused. This is what he is punished for, not his crime.

The critic who has developed this argument most convincingly is Robert Champigny in his book on the novel entitled *Sur un héros païen* (Gallimard, 1959). In it he states that Meursault is condemned

---

* This foreword to the American edition of *The Outsider* is reprinted as an afterword to the UK Penguin edition of the novel. See Albert Camus, *The Outsider*, Penguin, Harmondsworth, 1983, pp. 118–19.

because he rejects 'theatrical society', which he defines as a society not made up of natural beings but rather one in which hypocrisy holds sway. With his 'pagan' – that is, non-romantic, non-Christian – behaviour, Meursault is a living challenge to the 'collective myth'. His probable death by guillotine is, therefore, that of a free man, a heroic and edifying act.

This view of the novel seems to me partial and insufficient. There is no doubt that the way in which Meursault's trial is conducted is ethically and legally scandalous, a parody of justice, because what is condemned is not the killing of an Arab, but the antisocial behaviour of the accused, the way in which his psychology and morality is at variance with the norms of society. Meursault's behaviour shows us the inadequacies and defects of the administration of justice and allows us glimpses of the dirty world of journalism.

But to go from there to condemn the society that condemns him as being 'theatrical' and based on a 'collective myth' is really taking things too far. Modern society is no more theatrical than any other; all societies, without any possible exception, were, are, and will be theatrical, although the show that they put on will be different in each case. There can be no society, no form of coexistence, without a consensus that everyone in that society should respect certain forms or rituals. Without this agreement, there would be no 'society' but rather a jungle of completely free bipeds, where only the strongest would survive. With his behaviour, Meursault is also playing a role: that of a free individual in the extreme, who is indifferent to entrenched forms of sociability. The problem that the novel poses to us is rather: is Meursault's behaviour preferable to those that sit in judgement on him?

This is debatable. Despite what the author has implied, the novel draws no conclusion on this issue: it is left to the readers to decide.

The 'collective myth' is a tacit pact that allows individuals to live in a community. This has a price that men and women – whether they know it or not – must pay: they must relinquish absolute sovereignty, cut out certain desires, impulses and fantasies that could endanger others. The tragedy that Meursault symbolises is that of an individual whose freedom has been impaired to make life in society possible. It is this, the fierce, irrepressible individualism of Camus's character, that moves us and awakens our inchoate solidarity: in the depths of us all there is a nostalgic slave, a prisoner who would like to be as spontaneous, frank and antisocial as him.

But, at the same time, it is necessary to recognise that society is not wrong to identify Meursault as an enemy, as someone who would break up the community if his example were to become widespread.

His story is a painful but unequivocal demonstration of the need for 'theatre', for fiction, or, to put it more crudely, for lies in human relationships. Fake feelings guarantee social coexistence, for however empty and forced they might seem from an individual perspective, they are both substantive and necessary from a communitarian point of view. These fictitious feelings are conventions that cement the collective pact, like words, those sonorous conventions without which human communication would not be possible. If men were, like Meursault, pure instinct, not only would the institution of the family disappear, but also society in general, and men would end up killing each other in the same banal and absurd way that Meursault kills the Arab on the beach.

One of the great merits of *The Outsider* is the economy of the prose. When the book appeared, it was said that it emulated Hemingway's purity and brevity. But the Frenchman's language is much more premeditated and intellectual than the American's. It is so clear and precise that it does not seem written but spoken or, better still, heard. The absolute way in which the style is stripped of all adornments and self-indulgence is what contributes decisively to the verisimilitude of this implausible story. And here the characteristics of the writing and those of the character become intertwined: Meursault, too, is, transparent, direct and elemental.

What is most terrifying about him is his indifference to others. The great ideas or causes or issues – love, religion, justice, death, freedom – leave him cold, as does the suffering of others. The beating that his neighbour Raymond Sintes inflicts on his Arab lover does not provoke any feelings of sympathy; quite the opposite, he is prepared to offer him an alibi for the police. He does not do this out of affection or friendship but, one could say, out of mere negligence. By contrast, small details or certain daily episodes interest him, like the traumatic relationship between old Salmadano and his dog, and he gives his attention and even his sympathy to this. But the things that really move him have nothing to do with men and women, but rather with nature or with certain human landscapes that he has stripped of humanity and turned into sensorial realities: the hustle and bustle of his neighbourhood, the smells of summer, the beaches of burning sands.

He is an outsider in a radical sense, because he communicates better with things than with human beings. And, in order to maintain a relationship with humans, he must animalise them or objectify them. This is how he gets on so well with Marie, whose clothes, sandals and body strike a chord in him. The young woman does not awaken feelings in him, something durable; at best she awakens a string of desires. He is only interested in what is instinctive and animalistic in her. Meursault's world is not pagan, it is dehumanised.

What is curious is that, despite being antisocial, Meursault is not a rebel, because he has no concept of nonconformity. What he does is not tied to a principle or a belief that might lead him to defy the established order: that is just the way he is. He refuses the social pact, transgresses the rituals and forms that underpin collective life, in a natural way and without even any awareness of what he is doing (at least, until he is condemned). For those that are judging him, his passivity and lack of interest are clearly more serious than his crime. If he had ideas or values to justify his acts and behaviour, then perhaps the judges would have been more lenient. They could have contemplated the possibility of re-educating him, of persuading him to accept the norms of society. But, as he is, Meursault is incorrigible and cannot be reclaimed for society. Faced with him, all the limitations, excesses and absurdities that comprise the 'collective myth' or social pact are thrown into relief – everything that is false and absurd in communal life from the standpoint of an isolated individual of any description, not only someone as anomalous as Meursault.

When the attorney states that Meursault has nothing to do with 'a society whose laws he is unaware of', he is absolutely right. Obviously, from where the judge is sitting, Meursault is a kind of monster. But his case also reveals the monstrous, limiting aspects of society, since all societies, however open, always put obstacles and punishments in the way of the absolute freedom that each individual, deep down, aspires to.

Within the existential pessimism of *The Outsider*, however, there burns, albeit weakly, a flame of hope. There is a moment not of resignation but of lucidity that occurs in the beautiful final paragraph. Here, Meursault shakes off his anger towards the chaplain who had tried to domesticate him by offering to pray for him, and embraces, with serene confidence, his destiny as a man open to 'the tender indifference of the world'.

Camus's pessimism is not defeatist; on the contrary, it is a call to action or, more precisely, to rebellion. The reader leaves the pages of the novel probably with feelings for Meursault, but certainly convinced that the world is badly made and should change.

The novel does not conclude either explicitly or implicitly that since *things are the way they are* we should resign ourselves to accept a world organised by fanatics like the judge or pettifogging histrionic lawyers. We feel repugnance for both these characters. And we even find the chaplain disagreeable due to his inflexibility and lack of tact. With his disturbing behaviour, Meursault shows the precariousness and dubious morality of the conventions and rituals of society. His discordant attitude reveals the hypocrisy, lies, errors and injustices that social life entails. And at the same time it shows how the demands of living in a community lead to the mutilation or – to quote Freud, the great discoverer and explorer of the concept – the repression of individual sovereignty and certain instincts and desires.

Although the influence of Kafka is very apparent and although the philosophical novel or novel of ideas which were fashionable during the vogue of existentialism have now fallen into disrepute, *The Outsider* is still being read and discussed today, a time that is very different to the one in which Camus wrote. For this to be the case, there must be a more compelling reason than the fact that it is impeccably structured and beautifully written.

Like living beings, novels grow, and often age and die. Those that survive change skin and being, like snakes, or caterpillars that turn into butterflies. These novels say different things to new generations, very often things that the author had never thought of expressing. For readers today, above all in a Europe that is so much more prosperous, confident and hedonistic than the fearful, stunned and cataclysmic Europe in which *The Outsider* was first published, the solitary protagonist of this fiction can be appealing as an epicure, as a man at ease with his body and proud of his senses, who embraces his desires and elemental appetites without shame or pathos, as a natural right. The one seemingly lasting legacy of the revolution of May 1968 – that movement of idealistic, generous and confused young people at odds with their time and their society – is that human desires are now emerging from the hiding places where they had been confined by society, and are beginning to acquire acceptability.

In this new society that seems to be dawning, where desires have more freedom, Meursault would also have been punished for having killed a man. But no one would have condemned him to the guillotine, that obsolete museum piece, and, above all, no one would have been shocked by his visceral lack of interest in his fellow human beings or his rampant egotism. Should we feel pleased at this? Is it progress that the Meursault dreamed up by Camus half a century ago should appear to prefigure a contemporary attitude towards life? There is no doubt that Western civilisation has torn down many barriers and is now much freer and less repressive, with respect to sex, to the status of women, and to attitudes in general, than the society that (perhaps) cut off Meursault's head. But at the same time we cannot say that the freedom that has been won in different spheres has led to a marked increase in the quality of life, to an enrichment of culture for all or, at least, for the great majority. Quite the reverse, it would seem that in so many cases these barely won freedoms have been turned into forms of behaviour that cheapen and trivialise them, and into new forms of conformity by their fortunate beneficiaries.

The Outsider, like other good novels, was ahead of its time, anticipating the depressing image of a man who is not enhanced morally or culturally by the freedom that he enjoys. Instead this freedom has stripped him of spirituality, solidarity, enthusiasm and ambition, making him passive, unadventurous and instinctive, to an almost animalistic degree. I don't believe in the death penalty and I would not have condemned him to the scaffold, but if his head were chopped off by the guillotine, I would not shed a tear for him.

London, 5 June 1988

The Old Man and the Sea

Redemption through Courage

The story of *The Old Man and the Sea* seems very simple: after eighty-four days without any success, an old fisherman manages to catch a giant fish after a titanic struggle of two and a half days. He ties it to his skiff, but loses it the next day, in a no less heroic combat, to the jaws of the voracious sharks of the Caribbean. This is a classic motif in Hemingway's fictions: a man is caught up in a fight to the finish with an implacable adversary, after which, no matter whether he wins or loses, he achieves a greater sense of pride and dignity, becomes a better human being. But in none of his earlier novels and stories does this recurrent theme find as perfect an expression as in this tale, written in Cuba in 1951, with a limpid style, an impeccable structure and with a wealth of allusions and meanings to rival his best novels. He won the Pulitzer Prize for it in 1953 and also the Nobel Prize in 1954.

The apparent clarity of *The Old Man and the Sea* is deceptive, like certain biblical parables or Arthurian legends that, beneath their simplicity, contain complex religious and ethical allegories, historical references and psychological subtleties. As well as being a beautiful and moving fiction, this tale is also a representation of the human condition, according to Hemingway's vision. And, to some extent, it was also a resurrection for its author. It was written after one of the biggest failures of his literary career, *Across the River and into the Trees*, a novel full of stereotypes and rhetorical flourishes which seems to be written by a mediocre imitator of *The Sun Also*

Rises (*Fiesta*), and which the critics, above all in the United States, reviewed with ferocity, some of them, as respectable as Edmund Wilson, seeing in that novel the signs of the writer's irremediable decline. This cruel premonition was close to the mark, because the truth is that Hemingway had entered a period of waning creativity and output, ever more crippled by illness and alcohol, and with little energy for life. *The Old Man and the Sea* was the swansong of a great writer in decline and, thanks to this proud tale, he became again a great writer by producing what in the course of time – Faulkner saw this – would become, despite its brevity, the most enduring of all his books. Many of the works he wrote, which in their time seemed as if they would have a lasting effect, like *For Whom the Bell Tolls* and even the brilliant *The Sun Also Rises*, have lost their freshness and vigour and now seem dated, out of touch with current sensibilities, that reject their elemental macho philosophy and their often superficial picturesque nature. But, like a number of his stories, *The Old Man and the Sea* has survived the ravages of time without a wrinkle, and preserves intact its artistic seduction and its powerful symbolism as a modern myth.

It is impossible not to read the odyssey of the lone Santiago, battling against the gigantic fish and the merciless sharks along the Gulf Stream off the coast of Cuba, as a projection of the fight that Hemingway himself had begun to wage against the enemies that had already taken up residence within him. These enemies would first attack his mind and later his body, and would cause him, in 1961, impotent and having lost his memory and spirit, to blow his brains out with one of the guns that he so loved, and which had taken the lives of so many animals.

But what gives the adventure of the Cuban fisherman in those tropical waters its extraordinary breadth is that, by osmosis, the reader recognises in the struggle of old Santiago against the silent enemies that will end up defeating him, a description of something more constant and universal: that life is a permanent challenge, and that by facing up to this challenge with the bravery and dignity of the fisherman in the story, men and women can achieve a moral greatness, a justification for their existence, even though they might be defeated. This is the reason why when Santiago returns, exhausted and with bloody hands, to the little fishing village where he lives (Cojímar, although that name is not mentioned in the text) carrying the useless skeleton of the big fish eaten by the sharks, he seems to us to be someone who, through his recent experience, has gained enormously in moral stature, surpassing himself and transcending the physical and mental limitations of ordinary mortals. His story is sad but not pessimistic. Quite the contrary, he shows that there is always hope, that, even with the worst tribulations and setbacks, a man's behaviour can change defeat into victory and give meaning to his life. The day after his return, Santiago is more worthy of respect than he had been before setting sail, and that is what makes the child Manolín cry: his admiration for the resolute old man, even more than the affection and devotion that he feels for the man who taught him how to fish. This is the meaning of the famous phrase that Santiago utters to himself in the middle of the ocean and which has become the watchword of Hemingway's view of life: 'A man can be destroyed but never defeated.' Not all men, of course: only those – the heroes of his fictions: bullfighters, hunters, smugglers, adventurers of every hue – who, like the fisherman, are endowed with the emblematic virtue of the Hemingway hero: courage.

Now, courage is not always an admirable attribute, for it can be used irresponsibly or stupidly, like the lunatics for whom using violence or exposing themselves to violence is a way of feeling *manly*, that is, superior to their victims, whom they can flatten with their fists or wipe out with a bullet. This contemptible version of courage, a product of the most retrograde macho tradition, was not completely foreign to Hemingway, and it appears at times in his tales, above all in his accounts of hunting in Africa and his peculiar conception of the art of bullfighting. But, in its other aspect, courage is not found in exhibitionism and physical display, it is a discreet, stoical way of confronting adversity, without giving up or falling into self pity, like Jake Barnes in *The Sun Also Rises*, who endures in a quietly elegant way the physical tragedy that deprives him of love and sex, or like Robert Jordan in *For Whom the Bell Tolls* when faced by imminent death. Santiago in *The Old Man and the Sea* belongs to this noble lineage of brave men. He is a very humble man, very poor – he lives in a wretched shack and uses newspapers for bedding – and the butt of the village's jokes. And he is also alone: he lost his wife many years earlier, and his only company since then has been his memories of the lions that he saw walking along the beaches in Africa at night from deck of the tramp steamer where he worked, some American baseball players like Joe DiMaggio, and Manolín the boy who used to go fishing with him and who now, due to family pressure, has to help another fisherman. For him, fishing is not as it was for Hemingway and many of his characters, a sport, a pastime, a way to win prizes or of proving themselves by facing up to the challenges of the deep, but a vital necessity, a job which – through great hardship and effort – keeps him from dying of hunger. This context makes Santiago's struggle with the giant marlin extraordinarily human, as does the modesty and naturalness with which the old fisherman carries out his heroic deed: without boasting, without feeling a hero, like a man who is simply carrying out his duty.

There are many versions as to the origins of this story. According to Norberto Fuentes, who has made a detailed study of all the years that Hemingway spent in Cuba,* Gregorio Fuentes, who was for many years the skipper of Hemingway's boat, *El Pilar*, claimed to have given him the material for the story. Both would have witnessed a struggle similar to this that took place at the end of the forties, off the port of Cabañas, between a great fish and an old fisherman from Majorca. However, Fuentes also remarks that, according to some fishermen, Carlos Gutiérrez, Hemingway's first skipper, was the model for the story, while others attribute it to a local fisherman, Anselmo Hernández. But in his biography of Hemingway, Charles Baker points out that the central part of the story – the fight between the old fisherman and a great fish – had already been sketched out in April 1936, in an article published by Hemingway in *Esquire* magazine. Whatever the true origins of the story, whether it was completely invented or recreated from some living testimony, it is clearly the case that the central theme of the tale had

* *Hemingway en Cuba*, prologue by Gabriel García Márquez, Editorial Letras Cubanas, Havana, 1984.

been in search of its author ever since he began to write his first stories, because it distils, like an essence purified of all extraneous contamination, the vision of the world that he had been fashioning throughout his work. And doubtless for that reason he wrote it with all his very considerable stylistic control and technical mastery. For the context of the story, Hemingway used his experience: his passion for fishing and his long acquaintance with the village and fishermen of Cojímar: the factory, the Perico bar, La Terraza, where the neighbours drink and talk. The text is permeated with Hemingway's affection for, and identification with, the marine landscape and the men and women of the sea on the island of Cuba. *The Old Man and the Sea* pays them a great homage.

There is a turning point in the novel, a real qualitative leap, which turns Santiago's adventure, first with the fish and later with the sharks, into a symbol of the Darwinian struggle for survival, of the human condition, forced to kill in order to survive, and of the unexpected reserves of valour and resistance that human beings possess, which can be summoned when their honour is at stake. This chivalric concept of honour – respect for oneself, blind observance of a self-imposed moral code – is what finally makes the fisherman Santiago commit himself, as he does in his fight with the fish, to a struggle that, at an indefinable moment, is no longer just one more episode in his daily struggle to earn a living, and becomes instead an ordeal, a test in which the dignity and pride of the old man are being measured. And he is very conscious of this ethical and metaphysical dimension to the struggle – during his long soliloquy he exclaims, 'But I will show him what a man can do and what a man endures.' At this point in the tale, the story is no longer just recounting the adventure of a fisherman with a biblical name, it is recounting the whole adventure of humankind, summed up in that odyssey without witnesses or prizes, where cruelty and valour, need and injustice, and force and inventiveness are intertwined, along with the mysterious design that maps out the fate of each individual.

For this remarkable transformation in the story to occur – the shift from the particular to a universal archetype – there has been a gradual build-up of emotions and sensations, of hints and allusions that gradually extend the horizons of the tale to a point of complete universality. It manages this shift through the skill with which the story is written and constructed. The omniscient narrator narrates from very close to the protagonist but often lets him take over the account, disappearing behind the thoughts, exclamations and monologues through which Santiago distracts himself from monotony or anguish as he waits for the invisible fish that is dragging his boat along to get tired and come up to the surface so that he can kill it. The narrator is always completely persuasive, both when he describes objectively what is happening from a point removed, or when he allows Santiago to relieve him of this task. He achieves this persuasive power through the coherence and simplicity of his language that seems – only seems, of course – to be that of a man as simple and intellectually limited as the old fisherman, and through displaying a prodigious knowledge of all the secrets of navigation and fishing in the waters of the Gulf, something that fits the personality of Santiago like a glove. This knowledge explains the prodigious skill that Santiago displays in his struggle with the fish that, in this story, represents brute force that is defeated by the seafaring ingenuity and art of the old man.

These technical details help to reinforce the realist effect of a story which is in fact more symbolic or mythical than realist, as do the few but effective images that are used to map concisely the life and character of Santiago: those lions on the African beaches, those games of baseball that brighten up his life and the extraordinary legend of the striker DiMaggio (who, like him, was the son of a fisherman). Apart from being very believable, all of this shows the narrowness and primitiveness of the fisherman's life, which makes his achievement all the more remarkable and praiseworthy. For the person who, in *The Old Man and the Sea*, represents man at his best, in one of those exceptional circumstances in which, through his will and moral conscience, he manages to rise above his condition and rub shoulders with the mythological heroes and gods, is a wretched, barely literate old man who is treated as a joke by the village because of his age and lack of money. In a highly favourable review soon after the book was published, Faulkner stated that in this novel, Hemingway had 'dis-

Lolita

Lolita Thirty Years On

Lolita made Nabokov rich and famous, but the scandal surrounding its publication created a misunderstanding that is still with us today. Now that the beautiful nymphet is approaching, horror of horrors, forty, it is time to locate her where she belongs, as one of the most subtle and complex literary creations of our time. That does not mean, of course, that it is not also a provocative book.

But the fact that the first readers of the novel could only see the provocative parts and not its subtlety – something that is now apparent to any average reader – shows us how difficult it is for the true worth of a really original book to be appreciated. Four US publishing houses rejected the manuscript of *Lolita* before Nabokov gave it to Maurice Girodias at Olympia Press, a Parisian publisher that brought out books in English and had become famous for being subjected to numerous court appearances and book seizures for pornography and indecency. (Its catalogue was a bizarre mixture of cheap pornography and genuine artists like Henry Miller, William Burroughs and J. P. Donleavy). The novel appeared in 1955, and one year later it was banned by the French Ministry of the Interior. By then it had already circulated widely – Graham Greene started up a polemic by declaring it the best book of the year – and it had gained an aura of being a *maudit* novel. It never really managed to escape from this *maudit* label, and to some extent it deserves it, but not in the way we usually understand the term. But it was only after 1958, when the US edition appeared, alongside dozens of others throughout the world, that the book made an impact that spread much further than the numbers of its readers. In a short space of time a new term, a 'Lolita', appeared for a new concept: the child-woman, emancipated without realising it, an unconscious symbol of the revolution taking place in contemporary society. To some extent *Lolita* is one of the milestones, and one of the causes, of the age of sexual tolerance, the flouting of taboos by young people in the United States and in Western Europe, which would reach its apogee in the sixties. The nymphet was not born with Nabokov's character. It existed, without doubt, in the dreams of perverts and in the blind and tremulous anxieties of innocent girls, and a changing moral climate was beginning to give it credence. But, thanks to the novel, it took on a distinct form, shook off its nervous clandestine existence and gained the keys of the city.

What is extraordinary is that it is a novel by Nabokov that provoked such turmoil, affecting the behaviour of millions of people, and becoming part of modern mythology. Because it is difficult to imagine among the writers of this century anyone less interested in popular and contemporary issues – even in reality itself, a word that, he wrote, meant nothing if it were not placed between inverted commas – than the author of *Lolita*. Born in 1899, in Saint Petersburg, into a Russian aristocratic family – his paternal grandfather had been the Justice Minister of two Tsars and his father a liberal politician who had been assassinated by monarchist extremists in Berlin – Vladimir Vladimirovich Nabokov had received a refined education that made him a polyglot. He had two English nannies, a Swiss governess and a French tutor, and he studied in Cambridge before going into exile in Germany following the October Revolution. Although his most daring book, *Pale Fire*, came out in 1962, by the time *Lolita* appeared he had published most of his work. It was a vast, but little-known, body of work: novels, poems, plays, critical essays, a biography of Nikolai Gogol, translations into and out of Russian. It had been written firstly in Russian, then in French and finally in English. Its author lived in Germany, then in France, before finally opting for the United States, where he earned a living as a university professor and pursued, in the summers, his second great love: entomology, in particular, lepidopterology. He published several scientific articles and was, it seems, the first descriptor of three butterflies: *Neonympha maniola nabokov*, *Echinargus nabokov* and *Cyclargus nabokov*.

This work, which, thanks to the success of *Lolita*, would be revived in multiple re-editions and translations, is 'literary' to a degree that only one other contemporary of Nabokov – Jorge Luis Borges – would manage to achieve. By 'literary' I mean entirely constructed out of pre-existing literatures and possessing an exquisite intellectual and verbal refinement. *Lolita* has all these hallmarks. But in addition, and this was the great novelty within Nabokov's work as a whole, it is a novel in which the almost demonic complexity of its craftsmanship is garbed in an apparently simple and attractively brilliant story: the seduction of a young girl of twelve years seven months – Dolores Haze, Dolly, Lo or Lolita – by her stepfather, an obsessive forty-year-old Swiss man known only by a pseudonym, Humbert Humbert, and the passage of their love through the length and breadth of the United States.

A great work of literature always provokes conflicting readings; it is a Pandora's box in which each reader discovers different meanings, nuances and even stories. *Lolita* has bewitched the most superficial readers at the same time as it has seduced, through its torrent of ideas and allusions and the delicacy of its style, the most demanding of readers who approach each book with the insolent challenge that a young man once made to Cocteau: *Étonnez-moi!* (Surprise me!)

In its most explicit version, the novel is Humbert Humbert's written confession to the judges that are going to try him for murder, of his predilection for precocious girls, that began with his childhood in Europe and reached its climax and satisfaction in Ramsdale, a remote small town in New England. There, with the cynical intention of having easier access to her daughter Lolita, H.H. marries a relatively well-off widow, Mrs Charlotte Becher Haze. Chance, in the form of a car, facilitates Humbert Humbert's plans, knocking over his wife and placing the young orphan literally and legally in his hands. The semi-incestuous relationship lasts for a couple of years, until Lolita runs away with a playwright and scriptwriter, Clare Quilty, whom Humbert Humbert kills after a tortuous search for the couple. This is the crime for which he is going to be tried when he begins to write the manuscript that, within the lying tradition of Cide Hamete Benengeli, he calls *Lolita*.

Humbert Humbert tells the story with the pauses, suspense, false leads, ironies and ambiguities of a narrator skilled in the art of keeping the curiosity of the reader constantly aroused. His story is scandalous, but not pornographic or even erotic. There is not the slightest pleasure taken in the description of sexual activities – a sine qua non of pornography – nor is there a hedonistic vision that could justify the excesses of the narrator-character in the name of pleasure. Humbert Humbert is not a libertine or a sensualist: he is scarcely even an obsessive. His story is scandalous, above all, because he feels it and presents it as such, because he keeps talking about his 'madness' and his 'monstrosity' (these are his words). It is the protagonist's account of himself that gives his adventure its sense of being unhealthy and morally unacceptable, rather than the age of his victim who, after all, is only a year younger than Shakespeare's Juliet. And what further aggravates his offence and deprives him of the reader's sympathy is his unpleasantness and arrogance, the contempt that he seems to feel for all men and women, including those beautiful, semi-pubescent, little creatures that so inflame his desires.

Perhaps even more than the seduction of the young nymph by a cunning man, the most provocative aspect of the novel is the way it reduces all of humanity to laughable puppets. Humbert Humbert's monologue constantly mocks institutions, professions and everyday routines, from psychoanalysis – one of Nabokov's pet hates - to education and the family. When filtered through his corrosive pen, all the characters become stupid, pretentious, ridiculous, predictable and boring. It has been said that the novel is, above all, a ferocious critique of middle-class America, a satire of its tasteless motels, its naïve rituals and inconsistent values, a literary abomination that Henry Miller termed the 'air-conditioned nightmare'. Professor Harry Levin has also argued that *Lolita* was a metaphor that refers to the feelings of a European who, after having fallen madly in love with the United States, is brutally disappointed by that country's lack of maturity.

I am not sure that Nabokov invented this story with symbolic intentions. My impression is that within him, as in Borges, there was a sceptic who was scornful of modernity and of life, and who observed both with irony and distance, from a refuge of ideas, books and fantasies, where both writers could remain protected, removed from the world through their prodigious inventive games that diluted reality into a labyrinth of words and phosphorescent images. For both writers, who were so similar in the way they understood culture and approached the task of writing, the distinguished art they created was not a criticism of the existing world but a way of disembodying life, dissolving it into a gleaming mirage of abstractions.

And for anyone who wishes to go beyond the main plot of the novel, and consider its mysteries, try to solve its puzzles, work out its allusions and recognise the parodies and pastiches of its style, *Lolita* can be read as a baroque and subtle substitute for existence. This is a challenge that the reader can accept or reject. In any event, a purely anecdotal reading is very enjoyable in itself. But anyone who is prepared to read it differently discovers that *Lolita* is a bottomless well of literary references and linguistic juggling tricks, which form a tight network and are, perhaps, the real story that Nabokov wanted to tell. A story as intricate as that of his novel *The Defence* (which appeared in Russian in 1930), whose hero is a mad chess player who invents a new defensive game, or that of *Pale Fire*, a fiction that adopts the appearance of a critical edition of a poem and whose hieroglyphic story emerges, seemingly at variance with the narrator, through the interplay of the verses of the poem and the notes and commentary of its editor.

The search for the hidden treasures of *Lolita* has given rise to many books and university theses in which the humour and playful spirit with which both Nabokov and Borges transformed their (real or fictitious) erudition into art is almost always sadly lacking.

The linguistic acrobatics of the novel are very difficult to translate. Some, like the quotations in French in the original, just lie there, mischievous and rude. One example of many: the strange hendecasyllable that Humbert Humbert recites when he is preparing to kill the man who snatched Lolita away from him. To what and to whom does this refer: *Réveillez-vous Laqueue, il est temps de mourir*? Is it an actual literary quotation, or one made up, like so many in the book? Why does the narrator call Clare Quilty *Laqueue*? Or is he inflicting the name on himself? In an interesting book, *Keys to Lolita*, Professor Carl L. Proffer has solved the enigma. It is, quite simply, a convoluted obscenity. *La queue*, a tail, is French slang for a phallus; to die means to ejaculate. So the verse is an allegory that condenses, with its classic rhythm, a premonition of the crime that Humbert Humbert is about to commit, and his reason for the murder (the fact that the phallic Clare Quilty has possessed Lolita).

Sometimes the allusions or premonitions are simple digressions, for Humbert Humbert's solipsistic amusement, that do not affect the development of the story. But on other occasions they have a meaning that alters the story in significant ways. This is true, for example, of all the bits of information and references regarding the most disturbing character of all, who is not Lolita or the narrator, but the furtive playwright who is fond of the Marquis de Sade, the libertine, drunk, drug-addicted and, according to his own confession, semi-impotent Clare Quilty. His appearance disrupts the novel, sending the story in a hitherto unforeseeable direction, introducing a Dostoevskian theme: that of the double. It is thanks to him that we suspect that the whole story might be a mere schizophrenic invention by Humbert Humbert, who, the reader has been told, has spent several periods in mental asylums. As well as stealing Lolita away and dying, the function of Clare Quilty seems to be to place an alarming question mark over the credibility of the (assumed) narrator.

Who is this strange subject? Before materialising in the reality of the fiction, when he takes Lolita away from the hospital at Elphistone, he has already been infiltrating the text as a result of Humbert Humbert's persecution mania. There is a car that appears and disappears, like a will-o'-the-wisp, a hazy outline, lost in the distance, on a hill, after a game of tennis with the child-woman, and myriad signs that only the meticulous and ever-alert neurosis of the narrator can decipher. And later, when, on the trail of the fugitives, Humbert Humbert begins his extraordinary recapitulation of his travels across the United States – an exercise of sympathetic magic that attempts to revive the two years of happiness lived with Lolita, repeating their journey and the hotels they had stayed in – he discovers at every stage disconcerting traces and messages from Clare Quilty. They reveal an almost omniscient knowledge of the life, culture and obsessions of the narrator and a sort of subliminal complicity between the two. But are we talking about two people? What they have in common far outweighs what separates them. They are more or less the same age and they share the same desires for young girls in general, and Lolita Haze in particular, as well as both being writers (albeit with different degrees of success). But the most remarkable symbiosis can be found in the magic tricks that they perform at a distance, in which Lolita is merely a pretext, the elegant and secret communication that turns life into literature, revolutionising topography and the urban landscape with the magic wand of language, through the invention of small towns and accidents that trigger literary associations and surnames that generate poetic associations according to a very strict code that only they are capable of employing.

The culminating moment in the novel is not Humbert Humbert's first night of love – that is kept to a minimum and is almost a hidden detail – but the delayed and choreographed killing of Clare Quilty. In this extraordinarily intense, virtuoso description, which is a mixture of humour, drama, strange details and enigmatic allusions, every certainty that we had built around the fictive reality of those pages begins to teeter, suddenly riddled by doubt. What is happening here? Are we witnessing the conversation between the killer and his victim or rather the nightmarish doubling of the narrator? It is a possibility that is implied in the text: that, at the end of this process of psychic and moral disintegration, defeated by nostalgia and remorse, Humbert Humbert breaks, *stricto sensu*, into two halves, the lucid and recriminatory consciousness that observed and judged his own actions, and his defeated, abject body, the seat of that passion that he surrendered to without, however, surrendering to pleasure and indulgence. Is it not himself, that part that he detests about himself, that Humbert Humbert kills in this phantasmagoric scene, in which the novel, in a dialectical leap, seems to desert the conven-

The Tin Drum

The Drumroll

I read *The Tin Drum* for the first time, in English, in the sixties, in a neighbourhood in the suburbs of London where I lived among quiet shopkeepers who turned off the lights in their houses at ten at night. In this state of limbo tranquillity, Grass's novel was an exciting adventure, whose pages reminded me, as soon as I plunged into them, that life was also disorder, uproar, guffaws, absurdity.

I have reread it now in very different conditions, at a time when, in an unpremeditated and accidental way, I have found myself caught up in a whirlwind of political activities, at a particularly difficult moment in my country's history. In between a debate and a street rally, after a demoralising meeting where the world was changed by words, and nothing happened, or at the end of dangerous days, when stones were hurled and shots were fired. In these circumstances as well, the Rabelaisian odyssey of Oskar Matzerath with his drum and glass-shattering voice was a compensation and a refuge. Life was also this: fantasy, words, animated dreams, literature.

When *The Tin Drum* came out in Germany in 1959, its immediate success was attributed to different reasons. George Steiner wrote that, for the first time since the lethal experience of Nazism, a German writer dared face up, resolutely and clearly, to the sinister past of his country and submit it to an implacable critical dissection. It was also said that this novel, with its uninhibited, frenetic language, sparkling with invention, dialect and barbarisms, revived a vitality and a freedom that German language had lost after twenty years of totalitarian contamination.

Both explanations are probably correct. But from our current perspective, as the novel approaches the age at which, figuratively, its extraordinary protagonist begins to write – thirty years old – another reason appears as fundamental for understanding the impact that the book has continued to make on its readers: its enormous ambition, the voracity with which it looks to swallow up the world, history past and present, the most disparate experiences of the human zoo, and transmute them into literature. This colossal appetite to tell everything, to embrace the whole of life in a fiction, which can be found in all the major achievements of the genre and which, above all, defined the writing of literature in the century of the novel, the nineteenth century, can be found only infrequently in our age, which is full of temperate, timid novelists for whom the idea of writing with the ambition of Balzac or Stendhal seems naïve: don't movies do all that, and much better?

No, they do not do it better; they do it differently. Even in the century of the great cinematographic narratives, the novel can be a *deicide*, can propose such a minute and vast reconstruction of reality that it seems to compete with the Creator, breaking up and re-forming – correcting – what He created. In an emotional essay, Grass names Alfred Döblin as his master and model. Döblin, somewhat belatedly, is beginning to be recognised as the great writer that indeed he was. And without doubt *Berlin Alexanderplatz* has some of the tumultuous, fresh effervescence that makes *The Tin Drum* such a lively fresco of human history. But there is no doubt that the creative ambition of the disciple in this case far excelled that of the master, and that to find affiliations we must look to the best examples of the genre, where novelists, in the grip of an exaggerated and naïve frenzy, did not hesitate in opposing the real world with an imaginary world in which this real world is both captured and negated, summarised and abjured like an exorcism.

Poetry is intense; the novel is extensive. The number, the quantity, is an integral part of its quality because every fiction takes place and develops in time, it is time being made and remade under the gaze of the reader. In all the masterpieces of the genre, this quantitative factor – to be abundant, to multiply and to endure – is always present: generally a great novel is also a big novel. *The Tin Drum* belongs to this illustrious genealogy, as a world that is large and complex, brimming with diversity and contrasts, is erected in front of our eyes as readers, to the beat of a drum. But despite its vividness and sheer size, the novel never appears as a chaotic, dispersed world, without a centre (as occurs in *Berlin Alexanderplatz* or in the Dos Passos trilogy, *U.S.A.*), because the perspective from which the fictive world is seen and represented gives consistency and coherence to its baroque disorder. This perspective is that of the protagonist and narrator Oskar Matzerath, one of the most fertile inventions of modern narrative. He supplies an original point of view that suffuses everything he describes with originality and irony – thus separating the fictive reality from its historical model – as well as embodying, in his impossible nature, in his anomalous condition, between fantasy and reality, a metaphor for the novel itself: a sovereign world apart in which, however, the concrete world is refracted in essence; a lie in whose folds a profound truth can be seen.

But the truths that a novel makes visible are rarely as simple as those formulated by mathematics or as unilateral as those of certain ideologies. They are usually, like most human experiences, relative; they form imprecise entities in which the rule and its exception, or the thesis and antithesis are inseparable or have a similar moral weight. If there is a symbolic message embedded in the convulsive historic moments that Oskar Matzerath narrates, what might that be? That his decision, at three years old, not to grow any more, is a rejection of the world that he would have to be part of as a normal person, and that this decision, to judge by the horrors and absurdity of this world, is clearly a wise one. His smallness confers on him a kind of extraterritoriality, minimising him against the excesses and responsibilities of other citizens. His insignificant stature offers Oskar a marginal and thus privileged perspective from which to see and judge everything happening around him: that of the innocent. This moral condition becomes in the novel a physical attribute: Oskar, who is not involved in what is happening around him, is clothed with invisible armour that allows him to travel unscathed through the most risky places and situations, as becomes clear in one of the key moments in the novel: the siege of the Polish Post Office at Danzig. There, in the midst of the machine guns and the butchery, the little narrator observes, makes ironic comments and tells the story with the quiet assurance of one who knows that he is safe.

This unique perspective gives Oskar's testimony its very original tone, which is a mixture, like an exotic blend of mysterious fragrances, of strangeness and tenderness, patriotic irreverence and tremulous delicacy, outlandishness, ferocity and jokes. Like the impossible combination of Oskar's two intellectual totems – Goethe and Rasputin – his voice is an anomaly, a device that stamps on the world that it describes – or rather that it invents – its own very personal seal.

And yet, despite his evident artificiality, his existence as a metaphor, the little midget that beats his drum and tells the apocalyptic story of a Europe bled white and torn apart by totalitarian stupidity and war, does not have a nihilistic animosity towards life. Quite the reverse. What is surprising is that while his narration offers a relentless critique of his contemporaries, it expresses at the same time a warm sympathy for this world, which is clearly the only thing of importance to him. From his monstrous and defenceless smallness, Oskar Matzerath manages, in the worst moments, to transmit to us a natural and uncomplicated love for the good and entertaining things that the world also offers: play, love, friendship, food, adventure, music. Perhaps because of his size, Oskar has a much greater sensitivity to elemental things, to what is closer to the earth and to human clay. From down there, where he is confined, he discovers – like that night when, hidden under the family table, he observes the hesitant, adulterous movements of his parents' legs and feet – that in its most direct and simple, in its most earthy and coarse forms, life contains tremendous possibilities and is full of poetry. In this metaphorical novel, all this is wonderfully represented in a recurrent image in Oskar's memory: the warm encampment offered by his grandmother Ana Kolaiczek's four skirts when she squats down, which gives to those that seek shelter there an almost magical feeling of safety and contentment. The simplest and most rudimentary of acts, when passed through Oskar's Rabelaisian voice, can transubstantiate into pleasure.

A Rabelaisian voice? Yes, in its jocundity and its vulgarity, its quick-wittedness and its limitless freedom. Also, in the disorder and exaggeration of its fantasy and the intellectualism that lies beneath the cloak of vulgarity. When we read in translation, however good it may be (as in the case of the book I am reading), something of the texture and the flavour of the original is always lost. But in the case of *The Tin Drum*, the almost convulsive force of the account, the big, torrential voice of the narrator, breaks through the barriers of language and reaches us with overwhelming force. It has the vitality of the popular but, like *El Buscón*, it has almost as many ideas as images, and a complex structure organises this apparently chaotic monologue. Although the point of view is stubbornly individual, the collective is always present, the everyday and the historic, small, insignificant episodes of work or home life or major events – war, invasion, pillage, the reconstruction of Germany – albeit metabolised through the deforming prism of the narrator. All the values usually writ large, like patriotism, heroism or unselfishness with respect to a feeling or a cause, when filtered through Oskar, break and shatter like the way his voice shatters glass, and then appear as the senseless whims of a society bent on its own destruction. But, curiously, although we feel that this society is doomed, it is still, as it slides towards ruin, lively and human, full of people and things – landscapes above all – that we can empathise with. This is, without doubt, the greatest achievement of the novel: to make us feel, from the perspective of the humble people that are almost always the main protagonists, that life, in the midst of horror and alienation, is worth living.

Unlike the great stylistic versatility of the novel, which is full of verve and inventiveness, the structure is very simple. Locked up in a sanatorium, Oskar narrates episodes that refer to a near or an immediate past, with occasional flights to the remote past (like the amusing synthesis of the different invasions and dynasties in the history of Danzig). The story moves continually from present to past and vice versa, as Oskar remembers or fantasises, and this technique sometimes becomes rather mechanical. But there is another shift that takes place, that is less obvious: the narrator sometimes talks in the first person and at other times in the third person, as if the little dwarf with the drum were someone else. What is the reason for this schizophrenic doubling of the narrator, whom we see at times, in the course of a single sentence, approach us with the open intimacy of one speaking from the 'I' perspective and then retreat into the shadow of someone who is spoken or narrated by another person? In this novel, which is full of allegories and metaphors, it would not be wise to see the changing identity of the narrator as a mere stylistic flourish. It is clearly another symbol that represents the inevitable doubling or duplication that Oskar suffers (that all novelists suffer?) when he is, simultaneously, both narrator and narrated, the person who writes and invents and the subject of his own invention. Oskar's condition, split in two in this way, being and not being who he is in what he narrates, is a perfect representation of the novel: a genre that is and is not life, that expresses the world by turning it into something different, that tells the truth by lying.

Baroque, expressionist, committed, ambitious, *The Tin Drum* is also the novel of a city. Danzig rivals Oskar Matzerath as the protagonist of the book. The setting is described in both clear and elusive terms because, like a living being, it is continually changing, fashioning and refashioning itself in space and in time. The almost tangible presence of Danzig, where most of the story takes place, helps to give the novel its materiality, its palpable sense of living and breathing, despite the extravagance and even deliriousness of many of its episodes.

What city is this? Is the Danzig of the novel a true city that Grass has transposed like a historical document, or is it another product of his vibrant imagination, something as original and arbitrary as the little man whose voice shatters glass? The answer is not simple, for in novels – in good novels – as in life, things tend to be ambiguous and contradictory. Grass's Danzig is a centaur-city with its hooves buried in the mud of history and with its torso floating among the mists of poetry.

There is a mysterious link between the novel and the city, a relationship that does not exist in the case of theatre and poetry. Unlike these genres, which flourish in all cultures and in rural civilisations before the rise of the city, the novel is an urban plant which seemingly can only germinate and propagate in streets and neighbourhoods, in commerce and in offices, among the crowded, variegated, diverse throng of the city. Lukács and Goldmann attribute this link to the bourgeoisie, the social class in which the novel had found not only its natural audience, but also its source of inspiration, its primary resource, its mythology and its values: for is not the bourgeois century the century, par excellence, of the novel? However, this class-based interpretation of the genre does not take into account the illustrious precursors we find in medieval and Renaissance fiction – the romances of chivalry, the pastoral novel, the picaresque novel – where the genre has a popular audience (the illiterate 'common people' listened, spellbound, to the deeds of the likes of Amadis and Palmerín which were narrated in the markets and squares), as well as, in some instances, a courtly and aristocratic audience. The novel is urban in a comprehensive, totalising, sense: it embraces and expresses equally all the classes that together comprise urban society. The key word here is perhaps 'society'. However solitary and introverted they might be, characters in novels always need the backcloth of society in order to be believable and persuasive; if this multiple presence is not insinuated and does not operate in some way in the novel, then it becomes abstract and unreal (which is not the same as 'fantastic': the nightmares imagined by Kafka, even though they have few characters, are always firmly rooted in the social world). And there is nothing that symbolises the idea of society better than the city, the space of many people, a shared world, a gregarious reality by definition. That this should be the chosen ground of the novel is thus coherent with the novel's main aim, which is to simulate the life of the individual in a social context.

The city of Danzig in *The Tin Drum* has the immaterial consistency of dreams and, at times, the solidity of an artefact or of geography; it is a mobile entity whose past is embedded in the present, a hybrid and a fantasy, whose borders are uncertain and figurative. It is a city

Deep Rivers

Fantasy and Magic

In 1958, José María Arguedas published *Deep Rivers*, his best novel. Although it was deeply rooted in personal experience – the journeys through the mountains with his father, who was a lawyer, the periods of solitude when his father was travelling, the time he spent at the religious Miguel Grau School in Abancay, his memories of the Indian communes in Viseca, where he lived happily after escaping from his stepmother's house, and his memories of the large estates in Apurímac that he later visited – it is more than an autobiographical novel. It is a story so skilfully reworked that it has depersonalised the author's memories and offers instead a sovereign narrative world, which is what the best fictions always achieve. The book is seductive because of its elegant style, its delicate sensibility and the range of emotions with which it recreates the world of the Andes. Although the novel includes the different social groups in the sierra, at its heart are the cruel and innocent ceremonies of puberty and the early steps that a boy must take into the adult world, which is made up of rigid hierarchies and imbued with violence and racism.

The protagonist of the novel is a boy torn between two hostile worlds. The child of white parents, brought up by Indians and then returned to the world of the whites, Ernesto the narrator is a misfit, a solitary figure and also someone in a privileged position to evoke the tragic opposition between these worlds. At the beginning of the novel, in the shadow of the stone walls in Cuzco where the Indian and the Spanish worlds meet in harsh alliance, as they do in Ernesto (and in José María Arguedas), the boy's fate is sealed. He will not change, and throughout the story he is disturbed by the thousand and one forms of subtle or not so subtle conflict between two races and two cultures in the Andes. Subjectively identified with the Indians who brought him up and who, for him, represent a paradise lost, and yet far removed from them because of his social position that objectively places him among the whites in Abancay, whose views on the Indian population are anathema to him, the world around him poses an impossible dilemma for Ernesto. One has to live, of course, and since Ernesto cannot escape his predicament, he finds ways to make it bearable. He has two weapons at his disposal: the first is to take refuge in an inner world, in fantasy. The second is a desperate desire to communicate with the world outside of men and women: with nature. For this pariah child, with no roots in society, always in exile, the world is not rational but essentially absurd. That is why he displays a fatalistic irrationality and idealises plants, objects and animals, attributing to them not just human but also divine properties: he makes them sacred.

Every magical-religious vision – like that of Ernesto – is irrational, not scientific, because it presupposes the existence of a secret order within the natural and human order, outside rational and intelligent understanding. Such a world can be very refined, but it will always be *primitive* if we accept the premise that the transition from the primitive and tribal world to the beginning of modern culture is based, precisely, on the advent of rationality.

In *Deep Rivers*, as in all of Arguedas's work, there is a desire for a primitive, sociable world: the 'tribe' that Karl Popper talks about in *The Open Society and Its Enemies*, a collective not yet split up into individuals, magically immersed in nature, strongly united by a solidarity that stems from a shared faith in the same gods, in rituals and ceremonies practiced in common. This is contrasted to a caricature of the modern world in which individuals – like Ernesto in this novel – find themselves abandoned and alienated because they have lost the umbilical chord that binds them to society and are at the mercy of hostile forces that at every moment threaten to destroy them.

The magical-religious world depicted in the novel might be irrational and primitive, but it is very persuasive. This speaks well of the creative talent of Arguedas and not necessarily, as ideological critics would have us believe, of his skill as an ethnographer and folklore specialist. He doubtless had these skills when he worked as a researcher, but, fortunately, when he came to write novels, he did so with enough freedom to escape the rigid limitations that any 'scientific knowledge' of the Andes would impose. As a novelist and short-story writer, Arguedas built a world which was based on his 'scientific' knowledge of the Quechua world and on his own personal demons – his frustrations and desires, his suffering, emotions, passions, dreams and resentments – as well as on the flight of his fantasy. For that reason *his* Andean world is different to that of other novelists who wrote about the Andes and its traditional cultures, and is also very different to the historical and sociological reality of the Quechuan people. To read Arguedas's narratives as an ethno-historical manual, or through the rigid prism of political ideology, is to miss what is new about it: the creation of an imaginary world which has transformed into myth a heterogeneous material made up of personal memories, nostalgia and disappointments along with historical and social realities and a good dose of invention, and has transcended its 'model' – its space, its time and its sources – to live the autonomous life of those fictions that can persuade all types of readers of their uncertain truths, whose magic, made up of words and dreams, can help them identify and put up with their own particular truths.

Ernesto is also resistant to what other people believe and adore: his faith is not their faith, his God is not their God. Within this Christian world in which he is immersed, the solitary child establishes a personal religion, a surreptitious cult, a personal divinity. That is why he is so hostile to the ministers of the opposing faith: the head of his boarding school, a priest, the 'saint' of Abancay, is presented as the incarnation of human duplicity and injustice. A wave of fury breaks over the novel when this character appears. The masochistic speech that he delivers to the Indians in Patibamba and his unctuous and lying sermon to placate the women in revolt verge on caricature. Not even the local caciques who exploit the Indians or the soldiers that repress them are as harshly depicted in *Deep Rivers* as the priest who makes victims become resigned to their lot and opposes rebellion with dogma. This is understandable: the site of the novel, as we have said, is *interior* reality, where the religious element can exercise its subtle powers. Local caciques only appear fleetingly, although the problem of feudalism in the Andes is frequently referred to and is represented allegorically in the town of Abancay.

From his inner refuge, Ernesto participates in the struggle between the Indians and their masters. Two fundamental episodes in the novel refer to this age-old war: the uprising of the market women and the spread of the plague. These are the two moments of greatest intensity that send a current of energy throughout the book. The lava that flows from these volcanic craters seems to engulf the narrator, turning the timid retiring child into another person: in these episodes nostalgia is overcome by passion. For when the market women rebel and the citizens of Abancay take to their houses in terror, Ernesto is out on the street, happy and excited, singing alongside them in Quechua. It is curious how a novel that is so focused on the inner world, that draws so strongly on the contemplation of nature and on the unhappy loneliness of a child, can suddenly express an intolerable violence. Arguedas was not too bothered by the technical aspects of the novel, which is sometimes weak in its construction, but his intuition guided him to make the best use of his materials. These incidents of violence are structurally successful. From the first time that I read *Deep Rivers* I still remember the impact that these episodes had, lighting up the story like a fire: the image of the young girl in the plague-ridden town, with her 'tiny sex covered with enormous, white, insect-bitten swellings'*, or the lice that cover the heads and the bodies of those dying from the plague.

In the end, are we talking about a tormented conscience? A child beset by impossible contradictions that isolate him from others and imprison him in past realities kept alive by memory? A predominance of the natural order over the social order? A magical-religious world that owes as much to the personal fantasies and obsessions of the author as it does to Quechuan culture? People have read the

* *Deep Rivers*, University of Texas Press, Austria, p. 227

novel as a sort of distorted testimony, and have accused it of being politically immature or else have tried to impose their own interpretations and read it as an explicit and orthodox description of the struggle of the peasantry against feudalism and exploitation in the Andes. Arguedas himself did this, in his final years, at a time of increasing public demonstrations of political correctness: he added to the confusion by declaring to the First Meeting of Peruvian Writers, in Arequipa, that the entrance of the plague-ridden Indians from Patibamba into the city of Abancay was a literary premonition of the peasant uprisings headed by Hugo Blanco, years later. But these a-posteriori readings of the author are quite unnecessary: we are dealing with a novel, not an illustration of social struggles in the Peruvian sierra; a fiction that encompasses much more than the social problems of a historical moment, although these problems are not avoided. They are dealt with in that veiled, mythologised manner in which literature reflects the world. It is perfectly valid to ask any writer dealing with the Andes that they should pay heed to the injustices in the region, but not proscribe how they should do this. All the horror of the Andean region is contained in *Deep Rivers*, it is a given reality, without which Ernesto's troubled state would be incomprehensible. The particular tragedy of this child is an indirect but unequivocal testimony of that horror; it is one of its innumerable products. In his confusion, in his loneliness, in his fear, in his naïve embrace of plants and insects, in his constant retreat into the past, the imaginary, magical world, we see the roots of this evil. Literature bears witness to social and economic reality in this way, by refraction and through metaphor, registering the repercussions of historical events and great social problems on an individual and mythic level. This is the way that literary testimony remains alive and does not turn into the dead hand of ideology.

London, 17 August 1995

Neruda at a Hundred

When I was still a boy in short trousers, in Cochabamba, Bolivia, where I spent the first ten years of my life, my mother had on her bedside table an edition of *Twenty Love Poems and a Song of Despair* by Pablo Neruda, that had a blue cover with a stream of golden stars on it, which she read and reread. I had barely begun to read and, attracted by my mother's devotion to these pages, I tried to read them as well. She had forbidden me to do so, explaining that these were not poems for children. This ban made the verses extraordinarily attractive, making them seem rather disturbing. I read them secretly, without understanding them, excited, and intuiting that behind some of the mysterious exclamations ('My rough labourer's body tunnels into you/And makes the child leap up from the depths of the earth', 'Ah, the roses of the pubis!') there lay a world that was all about sin.

Neruda was the first poet whose poems I learned by heart: I would recite them in my adolescent years to the girls I fell in love with. He was the poet I most imitated when I began to scribble down verses, the epic and revolutionary poet that accompanied my years at university, and my political involvement in the group Cahuide during the sinister years of the Odría dictatorship. In the clandestine meetings of my cell, we would sometimes interrupt our readings of Lenin's *What is to be Done* and Mariátegui's *Seven Essays* to recite, in a state of trance, pages from the *Canto General* and *Spain in My Heart*. Later, when I became a more discerning reader than as a young man, very critical of propaganda poetry, Neruda continued to be one of my favourite writers – I even preferred him to the great César Vallejo, another icon of my youth – no longer as the writer of *Canto General*, but rather the Neruda of *Residence on Earth*, a book that I have reread many times, as I have done with a very small number of other poets, like Góngora, Baudelaire and Rubén Darío. Some of the poems in that collection – 'The Widow's Tango', 'The Single Gentleman' – still send a shiver down my spine and give me that sense of wonderful unease and shock that only the best literature can produce. In all aspects of artistic creation, genius is an inexplicable anomaly in our world of reason, but in poetry it is more than that: it is a strange, almost inhuman gift, something that has to be described with those much abused adjectives: transcendent, miraculous, divine.

I met Pablo Neruda in Paris in the sixties, in the house of Jorge Edwards. I still remember how excited I felt to be face to face with the very man who had written that poetry that was like an ocean of different seas and infinite species of animals and vegetables, unfathomably deep and enormously rich. I was struck dumb. I finally managed to blurt out a few admiring remarks. He received the praise with the naturalness of royalty and declared that it was a good night for us to eat the sausages that the Edwards had prepared for us. He was fat, friendly, gossipy, greedy ('Mathilde, get over to that dish right now and save me the best bits'), a good conversationalist, and he made an enormous effort to break the ice and make me feel at ease, as I sat there, overwhelmed by his imposing presence.

Although we ended up becoming quite good friends, I think that he was the only writer that I could never treat as an equal. When I was with him, despite the fact that he was always very warm and generous towards me, I always ended up feeling both intimidated and reverential. The man intrigued me and fascinated me almost as much as his poetry. His pose was anti-intellectual, contemptuous of the theories and complicated interpretations of critics. When someone floated an abstract, general topic, inviting a discussion about ideas – something that Octavio Paz shone at – Neruda's face fell and he immediately made sure that the conversation became trite and prosaic. He made a great effort to show that he was simple, direct and completely down to earth, a world away from bookish writers who preferred texts to life and who could say, like Borges, 'I have read a lot and lived only a little.' He wanted to make everyone believe that he had lived a lot and read very little, because he rarely mentioned literature in conversation. Even when he showed, with great pride, the first editions and the marvellous manuscripts that he'd collected in his splendid library, he avoided making any comments about literary value and instead focused on the purely material aspect of these precious objects filled with words. His anti-intellectualism was a pose, of course, because without reading a great deal and assimilating and reflecting on the best literature, he would not have been able to revolutionise poetic language in Spanish the way he did, or have written such diverse and essential poetry. He seemed to think that the worst risk a poet could run was to become confined in a world of abstractions and ideas, as if this might take away the vitality of the word, remove poetry from the public arena and condemn it to obscurity.

What was not a pose was his love of things, objects that could be felt, seen, smelt and eventually eaten and drunk. All of Neruda's houses, but in particular the house at Isla Negra, were creations that were as powerful and personal as his best poems. He collected everything, from figureheads to little matchstick ships in bottles, from butterflies to marine shells, from handicrafts to very early editions, and in his houses one felt enveloped by an atmosphere of fantasy and immense sensuality. He had an infallible eye when it came to detecting unusual and exceptional things, and when he liked something, he became like a capricious, difficult child who would not stop until he got what he wanted. I remember a marvellous letter that he wrote to Jorge Edwards, asking him to go to London and buy him a pair of drums that he had seen in a shop when he'd been passing through that capital city. Life was unliveable, he said, without a drum. In the mornings in Isla Negra, he sounded a trumpet, put on his naval beret and raised the flag on the mast that he had on the beach: the emblem was a fish.

Watching him eat was a wonderful spectacle. That time that I met him, in Paris, I interviewed him for the Radio-Television channel. I

128

asked him to read a poem from 'Residence of Earth' which I love: 'The Young Monarch'. He agreed, but when he found the page he exclaimed, in surprise: 'Ah, but this is a prose poem.' I felt a dagger to my heart: how could he have forgotten one of the most perfect compositions ever to come from the pen of a poet? After the interview, he wanted to go and eat Middle Eastern food. In a Moroccan restaurant in the rue de L'Harpe, he gave the fork back and asked for a second spoon. He ate with great concentration and happiness, brandishing a spoon in each hand like an alchemist mixing his vials, about to create the definitive potion. Watching Neruda eat, one realised that life was worth living, that happiness was possible and that its secret was sizzling in a frying pan.

The fact that he became so famous and so successful throughout the entire world, and could live so comfortably, stirred up envy, resentment and hatred that pursued him everywhere, and, on occasion, made his life impossible. I remember once in London indignantly showing him a newspaper from Lima, which contained an attack on me. He looked at me as if I was a child who still believed that storks brought babies. 'I have chests full of cuttings like that,' he said. 'I think that at some time or other I've been accused of everything disgusting under the sun.' But when this happened, he knew how to defend himself, and, at some points in his life, his poems were full of insults and ferocious diatribes against his enemies. But curiously, I cannot remember him ever saying anything bad about anyone, and only very rarely indulging in that favourite sport among writers which is to take fellow writers apart. One night, in Isla Negra, after an enormous meal, through half opened, tortoise eyes he looked at me and said that he had sent five signed copies of his latest book to five young Chilean poets. 'And not one of them wrote back to me,' he complained sadly.

This was in the last years of his life, at a time when he wanted everyone to like him because he had forgotten all the old enmities and grudges and was making peace with everyone. Although he remained loyal to the Communist Party and, out of this loyalty, had at certain moments sung the praises of Stalin and defended dogmatic positions, in his old age he began to be more critical of what had happened in the communist world and he became more tolerant and open. His poetry was no longer belligerent or resentful, and became serene, joyful and understanding, celebrating the things and the people of this world.

There is no other poetic work in the Spanish language as exuberant and as vast as that of Neruda, a poetry that has touched so many different worlds and stimulated so many different writing talents. The only comparable case that I know in other languages is the work of Victor Hugo. Like the œuvre of the great French Romantic, Neruda's work was uneven: it could be intense, surprising and strikingly original, but also facile and conventional. But there is no doubt that his work will last and will continue to bewitch future generations as it has bewitched our generation.

There was something childlike about him, with his obsessions and desires that he expressed without any trace of hypocrisy, with the healthy enthusiasm of a naughty boy. Behind his good-natured appearance, there was a man who was a keen observer of reality and also someone who, in exceptional circumstances, in a small group, after a well-lubricated meal, could suddenly reveal a heart-rending intimacy. And it was then that we could see, behind the Olympian figure, celebrated the world over, the small boy from the province of Parral, full of enthusiasm and amazement at the wonders of the world, this boy that he never stopped being.

Madrid, June 2004

How I Lost My Fear of Flying

There are certain naïve people who believe that a fear of flying is, or can be explained by, a fear of death. They are wrong: fear of flying is fear of flying, not of death, a fear as particular and specific as a fear of spiders, or of the void, or of cats, three common examples among the thousands that make up the panoply of human fears. Fear of flying wells up suddenly, when people not lacking in imagination and sensitivity realise that they are thirty thousand feet in the air, travelling through clouds at eight hundred miles an hour, and ask, 'What the hell am I doing here?' And begin to tremble.

It happened to me, after many years getting on and off aircraft as often as I change my shirts. I continued getting on these airborne missiles, but for a long time, I was sweating buckets on every flight, especially when we hit turbulence. My friend Saso, a most delightful air hostess who feels safer above the clouds than on terra firma, and who guffawed at my panic in the air, tried to cure me with the aid of statistics. She proved to me what everyone knows. That to travel by plane is infinitely safer than travelling by car, boat, train and even by bicycle or on skates, because every year many more people have accidents using those forms of transport. And even that going on foot, on a gentle and innocuous walk, is, statistically speaking, more dangerous than going in a plane. But, in my case, abstract statistics are incapable of stirring emotions or dispelling terror, so that even though rationally I was convinced by the figures that ploughing through the skies inside a plane is safer than sleeping in my own bed, I continued to have a terrible time on every flight.

My late friend, the Uruguayan novelist Carlos Martínez Moreno, who once travelled by plane with me, spent the whole flight clutching an edition of *Madame Bovary*, worn and tattered from so much handling, that he did not read, but stroked continually. It was an amulet that guaranteed him a peaceful and safe flight. He'd taken this book on his first flight and it would later accompany him on all other flights, because intuition, fantasy or madness told him that it was this novelistic talisman and not the smooth running of the engines or the skill of the pilots that kept the planes he travelled in free of all harm and mishap. But Martínez Moreno's remedy did not work for me, because of my strong scepticism of any form of witchcraft (especially its modern variants), or simply because I have yet to come across the spell that might convince me and convert me to the faith of witchcraft.

A Puerto Rican friend, a wealthy widow who travels the world, revealed to me that she had cured her fear of flying through whisky. She'd always take a good supply with her on board, hidden in a small bag, and at the second or third sip, the ship could turn somersaults or be tossed about by the wind and she'd be giggling and happy, impervious to everything. I tried to apply her formula, but it did not work for me. I am very allergic to alcohol, and gulps of whisky, far from taking away my fear of flying, just increased it, and gave me headaches, shivers and nausea on top. I would probably have needed to become a hardened alcoholic, seeing little green men, to achieve the indifference to flying that my Puerto Rican friend managed with a few sips of alcohol. The cure would have been more damaging than the illness.

At the other extreme to my Puerto Rican friend, some puritans argue that fear of flying is a result of heavy meals and an immoderate ingestion of spirits (wine and alcohol) on the journey. And for my serenity in the air, they recommended that I should abstain from eating and drinking wine on flights, and just drink large, and, for them, sedating, glasses of water. It didn't work. Quite the reverse, these forced diets made me very miserable, and added to my fear the demoralising torture of hunger and constant peeing.

Seconal, sanax and all those other pills invented to cure wakeful-
ness and abolish insomnia, are no use to me either. There are marvellous people (they merit both my admiration and my envy) who
become immediately somnolent on a plane and who sleep peacefully through the whole flight, lulled by the buzzing of the reactors.
And others who, in order to reach that same state, stuff themselves
with pills, which daze and anaesthetise them. But sleeping pills gave
me palpitations or the most dreadful nightmares in which I saw
myself sweating with terror inside a plane. So the relative, artificial
sleep induced by medicaments did not take my fear away, but rather
displaced it onto an oneiric and subconscious plane, and, as another
side effect, turned me into a depressed zombie by the end of the
flight.

The solution came in a most unexpected way, on a flight between
Buenos Aires and Madrid which, by chance, was commemorating
the first flight between those cities (by an Iberian Airline Douglas
DC4) on 22 September 1946. I bought at Ezeiza airport a copy of a
short novel by Alejo Carpentier that I had not read: *The Kingdom of
This World*. Nothing had prepared me for the surprise. From the first
lines of the story, which recreates the hallucinating life of Henri
Christophe and the building of the famous Citadel in Haiti, this
superbly written and even better constructed narration in which, as
in all literary masterpieces, nothing could be added or taken away,
absorbed me body and soul and took away my surroundings, trans-
porting me, for the ten hours or so of the flight, away from the frozen
starry night into a prodigious epic account of Haiti in the previous
century, where the most ferocious violence intermingled with the
most fevered imagination, and everyday and trivial events blurred
into miracles and legends. I read the final lines when the plane
touched down in Barajas; the book had lasted the flight, and had
taken away my fear for the entire journey.

It is a remedy that, from that time on, has never failed me, so long
as I choose for each flight a masterpiece whose spell is both total and
lasts for exactly the time that I am defying the law of gravity. Of
course, it is not easy to choose the right work, in terms of quality and
length, for each trip. But with practice I have developed a sort of

instinct to choose the right novel or story (poetry, plays or essays are not as strong antidotes against the fear of flying). I have also discovered that it is not necessary to have new works, for rereading can be just as effective provided the work in question can cast a spell that is as new and refreshing on third or fourth reading as it was the first time. Here is a list (as a token of my appreciation) of these reliable friends who in my recent, successful, attempts to emulate Icarus, helped me to conquer my fear of flying: *Bartleby* and *Benito Cereno* by Melville; *The Turn of the Screw* by Henry James; 'The Pursuer' by Cortázar; *Dr Jekyll and Mr Hyde* by R. L. Stevenson; *The Old Man and the Sea* by Hemingway; 'The Monkey' by Isak Dinesen; *Pedro Páramo* by Rulfo; *Complete Works and Other Stories* by Monterroso; 'A Rose for Emily' and 'The Bear' by Faulkner and *Orlando* by Virginia Woolf. Fortunately for me, the literary chemist store has limitless reserves of these medicines, so I still have plenty of plane journeys (and good reading) ahead.

Washington DC, 23 October 1999

Literature and Life

It happens quite often, in book fairs or bookshops, that a man will come up to me with a book of mine in his hand and ask me for an autograph, saying, 'It's for my wife or my young daughter, or my sister, or my mother; she or they are great readers and they love literature.' And I immediately ask: 'And what about you, don't you like to read?' The answer is almost inevitably: 'Yes, of course I like reading, but I'm very busy, you know.' Yes, I do know, because I've heard this dozens of times: that man, and thousands like him, have so many important things to do, so many obligations and responsibilities in their lives that they cannot waste their precious time spending hours on end absorbed in a novel, a book of poetry or a literary essay. According to this widespread conception, literature is a dispensable activity, a pastime, no doubt lofty and useful for the cultivation of feelings and manners, an adornment for people that have plenty of time for recreation and that has to be fitted in between sports, cinema, and games of bridge or chess. But it is something that can be sacrificed without a second thought when it comes to prioritising what is really important in life.

It is true that literature has increasingly become a female activity: in bookshops or lectures or readings by writers, and, of course, in university departments and faculties in the humanities, women quite obviously outnumber men. The explanation that has been given for this fact is that, among the middle classes, women read more because they work fewer hours than men, and also that many

135

women tend to consider that time spent on fantasy and illusion is more justifiable than do men. I am somewhat sceptical of interpretations that divide men and women into fixed categories, which attribute collective virtues and shortcomings to each of the sexes, so I don't subscribe wholeheartedly to these explanations. But it is true that, in general, readers of literature are on the decline and that most of these remaining readers are women. This is true almost everywhere. In Spain, a recent survey organised by the General Society of Spanish Authors came up with the alarming statistic that half of the population has never read a book. The survey also revealed that, of the minority that do read, the number of women who admit to reading is 6.2% higher than the number of men, and the tendency is for this gap to increase. I am sure that these differences apply to many other countries, including my own. And I am happy for those women, of course, but I am sorry for the men and for the millions of people who could read, but have decided not to do so. Not only because they do not know the pleasure they are missing, but, from a less hedonistic perspective, because I am convinced that a society without literature, or in which literature has been relegated, like certain unmentionable vices, to the margins of social life, and has become something like a sectarian cult, is a society condemned to become spiritually barbarous and even to endanger its freedom.

I would like to argue against the idea of literature as a luxury pastime and in favour of the view that it is one of the most enriching activities of the mind, an indispensable activity for the formation of citizens in a modern, democratic society, a society of free individuals, and, for that reason, it should be instilled in children from an early age by their families and be taught as a basic discipline throughout the education system. We already know that the opposite is true, that literature is shrinking and even disappearing from the school curriculum.

We live in an era of knowledge specialisation, due to the prodigious development of science and technology, and the fragmentation of knowledge into innumerable paths and compartments, a cultural trend that will only be accentuated in years to come. Of course, specialisation brings great benefits, offering much more detailed research and experimentation; it is the engine of progress. But it also has a negative effect: it elides all those common denominators of culture through which men and women coexist, communicate and feel a sense of solidarity. Specialisation leads to a lack of social communication, to the division of people into cultural ghettoes of technicians and specialists. They share a language, codes and information that are increasingly specialised and specific, which limits them in a way that the old proverb has warned us against: they can't see the wood for the trees. And knowing that the wood exists is what binds a society together, and prevents it from collapsing into a myriad of solipsistic parts. And solipsism – in nations or in individuals – produces paranoia and delirium, these disfigurements of reality that can cause hatred, wars and genocide. In our day and age, science and technology are increasingly divorced from broader culture, precisely because of the infinite complexity of its knowledge and the speed of its evolution, which has led to specialisation and the use of hermetic language.

Literature, by contrast, is, has been, and will continue to be for as long as it exists, one of the common denominators of human existence, through which human beings recognise themselves and talk to each other, no matter how different their professions or their plans for life, their geographical location, their individual circumstances or the historical moment that they are living in. Those of us who read Cervantes, Shakespeare, Dante or Tolstoy understand each other and feel part of the same species because, in the works that these writers created, we learn what we share as human beings, what is common to all of us beneath the wide range of differences that separate us. And there is no better defence against the stupidity of prejudice, racism, xenophobia, religious or political sectarianism or autarkic nationalism than this invariable truth that appears in all great literature: that men and women from across the world are equal, and that it is unjust that they are subject to discrimination, repression and exploitation. Nothing teaches us better than literature to see, in ethnic and cultural differences, the richness of our shared heritage, and to prize these differences as a demonstration of our diverse creativity. Reading good literature is enjoyable, of course; but we also learn, in that direct and intense way that we experience life through fictions, what and how we are, our human integrity, our actions and dreams and fantasies, alone or in the dense web of relations that link us to others, in our public persona and in the intimacy of our consciousness, that complex sum of contradictory truths – in the words of Isaiah Berlin – that make up the human condition. Not even other branches of the humanities – like philosophy, psychology, sociology, history or the arts – have managed to preserve this integrating and secular vision. For they too have succumbed to the irresistible pressure of the cancerous division and subdivision of knowledge, isolating themselves in increasingly segmented and technical areas of expertise, whose ideas and terminology are beyond the scope of ordinary men and women. This can never happen to literature, even though some critics and theoreticians try to turn it into a science, because fiction does not exist to investigate a particular area of existence. It exists to enrich life through the imagination, all of life, this life that cannot be dismembered, broken up, or reduced to schema or formulas, without disappearing. This is what Marcel Proust meant when he said: 'True life, life at last clarified and brought to light, the only life, furthermore, that is fully lived, is literature.' He was not exaggerating, influenced by his love of his own vocation. He merely wished to say that, thanks to literature, we understand and live life better and understanding and living life better means living and sharing it with others.

The fraternal link that literature forges between human beings, forcing them to speak to each other and making them realise that they have a common origin, that they form part of the same spiritual lineage, transcends the barriers of time. Literature takes us back to the past and links us to those who, in past times, plotted, enjoyed and dreamed through these texts that they have bequeathed us, texts that now give us enjoyment and fuel our dreams. This feeling of belonging to the community of human beings through time and space is the greatest achievement of culture, and nothing contributes more to its renewal with each generation than literature.

Borges always got annoyed when he was asked: 'What is the use of literature?' He thought it a stupid question and would reply:

'Nobody thinks of asking what is the use of the song of a canary or the crimson glow of a sunset!' Indeed, if these beautiful things exist and, thanks to them, life, albeit for a moment, is less ugly and less sad, isn't it rather small-minded to seek practical justifications? However, unlike birdsong or the spectacle of the sun sinking on the horizon, a poem or a novel are not simply there, fashioned by chance or by Nature. They are a human creation and it is thus valid to ask how and why they came about, and what they have given to humanity, to understand why literature, that is as old as writing itself, has lasted for so long. They were born, as formless ghosts, in the intimacy of a consciousness, the combination of the unconscious and a writer's sensibility and feelings. Poets and narrators then grapple with language to give these formless ghosts body, movement, rhythm, harmony and life. This is an artificial life, fashioned by language and the imagination, which has coexisted with the other, the real life, from time immemorial, and men and women seek out this imagined life – some frequently and others only sporadically – because the life that they have is not enough for them, is not able to give them everything that they want. Literature does not begin to exist when it emerges as the work of a single individual, it only really exists when it is adopted by others, and becomes part of social life, when it becomes, through reading, a shared experience.

One of its first beneficial effects occurs at the level of language. A community without a written literature expresses itself with less precision, with less nuance and clarity than another community whose principal mode of communication, the word, has been cultivated and perfected through literary texts. A humanity without readers, which has not been contaminated by literature, would be like a community of stammerers and aphasiacs, beset by tremendous problems of communication because of its coarse and rudimentary language. The same is true for individuals, of course. People who do not read, or read little or just read rubbish, might talk a great deal, but will say very little because they have a very limited and insufficient repertoire of words with which to express themselves. This is not just a verbal limitation; it is also an intellectual and imaginative limitation. It reveals a poverty of thought and knowledge, because the ideas and concepts through which we apprehend existing reality and the secrets of our condition do not exist outside the words through which our consciousness recognises and defines them. We learn to speak correctly, with depth, precision and subtlety, from good literature and *only from good literature*. No other discipline or branch of the arts can supersede literature when it comes to crafting the language through which people communicate. The knowledge transmitted to us by scientific manuals or technical reports is fundamental; but these do not teach us how to use words or express ourselves correctly. Quite the reverse, they are often very badly and confusedly written because their authors, who are often indisputably eminent in their field, are uneducated in literature and do not know how to use language to communicate the conceptual treasures that they possess. To speak well, to have at one's disposal a rich and varied language, to find the right expression for each idea and emotion that one wishes to express, means that one is better prepared to think, teach, learn and communicate, and also to fantasise, dream and feel. In a surreptitious way, words reverberate in all aspects of life, even those that seem far removed from language. And as language evolved, thanks to literature, achieving a high level of refinement and nuance, then it also increased the possibilities for human pleasure. With respect to love, it sublimated desires and conferred on the sexual act the status of artistic creation. Without literature there would be no eroticism. Love and pleasure would be impoverished, they would lack delicacy and refinement, and would not achieve that same intensity that literary fantasy can encourage. It is not far-fetched to say that a couple who have read Garcilaso, Petrarch, Góngora and Baudelaire feel greater love and pleasure than an illiterate couple who have become doltish by watching too much television. In a non-literary world, love and pleasure would be indistinguishable from animal desires, the crude satisfaction of basic instincts: copulating and drinking.

Nor are the audiovisual media in a position to supplant literature when it comes to teaching human beings to make assured and subtle use of the infinite riches of language. On the contrary, audiovisual media naturally tend to give words secondary importance in contrast to images, which is their primordial language, and to limit language to the spoken word, often with a bare minimum of dialogue, rather than the written word. Because if there are too many words, on the small or the large screen, or coming out of loudspeakers, the effect is always soporific. To say that a film or a television programme is 'literary' is an elegant way of calling it boring. And that is why literary programmes on the radio or television rarely reach a wide audience: to my knowledge, the only exception to this rule is Bernard Pivot's programme *Apostrophes* in France. This leads me to think as well, though I have my doubts, that not only is literature indispensable for a complete knowledge and command of language, but that the fate of literature is indissolubly linked to the fate of the book, that industrial product that many now declare to be obsolete.

One of these people is a man to whom we all owe so much in terms of developments in communication: Bill Gates, the founder of Microsoft. Mr Gates was in Madrid a few months ago and he visited the Royal Spanish Academy, which has embarked on what I hope will become a fruitful collaboration with Microsoft. Among other things, Bill Gates assured the members of the Academy that he would personally guarantee that the letter 'ñ' would never disappear from computer programmes. This was greeted with a sigh of relief by those four hundred million of us Spanish-speakers across five continents, for whom the loss of that letter in cyberspace would have created problems of Babel-like proportions. Now, immediately after this kind concession to the Spanish language, before he had even left the Royal Academy, Bill Gates declared in a press conference that he had to achieve his greatest goal before he died. And what might that be? To put an end to paper, and, thus, to books themselves which, in his view, are obstinately anachronistic. Mr Gates explained that computer screens can successfully replace paper in every function imaginable and that, as well as being lighter, being more portable and taking up less space than paper, reading information on a screen instead of in magazines and books has the ecological advantage of ending the destruction of forests, a cataclysm that has been caused by the paper industry. People would continue to read, of course, he explained, but on screen, and because of this there would be more chlorophyll in the atmosphere.

I was not present – I got the story from the press – but if I had been there I would have booed Mr Gates for declaring, quite shamelessly, that he was looking to put me, and so many of my colleagues, who write books, out of a job. Can the screen replace the book in every case, as the creator of Microsoft argues? I am not so sure. I state this in full knowledge that there is a major revolution taking place in the fields of communication and information which has lead to the development of new technologies like the Internet, which is an invaluable help to my own work. But to go from there to admit that the screen can replace paper when it comes to reading literature, is a step too far for me. I simply cannot conceive how any non-pragmatic and non-functional act of reading, that is not looking for information or some useful piece of instantly communicable knowledge, can derive from a computer screen the same feeling of intimacy, the same concentration and the same spiritual isolation that can be achieved by reading a book. This, perhaps, is a prejudice of mine, stemming from a lack of practice and from a lifetime of equating reading literature with reading books. Although I very happily surf the Internet looking for world news, I would never use it to read the poems of Góngora, a novel by Onetti or an essay by Octavio Paz, because I am sure that the effect would never be the same. I am convinced, though I can't prove it, that with the disappearance of the book, literature would suffer a severe, perhaps even mortal blow. The name would not disappear, of course; but it would probably be used to describe a type of text so far removed from what we understand as literature as soap operas are to the tragedies of Sophocles and Shakespeare.

There is another reason to give literature an important place in the life of nations. Without it, the critical mind, which is an engine of political change and the best champion of liberty that we have, would go into irremediable decline. Because all good literature asks radical questions of the world we live in. Every great literary text, often without the writer's intention, has a tendency towards sedition.

Literature has nothing to say to those people who are satisfied with their lot, who are content with life as it is. Literature offers sustenance to rebellious and non-conformist spirits and a refuge to those who have too much or too little in life; it wards off unhappiness and any feelings of lack or want. To ride alongside scrawny Rocinante and his scatterbrained owner across the plains of La Mancha, to sail the seas with Captain Ahab in pursuit of the white whale, to swallow arsenic with Madame Bovary or turn into an insect with Gregory Samsa is a clever way that we have invented to make up for the wrongs and impositions of this unjust life that forces us always to be the same, when we want to be many people, as many as it would take to assuage the burning desires that possess us.

Literature can only pacify momentarily this dissatisfaction with life, but, in this miraculous interval, in this provisional suspension of life afforded by literary illusion – which seems to transport us out of chronology and history and turn us into citizens of a timeless, immortal country – we do become these others. We become more intense, richer, more complex, happier, more lucid, than in the constrained routine of our real life. When, once the book is closed and the literary fiction is abandoned, we return to real life and compare it to the splendid place that we have just left, what a disappointment it is. We are faced with the awful truth: that the fantasy life of the novel is better – more beautiful and more diverse, more comprehensible and more perfect – than the life we lead when we are awake, a life that is weighed down by the limitations and obligations of our existence. In this sense, good literature is always - unintentionally – seditious and rebellious: a challenge to what exists. How could we not feel cheated, after reading *War and Peace* or *Remembrance of Things Past*, having to return to this world with its inconsequential pettiness, its rules and prohibitions that lie in wait for us and, at every turn, look to spoil our illusions. Even more, perhaps, than the need to maintain the continuity of culture and to enrich language, the main contribution of literature to human progress is to remind us (without intending to in the main) that the world is badly made, that those who argue the contrary – for example the powers that be – are lying, and that the world could be better, closer to the worlds that our imagination and our language are able to create.

A democratic and free society needs responsible and critical citizens, who are conscious of the need to scrutinise continually the world in which we live, and to try – although this is always a chimera – to make it more like the world that we would like to live in. Out of this stubborn desire to achieve this impossible dream – to marry reality with desire – civilisation was born and has developed, and through it we have defeated many – not all, of course – of the demons that once assailed us. And there is no better way of fostering dissatisfaction with life than good literature. And there is no better way of forming critical and independent citizens, who are difficult to manipulate, who are quick-witted and always questioning, than reading good books.

Now, to call literature seditious because the best fictions develop in their readers a clear sense of the imperfections of the real world does not mean, of course – as Churches and governments seem to think it means when they impose censorship – that literary texts immediately cause social upheaval or accelerate revolutions. Here we are entering a slippery, subjective terrain, and we need to move carefully. The socio-political effects of a poem, a play or a novel cannot be verified because they are not experienced collectively, but rather individually, which means that they vary enormously from person to person. That is why it is difficult, if not impossible, to establish precise rules. Also, if it is clear that a book has had an effect on society, it might have little to do with its aesthetic quality. For example, a mediocre novel, *Uncle Tom's Cabin* by Harriet Elizabeth Beecher Stowe, seems to have played a very important role in raising awareness in the United States about the horrors of slavery. But just because these effects are difficult to identify does not mean that they do not exist. Rather that they can be found indirectly, in so many ways, in the behaviour of people whose personalities have been shaped, in part, by books.

Good literature both temporarily assuages our human cravings and increases them: by developing a non-conformist, critical spirit towards life, we become more susceptible to unhappiness. To live dissatisfied, at war with existence, is to be constantly looking for trouble, to condemn oneself, like Colonel Aureliano Buendía in *One*

Hundred Years of Solitude, to fight battles knowing that they will all be lost. That is probably true. But it is also the case that without rebellion against the mediocrity and squalor of life, we humans would still be living in a primitive state, history would have stagnated, the individual would not have been born, science and technology would not have advanced, human rights would not be recognised, nor would freedom exist, because all of this came about through acts of rebellion against life, which was seen to be insufficient and intolerable. Literature has been fundamental in fostering an attitude that scorns life as it is and seeks, with the madness of Alonso Quijano, whose insanity, we should not forget, came about through reading novels of chivalry, to make the dream, the impossible, a reality.

Let us attempt a fantastic historical reconstruction and imagine a world without literature, a humanity that has not read poems or novels. In this agraphic world, with its miniscule lexicon in which grunts and ape-like gestures would probably prevail over words, there would be no adjectives based on literary creations: Quixotic, Kafkaesque, Pantagruelian, rocambolesque, Orwellian, sadistic and masochistic, among others. There would be madmen, victims of paranoia and persecution complexes and people with colossal and excessive appetites and bipeds who enjoy suffering and inflicting pain, of course. But we would not have learned to see behind this excessive behaviour, which is in conflict with supposed normality, essential aspects of the human condition, that is, of ourselves, that only the creative talent of Cervantes, Kafka, Rabelais, de Sade or Sacher-Masoch can show us. When *Don Quixote* appeared, the earliest readers made fun of this extravagant dreamer, just like the other characters in the novel. Now we know that the determination of the Knight of the Sorry Countenance to see giants where there are windmills, and to do all the crazy things he does, is the highest form of generosity, a way of protesting against the misery of this world and attempting to change it. The very notions of the ideal and of idealism, which are so imbued with a positive moral value, would not be what they are – clear and respected values – had they not been embodied in that fictional character that Cervantes's genius made so persuasive. And the same could be said of that small and pragmatic female Quixote, Emma Bovary – bovarism would not exist, of course – who also fought passionately to live that wonderful life of passion and luxury that she knew through novels, and who burned herself in that fire like a butterfly who flies too close to a flame.

Like those of Cervantes and Flaubert, the inventions of all great literary creators both break down the walls of our realist prison and transport us into realms of fantasy, and also open our eyes to hidden and secret aspects of our condition and equip us to explore and better to understand the depths of human behaviour. When we say 'Borgesian', we immediately move out of routine and rational reality into a fantastic, rigorous and elegant mental construction, almost always labyrinthine, full of literary references and allusions. This singular world is not strange to us, however, because we recognise in it hidden desires and intimate truths about ourselves that only became apparent thanks to the literary creation of a Jorge Luis Borges. The adjective Kafkaesque comes straight to mind, like the flash gun of one of those old tripod cameras, every time we feel threatened, as defenceless individuals, by those oppressive and destructive institutions that have caused so much pain, abuse and injustice in the modern world: authoritarian regimes, vertical parties, intolerant Churches and stifling bureaucracies. Without the novels and short stories of this tormented Jew from Prague who wrote in German and was ever watchful, we would not have been able to understand so clearly that feeling of defencelessness and impotence that isolated individuals or persecuted and discriminated minorities experience when faced with all-embracing powers that can annihilate them and wipe them out, without their executioners ever having to show their faces.

The adjective 'Orwellian', a first cousin of 'Kafkaesque', alludes to the oppressive anguish and the sensation of extreme absurdity generated by the totalitarian dictatorships of the twentieth century, the most refined, cruel and absolute dictatorships in history, given their control over the actions, thoughts and even dreams of members of society. In his most famous novels, *Animal Farm* and *1984*, George Orwell described in cold and nightmarish tones a humanity under the control of Big Brother, an absolute master who through an efficient combination of terror and modern technology, has eliminated liberty, spontaneity and equality – in this world, some are 'more equal than others' – and has turned society into automatons. Not only behaviour is controlled by the dictates of power; the language, as well, 'Newspeak', has been cleansed of all individualism, subjectivity and inventiveness, and has become a string of platitudes and clichés that endorse the individual's slavery to the system. It is true that the sinister prophecy of *1984* did not come about in reality and that, as happened with fascist and Nazi totalitarianism, Communism disappeared in the USSR and began to lose its grip in China and in the present-day anachronistic societies of Cuba and North Korea. But the term 'Orwellian' is still current, a reminder of one of the most devastating political and cultural regimes in the history of civilisation, that the novels of George Orwell helped us to understand in all its complexity.

So the unreality and the lies of literature are also a precious way of understanding the most profound truths of human reality. These truths are not always flattering; sometimes the reflection of ourselves that appears in the mirror of novels and poems is monstrous. That happens when we read the horrific sexual butchery imagined by the Divine Marquis or the gloomy lacerations and the sacrifices that people the *maudit* books of a Sacher-Masoch or a Bataille. Sometimes the spectacle is so offensive that it is irresistible. And yet the worst thing about these pages is not the fevered description of blood, humiliation and abject tortures and convulsions. It is the realisation that this violence and excess is not alien to us, but is the very stuff of humanity. These monsters thirsting for transgressive, excessive behaviour live deep within us, and from the shadows where they live, they wait for an appropriate moment to appear, to impose their rule of unfettered desire which destroys rationality, community and perhaps even existence. It is literature, not science, that has been the first to explore the depths of human behaviour and discover its terrifying destructive and self-destructive potential. So a world without literature would be blind in part to these terrible depths where the reasons for unusual behaviour can frequently be found. Such a world would be unjust towards individuals who are different, in the same way that not long ago people thought that those who were dumb or who stammered were possessed by the devil. It might even continue the practices of certain Amazon tribes that subscribed to the notion of physical perfection to such a horrifying degree that they used to drown newborn children with physical defects.

Uncivilised, barbarous, devoid of sensitivity and clumsy in speech, ignorant and instinctual, without passion or eroticism, this world without literature in the nightmare that I am describing would mainly be characterised by conformism and a general submissiveness to the established order. It would also be in this sense an animal world. Basic instincts would decide the daily routines in a life determined by the struggle for survival, fear of the unknown and the satisfaction of physical needs. There would be no place for the spirit. And in the stifling monotony of life, a pessimistic feeling would always be casting its shadow: that human life is what it is supposed to be and will always be, without any possibility for change.

When one imagines a world like this, there is a tendency to identify it immediately with primitive peoples, with small magical-religious communities that live on the margins of modernity in Latin America, Oceania and Africa. But the truth is that the extraordinary development of audiovisual media in recent times allows us to imagine a possible scenario in a mediated future: a very modern society, bristling with computers, screens and speakers, and without books, or, rather, where books – literature – would have become what alchemy was in the age of physics: an anachronistic curiosity, kept alive in the catacombs of a media society by a neurotic minority. I fear that this cybernetic world, despite its prosperity and power, its high standard of living and scientific achievements, would be profoundly uncivilised, lethargic and lacking in spirit, a resigned, robotic world that would have abdicated its freedom.

Of course it is highly improbable that this terrifying prospect could ever become a reality. History is not written in advance, there is no predetermined fate that has decided for us what we are going to be. It depends entirely on us as to whether this macabre utopia takes shape or fades away. If we want to prevent literature – this source that powers our imagination and our sense of dissatisfaction,

148

that refines our sensibilities and teaches us to speak with elegance and precision, that makes us free and gives us richer and more intense lives – from disappearing or being relegated to the attic alongside the things we no longer use, then we must act. We have to read good books and to encourage and teach those that follow us – in families and in lecture halls, in the media and in all aspects of our lives – that reading is absolutely essential, for reading pervades and enriches all aspects of our lives.

Lima, 3 April 2001

A Dream Factory

For some aberrant reason, the idea of a museum is associated in everyday language with notions such as obsolete, anachronistic, in decline and even extinct. To call someone a 'museum piece' is a kind way of saying that this person is more dead than alive, a walking corpse, someone who has fallen behind the times and remained stuck in some earlier moment. But conserving certain archaeological, artistic or scientific artefacts of the past as cultural relics is just one, and by no means the most important, function that a museum fulfils. In the concrete case of an art museum, the main function is to enrich our lives with all the vitality and creativity of men and women who came before us, offering a more rounded picture of current concerns by showing how our predecessors dealt with life, the ways they heightened, or protected or intensified their existence.

A museum of art worthy of its name does not enlighten us as to the achievements, but rather as to the unachievable aspirations of earlier generations, the capacity that cultures, that are forerunners to our own, had for dreaming and desiring: that imaginary rebellion against the limitations of the human condition that takes place in every period and society. Impossible dreams, unsatisfied desires are the stuff out of which the imaginary cities of fiction have been built, that counter-reality fashioned out of great deeds, emotions or delirium which, because they cannot find expression in the real reality of history, achieved citizenship in the illusory lands of fiction, that vast invented land in which literature and art are important provinces.

153

A painting by Goya or Velázquez, or a novel by Cervantes, are rooted in a world that their authors lived to the full – suffering and enjoying this life with an extremely fine-tuned sensibility – but these works have transcended their time and their creators and have achieved the timeless status of great art. This is because the richness of their composition and the persuasive power of their imaginary worlds freed them from their models – those kings, bandits, go-betweens, spirited women, rogues and adventurers that they purportedly reproduced from the real world whereas, in fact, they were inventing them – and replaced these models with their own bewitching characters. Spain in the sixteenth, seventeenth or eighteenth century was not like that; or rather, it was as it appears on these canvases or in these chapters only in the fantasy and imagination of the Spaniards of those times who wanted to see themselves in this way. The artistic and literary genius of Velázquez, Goya and Cervantes was able to intuit this feeling and transform it into painted images or stories that both drew from their contemporaries' thirst for unreality and also added their own indelible touch. The most important thing about their work is not what they drew from real life, but what they managed to add to it, in such a subtle and convincing way that now there is no way of disentangling these two strands. In *Las Meninas*, in the unsettling nightmares of Goya that decorated the Quinta del Sordo, and in the adventures of Don Quixote and his squire, fiction ended up prevailing over the reality that inspired it.

There are people who go to galleries to *study* a period, find out about customs and important events, get to know the faces of their forebears and the fashions of the women. They are perfectly entitled to do so, of course, and there is no doubt that a museum can also offer (if one takes great care) some lessons in history and sociology. But using museums in this way distorts what they contain, in the same way as someone might read a novel just to list the foreign phrases, idioms and neologisms that were in use at the time it was written. We go to a museum as we go to the cinema or to the opera, to step out of real, pedestrian life and live a sumptuous unreality, to have our fantasies embodied in other people's fantasies, to travel outside ourselves, to discover the ghosts that are lurking in our innermost being, to change skin and to become other men and women in other times and other places, to flee the precise limitations of the human condition and what is possible so that we can become for some eternal moments or hours many other people while remaining ourselves, ubiquitous, without moving from where we are, eternal, though we are mortal and all-powerful without losing our miserable smallness. Because an art museum is not really a laboratory or an historical archive, it is a dream factory.

The Prado Museum, along with a handful of similar museums – the Louvre, the Hermitage, the National Gallery, the Uffizi, Pinacoteca Gallery in the Vatican, the Munich art museum and very few others – is one of those places where, thanks to a combination of historical circumstance, chance and the initiative of certain immensely wealthy, powerful, tasteful or far-sighted individuals, an art collection has been put together that is so extraordinarily important and diverse that it far exceeds any attempt to quantify it economically or see it as the property of a single nation. It becomes, instead, a representative of an entire civilisation and the patrimony of the world. André Malraux put it well in *Les Voix du silence* (*The Voices of Silence*): 'Above all, a museum is one of those places which shows man at his best.'

It would be unjust if we were to consider that because the immense majority of the painters and sculptors exhibited there are European, the Prado should not be considered a universal collection and be seen just as representative of the Old World. The art it exhibits is a fine example of the universal reach of this Western culture whose aesthetic ideals, along with its most conspicuous values – freedom, tolerance, human rights – have permeated the whole world, affecting all living cultures, even the most exotic, including men and women of every hue. Because the first message that hits a visitor to the gallery is that the world of artistic imagination, at this level of skill and daring, lacks borders, transcends space and time, and is firmly rooted - beyond the stories that the works tell and the fleeting times that they allude to – to a single common denominator that is the human condition, the tragic fate of men and women to have been given, at once, the ability to fantasise and to desire a richer and more diverse life, and the limitations of having just one destiny, which falls well short of our dreams. Art and literature were born to fill that chasm between reality and desire, and there is no better proof of the extraordinary strength with which humanity has rebelled against its fate, creating another world, another life, another humanity better than, and different to, reality, than the prodigious universe of images confined to the walls of the Prado Museum.

To understand the essentially fictitious nature of this alternative reality that is art it is not necessary to immerse oneself in the work of the great visionaries, like *The Garden of Delights* by Hieronymus Bosch, who gave shape to all the celestial and hellish terrors of medieval philosophy, blending them with his personal nightmares, or *The Triumph of Death* by Pieter Brueghel, whose apocalyptic imagination catches the decisive moment when human beings face what is beyond, or Goya's *Caprichos*, which plum the gloomy depths of the subconscious. Simply pause and look at the so-called 'realist' painters, for example the still lifes in which Juan Van der Hamen y León, Tomás de Yepes, Sánchez Cotán or Zurbarán purport to reproduce fruit, vegetables, cooking items or hunting pieces with such prodigious objectivity that they appear self-sufficient, not the creation of a controlling mind, hand and brush. But it is clear that they are also pure subjectivity, perhaps more so than the great mythological or biblical fantasies, because they manage to persuade us that they are 'pieces of reality', portraits of what exists – ornaments, utensils or items of food – whose very perfection lifts them out of this imperfect real world of their models, which is subject to deterioration, ageing and extinction, a world that they can deny each day with their eternal freshness and youth. The four plates and the bare wooden table in Zurbarán's *Still Life*, with its light and shade and its delicate contrasts of colour, is as mysterious and magical as a fantastic picture by Caravaggio or the intense spirituality of an El Greco. It is the discreet or flagrant alterations to reality, the creation of self-contained worlds which is the true domain of art, that element added by the artist to the materials that their time, their society, their own biography of heroic or petty deeds placed at their disposal, which through their skill and creativity they managed to transform into something different, something that we will later clearly associate with them. The way that Rubens rounds and thickens the female body in pink hues, fashioning it into sensual courtly, historic or mythological images; the way that El Greco slims and elongates and diffuses the human form in pale and iridescent light, in search of transcendence; or how in Goya men and women become animalised and degraded when they become a collective, a stupid and fanatical mass.

These wonderful fictions and many others like them – Flemish, Italian, English, German, French as well as Spanish – housed by the Prado, all had their origins in a defiance of the real world, but they have gradually become part of the real world through us, they have been subtly contaminating reality with their forms and values. Like in the Borges story, 'Tlön, Uqbar, Orbis Tertius', in which a group of romantic dreamers manage to smuggle a completely invented world into reality, the rich imaginative reality of these artists in the Prado is there, at our service, to show us that the imaginary, this subterfuge of unsatisfied desires, is also of this world, an achievable experience. In the halls and corridors of the Prado, there is sustenance for all the demands of body and soul, the walls are full of myriad examples of how to combat adversity with the arm of fantasy, of how to defeat dissatisfaction by gorging oneself on beauty, of how to overcome the grey mediocrity of existence by turning it into the terrifying or majestic lives depicted there. The dazzling riches of the Prado is the best example there is that museums are not mausoleums but rather a city of living, vibrant beings, in constant movement, where reality and desire meld to create the life that we do not have, that we long for and that we can only achieve, vicariously, in the mirages of fiction.

London, January 1996

Grosz: A Sad and Ferocious Man

Here comes Grosz,
*The saddest man in Europe.**

In the spring of 1985, during one of those exhausting book tours I agree to for reasons which are still beyond me, I escaped for a couple of hours to the Palazzo Reale in Milan, to see an exhibition dedicated to *Gli anni di Berlino* of George Grosz. Three months later, in the torrid Italian summer, I made a special trip to see the exhibition once again in the fantastic (artistically speaking) city of Ferrara. And, some time later, I was lucky enough to see it for a third and final time in the exhibition hall in the Mairie in Paris.

I already knew that Grosz was an artist whose work and life were very important to me, more than most modern painters that I admire or remember, for reasons to do with his talent, of course, but also because his work illustrates an important aspect of artistic creation: the relationship of art and fiction to history and life, to truth and lies, the type of testimony that fiction offers on the objective world. And I also knew – and I would know it more clearly in the following years, as I travelled the world in search of accessible material by or on Grosz – that my fascination for what he painted, drew, wrote, and did or did not do in his sixty-six years, could be explained through certain affinities and differences that I will try to explain in this essay. These might help to clear up some misunderstandings about the nature of fiction in art and about one of the most interesting artists of the twentieth century.

* Poem written by Grosz in 1918. See Uwe Schneede, *Georg Grosz. The Artist in His Society*, New York, 1985, p. 47.

Grosz (his real name was Georg Ehrenfried Groß) was born in Berlin on 26 July 1893, but spent his early years in a small town in eastern Pomerania, Stolp, where his father looked after the Masonic Lodge. Gloomy stories, of coffins and mummies guarded by masons in that house, excited the imagination of the Stolp children and perhaps sowed in Grosz the first seeds of what would later become his obsession with death, a recurring presence in his paintings and drawings.

His father must have been rough, and perhaps brutal, because in his autobiography (*Ein kleines Ja und ein großes Nein*, a book where there are as many omissions as there are memories) Grosz mentions that he scared him and his sister Marta by showing them dancing skeletons in the garden. He died when the boy was six years old.

The family returned to Berlin, where they faced penury and danger in the streets, in the working-class neighbourhood of Wedding, until his mother managed to return to Stolp as a cook in the hussars' barracks. Grosz spent his childhood and his adolescence there, and he studied in the local school until 1908 when, just before the end of his secondary studies, he was expelled for hitting a teacher.

Among the hussars of Prince Blücher, in Stolp, he doubtless learned to hate with all his heart (that extreme hate which, as the saying goes, is akin to love) Prussian officers, one of the main characters of the world that he immortalised (others are capitalists, criminals, religious people, the proletariat and whores). It was the Prussian officers that he perhaps caricatured with the greatest ferocity and vehemence. I use the word 'hate' advisedly, because without that destructive and exasperated passion that the word implies, Grosz's work would not have been possible; nor would it have been possible without the extreme simplifications that a unilateral and schematic view of reality tends to convey.

He studied painting for two years (1909–1911) at the Royal Academy of Art in Dresden, where stultifying teachers versed in the classics made him copy plaster statues and Hellenic marbles, and where his instructor, Richard Müller (who would later collaborate with the Nazis) thought that Van Gogh's sunsets were 'shit' and that the expressionist Emil Nolde was a 'filthy pig'. At that time, Grosz dreamed of being a local epic painter, of military triumphs, in the style of Grützner. And he was a voracious reader of adventure stories – James Fenimore Cooper, Karl May, Sherlock Holmes stories, *Robinson Crusoe* – as well as the popular serial novels full of horror and crimes that he confessed to having an early fascination for, alongside the terrifying and magical acts performed in fairs and circuses. All of this would help to form his artistic personality as much as, or even more than, his time at the Academy.

After he received his diploma, in 1911, he moved to Berlin, where he continued studying graphic art for a time, at the School of Arts and Crafts, while he sent drawings and caricatures to different publications. He had also begun to illustrate books. His first work accepted for publication, in 1910, in the magazine *Ulk*, depicts two stylised gentlemen watching an elegant couple go by: a conventional, bourgeois, scene, a thousand miles from the world that he would invent in the following years. But, from 1911, there begin to appear traces of the apocalyptic vision that would later be fuelled by the butchery of the First World War, the social and political struggles of the Weimar Republic (1918–33), and the intense Berlin years of Dadaism, revolution, artistic experimentation, anarchy, utopian dreams and bohemian life that preceded Hitler's and Nazism's coming to power on 30 January 1933.

Among these most visible traces are violence associated with sex, suicide and crimes. Some critics interpret this macabre propensity as a metaphorical description of a repressive society, the Imperial Germany of Kaiser Wilhelm II, in which the strict and narrow moral codes that sought to curb the instincts, desires and fantasies of good citizens had instead the opposite effect of increasing neuroses and encouraging perversion and sexual violence. But it is also possible to detect in Grosz's drawings in these years – peopled by strangled women (*Ehebruch* (*Adultery*), 1913), decapitated women, caught in adultery or dismembered, families that sacrifice themselves (*Das Ender der Straße* (*The End of the Road*), 1913), deformed beings (*Abnormitaten*, (*Monsters*), 1913), men attacking other men with axes, knives or guns, or maddened crowds that seem about to tear each other apart or else explode (*Pandemonium* (1915–16) – a Baudelairian *maudit* aesthetic, full of excess, extravagance, distortions and human ferocity, which the society of his time seemed to condemn, but in truth found seductive and stimulating. Because all these mutilations, ugliness and crimes are not depicted in an accusatory manner, but rather with an (albeit implied)sense of indulgence, akin to the festive way that Edgar Allan Poe wrote his horror stories. Grosz sketched an imaginary portrait of Poe in 1913, *Wie ich mir Edgar Allan Poe vorstelle* (*How I Imagine Edgar Allan Poe*), and his work would inspire him to draw that same year *Der Doppelmord in der Rue Morgue* (*The Double Crime in the Rue Morgue*). But whereas the work of Poe, Barbey d'Aurevilly and other horror writers tends towards rather unreal, abstract fantasies, in Grosz horror is always firmly rooted in real life. 'I can paint a devil, but I can't paint an angel,' he once said.* That's right; but his devils always give the impression of being of flesh and blood.

The 1914–18 war had a traumatic effect on Grosz's life. It accentuated the pessimistic and anarchic aspects of his personality and it furnished him with many experiences – images, rage – that would help shape the extreme, apocalyptic, dissolute and dogmatic nature of his artistic vision. How he was involved in the war itself is not at all clear. When the conflict broke out, Grosz enrolled as a volunteer in the grenadiers of the second Kaiser Francis. Six months later, in May 1915, he was exempted from service for medical reasons. From what he has said, and from what has been unearthed, it would seem that he spent most of this time suffering from sinusitis in hospitals behind the lines, where the wounded and mutilated were sent and where, of course, the pestilence, suffering and squalor were indescribable. There the war had nothing heroic to it: it appeared exclusively in all its savagery and stupidity. He was called up again on 4 January 1917, but was almost immediately interned in a psychiatric hospital in Gorden, suffering from a nervous breakdown, as a result of which he was officially declared as unfit for the army in April of that year. It seems that a famous Berlin sexologist, Dr Hirschfield, and a tycoon and patron of the arts, Count Harry Kessler, pulled some strings to have him returned to civilian life,

* M. Kay Flavell, *George Grosz. A Biography*, New Haven and London, p. 300.

away from a war that – as his letters and drawings of this time reveal – he abhorred with all his being.

In those years of the First World War, he contracted – the way you contract a disease – a furious indignation against his country and against his compatriots, that is well illustrated in this extract from a letter of 1916 to Robert Bell: 'Day by day, my hatred for Germans grows with the irremediably ugly, anti-aesthetic (yes, anti-aesthetic) and horrible appearance of most Germans in Germany. To put it as crudely as I can: "I feel no kinship at all with such a mess."'* In this rather 'unpatriotic' state of mind, he painted his first masterpieces, among which were some oil paintings, a technique that he had begun to use in 1907. One of the most vigorous of these paintings, dating between 1917 and 1919, has either been lost or was one of his numerous 'degenerate' works destroyed by the Nazis: *Deutschland, ein Wintermarchen* (*Germany, a Winter's Tale*). Even seeing it as a reproduction, the powerful language and the fevered imagination jolts us. His world is already there in place, in a picture that revolves around a uniformed bourgeois character, a monster of indifference and egotism, who sits in the centre of the picture, armed with a knife and fork, surrounded by food, beer and reactionary newspapers, satisfying his needs while all around chaos ensues. At his feet, three puppets – a priest, a soldier and a schoolteacher – represent the institutions that defend his interests and privileges. None of the four individuals seems too perturbed by the surrounding devastation: fires, landslides, and the disappearance of the law of gravity, because everything is turning, getting muddled and falling down. It's true that there's a spark in the little eyes of the bourgeois; but perhaps it isn't fear, but rather excitement at the proximity of his pleasure. A naked woman, with fat thighs and buttocks and pendulous breasts, comes through the chaos unscathed. The painter himself has slipped into the bottom left-hand corner of the picture: a frowning man who is watching the end of the world quite unperturbed. That's how he would also later describe himself in an ink drawing of 1917: *Straßenszene mit Zeichner* (*Street Scene with Arist*). He's drawing with his pipe in his mouth, sitting in the midst of the city bustle, looking not at his

* Schneede, p. 31.

paper but at the distorted landscape surrounding him: buildings, many crosses, and a little deformed man looking covetously at a naked woman, with a skull's face, whose sex seems to be a spider. The artist, immersed in this world, also keeps his distance from it: he is creating, not describing, it.

Another of Grosz's great paintings, the *Widmung an Oskar Panizza* (*Dedicated to Oskar Panizza*) is also a visionary representation in which death – a skeleton sitting on a coffin – is leading an infernal procession, like those in the nightmares of a Brueghel or a Hieronymus Bosch, painters much admired by Grosz. Within the bloody glow that bathes the picture, emanating from fires devouring buildings, a maddened crowd dehumanised by excesses and fear – with animal faces, or faces stripped of skin – is dying in a holocaust. Among them, some ridiculous characters are behaving in an absurd way: they are waving flags, brandishing sabres or crucifixes, blowing bugles. In the midst of the flames and the general dissolution, you can make out female forms. Everything is measured and oblique, everything is criss-crossed by planes that introduce geometric confusion and disorder into the old rational symmetry of the world.

John der Frauenmörder (*John The Lady Killer*, now in the Kunsthalle in Hamburg) dates from 1918. In this oil painting, with its contrasting strong colours made fashionable by Expressionism, we find on the same plane the victim, a naked woman with her neck severed, and her assassin, a stiff, well-dressed little man who is fleeing through the streets of a burning city. The insufferable tension in the picture comes from the subtle blend of story and language; the oblique planes emphasise the violence of the bloody corpse, and the flames in the buildings suggest instability and change, as does the instability of the perspective. And the green, yellow and black tones of the criminal express his cruelty as much as the murdered body of his victim. The image of women with their throat slit obsessed Grosz in this period, and in 1918 alone he produced three very similar pictures. His best works of the war and the post-war period would be like these paintings: blood-drenched incidents involving individuals or larger groups.

Although among his great work one must always single out at least a dozen oil paintings, Grosz's genius lay not so much in his paintings as in his work as a graphic artist: a cartoonist, caricaturist, engraver, illustrator, poster designer, publicist, and a designer of book covers and theatre costumes and sets. As Orwell did in his newspaper articles, radio broadcasts and book reviews, Grosz invested in these 'minor' genres all the energy, imagination and rigour that other creators put into the 'major' genres, making them distinctive, lasting works of art. This is one of the achievements that I admire most in him, and in Orwell, who is similar to Grosz in a number of ways, including his ideas about politics. He used the forms that were most accessible to the general public, the most advanced technologies, to express his inner world, his obsessions and his fury, without sacrificing his moral independence and the right that every artist has to be a critic and to experiment with form.

Like Orwell, Grosz always found repugnant any idea of 'Art' with a capital 'a', reserved for an elite of pretentious people, light years away from ordinary men and women. According to his son Marty, every time reverential admirers praised his 'artistic' achievements, Grosz hurled abuse at them: *'Kunst ist Scheiße'* ('Art is shit').* The media that he worked in were a way of opposing dominant ideas about specialisation in art, looking instead to re-establish the link that once existed between the artist and the whole of society, when 'art', which was inseparable from magic and religion, was one of the basic needs of life. The choice of popular 'genres', however, did not mean that Grosz, unlike other artists who were committed to producing 'popular art', did not pay attention to technique. Instead, he worked intensively to create a language that was direct and accessible but also intense and original.

The arrival of Dadaism in Berlin in 1918 – from Zurich and the work of Richard Huelsenbeck – gave Grosz an appropriate climate – a philosophy and certain techniques – to give full rein to his anarchism and iconoclasm, to his fury and virulence against the political regime and the institutions of the nascent Weimar Republic, and to his revolutionary dreams, that were more destructive than construc-

* Marty Grosz, in George Grosz, *Gli anni di Berlino*, Mazzotta, Milan, 1985, p. 16.

tive, and would keep him in the Communist party until 1925. (He joined the party in 1918, along with other Berlin Dadaists like John Heartfield, Wieland Herzfelde and Erwin Piscator.) From that time he contributed to all the Dadaist magazines, manifestos and shows, he printed his first collections of lithographs, edited and illustrated innumerable avant-garde and revolutionary publications, was involved in scandals, married Eva Peter, his lifelong companion, organised individual exhibitions, was tried and fined three times for blasphemy and insulting the army, and lived to the full all the excesses, madness, fun and the political and cultural polemics of the twenties. These years prepared the ground for the second great European apocalypse, but they were also extraordinarily dynamic in artistic terms.

These are Grosz's great years. He was the leading artist in Berlin, in Germany, throughout the Weimar period. His two folders of lithographs, *Erste George Grosz-Mappe* and *Kleine Grosz-Mappe* date from 1917; the third, much more political than the previous two, *Gott Mit Uns (God is with Us)*, is from 1920. As would happen later in his career, these engravings had already appeared before as drawings in different exhibitions and publications.

In these years, Grosz would achieve a solid reputation, but he would also be subject to irate criticism from conservative sectors, which attacked him for his obscenity, anti-militarism and blasphemy, and, at times, even from his comrades in the Communist Party, who felt obliged to keep their distance from his iconoclastic excesses. The party publication *Die Rote Fahne (The Red Flag)*, for example, condemned as 'perverse' and 'idiot forms of *kitsch*' the paintings and objects of the First Dadaist Exhibition in Berlin (July and August 1920), in which Grosz exhibited nine engravings/lithographs from *Gott Mit Uns*, for which he was taken to court and fined three hundred marks (the court also ordered the destruction of the plates).

Grosz's world is, indeed, too individualist, arbitrary, obsessive and violent to serve the interests and objectives of a political party, even a party looking to reconstruct society root and branch. He very rarely offered a positive view of the proletariat and any future classless society. His 1919 drawing *Wie der Staatsgerichtshof aussehen musste* (*How Courts Should Act*), in which, beneath a portrait of the revolutionary leader Karl Liebkneth, a court of workers and peasants is trying a handful of generals in chains, is unusual in this respect. Instead, almost all his work of this period seems to be intent on satirising and expressing disgust at the military, the bourgeoisie, leaders and religious people, and describing, in extremely minute detail, degenerate and criminal elements.

A pen-and-ink drawing from 1917, *Als alles vorbei war, spielten sie Karten* (*When that finished, they started playing cards*), which would appear in his book *Ecce Homo* (1923), with the title *Apachen* (*Apaches*), shows three horrifying individuals around a table, playing cards with icy tranquillity, after having murdered and dismembered a woman. A leg of the victim is sticking up out of one of the murderer's chairs and the blurred mutilated body is in a corner. On the floor of the squalid room there is a woman's boot, a basin and the axe and knife used for the crime. We can't talk about 'black humour' here, because there is no humour, just macabre blackness, a life reduced to its essential cruel and grotesque components. And yet there is something about these three ferocious figures, their amorphous size, their rigid, slumped forms, their dead eyes, that is rather pathetic, a hint of humanity that seems to be accusing us. The design is simple and precisely realist.

The word 'realist' is inevitable when it comes to describing Grosz's world, as well as saying that it is urban, cataclysmic, full of sensuality, sex, blood, egotism, exploitation and cruelty. Also that it is elemental and primary, without nuance, ambiguity, generous gestures, compassion or lofty feelings. The people that inhabit this world are stupid puppets, vulgar bipeds thirsting for material pleasures, like eating, drinking, fornicating, exploiting their neighbours, going to war, as well as baroque excesses like slaughtering and decapitating other human beings. Is this life? Was this Berlin in the twenties? Of course not. Why use the word realist, then, to describe such an extravagant caricature? Because even though it is completely deformed and stripped of all positive aspects and complexity, the life reflected in Grosz's 'fiction' is rooted in this common fund of shared experience, and we can recognise in it something that we are *as well.* The animate and inanimate beings of this world are joined by a very thin umbilical chord to the beings in our world – their carnal desires and the space they move in – and the artist's skill has given them a persuasive power that overcomes any reservations we might have about their evil, their mechanised being or their ugliness (that is their unreality).

In an autobiographical text from 1925, entitled *Abwicklung (Liquidation)*,* Grosz tells us that in order to make his objects as rough and virulent as possible, he studied the crudest impulses of artistic creation, the graffiti in public urinals and street doodles, which expressed very directly 'the most powerful instincts'. He also felt that children's drawings stimulated him 'through their lack of ambiguity'. In his early exercise books and notebooks there are copies of slogans and images that he has seen in city streets. Indeed, in many of Grosz's drawings in the twenties, especially in the first years of the decade, there are many echoes of these spontaneous, inexperienced attempts at producing images. Grosz looked for inspiration and models that chimed with his own view of life. The elemental and dogmatic views that he upheld required, for the sake of coherence, an equally simple and primary form: little men that seem like the stick figures that children doodle, or obscene graffiti where, in the loneliness of public toilets or in the darkness of the night, certain people give expression to filthy and disgusting feelings. The outlook and the form complement each other so successfully that they create an entire reality, different to that other reality – the real world – but linked to it by a powerful mixture of contrasting feelings: repulsion and fascination, hatred and desire, attraction and a desire to escape.

Grosz's world is very personal, but not solipsistic, as would be the case, in those years, with many other artists, above all those that abandoned figurative art. In his work there are many aspects that would appeal not just to his progressive contemporaries, but also to very large numbers of apolitical people. Take, for example, his criticism and condemnation of militarism, the old military caste that, despite the fall of the empire, continued to dominate the army and was a very troublesome legacy for the republican regime. They were

* Published in *Das Kunstblatt*, vol. 8, no. 2, Verlag Gustav Kiepenheur, Berlin, 1924.

responsible for losing the war and for the limitless sufferings of the German people. The merciless satires and caricatures that Grosz launched against the rituals, personalities, mythology and emblems of the military world were interpreted as being ideological. But it was not historical materialism and the class struggle that were the real sources of inspiration, but rather an irresistible desire to provoke and offend the people who best symbolise, in any regime, those aspects of the world most odious to an individualist, seditious and anarchic spirit such as his: force, discipline, hierarchies and order.

The collection *Gott Mit Uns* contains his best anti-militarist prints. Perhaps the most famous of these is *K.V.* (*Die Gesundbeter*) (*The Quack Doctors*), which is in the Museum of Modern Art in New York. (*K.V.* stands for *kriegsverwendungsfahig*: fit for active service). An army doctor declares as 'fit for service' a skeleton that he is examining with a stethoscope. The picture is framed by high-ranking officers standing around smoking and chatting, indifferent to the farce that they are party to, and by upright, automaton soldiers. The two generals in the foreground, seen in profile, have that look that is common to many of Grosz's characters, somewhere between a clown and a wild beast: bald heads, walrus moustaches, bull necks enclosed in stiff uniform collars, epaulettes, monocles, open jaws, butcher's teeth, doll-like stiffness. There is something profoundly stupid, as well as carnivalesque, about these stunted human beings that seem to be enslaved by rituals that are absurd and yet can cause immense grief and violence. The tone is sarcastic, and the scene is also very claustrophobic, with the bare walls and barred windows through which one can glimpse skyscrapers, chimneys and clouds of smoke.

It is not just the ferocity and insolence of the artist's vision that is so impressive in this and in other drawings. It is true that they can be seen as a bilious attack on a certain state of affairs, an important moment in history. But if the vigorous energy of this work depended just on its historical content, then it would have become more anodyne or have disappeared altogether with the passing of time. The fact that it makes such an impact today, when 'German militarism' is now a thing of the past, is because this drawing also offers its own coherent and tightly structured world, full of colourful and terrifying buffoons and horrifying victims that have a life of their own. It is a creative response to real life: the deceitful world of fiction. A life without which the other life, the one that we live and not the one we dream, would be much more difficult to endure. That is why certain exceptionally talented people, like Grosz, have invented, with all the force of their imagination and technique, this parallel and autonomous life found in great artistic fictions.

Until he left Germany in 1933, and above all in the immediate post-war years, military men constantly appear in Grosz's world, in all their ridiculousness, ordering massacres, playing the macabre game of war, repressing workers, killing communists or simply exhibiting their ugly loud-mouthed faces, pitted with duelling scars, along with their dress swords, pistols, helmets and medals, often including swastikas. And in squalid, plebeian contrast to this military aristocracy stifled in their operatic parade uniforms, we find the former soldiers, turned by the war into mere shadows of human beings, armless, eyeless, leaning on their prosthetic limbs, starving, dragging their wretched figures through the streets, begging or selling knick-knacks in café or brothel doors.

But these former soldiers, like the proletariat – whom we glimpse only rarely, always in the background, tied to an execution post, run through by a bayonet, setting out at dawn for the factory, or sweating in the factories to make the bosses rich – are, compared to the military, secondary figures in the farcical world of Grosz. This is a world of oppressors rather than victims.

By contrast, the capitalist is also a prominent figure and is always centre stage, as in the marvellous sketch in the sixth issue of *Die Pleite* magazine (January 1920), where we find a general and a bourgeois gentleman dangling from scaffolds, shaking hands and wishing each other a happy New Year. The capitalist is described – invented – with the same tremendous excess as the military man. He is also a repulsive puppet. Whether he is a millionaire or a small-scale landlord, he is always seen as unsatisfied in his desires, always desperate for more money, more drink, more food and more women. He preens himself like a coquette, but he oozes vulgarity. He surveys his companies with shameless delight, stating, implacably, 'I will destroy everything that prevents me from being the absolute master of this' (an illustration for Schiller's *Die Rauber* (*The Robber*)), or, brandishing a cigar, smoking, his hands in his waistcoat, his head in the clouds, showing the wretched of the world his immense stomach in which even his entrails are shaped like his factories (the illustration for *Die Drie Soldaten* (*The Three Soldiers*) by Bertolt Brecht in 1930).

Capitalists make an appearance in cafés, count their money wads with their little eyes gleaming with greed, they dress in furs, watch-chains gleam in their waistcoats, they disport walking sticks and umbrellas, dress coats, cravats, top hats, round metal glasses, stiff collars, carnations in their buttonholes, walking their dogs in the street, kneeling in front of military men, kissing their swords and boots, eating and drinking until they are sick, spending their nights in nightclubs, frolicking with whores or with their wives whom they treat like whores. Among their fantasies are sadism and masochism and they are inveterate *voyeurs*. They play cards, speculate on war, preach sacrifice to their workers, they are patriots, nationalists and Nazis. In the intimacy of their bedrooms, they like to loosen their braces, unbutton their flies, stretch their legs and look covetously at the ample flesh of their lovers or wives or prostitutes.

Grosz's best collection – *Ecce Homo*, eighty-four lithographs and sixteen watercolours (Berlin, 1923) – mainly concentrates on these men. Here the bourgeois reigns, repellent, abusive, egotistical, hypo-critical, a mediocre monster drunk with power and sensuality. In the most caustic of these images, the watercolour *Kraft und Anmut* (*Force and Grace*, 1922), you can see him with his hands in his pockets, in an elegant brown suit and a green tie, his jutting chin defying the world. Is he looking through the window at the properties that he has already acquired, or at those that will soon fall into his grasp? His posture, his expression, his square face, the muscles in his enor-mous neck, his open legs all signal an absolute confidence in himself, the security of someone who has possessions and who is in charge. Behind him, on the yellow quilt and the maroon cushions, in quiet desperation, or stretched out in a suggestive pose, is the third central figure in this crude and strident social trinity envisaged by Grosz: the prostitute. She wears pink slippers and black stockings, she has coloured ornaments on her white slip, which reveals some thigh and the mounds of her breasts. Her eyes reflect the tiredness of pleasure, her mouth is half open and, by the way that she is showing them off, she seems to be proud of her hairy armpits. This blatant vulgarity represents 'Grace' in Grosz's twisted world.

This paradise of militarism, exploitation and other bourgeois vices is also a relentlessly macho world, cruel to women. Women exist to be observed naked, to be fondled, hit, humiliated, murdered or cut up like a piece of meat. Because here women, as in the sermons of Puritan fanatics excoriating 'sins of the flesh', seem to possess the sinister gift of bringing out the worst in men, of turning them into beasts, as literally occurs in a 1928 drawing, *Ruf der Wildnis* (*The Call of the Wild*), in which five people looking at a dancer shaking her thighs grow the mouths and snouts of pigs. It comes as no surprise to learn, therefore, that the young Grosz was fascinated by the mythical figure of Circe, who turned men into pigs. There are at least two drawings dedicated to her, from 1912 and 1913: in one she is a modern woman with a hat, and in the other she has high heels and is smoking a cigarette, enthroned, in Olympian fashion, above groups of animalistic men, who are cowering at her feet. Women appear in Grosz's world stretched out in voluptuous poses, showing their sex or their buttocks to bourgeois males with their flies undone who observe them as potential victims or as mere instruments of pleasure. They also appear in transparent dressing gowns and petticoats, in black stockings, half naked but wearing hats, jewels, chains and crosses. All these are the marks of the courtesan or professional woman of pleasure, or of bourgeois ladies who have become corrupted: these are the only parts they are allowed to play by the shadowy lustful males who dominate the world. Even when they get dressed and go out, to sit in a café or go for a walk, they cannot escape their nature and condition: their clothes are transparent and reveal their fat thighs, their heavy breasts and their enormous buttocks. Their appearance is the same, like the soldiers and the bourgeois men, whether they are gyrating at the top of a rope, doing acrobatics, gossiping in cafés, flirting in parties or opening their legs in the bedroom: plump, bags under their eyes, painted, pure flesh without brains or spirit, shameless, vulgar and artificial.

Grosz grew up in a rural area of a region that was the bastion of very strict Protestantism, where families respected the pious customs of Wilhelm's Germany. In his autobiography he remembers that in his youth convention dictated that the female form should be hidden by demure bodices, girdles and layers of clothing, without even an ankle showing, and that 'decent women' were not even allowed to cross their legs. He also recounts in great detail the miraculous, unreal experience of seeing as a child a friend's aunt undressing, thus discovering the intimacy of the female form. Whether it is true or false, the anecdote reveals the tremendous repressive atmosphere surrounding sex and the twisted, overheated effect that this had on male erotic fantasies. Without this background, one cannot understand how the depiction of women, sex and desire in Grosz's drawings from the Berlin years could be so grotesque and violent, and so much like a sermon on chastity delivered by a preacher.

That is why some critics call him a 'moralist'. He does not seem to have been so in the post-war years, when the republic ushered in a spectacular liberation in behaviour, especially in the artistic, bohemian world of Berlin. Although he was a very dedicated worker, he enjoyed on at least several occasions those alcoholic and cocaine-fuelled binges where everything was possible, and he wrote about an orgy in his studio that lasted twenty-four hours. But it is certainly the case that when he came to paint, and doubtless contrary to his rational beliefs, there welled up from some inner place someone who was frightened by and furious at the mysteries of sex, someone who never felt himself on equal terms with women, or who had never rid himself totally from the inhibitions that are always at the root of the apocalyptic desires, the violence and the humiliation associated with physical love. Although he knew of Freud's efforts, which were very fashionable in Germany at the time, to have the different aspects of sex treated naturally, as an essential part of life, he could not have taken them very seriously. (He dedicated a sardonic watercolour to him in 1922, *Professor Freud gewidmet*, in which we see this elegant gentleman with his tongue hanging out, surrounded by ample naked and half-naked ladies).

In any event, in Grosz's fictional world, women and sex have nothing to do with love, for there is no place for that, or with pleasure, if we take pleasure to mean something that enriches the life of men and women, but rather they are the exclusive domain of the violence, cruelty and animal instincts of a world in which the only possible relationship between the two sexes appears to be one of domination and destruction. The word 'libertinism' that in the eighteenth century came to describe the delicate ways in which a culture free from sexual taboos staged the act of physical love through a series of games and rituals, dignifying it, sublimating it and turning it into an elegant and imaginative art, where men and women play the leading roles, is at the opposite extreme to the elemental and paroxysmic erotic world of Grosz. With very few exceptions, like the splendid pen-and-ink drawing of 1912 entitled *Orgie*, in which several couples intertwine in an enthusiastic pagan celebration of instinct,* there are no games, ceremonies, play, enjoyment, humour or feeling: just copulation, blood and animality.

Perhaps Grosz was taking his revenge on these unconscious manifestations of his Puritan education, by making religious people another puppet in his artistic world. Because blasphemy has an equally prominent place as murder, suicide and female buttocks, especially in the drawings of *Hintergrund* (*Backcloth*), where the vitriol is directed at priests and at Christianity. It is true that these drawings and cartoons are not as strongly focused as his diatribes against soldiers or bankers. The pastor or priest can be seen supporting the execution of workers by executioners dressed as bosses (*Das Vaterunser* (*The Paternoster*), 1921). In the midst of infernal cataclysms, he raises his cross and gives blessings, as if justifying or denying the horrors. The enemy of truth and compassion, he is a naïve or blasphemous cynic, who finds it amusing to balance a cross on the end of his nose (*Seid untertan der Obrigkeit* (*Obedience to Authority*), 1928), and a militarist: he delivers bellicose sermons and what comes out of his mouth are not words but bullets, sabres and

* Reproduced in Hans Hess, *Georg Grosz*, London and New Haven, 1985, p. 31.

173

mortars (*Das Ausschüttung des heiligen Geistes* (*The Dividends of the Holy Spirit*), 1928). He is also seen as servile to the powers that be – capitalists and the military. Hypocritical, grim and shadowy, he is another of the 'pillars of society'.

This is the title of one of the most vivid oil paintings that Grosz produced in 1926, his most fertile year for painting, *Stutzen der Gesellschaft*, now in the Nationgalerie in Berlin. Out of the by now quintessential background of fires and soldiers advancing swords in hand, four figures emerge. There is an intellectual who is waving an olive branch, clutching his pencil and newspapers, wearing a chamber pot on his head, a pathetic emblem of the importance of his ideas. A social democrat has a little national flag and a badge proclaiming, '*Socialismus ist Arbeit*' ('Socialism is work'), but out of the top of his head comes not arguments but a pile of shit. But it is the terrifying Nazi bourgeois capitalist in the foreground who is the most unforgettable image. He looks horrendous – with a carnivorous mouth, a monocle, a scar and an open skull that contains a lancer on horseback instead of his brains – and in each hand he carries a symbol of his ideals: a glass of beer and a sabre. Above the three of them, with his arms outstretched and the expression of a predator surveying carrion, we find the religious figure, dressed in a black habit: his ferocious smile makes it very clear that he approves of the posturing and the horror around him, and that perhaps he even lives off it all.

The extraordinary force of the picture transcends its critical focus and historical references and comes across to us as an autonomous fictive reality, the product of a corrosive imagination and an immense artistic skill. A reality depicting alienation, barbarity, theatricality and stupidity, drawn in aggressive colours that seem to be forced to coexist despite being essentially repellent, and full of an exaggerated number of figures, objects and narratives in a reduced space. We feel the claustrophobia, the violence and the madness of a humanity that has lost its direction and is heading towards inevitable catastrophe.

In these years – from 1925 to 1928 – Grosz went back to painting after a long period working almost exclusively as a graphic artist. In

174

this period he produced some of the most remarkable oil paintings of our time. Like *Sonnenfinsternis* (*The Eclipse of the Sun*) of 1926, in the Hecksher Museum, Huntington, New York, in which the capitalist and the general (in this case, Marshal Hindenburg, the President of the Republic) are giving orders to a group of bare-headed politicians. Or *Agitator* (*The Demagogue*) of 1928, in the Stedelijk Museum, Amsterdam, and a number of important portraits and self-portraits, in particular – a work of genius – the portrait of his friend, the writer and critic Max Herrmann-Neisse, of 1925 (in the Kunsthalle Mannheim).

Grosz made many pencil and charcoal sketches in preparation for this painting, which he worked on very carefully and slowly, according to his correspondence and the accounts of friends who visited his workshop. The result is a work that is both disconcerting and dazzling, a key element in his fiction: a little worm-like man, hunched up and getting smaller and smaller in front of our eyes. His bald head has shrunk almost to the top of the backrest of the chair, embroidered with red, blue and yellow flowers, where he is sitting. Very likely, if we kept watching him, he would carry on shrinking into a tiny figure, or even disappear, as in a fantasy story. His funeral garb, his large bony hands, the red ring on his finger, the slippers and gleaming bald head, his puckered mouth and blood-red lips, the way his head sinks into his curved chest: everything about him is strange, violates the norms, and yet at the same time there is something about this little gnome that we identify straight away, the inexorable life within him, perhaps the life of ideas, dreams and desires that inhabit his wretched body, or simply the life force that is his will to live, to defy the death that has already paid him a call and has begun to devour him. Grosz's passion for macabre, grotesque and fantastic imagery can clearly be seen in this work, yet it does not lose its 'realist' appearance. This is one of the peculiarities of his art: it can be caught up in a mad flight of fantasy without ever departing from lived experience, without sinking into artifice or abstraction. Among the innumerable 'monsters' that emerged from Grosz's pencils and brushes, few are as original and strange as this portrait.

During his years in Berlin, Grosz designed sets and costumes for several theatre productions, the most famous of which was the production staged by his friend Erwin Piscator, an adaptation of the Czech novel by Haroslav Jasek, *The Good Soldier Schwejk*. Along with supplying more than three hundred drawings for the cartoon film that Piscator used as a backcloth for the show – and which commented on, illustrated and, on occasion, took part in the action – Grosz, along with Bertolt Brecht, provided many ideas and suggestions for what would be remembered as one of the most memorable productions of the Weimar period. According to one critic, Grosz contributed above all else a sense of 'ferocity' as well as accentuating the anti-militarism of the piece.* Although the film has been lost, there remain seventeen lithographs, based on drawings of the *mise en scène* that Grosz edited in 1928, with Malik, in a folder entitled *Hintergrund*. Among these is the drawing that caused a scandal and led to a long court case where Grosz was found guilty of blasphemy.

It is called *Maul halten un weiter dienen* (*Close Your Mouth and Do Your Duty*), and shows Christ on the cross with a gas mask and soldiers' boots. One of his hands, raised aloft despite his bindings, is holding a black cross. Between his head and the inscription INRI is a shining halo. You can see his ribs through his skeletal body and in his side is the bleeding lance wound. The extreme weakness of the dying figure is shown in his buckling knees, no longer able to bear the weight of his fragile body. I have always been haunted by this small drawing. It is both terribly irreverent but also a savage plea for good sense and rationality to emerge from these depths of neglect and shame, an unadorned testimony to human suffering, not an act of blasphemy. Grosz detested romanticism, and in this period he always stated that one should accept life in all its cruel reality, without idealising it. 'My opinion is that one should always have the courage to face up to the senselessness of everything that happens. The only sense in the world is the sense that one gives it. That for me, with a few nuances, is the domain of my art,' he wrote to Wieland Herzfelde on 6 June 1933,† a sentence that encapsulates his attitude towards art and life. But this picture shows how artistic creation can-

* Andrew De Shong, *The Theatrical Designs of George Grosz*, Michigan, 1982.
† Flavell, p. 128.

not be controlled by reason alone, even in someone as reluctant to express 'emotion' as Grosz. For in that Christ in uniform, exposed to the horror of war in the trenches – the mud and mustard gas – who protests with the only thing that he has left to him– the human suffering inflicted on him by his killers – we see not just a provocative image but rather a moral allegory and a plea to society, to alienated men and women, to change direction. In the explosive conditions of extreme radicalisation that the Weimar Republic was experiencing in the final years of the decade, it would have been difficult for anyone to give such a pacifist and humanist reading of this Christ with his mask and boots, and it would not have been an interpretation that even Grosz would have accepted, because he was convinced that this was just another of his sacrilegious attacks on institutions and idols. That is perhaps the reason why, in 1930, he made a statue of this same image for an exhibition in Berlin organised by the IFA, the front organisation for the Communist Party. (The statue was confiscated by the police.) But, taken out of this radical context, this pathetic, alarming little figure has acquired an emotional and ethical resonance very different from how it was initially conceived. Something deeper and more permanent is now being expressed through it, with an energy and a subtlety that Grosz would only achieve on rare occasions.*

Although he continued working occasionally with the Communist Party, Grosz had stopped being an activist in 1925, and for some time, albeit discreetly, he had voiced his contempt and scepticism for the 'masses' and had openly rejected all forms of 'collectivism'. In his autobiography, he states that his disillusionment with communism and Marxism began with his visit to the USSR, where he spent six months in 1922. He was there to do a book with the Danish writer Martin Andersen-Nexo (who ended up writing it on his own). The journey was eventful, full of colourful incidents. Grosz met a very sick Lenin in the Kremlin, along with a number of figures from the Revolution, including Bujarin, Lunacharsky and Radek, and he heard Trotsky speak. Grosz was at one point drawn to Construc-

* As can be seen in his collection *Mit Pinsel und Schere: 7 Materialisationen*, Berlin, Malik, 1922.

tivism, the art form that looked to embrace modern technology and industry and replace man by machines (or turn man into a machine). Constructivism was all the rage in Moscow, and Grosz offers an amusing sketch of the extravagant Tatlin, the mentor of that school, whom he visited in his ramshackle house full of balalaikas and chickens. But the chaotic state of the country, the hunger, the arrogance of the commissars, the signs of authoritarianism – and perhaps above all, his intuition of the absolute control that would be exercised over all aspects of society as the state, in the hands of the Party, began to spread its tentacles – revealed to him another side of that revolution that he and his left-wing friends in Berlin had viewed with so much hope. And they showed him that, however many gains they might achieve, in communist societies there would never be a place for iconoclastic and uncontrollable people like him. This journey, without doubt, began the process that, as happened with Orwell, would lead him to become as radically opposed to communism as he was to fascism.

But this was a gradual and somewhat tortuous process; when he got back to Berlin, and in the years immediately following his visit, he did not make public his negative impressions of the USSR, perhaps to keep his distance from the violent anti-Soviet sentiments of the conservatives and the Nazis, who were becoming increasingly numerous in German society, that he would continue to attack with the same vehemence as before. He stayed another three years in the party and even became the president of the recently formed *Rote Gruppe* (Red Group) of the Communist Union of German Artists in 1924. He contributed posters and drawings to the electoral campaigns of the party and until the end of the decade, with some strained moments, he remained a loyal 'travelling companion'. In 1925 he published with Wieland Herzfelde *Die Kunst ist in Gefahr* (*Art is in Danger*), a collection of essays close to the aesthetic line of the Communist Party. There he argued that 'the artist cannot ignore the laws of social development, which is now the class struggle', and that painters had no other option but to choose between 'displaying technique and propaganda and class struggle'. Luckily, when he came to paint and draw, Grosz did not take any account of his own ideas in favour of this 'tendentious art' and continued to follow, above all, his own impulses and deeper instincts. His art was 'tendentious' to the highest degree, of course, and his vision of social reality was absolutely dogmatic and Manichaean, but it was also individualist and arbitrary in a way that was completely incompatible with the teachings and propaganda that the Communist Party expected of its artists. In one court of law where he was being tried, Grosz declared in 1928: 'When I am creating a drawing, I am not interested in any laws'.* That's true. Among these 'laws', of course, were his own political convictions. But when, in the intimacy of his studio in Sudende, these came up against his fantasy and his sense of unbridled freedom, it was fantasy and freedom that prevailed.

Some critics, including the well-informed Uwe M. Schneede, quote a letter that Grosz sent to his brother-in-law, Otto Schmalhausen, on 27 May 1927 as proof that his break with the revolution and the left could be due to financial considerations. 'My plan (taking into account the advice of Flechtheim†) is the following: to painting a series of 'commercial' landscapes, avoiding causing offence. If I sell them, then, in the winter, I'll be able to work on my favourite themes.' But this implied criticism is not born out by the facts. It was precisely his most pugnacious and virulent paintings and drawings that brought him prestige among the most enlightened sectors of Weimar Germany's bourgeoisie and aristocracy, who, like the elites of other European societies in the mad years of the inter-war period, discovered the refined pleasure of being artistically insulted, ill-treated and scandalised by Dadaists, Surrealists and revolutionaries of all complexions, and subscribed to their magazines and theatres, bought their paintings and went along happily to their shows. If its financial fate had depended on the proletariat, then all this rich literature and this splendid iconoclastic art in Europe at the beginning of the century would have vanished without trace. From this despised elite came the buyers and also Grosz's backers, like the generous Doctor Felix J. Weil and Count Harry Kessler who, even in his most

* Quoted by Uwe M. Schneede, *George Grosz: His Life and Work*, Universe Books, New York, 1979, p. 108.
† The successful Berlin *marchand* and gallery owner.

revolutionary moments, continued to help him economically, paying for trips and giving him a monthly income. It was this ferocious and insulting Grosz that the clientele admired, not the docile painter of landscapes that he did indeed begin to work on at the end of the twenties.

The evolution or, perhaps, the involution that Grosz's work experienced, and which would continue after his move to the United States, is too profound and complex to be interpreted as a simple mercenary calculation which would also have been completely counterproductive, and would have undermined his artistic prestige. In any event, the fact is that when in 1930 he published, not with his communist friend Wielan Herzfelde's publishing house, Malik Verlag, but with Bruno Cassirer, the sixty drawings of the series *Über alles die Liebe* (*Love above All Else*), something had changed in his world, even though outwardly all seemed to be the same. In his brief introduction to this work, Grosz says: 'The devil will know why, but when one looks at them up close, people and things become inadequate, ugly and often ambiguous and senseless.' However, in the watercolours and drawings of this collection, the reverse is true; people and things have become beautiful and more concrete. The world has lost its mystery, and objects and human beings seem to occupy firm and stable places in a world that has become static.

There are no demonic priests, and the few soldiers that crop up are not malevolent but seem instead cheerfully ridiculous. The bourgeois has softened his manners, and ladies have become much more decorous: they now play tennis, and when they are in dance halls, in cafés, on walks and even in the bedroom, they no longer display their buttocks, their breasts and their vaginas to such an extent. As well as being more dressed than undressed, they are also less fat than before, and sometimes have slim bodies that show off to great effect the tailored coats and high-heeled shoes that are the dominant fashion of the day. Dandyism, hedonism, frivolity, snobbery and cunning have replaced the slashed throats, dismemberments, sadism, masochism and voyeurism. Politics and nightmares have disappeared, and sex, crime and assaults can only be glimpsed in the distance, remote grounds for muted fury and innocuous venom.

There is a sense of general prosperity. Instead of cripples, beggars and unemployed people, the streets are full of friendly construction workers, and even the few remaining prostitutes, in their discreet brothels, are a bit like young society ladies. Instead of raping or killing them, gentlemen now kiss the ladies, sit them on their knees and talk to them like equals. Naughty old buffers spy on maids, as in popular farces. Evil, cruelty and violence have fled the fictive world of Grosz and their place has been taken by irony, humour, conformity, understanding and benevolence.

Just as his fictional world was transformed, so his life became radically different when he travelled to the United States. It was a childhood dream and a political necessity. He travelled just in time, since eighteen days after his departure, on 30 January, Hitler came to power. Few artists were as detested by the Nazis, and for good reason. In his last year in Berlin a group of brown shirts came to his studio in Berlin. He was saved by his acting ability: the thugs went away thinking that he was the butler. In the famous inquisitorial fire of 10 May 1933 at the gates of the University of Humboldt, the forty odd books that he illustrated as well as his own books became fuel for the flames. Five oils – including the portrait of Max Herman-Neisse – two watercolours and thirteen prints were included in the Degenerate Art Exhibition organised by Goebbels and exhibited throughout Germany to show how obscene, sacrilegious, anti-patriotic, pro-Jewish and pro-Bolshevik 'modernist' art was (and, indeed all these adjectives applied to Grosz). The regime's attack on his work was systematic and savage. Max Pechstein calculates that 285 works by Grosz disappeared or were destroyed by the Nazis. In March 1938 they took away his German nationality and, as they had nothing left of him to attack, they seized his wife's few possessions. Grosz had already decided that he would, 'along with his citizenship, discard his German identity, as if it were an old coat'. (He says this in his autobiography.) That year, he was given US nationality.

Editor's note. For reasons of space, we are not including the analysis of the years spent in the United States. In these years, according to Vargas Llosa, the world depicted in Grosz's art, showed 'good sense, intelligence and reason, and perhaps even goodness and generosity'.

A dogmatic vision has tragic consequences in politics, because dogmas restrict and distort human reality, which is always more subtle and complex than ideological schemata and Manichean world views. But such a vision can be a marvellous stimulus for creating a work of art, which is always a *fiction*, that is, a condensation of reality. When a schematic view of humanity – and here we think of Grosz in art and Brecht in literature – is expressed with great technical and formal skill, then it can become a powerful and persuasive reality, an alternative world to lived experience. And although it is a fraud, it can often impose itself on reality and become that reality. Grosz produced his best work when he hated and wounded without compunction, when he dreamed of crimes and the apocalypse, when he divided the world into devils – soldiers, priests, prostitutes, bureaucrats and capitalists – and saints – revolutionaries and workers – and expressed all this in seductive and deceitful images.

In the worlds of art and literature – the worlds of fiction – people sometimes discover that their own secret utopias have been expressed, their deepest cravings have to some degree been satisfied. I find this with Grosz, above all the Grosz of the Berlin years. To admire his work, I do not have to burden it with ethical and political considerations, or psychological readings, because although these aspects might well be important, they do not address the central issue: that Grosz *used* all of this material to construct his own world, based on his own creative egotism.

Great artistic works are always mysterious and complex, so it is always risky to gauge them in ideological, moral or political terms, although not to do so would be to avoid something that is also undeniable: that a work is not created and does not resonate in a void, but rather within history. Some works can be understood quite easily and thus lend themselves to different interpretations. Other works, like those of Grosz, are much less easy to read, which is why critics often seem uneasy with him. Some critics analyse his work purely in artistic terms, talking about form and colour and composition, ignoring the ferocious distortions and violence of his world. And those that merely explore the content are often loathe to accept that his images are contradictory, at once a violent attack on, but also a celebration of, a world with which – doubtless despite himself – he closely identified.

Grosz was not a 'social artist'. He was a *maudit*. In today's shifting and superficial definitions of art, all original works must be described as *maudit*, eccentric and marginal, and so the term seems rather meaningless. But this was certainly not the case when Baudelaire used the word. What I mean is that Grosz's work is absolutely authentic, and expresses an unrestrained freedom. His fantasies stirred the bilge of society and the human heart, and his invention of reality has, over time, become more powerful and truthful than reality itself. When we talk of the 'Berlin years' today, we are not thinking of the years that Germany suffered and enjoyed, but rather the years that Grosz invented.

Berlin, March 1992

Two Friends

The famous Yellow House in Arles that Vincent Van Gogh hired, furnished and filled with his own paintings to receive his friend Paul Gauguin in the autumn of 1888, no longer exists. It disappeared in an Allied bombing raid on 25 June 1945, and on the site now is a modest hotel called the Terminus Van Gogh. The owner, an alert little old lady of eighty-four, has a photograph of the bombed house. She had witnessed the bombing raid, which almost cost her her life. The surrounding area has not changed much, however, and you can recognise straight away the house next door that appears in one of the Dutchman's paintings.

The large, circular Place Lamartine is still there, as are the massive green plane trees by the Cavalry Gate, set into the wall of the old city. The Rhône probably hasn't changed much either as it flows slowly and majestically a few yards from this terrace, flanking the Roman town. What has disappeared is the small police station – replaced by a Monoprix store – along with the brothel of Madame Virginie, known then as the Number One House of Tolerance, which, in those two months that they lived together, the friends visited two or three times a week, Van Gogh always to sleep with a girl called Rachel. The shabby street where the brothel was located has been dug up and replaced by a wide avenue. This was then a very poor neighbourhood on the outskirts of town, with beggars, prostitutes and cafés full of the dregs of humanity, but in the century or more that has gone by, the area has become gentrified and it is now the home of discreet and anodyne middle-class people.

The two months that Van Gogh and Gauguin spent here, between October and December 1888, are the most mysterious in their lives. The details of what really happened between the two friends in those eight weeks have escaped the stubborn investigation of hundreds of researchers and critics who, from the few objective facts, try to clarify the unknown, sometimes with rather wild hypotheses and fantasies. The letters of the two men are evasive about their time together, and when at the end of his life Gauguin referred to this period, in *Avant et Après*, some fifteen years had gone by, syphilis had wreaked havoc with his memory, and his testimony was suspect because he was trying at all costs to counter the rumours, which were then widespread in France, that he had been responsible for Van Gogh's final collapse into madness. What we do know is that in this now phantom house, the two men dreamed, painted, argued and fought, and that the Dutchman was on the point of killing the Frenchman, whose trip to Arles he had waited for with the impatience and the hopes of a lover.

There are no hints of a homosexual relationship between the two, but the relationship was certainly passionate and very highly charged. Van Gogh had met Gauguin a few months earlier, in Paris, and was fascinated by the overwhelming personality of this artist-adventurer who had just returned from Panama and Martinique, with some paintings that were full of light and primitive life, like the life that he himself looked to lead so as to counterbalance 'the decadence of the West'. So he asked his brother Theo to help him convince Gauguin to come with him to Provence. There, in that yellow house, they would establish a community of artists, and they would be the pioneers. Gauguin would be the director and new painters would come to join this brotherhood or commune, where everything would be shared, where they would live for beauty, and where private property and money would not exist. This utopia obsessed Van Gogh. At first, Gauguin was opposed to it and came to Arles reluctantly, lured by the economic incentives offered by Theo, because the truth was that he was very happy in Pont-Aven, in Brittany. This can be seen in the fact that in several of the sixteen paintings that he completed in Arles, his Arles inhabitants are wearing Breton clogs and caps. However, after the tragedy of Christmas Eve, 1888, it would be Gauguin and not Van Gogh who would dedicate the rest of his life to try to bring to fruition the Dutchman's utopian dream, and would set off for Polynesia, a land that had fascinated Van Gogh when he read about it in a novel by Pierre Loti, *Le Mariage de Loti*, a novel that he made Gauguin read during his stay in Arles.

Was it his excessive obsequiousness and the extraordinary lengths to which Van Gogh went to make him feel comfortable and happy in Arles that turned Gauguin against his companion? It is quite possible that the rather hysterical effusiveness of the Dutchman began to get on his nerves and made him feel imprisoned. But he was also irritated by his messiness, and by the fact that he took more money than had been agreed out of the common kitty for his 'hygienic activities' (which is what he called his visits to Rachel). They had divided up the tasks. Gauguin cooked and Van Gogh did the shopping, but the cleaning, that they shared, always left much to be desired. There was one definite argument over the *pointilliste* Seurat; Van Gogh, who admired him, wanted to invite him to the Studio of the South, the name given to the utopian community, and Gauguin refused, because he hated the artist.

Their aesthetic differences were more theoretical than practical. Van Gogh declared himself an out-and-out realist and looked to set up his easel in the open air, so that he could paint natural scenes. Gauguin maintained that the true raw material of a creator was not reality but memory, and that one should look for inspiration not in the world outside but rather from within. This dispute, which apparently provoked tremendous arguments between the two friends, has been resolved over time: neither of them illustrated their theories in their paintings, which now appear to us, despite being so different, equally full of invention and imagination as well as being firmly rooted in reality. In the first few weeks that they lived together in Arles, the good weather allowed them to put into practice Van Gogh's theories. They both installed themselves outside to paint the same topics: the Alyscamps countryside, the great Roman and palaeo-Christian necropolis, the gardens of the Hôtel-Dieu, the public hospital. But then torrential rains set in and they had to stay cooped up in the Yellow House, painting mainly with their imagination and from memory. Being cooped up like this because of the inclement weather – it was the windiest and wettest autumn in half a century – must have created an atmosphere of claustrophobia and extreme tension, which often translated into violent arguments. That was the time that Gauguin sketched the portrait of his friend painting sunflowers that left the Dutchman dumbfounded: 'Yes, that's me. But already mad.'

Was he? There's no doubt that in the hazy world that we call madness, there is a place that cannot be precisely defined which corresponds to Van Gogh's mental state that autumn, although the diagnoses of 'epilepsy' that doctors treating him first in Arles and later in Saint-Rémy came up with leave us somewhat perplexed and sceptical about the true nature of his illness. But it is a fact that when living with Gauguin, something that he had invested so much in, turned sour, this brought on a crisis that he would never get out of. It is a fact that the idea that his friend would leave before the date he had promised (a year) was unbearable for him. He moved heaven and earth to keep him in Arles, but this had the opposite effect on Gauguin, convincing him to leave as soon as possible. This is the context for the episode on the night before Christmas Eve, 1888, for which we have only the improbable testimony of Gauguin to rely on. An argument in the Café de la Gare, while they were having an absinthe, ended abruptly: the Dutchman threw his glass at his friend, who only just managed to take evasive action. The next day, Gauguin tells him that he is going to move into a hotel because, he says, if a similar incident happened again, he would be likely to react with equal violence and wring his neck. At nightfall, when he was walking through Victor Hugo Park, he heard footsteps behind him. He turned, and saw Van Gogh with an open razor in his hand. When Van Gogh saw that he had been discovered, he ran away. Gauguin spent the night in a neighbouring guest house. At seven in the morning, he went back to the Yellow House and found it surrounded by neighbours and police. The previous evening, after the incident in the park, Van Gogh had cut off part of his left ear and had taken it, wrapped in a newspaper, to Rachel at Madame Virginie's. Then he returned to his room and fell asleep, in a pool of blood. Gauguin and the police took him to the Hôtel-Dieu, and Gauguin left for Paris that same night.

Although they never saw one another again, in the months that followed, while Van Gogh spent an entire year at a clinic in Saint-Rémy, the friends from Arles exchanged several letters, in which the episode of the mutilation of the ear and their time in Arles are conspicuous by their absence. When Van Gogh committed suicide a year and a half later, in Auvers-sur-Oise, putting a bullet into his stomach, Gauguin made a very short and edgy comment, as if the whole matter was something far removed from him ('It was fortunate for him, in terms of his suffering'). And subsequently, in the years that followed, he would avoid talking about the Dutchman, as if he always felt uneasy about the topic. However, it is clear that he did not forget him, and that his absence was very present in the fifteen remaining years of his life, perhaps in ways that he was not even always conscious of. Why else, if not, did he attempt to sow sunflowers, in front of his cabin in Punaauia, in Tahiti, even when everybody assured him that this exotic flower could never acclimatise to Polynesia? But the 'savage Peruvian', as he like to call himself, was stubborn, asked his friend Daniel de Monfreid for seeds, and worked the land so persistently that finally his indigenous neighbours and the missionaries of that remote place, Punaauia, could enjoy those strange yellow flowers that followed the movement of the sun.

All this happened more than a century ago, sufficient distance for the story to become enriched by the fantasies and lies that all human beings, not just novelists, are prone to. The friendly octogenarian who presides over the small Hôtel Terminus-Van Gogh, in the Place Lamartine, with whom I got on really well in the half an hour that she sat on this sunny terrace, told me, for example, some delightful inaccuracies about the Yellow House, that I pretended to believe completely. Suddenly, as a homage to those two friends who ennobled this piece of land, I decided to drink an absinthe. I had never before tried this drink that has such an illustrious Romantic, sym-bolist and *modernista* ancestry, the drink that Verlaine, Baudelaire and Rubén Darío drowned in, and which Van Gogh and Gauguin imbibed like water. I had imagined it as an exotic, aristocratic spirit, a green viscous colour, which would have a dramatic effect on me, but I was brought instead a rather plebeian pastis. The horrible drink smelt of pharmaceutically prepared mint and sugar and, when I rather unwisely forced it down me, I started retching. Yet one further proof that dull reality will never live up to our dreams and fantasies.

Arles, June 2001

Traces of Gauguin

The Marquesas are the most isolated islands – the furthest from a continent – of all the islands floating in the seas of the world. To get to Hiva Oa, you have to fly first to Tahiti (twenty-four hours from Europe and twelve from the American continent) and then, in Papeete, get into a tiny plane that is buffeted for about four hours by stormy clouds, and finally, after a stop in Niku Hiva, you land in Atuona. The landscape is magnificent: soaring mountainsides and peaks covered in green, rising out of a rough sea, with great foaming waves which seem to be battering Hiva Oa, intent on destroying it.

Atuona, the capital of the island, is now even smaller than in Gauguin's time. Now it has less than a thousand inhabitants and, in 1901, when he stepped on shore, there were two hundred more people. It is still a single small street that leads from Traitor's Bay two-thirds of a mile to the slopes of the imperious Mount Temétiu. In some parts you need a lot of imagination to follow Gauguin's travels in Tahiti: Papeete and Punaauia are now modern and prosperous and overrun by tourists. In Atuona, by contrast, the traces of the last two years of his life that he spent here are everywhere to be seen. The landscape, of course, has barely changed. The town, which has some new houses but has lost a lot of the old buildings, is still a small human settlement engulfed by nature, which seems to have kept it apart from time and the trappings of the modern world. In Atuona, it isn't the clocks but rather the cock crowing that wakes up the inhabitants, and life still continues in slow motion, in a warm and happy lethargy.

Mr Maitiki, who gave Gauguin lodgings in his first weeks on the island, is buried in the Make Make cemetery, not far from his grave, and his descendants are still involved in trade, as he was. A great-grandson of Monsieur Frébault, who was there at his death, is the president of the Friends of Gauguin Society, and he acts as my guide. He's an athletic islander, and his body is covered with the fine tattoos that, from time immemorial, the islands have been famous for, and which was one of the attractions that drew Gauguin here. But Gauguin, alas, could hardly see those delicate tattoos because of the calamitous state of his eyes – as well as lacerating his legs and damaging his heart and brain, syphilis had greatly affected his eyesight in his final years – and because the implacable Bishop Martin, his mortal enemy, who was bent on Westernising the Kanakas and the Maori, had banned them. Now the bones of Monseigneur Martin and Koke (the name given to Gauguin by the local people) rest a few yards from each other in the heights of Atuona, facing the open seas that brought in whaling ships to press-gang local Indians as crew members, and also terrifying tsunamis that devastated Atuona on several occasions in the nineteenth century.

There's no trace left of Ben Varney, the storekeeper, who was a very close friend of Gauguin and possibly went back to die in his homeland, the United States. But the store is still there, almost intact, a two-storey building with wooden railings and a corrugated iron roof, where Koke came to buy the little that he ate and the great deal that he drank, absinthe for him and his friends, and rum for the indigenous people that Monseigneur Martin had forbidden to drink alcohol. Gauguin fought against this prohibition, leaving outside the door of his house – la Maison de Jouir – a small barrel of rum for all the local people to help themselves.

His dear friend and neighbour Tioka, with whom he exchanged names – a Marquesa custom signifying brotherhood and reciprocity – died here, and although his house no longer stands, his family house does, identical to the dwellings that wealthy townspeople built in Atuona in those days. It's on the other side of the stream where Gauguin used to bathe naked, an act which scandalised the neighbouring missionaries and nuns and outraged the local policeman Claverie, who would have put him in prison – this was his dream – if Gauguin had not died beforehand. Gauguin's house no longer exists – the House of Pleasure has been rebuilt in another place – but the former site has been identified thanks to the well that the painter helped to dig out with his own hands. This was the house that the girls from the nearby Santa Ana College came to in secret when the Cluny nuns were not keeping an eye on them. The college has grown since then, but it still has a very pretty garden full of bougainvilleas, mangoes and coconut palms, and a myriad laughing and talkative young girls who are not put off at all by the presence of an outsider. When I mention Gauguin, the friendly Mother Superior blushes and changes the subject. Those wilful little girls ignored the ban and went to look around the house of this corrupting devil and see the pornographic postcards that were up on his walls: forty-five exactly, showing every imaginable position, which he had bought in Port Said on a stopover on the boat journey that brought Gauguin to Polynesia.

His sexual exploits, which his biographers have fantasised over at length, were a thing of the past when Gauguin arrived in Atuona. His precarious health did not permit too many excesses. It's true that he bought a girl, his *vahiné*, Vaeoho, from an indigenous family in the Hekeani Valley. The family asked for a number of goods in exchange for her, that he had to buy on credit from the shopkeeper Ben Varney. Vaeoho gave him a child, whose descendants, spread throughout Hiva Oa, now flee from journalists and critics as if they had the plague (they're surely right to do so). However, this marriage did not last long because as soon as she knew she was pregnant Vaeoho, who found his legs revolting, left him. Apart from a bit of more or less harmless dabbling with the girls from the mission who visited him, and an adventure with the red-haired Tohotaua, who was a model for his final paintings, it is inconceivable that, given his physical and mental condition when he reached the Marquesas Islands, he could have indulged in the same excessive behaviour as in Tahiti or in France. On Atuona, the only excesses open to this human wreck were in his imagination. And he did not hesitate in using this imagination to develop impossible projects: delirious religious essays arguing a so-called revolutionary interpretation of anti-Catholic Christianity, and political-judicial campaigns to exempt the indigenous people who lived far from Atuona from the obligation of sending their children to the school, to lift the ban on their purchasing alcohol and to exempt them from paying a road-building tax with the impeccable argument that the state had never built on the island of Hiva Oa one single yard of road (a fact that remains true today, one hundred years later). It was these manifestations of rebellion against colonial society that allowed his enemies – the church and the police – to enmesh him in a court case that he lost, a judgement that would have led not just to him losing his house and his few belongings, but also to a term of imprisonment, had his heart not stopped at an opportune moment.

In Tahiti, although there is an official cult to his memory and his work, many Tahitians put in a number of provisos when they talk about him. His behaviour towards native women was, who could deny it, abusive and sometimes brutal, and some people still repeat that as well as being a paedophile – he liked girls, young girls of thirteen or fourteen – he gave syphilis to many of his lovers. And, besides, could one speak of him as a *Tahitian* painter? I hasten to agree with them: the Tahiti of his paintings is much more a product of his fantasy and his dreams than of the real model. But is that not a point in his favour, the best way to show his credentials as a creator? Here on the Marquesas Islands, by contrast, I have not found in any conversation the slightest reticence among the native inhabitants in expressing their appreciation and admiration for Koke. Quite the reverse. Everyone knows who he was, what he did, where he is buried, and they tell stories that reveal a warm and friendly attitude towards him, a sense of kinship. Perhaps it isn't Gauguin at all, but rather the way that the Marquesas people have of understanding and dealing with their fellow men and women: by opening their arms and their heart to them. And wasn't it this, precisely, that Gauguin came looking for here, in the last journey of his incessant life? He spoke of primitive and intense civilisations, as yet uncorrupted by the abuse of reason and ecclesiastical laws, where beauty would not be a monopoly of artists, critics and collectors but rather a natural manifestation of human life, a shared state of mind, a universal religion. But, probably, behind these big words and schematic generalisations, there lay something much more simple and elusive: a society where happiness was possible. A society where one could live in peace and not in a state of permanent nervousness, without having to struggle for food, money and success, where one could concentrate on one's vocation and not all the everyday worries that get in the way of this vocation. Paradise is not of this world and those who set out to look for it or construct it here are irremediably condemned to failure. But it is likely that out of all the places in the world that he went to look for it, Gauguin had never been so close to reaching that shimmering mirage that he had pursued all his life, as in this place where he arrived already half dead, where, in truth, he had come not to live but to die. It is enough to feel the gentle warmth that bathes Hiva Oa, and to look out on its mountain slopes or its rough seas, and listen to the melody with which the native people sing their words, and see them walk with a dance in their steps, unhurriedly and with supernatural grace, to feel that, despite everything, Koke, the wretched dreamer, was not completely on the wrong track when he came here in pursuit of his unrealisable dream.

Atuona, January 2001

The Men-Women of the Pacific

When Gauguin arrived in Tahiti for the first time, in June 1891, he had his hair down to his shoulders, wore a cockade with red fur, and his clothes were flamboyant and provocative. He had dressed like this ever since he had given up his career on the Stock Exchange in Paris. The indigenous people of Papeete were surprised at his appearance and believed he was a *mahu*, a rare species among the Europeans in Polynesia. The colonists explained to the painter that, in the Maori tongue, the *mahu* was a man-woman, a type that had existed from time immemorial in the cultures of the Pacific, but which had been demonised and banned by common consent by both Catholic and Protestant missionaries, engaged in a fierce battle to indoctrinate the native peoples, during the intense period of colonisation in the mid-nineteenth century.

However, it proved well-nigh impossible to root out the *mahu* from indigenous society. Concealed in urban settlements, the *mahu* survived in the villages and even in the cities, and re-emerged when official hostility and persecution abated. Proof of this fact can be found in Gauguin's paintings in the nine years that he spent in Tahiti and the Marquesas Islands, which are full of human beings of uncertain gender who share equally masculine and feminine attributes with a naturalness and openness that is similar to the way in which his characters display their nakedness, merge with the natural order or indulge in leisure.

In his book of fantasised memoirs, *Noa Noa*, Gauguin relates a quasi-homosexual experience that he said inspired his painting *Pape Moe* (*Mysterious Waters*), in which an androgynous young person is bending over to drink from a forest waterfall. In fact, Gauguin's Tahitian paintings would be very different and would seem much more arbitrary, without the strong presence of the *mahu* in the indigenous community that he was so close to. They are the raw material, the secret root, of his women with their solid thighs and broad shoulders, who stand firmly on the ground, and of his effeminate young men, in languid poses who seem to exhibit themselves as they stretch out to pick fruit from the trees, and who adorn their long hair with diadems of flowers. It is true that he invented these unmistakable characters; but he based them on a human reality about which, curiously for a man so loquacious on other topics, he always maintained a stubborn reserve.

It is risky to translate *mahu* as homosexual because, even in the most permissive societies of our age, homosexuality is still surrounded by prejudice and discrimination. Such prejudices did not exist among the Polynesians before the emissaries of Christian Europe censored a practice that, before their arrival, was recognised and universally respected and accepted as a legitimate variant of human diversity. The extraordinary sexual freedom of the Maoris of the islands has been the subject of countless studies, testimonies and caricatures ever since the first European ships reached these islands of paradisiacal beauty. Only now that Western society has gradually made sufficient advances to allow a similar sexual freedom and tolerance to that enjoyed by Polynesian cultures can we realise how civilised and lucid these small Pacific Maori communities were, at a time when the powerful West was still mired in the savagery of prejudice and intolerance. It was not just a question of sexual freedom; there was also a widespread practice among native communities of adopting orphaned or abandoned children, a custom that is still maintained. (Mr Tetuani of Mataiea, where Gauguin lived for several months, had twenty-five adopted children.)

The *mahu* might be a practising homosexual or remain chaste, like a girl making a vow of chastity. What defines them is not how or with whom they make love, but that, having been born with the sexual organs of a man, they have opted for femininity, usually from childhood, and that, helped by their family and community, they have become women, in their way of dressing, walking, talking, singing, working and often, but clearly not necessarily, of making love.

One of the reasons why, despite the prohibitions of the Churches, the *mahus* survived in Maori society during the nineteenth century was that they could count on the hidden complicity of the European colonists. They hired *mahus* to work as domestic servants – cooks, childminders, launderers, etc. – because for these household tasks the *mahus* were generally competent and, according to public opinion, 'irreplaceable'. But in certain dances, songs and public ceremonies the *mahus* were also indispensable, because some songs, dances and performances are strictly for them, traditional expressions of what we might call that third sex, that are markedly different from male and female expressions.

Is it true that today, unlike what happened in traditional Polynesian society, ninety per cent of *mahus* are of humble origin, and that there is something like a relationship of cause and effect between the *mahu* and the poorest and most marginal sectors of indigenous society? (I hasten to add the proviso that 'poverty' and 'marginality' are concepts that, in Tahiti and the Marquesas Islands, bear little relationship to the extremes of injustice and inhumanity that these words express, for example, in Latin America). It must be the case, since I was given the information by a sociologist from the University of Papeete, who has studied Maori society for many years. He also told me that whereas in the past it was often the case that if a family had a number of boys, their own parents would decide to educate one of the boys as a girl, today nobody is a *mahu* through parental imposition, but through their own free choice.

In any event, even though the majority of the *mahus* are of humble origin, there are a number among the native middle classes of the islands. I have seen them, for example, in university lecture halls, mingling with the other students, as customers or employees in restaurants and cafés, and in the Protestant and Catholic services on Sundays, dressed up in beautiful clothes and headgear, without attracting any impertinent glances apart from mine.

I confess my admiration for the absolute normality with which I have seen the *mahus* move around, from the streets, hotels and offices of modern Papeete to remote rural areas in Atuona, on the island of Hiva Oa, or on the Marquesas. The cook in the hotel I stayed in on Atuona was a *mahu* called Teriki who told me that she had realised around eleven or twelve that she wanted to be a woman. Her parents did not place any obstacles in her way; quite the reverse, they helped her from the outset, dressing her as a woman. She assured me that she has never been ill-treated or ridiculed by anyone on Atuona, where she and the other *mahus* – ten per cent of the male population, she assures me – lead a normal life. It's true that they had some difficulties at first with the friendly Father Labró of the Catholic mission, but Teriki and other *mahus* on the island explained their case at length, and from then on 'the parish priest accepted us'.

However, a curious character that I got to know on Papeete, called Cerdan Claude, assured me that, contrary to appearances and the evidence of my own eyes, the *mahus* were not widely accepted in Polynesian society. According to him, modernity has also brought machismo and homophobia to Polynesia, above all at night, when it was not unusual to find gangs of thugs bursting into the prostitute district around the port of Papeete looking for *mahus* to harass and beat up. Cerdan Claude is sixty, and is gaunt and mysterious like a character out of Conrad. He was born in a Foreign Legion camp in Algeria, but he has never been a legionnaire. He has travelled the world, was once a boxer, has spent more than thirty years in Tahiti and now writes novels. His latest is a documentary novel on the world of the *rae rae*, a word that I thought synonymous with *mahu*, but he assures me that between the two terms there is a 'metaphysical distance'. His long explanation of the difference leaves me confused. I finally deduce that while the *mahu* is the man-woman with traditional roots in Polynesian society, the Tahitian *rae rae* is its modern, urban expression, having more in common with the snipped and tucked drag queens of the West, with their hormone and silicone injections, than with the delicate cultural, psychological and social re-creation that is the *mahu* of Maori tradition. The *mahu* is an integral part of society, while the *rae rae* lives on its margins. Cerdan Claude seems to know very well the nocturnal world of prostitution inhabited by the *rae rae*, a world in which he moves freely; he adopts a beneficent, rather paternal attitude towards them. They tell him about their sorrows and desires and he gives them advice on how 'to deal with the problems of life': he says it with such conviction that I believe him.

The 'Piano Bar' in Papeete, where Cerdan Claude takes me one night, is an enormous, smoky discotheque, where the *rae rae* and heterosexual couples socialise in perfect harmony. They mingle all the time. It is not easy to detect the borders that separate the sexes – my impression is that very little or nothing separates them – at least to my layman's eye. Cerdan Claude, by contrast, has a very sharp eye, and knows everyone by name. The *rae rae* come, one after the other, to greet him and kiss him on the cheek, and he receives them like a kindly grandfather. He introduces me to everyone and encourages them to talk to me about their lives and have their photograph taken by my daughter Morgana, something which they are delighted to do, brimming over with good humour and childish curiosity. Anne, the son of a New Zealand man and a Tahitian woman, is a beautiful, willowy girl who, she says, had difficulties with her parents when, as a boy, she started to dress as a girl. But now she gets on very well with them and they do not object to her sexual orientation. It is difficult to imagine that this smiling young woman was once a man. But she was, and still is, in part, as she tells me with great charm and no hint of vulgarity. She has been under the surgeon's knife, which retouched her nose and implanted the upright breasts that she displays, but she has still to replace her phallus and testicles with an artificial vagina, because the operation is very expensive. She is saving and she will have it done. She had just spent a couple of years in Paris, where she got some good modelling jobs, but the violence in the city – where, one night, an Arab threatened her with a knife – and the cold made her return to warm and peaceful Polynesia. When she leaves us, the boys at the 'Piano Bar' swarm around her like flies, asking her to dance. I heard her utter this patriotic phrase, the most

The Painter in the Brothel

Jean-Jacques Lebel, a writer and avant-garde artist who used to organise 'happenings' in the sixties, had the very daring idea back then to stage 'with absolute fidelity', *Desire Caught by the Tail*, a delirious theatre piece written by Picasso in 1941 in which, among other crazy things, a female character, La Tarte, urinates on stage for ten consecutive minutes, squatting over the prompter's booth. (To achieve this effect, Lebel informs us, the liquefying actress had to drinks pints of tea and great infusions of cherries.) He talked to the painter at the beginning of 1966 about the project and Picasso showed him a whole raft of erotic drawings and paintings, from his Barcelona period, that he had never exhibited. From that moment Lebel decided that one day he would organise an exhibition that would show, without any euphemisms or censorship, the power of sex in Picasso's world. This idea has finally become a reality, almost four decades later, in a vast exhibition of 330 works, many of them never exhibited before, in the Jeu de Paume in Paris, where it will stay until the end of May, before moving on to Montreal and Barcelona.

The first question to ask, after going round this exciting exhibition (never has that adjective been more appropriate), is why it has taken so long to organise. There have been innumerable exhibitions on the work of this artist, whose influence can be found in every branch of modern art, but, until now, nothing specific on the theme of sex which, as this exhibition curated by Lebel and Gérard

Régnier so very clearly demonstrates, obsessed the painter in a very productive way. Especially at certain extreme moments in his life – in his youth and old age – he experimented and expressed himself in this area with remarkable confidence and daring, in drawings, sketches, objects, engravings and canvases that, despite their unequal artistic value, reveal his most secret and intimate motivations – his desires and erotic fantasies – and throw a new light on the rest of his work.

'Art and sexuality are the same thing,' Picasso said to Jean Leymarie and, on another occasion, he pointed out that 'there is no such thing as chaste art'. Perhaps such remarks might not be true for all artists, but they are quite clearly appropriate for him. Why, then, did Picasso himself help to hide for quite a long time this aspect of his artistic production, that is a constant in his work, even though at times he chose to keep it a secret? For ideological and commercial reasons, says Jean-Jacques Lebel in an interesting interview with Geneviève Breerette. During his Stalinist period, when he painted the portrait of Stalin and denounced the 'massacres in Korea', eroticism would have been a source of conflict between Picasso and the Communist Party, to which he was affiliated, which espoused the aesthetic orthodoxy of socialist realism, in which there was no room for the 'decadent' celebration of sexual pleasure. And late, following the advice of his *marchands*, he admitted that he kept this aspect of his work hidden for fear of offending the puritanism of US collectors, thus cutting off this lucrative market. These are human weaknesses that geniuses are not exempt from, as we know.

In any event, it is now possible to consider every facet of Picasso's work, a universe with so many constellations that it makes us giddy. How could one hand, the imagination of a single mortal, produce such extraordinary creativity? There is no reply to this question; Picasso leaves us speechless, as do Rubens, Mozart or Balzac. The development of his work, with its distinctive stages, themes, forms and motifs, is a journey through all the schools and artistic movements of the twentieth century, which he learned from and to which he contributed in his own completely distinctive way. Then he looked to the past, bringing that past back into the present in a number of very finely observed re-creations, caricatures and rereadings that showed just how contemporary and fresh the Old Masters were. But sex is never absent, in all the periods that critics have divided and organised Picasso's work, even in the Cubist years. Sometimes it is a discreet, symbolic reference, working through allusion. At other times it is insolently open and crude, in images that seem to challenge the conventions of eroticism, refinement and the chaste ways that art has traditionally described physical love, to make it compatible with established morality.

The sex that Picasso reveals in most of these works, especially in the years of his youth in Barcelona, is elemental, not sublimated by the rituals and baroque ceremonies of a culture that disguises, civilises and turns animal instinct into works of art, a sex that wants desire immediately satisfied, without delay, subterfuge, fuss or distractions. Sex for the hungry and the orthodox, not sex for dreamers or refined people. That is why it is a completely macho sexual outlook, where there is no male homosexuality and where lesbianism is just there for the pleasure of the male onlooker. Sex for men, primitive, rough, where the phallus is king. Women are there to serve, to not have pleasure themselves, but to give pleasure, to open their legs and submit to the whims of the fornicating male. They are often depicted kneeling, engaged in fellatio, which could be seen as an archetypal image of this sexual order: the woman gives pleasure but also yields to and adores the all-powerful macho. The phallus, these images proclaim, is above all else power.

It is natural that the privileged location for this sort of pleasure is the brothel. There are no sentimental distractions in the way of this drive that looks to sate an urgent need and then forget about it and go on to something else. In the brothel, where sex is bought and sold, where there are no entanglements and no excuses or alibis are necessary, sex is revealed in all its naked truth, as pure present, as an intense and shameless spectacle which does not linger in the memory, pure and fleeting copulation, immune to remorse and nostalgia.

The repeated images of this brothel sex, its vulgarity and lack of imagination, that fill so many notebooks, cards and canvases, would be monotonous without the cheerful touches that we find, jokes and exaggerations that show a state of mind brimming over with enthusiasm and happiness. A humanised fish – a *mackerel*! – is licking a young woman who is compliant but bored to death. And in all this work, even the rapid sketches he did in the middle of some party, on serviettes, menus and newspaper cuttings, to please a friend or to record a meeting, there is evidence of his extraordinary craft, that piercing gaze that can set down in a few essential brushstrokes the mad vortex of reality. The apotheosis of the brothel in Picasso's work is, of course, *Les demoiselles d'Avignon*, which is not in this exhibition, although many of the first sketches and drafts of this masterpiece are here.

With the passing of the years, the rough sexual edges of youth were smoothed out, and desire began to be expressed in mythological characters. All the Minotaurs painted in the thirties gleam with vigorous sensuality, with a sexual power that displays its bestiality with grace and shamelessness, as a proof of life and artistic creativity. By contrast, in the beautiful series of prints dedicated to *Rafael and Fornarina* from the late sixties, the loving interaction between the painter and his model under the lascivious gaze of an old pontiff who is resting his flaccid limbs on a chamber pot, is imbued with a deep sadness. What is represented here is not just the joyful physical love of the young people, the voluptuousness that is part of artistic endeavour. There is also the melancholy of the observer, who, with the passing of the years, is no longer competing in the jousts of love, an ex-combatant who must resign himself to enjoy looking at other people's enjoyment, while he feels life slipping away. And that the death of his sexual drive will soon be followed by the other, the definitive death. This theme is recurrent in the final years of Picasso's life, and the exhibition in the Jeu de Paume has a number of pictures in which this inconsolable nostalgia for a lost virility appears with a wrenching insistence, the bitterness of knowing that the fateful wheel of time no longer allows one to bathe in the source of life, to experience that explosion of pure pleasure in which human beings glimpse immortality and which the

French ironically call 'the little death'. Figurative death and real death, orgasm and physical extinction, are the protagonists of the dramatic painting that Picasso kept on producing almost until the final death rattle.

Paris, March 2001

When Paris was a Fiesta

It is not an exaggeration to say that I spent the whole of my adolescence dreaming of Paris. I lived then in the claustrophobic world of Lima in the fifties, convinced that it was impossible to become a writer or an artist without knowing Paris, because the capital of France was also the universal capital of thought and the arts, the centre that conveyed to the rest of the world new ideas, new forms and styles, the experiments and issues that would do away with the past and lay the foundations of what would become the culture of the future.

Given the poverty of literature and the arts in present-day France, those beliefs might now seem rather stupid, the naïveté of a provincial and underdeveloped young man, seduced at a distance by the romantic myth of Paris. But the truth is that the myth was still very close to the reality in 1959, when, in a trance, I finally began my stay in Paris, which would last for almost seven years. The great intellectual figures whose ideas and works reverberate throughout almost the entire world were still alive, and many of them at the height of their creativity, from Sartre to Camus, from Malraux to Céline, from Breton to Aragon, from Mauriac to Raymond Aron, from Foucault to Goldmann, and from Bataille to Ionesco and Beckett. The list is a long one. It is true that the *nouveau roman* of Claude Simon, Robbe-Grillet, Nathalie Sarraute and company that was in vogue at the time, passed like a will-o'-the-wisp, without leaving many traces, but that movement was just one among many, like the Tel Quel group, organised under the influence of the brilliant sophist Roland Barthes, one of whose university courses I took at the Sorbonne, with a mixture of fascination and irritation. Barthes listened to himself talking, as spellbound by his own words as we, his audience, were, and his lectures were a mixture of massive erudition and intellectual frivolity.

I don't know whether in the sixties Paris was still the capital of culture. But to judge by the magnificent exhibition at the Royal Academy in London entitled 'Paris, Capital of the Arts 1900–1968', it certainly was, at least in this sense: no other capital in the world had the same ability to attract and assimilate so much artistic talent from all parts of the world. Along with the Romanians Cioran and Ionesco, the Greek Castoriadis, or the Swiss Jean-Luc Godard, innumerable musicians, filmmakers, poets, philosophers, sculptors, painters and writers left their own countries, of necessity or by their own free will, and took up residence in Paris. Why? For the same reasons as those expressed by the Chilean Acario Copota, who considered that for any writer in the making, it was essential to take 'a breather in Paris'. Because, apart from the stimulating atmosphere of creativity and freedom, Paris was, culturally speaking, an open city, hospitable to foreigners, where talent and originality were welcomed and adopted with enthusiasm, regardless of origin.

One of the most instructive aspects of the Royal Academy exhibition is to see how, throughout the twentieth century, the most fertile and novel tendencies in art in Europe and many parts of the Western world – above all in the United States and Japan – passed through Paris or found in France the recognition and encouragement to establish themselves on the world stage. This happened with Picasso, Miró and Juan Gris; with Mondrian and Giorgio di Chirico; with Diaghilev, Nijinsky and Stravinsky; with Brancusi, Beckmann and Max Ernst; with Giacometti, Henry Miller and César Vallejo; with Huidobro, Gino Severini and Isadora Duncan; with Chagal, Lipchitz, Calder and Foujita; with Van Dougen, Diego Rivera, Kupka and Natalia Goncharova; with Lam, Matta and Josephine Baker; with Modigliani and Man Ray; with Julio González, Torres García, Naum Gabo and hundreds, thousands, more. Perhaps it would be fanciful to say that all this extraordinary burgeoning of talent was the creation of what another lover of Paris, Rubén Darío, called the 'face of Lutetia'. But that is not to say that the atmosphere and cultural dynamism of the City of Light itself did not contribute decisively to the full development of their creative potential.

In Paris one felt at home, because Paris was a home for all. And French culture was what it was because it did not belong only to Paris, but to the whole world; or rather it belonged to those who, seduced by its richness, generosity, variety and universality, made it their own, as I did as an adolescent in Lima, when I rushed to the Alliance Française to read in the original the authors that had dazzled me. And, in turn, one could see in the galleries of the Royal Academy that the open-door policy towards 'foreigners' had the very positive result of incorporating their inventiveness, daring, insolence and radicalism into French culture. From post-Impressionism to 'happenings', including Cubism, Dadaism, Surrealism and all the avant-garde movements, in the field of art Paris is a Borgesian aleph, a microcosm that reflects the whole cosmos, the place that attracted or initiated the most influential cultural and artistic practices of the century.

How could it have happened that this international capital of the arts, the land that was open to the world and attracted artists from all over the world, could have declined so rapidly, and succumbed to a ridiculous, chauvinist provincialism, that, in a picturesque alliance between the far right and the far left, frenetically reclaims 'cultural exceptionalism' as a way of preventing foreign (for foreign read American) artistic products from staining the sacrosanct 'cultural identity' of France?

I read the answer to this question that had been plaguing me ever since I left the Royal Academy in low spirits, in a luminous article entitled 'Cultural Extinction' written by Jean-François Revel. The text, written with his usual sparkling irony and devastating intelligence, demolishes the arguments in favour of cultural protectionism with irrefutable examples. To defend oneself against foreign influences, he says, is not the best way to preserve one's own culture; it is, rather, the best way to kill it. And he compares the example of Athens, an open city, where arts, letters, philosophy and mathematics circulated freely, with that of Sparta, which jealously guarded its exceptionalism and which achieved 'the feat of being the only Greek city not to produce a single poet, orator, thinker or architect'. Sparta defended its culture so successfully that that culture became extinct.

Revel also reminds us that cultural nationalism, a thesis normally propounded by ignorant people who see culture simply as an instrument of power and political propaganda, is profoundly anti-democratic, a grotesque scenario characteristic of totalitarian regimes. These regimes have always put fences around cultural life and subjected it to the control and the beneficence of the state. For that reason, cultural nationalism is inapplicable to an open society, which means that, despite all the noise and periodic campaigns in support, it will find it difficult to prosper in France so long as French society continues to be democratic, which it will doubtless remain for the foreseeable future. Because the only way in which cultural protectionism can translate into an effective policy is through a rigorous system of discrimination and censure against cultural products, something that would be intolerable for an adult, modern and free society.

What would have happened, asks Revel, if, instead of inviting Italian painters to Paris, the French kings in the sixteenth century had thrown them out, in defence of 'national identity'? And what of the enormously fertile influence of Spanish literature in France in the sixteenth century, even when the two countries were at war?

If France had not traditionally opened its borders to 'foreign products', there could never have been an exhibition like this in the Royal Academy, which is an involuntary manifesto in favour of the free circulation of art and artists throughout the entire world, with no barriers in place. And without this openness, France would never have managed to excite so many young people the world over, like me in Lima in the fifties, with the idea that there, in that splendid, distant land, beauty and genius were cultivated in greater measure than in other parts, as was demonstrated by those poets and writers who spoke to us with a voice so clear and strong that it reached even the furthest corners where we felt isolated, and those artists, filmmakers and musicians whose works seemed to be pitched exactly to satisfy our most demanding desires and dreams.

Botero at the Bullfight

The premiere of *Blood and Sand* with Tyrone Power and Rita Hayworth, in Cochabamba, Bolivia, in the mid-fifties, was a major event in my life. I saw the film seven times, in the morning and matinée screenings in the Acha Cinema, and from that moment on, for many years I dreamed of becoming a bullfighter. This desire had surfaced in my imagination ever since my uncle had taken me to my first bullfight, in the small ring in Cochabamba, yet it was not the real bullfight, but rather the one imagined by Blasco Ibáñez and Hollywood that turned this desire into a desperate need.

Was this childhood bullfighting obsession part of a generational epidemic spreading throughout Latin America? Because at the time when I was fighting Bolivian tricycles, a few thousand kilometres away, in another provincial city in the Andes, the green and winding Medellín, Fernando Botero enrolled in a bullfighting school and, for two years, took classes to train as a matador. His uncle Joaquín, a fanatical bullfighting aficionado, took him to the school, just as he had taken him along to see many fights with mature and novice bulls in the brand-new Macarena bullring and in the surrounding mountain towns, at a time when he had not even begun to dream about becoming a painter. The spectacle, the excitement, the colour, the indescribable blend of primitive savagery and exquisite refinement of these bullfights would become firmly lodged in his memory from that time on.

This is why it is not surprising that the first drawings Botero produced in the Jesuit College in Medellín were sketches of bulls. And it is perhaps a premonition that his first more or less personal work is a watercolour of a bull. We will never know, of course, if his defection from the bloody ceremonies of the bullfight in favour of the more gentle ceremonies of brush and easel, was a tragedy or a fortunate escape for the art of Manolete and Belmonte. But there is no doubt that it was a happy moment for the art of Goya and Velázquez. Furthermore, over the years, the skilled brushes of this artist would provide the most enthusiastic and complete homage to bullfighting of any modern painter (and I am not forgetting all the marvellous work that Picasso produced).

Although it was a central experience of his childhood and a significant presence in his early artistic expression, this theme – the bullfight – seems largely to disappear from his painting until the eighties. Botero remained a fan and went to all the fights he could, but bulls and bullfighters are not the subjects he treats in the difficult years of his childhood, when the Mexican muralists were his models, or in later years, when he carefully studied the classics in Spain, France and, above all, Italy. They crop up on occasion, but as furtive shadows, after that providential afternoon in 1956, in a park in Mexico, when, while he was doodling, he inflated the mandolin that he was drawing and suddenly discovered, miraculously, the sumptuous secret world of opulence in this object, and also his painting method. In 1982 or 1983, already famous and with a vast œuvre recognised worldwide, he went back one afternoon to see a bullfight in the Macarena bullring, in the city of his birth. And, he says, he immediately felt that here was a familiar and stimulating world to explore: 'From then I started one painting after another, to the point where I became very taken with the subject, and for three years I just painted bulls. Then I began to paint other topics, but also bulls.'* In fact, they became his obsessive and almost exclusive passion to this day. The twenty-five paintings on bullfighting themes exhibited in the Malborough Gallery, New York, in 1985, would grow to eighty-six works (drawings, watercolours and oils) on the same topic,

* Fernando Botero, *La corrida, oleos, acuarelas, dibujos*, exhibition catalogue, Hospital de los Venerables Sacerdotes, Seville, 1992, p. 19.

exhibited in Milan in 1987 and in the Hospital de los Venerables Sacerdotes in Seville in 1992. This sequence will reach a sort of apotheosis this autumn in 1992, when the hundreds of his works on the
reality and the myth of bullfighting will fill the Grand Palais in Paris
(while, at the same time, his monumental sculptures will line the
Champs-Elysées, from the Place de la Concorde to the Rond-Point).

It is not possible today to see the bullfight with the same clear conscience with which aficionados went to the bullrings when Botero
and I dreamed of donning the bullfighter's suit and facing up to a
fierce Miura bull armed with a red cape. Culture and sensibilities
have evolved to such a degree that it is more and more difficult to
find arguments that do not seem to ourselves – who have experienced moments of overwhelming intensity watching a good bullfight – fallacious and inconsistent. I know them all, from the one
about traditions and customs, national traits and cultural identity to
the argument that goes, 'Will we have to give up steaks and ham as
well?', to say nothing of the idea that 'animals don't have feelings
like humans' or the notion of fair play: doesn't the bull also have a
chance to gore the bullfighter? I have used them in thousands of
arguments, defending the bullfight to the death against its detrac-
tors, but I believe them less and less. Because there is no rational
argument that can justify the cruelty behind this beautiful spectacle,
the inhumanity that underlies the indescribable grace, elegance,
courage and drama that a great bullfight can achieve.

Because, unlike what happens to the bullfight when Botero turns
it into oils, drawings, prints and sculptures and frees it from all
moral contingency, reducing it to pure sensation, to *healthy* pleasure,
what in real life attracts and bewitches us in the bullfight is its dirty
beauty, the way in which it transgresses certain basic laws, like the
law, essential to the survival of the community, which argues for the
preservation of life, the defence of life against death in all circumstances. The bullfight is a festival of death, inflicting and accepting
death, defying and becoming intoxicated by death, playing with it,
with proud contempt for one's own life and the life of others. The
beautiful images that can be displayed when the person executing
this terrible dance does it with skill and inspiration, and is aided by

213

the animal – that we then call noble and thoroughbred – does not diminish one iota the violence of the spectacle, or justify it in moral terms. It simply offers an aesthetic alibi to the ferocious pleasure that it gives us, clothing in civilised garb the appetite that, deep within us, links us to our remote ancestors and their savage rites, in which they could unleash their worst instincts, the instincts that need destruction and blood to be sated.

All this appears in a luminous manner, by contrast, when we put the real bullfight alongside the extraordinary bullfight saga that Botero has been developing over the last ten years. Few artists in the history of painting have worked on a topic with such detail and sympathy as he has done with the bullfight, reconstructing it in all its variety and richness, with its cast of characters, its setting and its myths, its colour, rituals and emblems. Here we find the swords, the picadors, the banderilleros, and the bullfighter's assistants, the officials, the lowly picador assistants and the lively women in the stands, and the beauties in the enclosures where the matadors go to celebrate their triumphs or to console themselves when they fail. And here are the horses, the blindfolded draught horses bowed under the weight of the picadors, and the bulls charging, going under the cape, or dying with a sword of steel in their entrails.

They are also very beautiful images, and some of them, like the oil painting from 1988, *La cornada* (*Being Gored*), one of the great artistic achievements of Botero's entire œuvre, almost agonisingly perfect. However, even the most inexperienced spectator can see immediately that an unbridgeable gap separates this bullfighting world from the world that inspires it. This is a fictional world: without deception, malice or instinct, purely sensory and benevolent, which celebrates life, not death, and which lives pleasure with the serene self-confidence of the hedonist. Unlike the disturbing bullfighting visions of Goya, which explore the human depths, or those of Picasso, which are always invaded by the irrationality of desire and the violence of sex, Botero's bullfight is a civilised celebration of the senses, in which a discreet intelligence and a flawless technique have skilfully remade the world of the bullfight, purifying it, stripping it of all that burden of barbarism and cruelty that links the real bullfight to the most irresponsible and terrifying aspects of human experience.

It is wrong to think that Botero fattens people and things just to make them more colourful, to give them more substance, to make them more rounded and imposing. In fact the swelling that his brushes impress on reality has an ontological effect: it empties the people and objects of this world of all sentimental, intellectual and moral content. They are reduced to physical presences, to forms that refer in a sensory way to certain models of real life, but which contradict and disown this real life.

At the same time it removes them from the river of time, from the nightmare of chronology and places them in an eternal immobility, in a fixed and everlasting reality. From that vantage point, splendid in their multicoloured attire, innocent and bovine in their abundance, frozen at some instant in their lives, when they were still part of history – driving in a goad, drawing the bull away, adorning themselves with capes or, most frequently, looking at the world, looking at us, with that stony absorption, with a sort of metaphysical indifference – they pose for us, offering themselves for us to admire.

The truth is that it is impossible not to envy them. How superior and perfect they seem, compared to us, miserable mortals, who are slowly ravaged and finally obliterated by time. They do not suffer, they do not think, they are not prey to thoughts that hinder or distort their behaviour; they are pure presence, existences without essences, a life that is lived for itself with an enjoyment that is limitless and without remorse.

Among modern painters, Botero represents as few others the classical tradition, in particular his favourite models, the painters of the Italian Quattrocento, who did not paint to express any disagreement with the world or to protest against life, but rather to perfect the world and life through art, offering certain models and ideal forms that men and women and society should seek to emulate in order to become better and less unhappy. As in the great Renaissance canvases, in Botero's painting there is a profound acceptance of life as it is, of the world we have been given, and a systematic attempt to translate this reality into the realm of art purged of everything that might sully, impoverish or corrupt it. This might be a chimerical quest, at a time when no one believes any longer that art makes men and women better and happier: the suspicion is, rather, that an acute sensibility is a passport to unhappiness. However, this does not devalue, but rather reinforces the singularity of this tireless artist who, while he has always retained an affable and rather shy Andean demeanour, a provincial circumspection, has, throughout this whole creative career, been able to swim against the tide: being a realist when fashion demanded that painters should be abstract, finding sources of inspiration in regional and local topics when it was obligatory to drink from cosmopolitan wells, daring to be colourful and decorative when these notions seem antithetical to the very meaning of art and, above all, painting to express his love and contentment with life when the greatest artists of his time painted to express its horror and impossibility.

With Botero we can go to the bullfight to enjoy the blood and the death, without any guilty conscience.

London, August 1992

CULTURE AND POLITICS

Nationalism and Utopia

A recurring theme in a book of essays that Sir Isaiah Berlin has just published – *The Crooked Timber of Humanity: Chapters in the History of Ideas** is very topical: the question of nationalism. With its awareness of history, its passion for region and landscape, its defence of local tradition, language and customs, and the way that it offers an ideological mask for chauvinism, xenophobia, racism and religious dogmatism, nationalism will doubtless, in the next few years, be the great political force that will resist the internationalisation of our social and economic lives brought about by the development of industrial civilisation and democratic culture.

How and where was this ideology born that vies with religious intolerance and revolutionary extremism in causing the worst wars and social cataclysms in history? According to the old and wise professor, it came into the world, initially in a benign form, as a response to the utopian dreams of the perfect society – which once existed in a former Golden Age or which will be constructed in the future in accordance with reason and science – that is one of the most constant motifs of Western thought.

In the eighteenth century, a Neapolitan philosopher and historian revolutionised the belief that Rome and Greece offered a sort of static paradigm of human evolution, which all societies should aspire to. In his *Scienza nuova*, Giambattista Vico argues that this is simply not

* John Murray, London, 1991.

true. He states that history is movement and that every age has its unique form of society, thought, beliefs and customs, religion and morality, that can only be understood properly on its own terms by true historians who can combine documentary and archaeological investigation with sympathy and imagination, which he called *fantasy*. In this way, Vico dealt a severe blow to the ethnocentric view of human evolution and laid the foundations for a relativist and plural conception of evolution in which all cultures, races and societies had the right to the same consideration.

But the real cradle of nationalism is Germany, and its earliest exponent is Johann Gottfried Herder. The utopia that he was reacting against was not located in a remote past but rather in an overwhelming present: the French Revolution, daughter of the *philosophes* and the guillotine, whose armies were advancing throughout the entire continent, levelling and integrating the continent under the weight of the same laws, ideas and values, which were proclaimed as superior and universal, standard bearers of a civilisation that would soon encompass the entire planet. Against this threat of a uniform world that would speak French and be organised according to the cold and abstract principles of rationalism, Herder erected his own little citadel that was formed by blood, earth and language: *das Volk*. His defence of the particular, of local costumes and traditions, of the right of all peoples to have their identity recognised and respected, has a positive aspect. It is not racist or discriminatory – as these same ideas would become in the writings of Fichte, for example – and can be interpreted as a very human and progressive vindication of small and weak societies when faced by powerful societies with imperial designs. Furthermore, Herder's nationalism is ecumenical; his ideal is a diverse society in which all the linguistic, folk and ethnic expressions of humanity can coexist, without hierarchies or prejudice, in a kind of cultural mosaic.

But these dispassionate, beneficent ideas can become charged with violence when they fall on a terrain that has been fertilised by resentment and wounded national pride and, above all, by Romantic irrationalism. According to Berlin, Romanticism was a delayed rebellion against the humiliations inflicted on the German people by the armies of Richelieu and Louis XIV, which held back a Protestant renaissance in the north. And the modernising designs of Frederick the Great in Prussia, who imported French staff, also contributed to the pent-up hostility against this disparaging and haughty French nation, which saw itself as the arbiter of intelligence and taste, and it made people reject everything that came from France, in particular the ideas of the Enlightenment.

With its exaltation of the individual, of history and of local issues as opposed to the universal, timeless philosophy of the Enlightenment, the Romantic movement gave nationalism a major boost. It swathed it in multicoloured, strident images, supplied it with a heated rhetoric and put it within reach of a general public, through plays and novels and poems that focused on picturesque and emotive local traditions. A positive affirmation of local values later turned into contempt for outsiders. The defence of German singularity soon became an affirmation of the superiority of the German people – and for German, read Russian, or French or Anglo Saxon – which had a historical mission that, for racial, religious or political reasons, it had to carry out on the world stage. Other nations would have to comply or else be punished for their non-compliance. This is the road that led to the great disasters of 1914 and 1939. And also the road that caused Latin America to maintain the absurd balkanisation of the colonial period and fight bloody wars to preserve or alter boundaries which, in any event, were pure inventions, without any ethnic, geographic or traditional basis.

The thesis of Sir Isaiah Berlin, which is magnificently argued throughout the eight essays brought together in this book (and we must thank Henry Hardy for this: he has made sure that the vast work of the Latvian professor has not remained scattered in myriad academic journals), is that nationalism is a doctrine or a state of mind, or both, that comes about as a reaction to the utopia of a universal and perfect society. We might add that nationalism is also a utopia, no less real or artificial than other utopias that argue for a classless society, the republic of the just, the republic of racial purity or of preordained truth.

The very idea of nation is fallacious, if we conceive it as an expression of something homogeneous and perennial, in which language, tradition, habits, customs, beliefs and shared values go to make up a collective personality that is clearly differentiated from other groups. In this sense, there are no nations, nor have there ever been nations, in the world. The societies that are closest to this fantasy model are archaic and barbarous societies, which have been kept out of modernity, and almost out of history, by despots and isolation. All other societies offer a sort of framework, in which different ways of being, speaking, believing and thinking can coexist. How we decide to live has more to do with individual choice than with tradition or family or the language we were brought up in. Not even language, perhaps the most genuine marker of social identity, can be said to be synonymous with nation. Because almost all nations speak different languages – even if one is official – and because, with very few exceptions, almost all languages escape national borders and find their own way in the world.

No nation has evolved from the natural and spontaneous development of a single ethnic group, religion or cultural tradition. They all came about as a result of political arbitrariness, dispossession or imperial intrigue, crude economic interests, brute force combined with good fortune, and they all, even the oldest and most distinguished of them, have erected their borders on a devastated terrain of destroyed or repressed or fragmented cultures, incorporating people who have been thrown together through wars, religious strife or out of a simple survival instinct. Every nation is a lie that time and history have given – as in old myths or classical legends – an appearance of truth.

But it is the case that the great modern utopias – Marxism and Nazism, that looked to abolish borders and reorder the world – proved to be even more fragile and transitory. We can see this in particular today, with the rapid collapse of Soviet totalitarianism, as nationalism is reborn from the ashes in countries formerly under Soviet rule and threatens to become the great ideological rallying cry for people looking to reclaim their sovereignty.

It is important, therefore, at the threshold of this new historical period, to remember that nationalism is no more compatible with democratic culture than is totalitarianism. If proof is needed, read the splendid essay that Isaiah Berlin dedicates to Joseph de Maistre, a reactionary par excellence and the father of all nationalisms. Berlin sees him not as he is usually depicted, as a retrograde, a thinker who turned his back on the present, but rather as a terrible visionary and prophet of the obscurantist apocalyptic events that Europe would suffer in the twentieth century.

Nationalism is the culture of the uncultured, the religion of the demagogue, and a smokescreen behind which prejudice, violence and often racism can be found lurking. Because at the root of all nationalism is the conviction that being part of a specific nation is an attribute, something distinctive, an essence shared by similarly privileged people, a condition that inevitably establishes a difference – a hierarchy – with respect to other people. It is the easiest thing in the world to play the nationalist card to whip up a crowd, especially if that crowd is made up of poor and ignorant people who are looking to vent their bitterness and frustration on something or someone. Nothing better than the pyrotechnics of nationalism to distract these people from their real problems, to prevent them from seeing who are their real exploiters, by creating a false illusion of unity. It is not by chance that nationalism is the most solid and widespread ideology in the so-called Third World.

Despite this, it is true to say that along with the crumbling of the collective utopia, we are also witnessing today the slow decline of the nation, the discreet removal of borders. Not as a result of an ideological offensive, another utopian assault, but rather as a consequence of the growth of trade and commerce that has brought down national barriers. The flexibility of democratic societies has allowed the internationalisation of markets, capital and technology, and the development of the great industrial and financial conglomerates that have spread across countries and continents. And as a result of all this, there have been moves towards economic and political integration, in Europe, Asia and the Americas, which are beginning to transform the face of the planet.

This widespread internationalisation of our lives is perhaps the best thing that has happened in the world to date. Or, to be more precise, because the progress towards this goal is not irreversible – nationalists could interrupt it – the best thing that *could* happen. Through this process, poor countries will become less poor, since they will fit into markets where they can use their comparative advantages to good effect, and prosperous countries will achieve new levels of scientific and technological development. And more important still, democratic culture – the culture of the sovereign individual and civil and pluralist society, the culture of human rights and the free market, of private enterprise and the right to criticise, the culture of decentralised power – will grow stronger where it already exists and will extend to countries where now it is a mere caricature or a simple aspiration.

Is there a certain utopian ring to all this? Of course. And, even in the best of cases, all this is all a distant possibility, which will not be achieved without setbacks. But, for the first time it is there, within our grasp. And it is up to us whether it becomes a reality or it disappears like a will-o'-the-wisp.

Cambridge, November 1992

The Man Who Knew Too Much

If in addition to his brilliance, Isaiah Berlin (1909–97) had not been so well liked and held in such high regard, then it is quite possible that he would never have been the universally recognised intellectual figure that he had become by the time of his death, and that most of his work would remain unknown to the majority of his readers outside a handful of academic colleagues and students in Oxford and in American universities where he taught. Throughout his life he showed an Olympian lack of interest in whether or not his essays were read or published – he sincerely believed that they were not important enough to merit that honour – and he also decided not to write his autobiography or write a diary, as if he were not remotely concerned about the image that he might leave for posterity (*'Après moi le déluge'*, he liked to say).

Those of us who did not attend his classes and yet still feel ourselves to be his students will never be able to thank enough Henry Hardy, the philosophy postgraduate at Wolfson College (that Isaiah Berlin founded and ran in Oxford between 1966 and 1975), who, in 1974, proposed to his supervisor that he should collect, edit or re-edit his writings. However incredible it might seem, up until that date, he had published only three books, on Marx, Vico and Herder, and his four essays on freedom. The rest of his vast written work was unpublished, packed in dusty boxes in his office, or buried in scholarly journals, *Festschriften*, in folders containing testimonials, speeches, reports, reviews, obituaries – or in archives of official institutions, feeding the worms. Thanks to the persuasive gifts of Hardy, who managed to overcome Isaiah Berlin's tenacious reticence to excavate his own bibliography, which he did not think was justified, and to Hardy's titanic research and rigorous editing, between 1978 and 1999 there appeared *Russian Thinkers, Concepts and Categories, Against the Current, Personal Impressions, The Crooked Timber of Humanity, The Magus of the North, The Sense of Reality* and *The Roots of Romanticism*, the books that really cemented the prestige of Isaiah Berlin inside and outside the university. In the near future, his voluminous correspondence will also be published. Without the devotion and tenacity of Henry Hardy, this master of liberal thought that we know today would not exist. And without Michael Ignatieff, another friend and persistent follower of the professor from Latvia, he would still be a mere ghost, without flesh or blood, shielded behind a scattered bibliography.

Just as the volumes compiled by Hardy proved to the world that the insinuations of his rivals were absolutely false, when they put around the idea that Isaiah Berlin was merely a brilliant conversationalist, a salon philosopher, without the patience or the energy to undertake work of great intellectual scope, so, thanks to Ignatieff – a journalist and historian, born in Canada, a graduate of Toronto and Harvard, now resident in England – we now know* that the author of *The Hedgehog and the Fox* had an interesting and, at times, dramatic and adventurous life. His life was not just spent, as might first appear, submerged in the rituals and the peaceful cloisters of the elegant unreality of Oxford, for he was involved, sometimes directly and sometimes indirectly, in the great events of the century, like the Russian Revolution, the persecution and extermination of Jews in Europe, the creation of Israel, the Cold War and the great ideological conflicts between Communism and democracy in the post-Second World War period. The character that emerges from Ignatieff's book – an affectionate and loyal book, but also an independent work because, true to Berlin's ethical principle par excellence, that of fair play, he does not hesitate in pointing out his errors and defects along with his virtues and excellent qualities – is still very attractive, a

* *A Life: Isaiah Berlin*, Chatto & Windus, London, 1998.

modest, cordial, amenable and sociable man, around which the legend that followed him throughout his life was built. But the picture is also more complex and contradictory, more human and more profound, of an intellectual who, despite having received major honours in his county of adoption, Great Britain – President of the Royal Academy, Rector of an Oxford college, recipient of a knighthood from the Queen and of the Order of Merit – always felt deep within himself that he was an expatriate and a Jew, supporting a tradition and a community that had been, since time immemorial, the object of discrimination, unease and prejudice, a condition that contributed decisively to the insecurity that shadowed him through every period of his life and also, doubtless, shaped his prudent outlook, his desire to integrate into society and to go unnoticed, away from the glare of power and success, and also shaped his systematic defence of tolerance, pluralism and political diversity and his hatred of fanaticism of any form. Behind the inexhaustible conversationalist who, it seemed, bewitched guests at dinners and parties with the quality of his stories, his fluency and his extraordinary memory, there hid a man torn by the moral conflicts that he described before, and better than, anyone else: freedom and equality, justice and order, the atheist Jew and the practising Jew, and a liberal fearful that unrestricted freedom might lead to 'the wolf eating the lambs'. The clear, serene and luminous thinker suggested by his writings comes out in the portrait painted by Michael Ignatieff. But beneath the shining clarity of his ideas and his style there appears a man overwhelmed by doubt, who made mistakes and was tortured by these mistakes, who lived in a state of discreet but constant tension that prevented him feeling totally integrated into any society, despite all appearances to the contrary.

Although he never considered writing his autobiography, Isaiah Berlin agreed to talk to his friend Michael Ignatieff, in front of a tape recorder, about all the events in his life, on condition that Ignatieff would only publish the results of his research after Berlin's death. The conversation lasted ten years and ended in the final week of October 1997, a few days before his death, when Sir Isaiah, very fragile and racked by illness, invited his biographer to Headington House, his country house in Oxford, to correct some facts that his memory had clarified, and to remind Ignatieff, insistently, that his wife, Aline, had been the centre of his life, and that he was for ever in her debt. Ignatieff rounded off these personal memoirs with very detailed research in Russia, the United States, Israel and England, interviewing hundreds of people associated with Berlin, and combing newspapers, books and archives, so his biography, without being definitive, is certainly a very complete account of the life of the great thinker, linking it to the development of his interests, convictions, ideas and intellectual work. It is a literary biography, in which the life and the work are melded.

Although Isaiah Berlin spent only his first twelve years in Russia (he was born into a well-off Jewish family in 1909 in Riga, at a time when Latvia belonged to the Russian Empire), the experiences of those early years of his childhood, affected by tremendous social convulsions and family upheavals, left an indelible impression and shaped two aspects of his personality: his horror of totalitarianism and dictatorships, and his Judaism. The main event of this childhood was, without doubt, the Bolshevik revolution which he saw close up in Petrograd, where his family had taken up residence after fleeing from the insecurity and the threats that the Jewish community was subject to in Riga. In Petrograd he witnessed, at the age of seven and a half, scenes of street violence that made him immune for ever to revolutionary enthusiasm and 'political experiments'. In this period, his hostile attitude towards Communism was born, and he remained faithful to it throughout his life, even at the time of the Cold War, when the great majority of the intellectual community of which he was part was Marxist or close to Marxism. He never yielded to this temptation; and his anti-Communism led him to extreme positions that were rare in him, like defending the United States during the unpopular Vietnam War and refusing to sign a protest against Washington in response to the Bay of Pigs invasion of Cuba (Castro 'may not be a Communist', he wrote to Kenneth Tynan, 'but I think that he cares as little for civil liberties as Lenin or Trotsky'*). This attitude led him to commit an act that was not very consistent with his pluralist ethic: he used his aca-

* Ignatieff, p. 234.

demic influence to block the appointment to a Chair in Politics at the University of Sussex of Isaac Deutscher, an exiled Jew like himself, but an anti-Zionist and a left-wing intellectual, the author of the most famous biography of Trotsky. His somewhat dubious response to those who accused him of behaving in this affair like 'the anti-Communist witch hunters' was that he could not support for a Chair anyone who subordinated scholarship to ideology.

Fleeing once again, this time not only from fear but also from hunger, the Berlin family returned to Riga for a short time in 1920, and on the train they were subjected to insults and attacks from anti-Semitic passengers and officials, which, according to Berlin, made him realise for the first time – and for ever – that he was not Russian or Latvian, but Jewish, and would always be so. Although he was an atheist and was educated in England in a secular environment, he was always committed to the community and the culture of his ancestors, even to the extreme of strictly observing Jewish religious rituals at home. He was a curious practising non-believer. And, as a Zionist, he collaborated closely with one of the founders of the State of Israel, Chaim Weizmann, although, unlike a number of his relatives, he never thought of emigrating and becoming an Israeli citizen. A lot of this work was done during the Second World War, when Isaiah Berlin was serving as an analyst and political adviser to the British government, in New York and in Washington, which must have caused him much anguish and many moral dilemmas, given the tense and sometimes antagonistic relationship that existed between the Foreign Office, that was pro-Arab, and the Zionist leaders. Knowing in detail these contradictions in Isaiah Berlin's personal life helps us to understand the secret root of one of his most famous theories: that of 'contradictory truths'.

The Latvian Jewish community into which Isaiah was born spoke Russian, Latvian and German, and although the child learned these three languages, he identified most with Russian culture, a language and a literature that he studied all his life. In England, while he was educated at a most distinguished Christian public school, St Paul's in London, and then, thanks to his outstanding grades, at Oxford, he continued studying Russian alongside philosophy, so that although the umbilical cord that bound him to Russia was cut at twelve years of age, when he became a British citizen and was assimilated into the life of his second country, his intellectual sympathy and love for Russian language and literature remained. We can see this in the remarkable assurance and knowledge that he brought to his many essays on Russian writers and thinkers (*Russian Thinkers* is, for me, his best book), like those dedicated to Tolstoy, Turgenev, or his admired model, the liberal Alexander Herzen. On his return to Russia for a few months in 1945 as a British diplomat – a journey that would have an incalculable effect on his emotional and political life – the two great writers that he met, Boris Pasternak and Anna Akhmatova, were literally astonished at the fluent elegance with which this professor from another world spoke the cultured Russian of former times, and also that he was so well acquainted with a literature and authors that were beginning to become ever more invisible or remote in this society that was subject to the iron censorship of Stalin.

The Second World War radically changed the private world of Isaiah Berlin. Without it, it is very likely that his life would have been spent, like those of other dons in Oxford, among the halls where he first gave classes on philosophy and later on political and social ideas, in libraries and in his rooms in the most prestigious and traditional of all the colleges in the university, All Souls, where he had been elected as a Fellow at the incredible age of twenty-three (the first Jew to be given a place at that college). But when the war broke out, this 'asexual and erudite' life underwent an abrupt transformation: the young don, whose fame as a polyglot and specialist in European cultures – Russian and German in particular – was already widespread in academic circles, was sent to the United States by the British government, to New York and Washington, to act as an adviser to the Foreign Office and the Embassy in its dealings with the White House. Between 1941 and 1945, Sir Isaiah did extraordinary work for his country of adoption, not just through his analyses of the international situation and the delicate diplomatic relations between the Allies, which are perhaps the most read among all the Foreign Office briefing papers (in 1944 Churchill himself was so impressed by them that he wanted to know who had written them. The Foreign Office response described him as 'Mr Berlin, of Baltic Jewish extraction, a philosopher'. Churchill wrote to Eden, 'The summaries are certainly well written', and Eden replied in his own hand that he thought the papers had 'perhaps a too generous Oriental flavour'.* He also established a network of contacts in the highest social, academic and political circles in the United States, thanks to his personal charm and ease in society: a pyrotechnic conversationalist, he was the toast of diplomatic dinners and meetings, and, apart from hypnotising and amusing people with his anecdotes and his knowledge, he left his interlocutors with the rather gratifying impression that, by spending time with him, they were immersing themselves in high culture. This snobbish aspect of his life – which was always full of social engagements, dinners, galas and receptions in the highest echelons of society – curiously did not affect in any way his intellectual work, in which he never made concessions or lapsed into banality. It is not out of the question to see this somewhat frivolous aspect of his personality as a compensation, a substitute, for sex, of which it appears he had little or no experience until his later years. All his friends in Oxford were sure that he was a confirmed bachelor.

Perhaps this is the reason why he was so affected by an entire night that he spent in 1945, in a soulless flat in Leningrad, with the greatest living Russian poet, the unfortunate Anna Akhmatova. Isaiah Berlin had been sent for a few months to the British Embassy in Moscow and he took a nostalgic trip to Leningrad, in search of books and memories of his childhood. In a bookshop, someone overheard him asking after the poet and offered to take him to her flat, which was close by. Anna Akhmatova was fifty-six years old, twenty years older than Berlin. She had been a great beauty and a very famous poet before the Revolution. She was now in disgrace, and, since 1925, Stalin had not allowed her to publish a single line or give readings. Her tragic life was one of the saddest stories of those terrible years: the Soviet regime shot her first husband and imprisoned her third husband in a Siberian labour camp. Her son Lev, a talented young man with whom Isaiah Berlin spoke briefly on that night,

* Ignatieff, p. 125.

would be sent to the Gulag for thirteen years, and the Soviet commissars blackmailed Akhmatova, offering to keep him alive if she wrote abject odes in adulation of the dictator who was tormenting her. Because the suffering of the poet greatly increased after that night, Isaiah Berlin would always feel remorse that he had been involuntarily responsible for this. (In the archives of the KGB, there is memorandum on the conversation, in which Stalin remarks to the cultural commissar Zhadanov, 'So now our nun is consorting with British spies, is she?'*)

He always emphatically claimed that the eleven or twelve hours that he spent with Akhmatova, were chaste, full of intense and sparkling conversation, and that in the course of the night she recited to him a number of the celebrated poems from the book *Requiem* that – in defiance of persecution – she was writing from memory, a book that would come to represent one of the highest testimonies of spiritual and poetic resistance against the Stalinist tyranny. The talk was of literature, of the great pre-Revolution authors, many of them dead or in exile, about whom Berlin could give her information, and, discreetly, they touched on Anna's very difficult situation, her life always in the balance, seeing repression all around her and waiting for it to fall on her at any moment. But it is a fact that, although there was not the slightest physical contact between them, at noon the next day the austere Isaiah Berlin returned to the Hotel Astoria jumping with joy and proclaiming, 'I am in love, I am in love!' From that moment right up to his death, he would always state that this had been the most important event in his life. And Akhmatova's reflections on that visit can be found in the beautiful love poems in *Cinque*. A story of impossible love, of course, because, from then on, the regime cut all communication and contact between the poet and the outside world, and in the following seven years, Berlin could not find out where she was living. (When he asked the British Embassy in Moscow to make enquiries for him, he was told that it would better for Akhmatova if he did not even try to contact her.) Many years later, in 1965, at the beginning of the thaw in the Soviet Union, Isaiah

* Ignatieff, p. 167.

Berlin and other dons proposed the great Russian poet for an honorary doctorate in Oxford, and the Soviet authorities allowed her to travel to England to be awarded the doctorate. She was by now an old woman, but her prolonged ordeal had not broken her. Their meeting was cold, and when she looked around the sumptuous residence, Headington House, where Berlin lived with his wife Aline, she remarked caustically: 'So the bird is now in its golden cage'.*

The fact that the confirmed bachelor Sir Isaiah would, in 1956, come to marry Aline Halban, who belonged to an aristocratic and very wealthy French Jewish family, was not just a surprise to his innumerable friends; it was the culmination of a bizarre sentimental adventure that could provide rich material for a delightful picaresque comedy. When his diplomatic mission ended in 1945, Isaiah Berlin returned to Oxford, to his classes, his lectures, his intellectual work. He was beginning to be known on both sides of the Atlantic, and from that time on began to spend terms or semesters at North American universities, above all Harvard, as well as making periodic journeys to Jerusalem. He was showered with distinctions, and the British establishment opened their doors to him. And then, well into his forties, sex seems to have erupted in his life, in a manner that one could only describe as tortuous and academic: through adulterous liaisons with wives of his university colleagues. An irresistible humour fills the pages in which Ignatieff – with great affection and indulgence – describes a first affair, lasting several years, with meetings in churchyards, libraries, corridors and even in his parents' house. Overcome one day with remorse, Berlin went to the husband and told him the truth: 'I'm in love with your wife.' The aggrieved husband dismissed the matter with an emphatic 'That's not possible,' and changed the subject.†

The second adventure was the serious one. Aline was married to an eminent physicist, Hans Halban, an Austrian by birth, who had worked on French nuclear programmes before coming to Oxford. She was attractive, cultured, rich and passionate about music and social life, like Isaiah himself. The close friendship forged as a

* Ignatieff, p. 233.
† Ignatieff, p. 211.

result of these shared interests began to evolve in a 'guilty' manner. The physicist found out what was happening and tried to put an end to Aline's outings. Isaiah Berlin paid him a visit. While (I am sure) they had tea, they discussed the problem that had arisen. Aline waited in the garden to hear the outcome of the conversation. The philosopher's logic was persuasive, and the physicist recognised this. They both went out to the garden to walk among the rose bushes and the hydrangeas and inform Aline of their agreement: she could see her lover once a week, with the approval of her husband. And so it seems that friendly triangular harmony persisted until Hans Halban had to return to Paris. The couple decided to divorce, and Isaiah and Aline were free to marry. The marriage was a happy one. In Aline, Sir Isaiah found more than a tender wife: she was his accomplice, who shared his tastes and interests and helped him with his work, a woman capable of organising life with the confidence that comes with wealth and experience, and creating an agreeable, well-ordered existence in which social life – summers spent in Parragi in Italy, the music festivals at Salzburg, Pesaro and Glyndebourne, the dinners and outings with distinguished people – coexisted with the mornings and afternoons spent reading and editing his essays.

His intellectual work, which was rich, dense and extraordinarily acute, was concentrated in essays and articles, lectures and reviews, not in great syntheses, organic works or ambitious long-term projects. This was not due, as Ignatieff convincingly argues, to the dispersed life, full of many different obligations, that Berlin always led: brevity and small scale were his unmistakable hallmark. In the eighties, as if to prove those critics wrong who reproached him for not bringing out a major work on a wide-ranging theme, he decided to expand the 1965 lectures he had given in Washington on the origins of Romanticism (published posthumously as *The Roots of Romanticism*) and worked for many months in the British Library, filling hundreds of file cards. In the end, he gave it up: big projects were not his style. He lacked the ambition, the enormous faith in himself, that touch of obsession and fanaticism that produce masterpieces. The essay was more conducive to his modesty, his sceptical view of himself, his complete disregard for being, or appearing to be, a genius or a sage, his conviction – that was not a pose but something he felt very deeply – that what he had done, or was capable of doing, counted in the end for very little in the dazzling ferment of universal thought and literary creation.

That was not true, of course. Because in these relatively short texts that interpreted and reread the great thinkers, historians and writers of modern Europe, this born essayist – he is similar in this respect to another great liberal thinker, José Ortega y Gasset – has left a work that is seminal to the culture of our time. A work that ranks among the finest in the liberal tradition, a tradition that he brought up to date in a way that few other contemporary thinkers could match. Probably only Popper and Hayek have done as much as him, in our times, for the culture of freedom. Of the three, the most artistic, the best writer, was Isaiah Berlin. His prose is as transparent and readable as that of Stendhal, another polygraph who did not write but rather dictated his texts, and, quite frequently, the richness and animation of his ideas, his quotations and his examples, the liveliness and elegance with which he organised his thought, give his essays a novelistic quality, full of throbbing life and infectious humanity.

I saw him twice in my life. The first time, in the eighties, at a dinner at the house of the historian Hugh Thomas, at which the star guest was the Prime Minister, Margaret Thatcher. They sat Sir Isaiah next to her, and, throughout the whole evening, the only one of the intellectuals present to whom she made a real attempt to show respect and affection was Berlin. He seemed rather overwhelmed and happy. At the end of the dinner, when Mrs Thatcher left, after a couple of hours of subtle cross-examination from the dinner guests, Isaiah Berlin declared, 'Nothing to be ashamed of'. The second time was in Seville, in 1992, at a congress devoted to the fifth centenary of the discovery of America. People showered him with compliments, which he accepted blushingly but gratefully. I had written a series of articles on him, which would later become the prologue to the Spanish edition of the *Hedgehog and the Fox*, in which I committed the gaffe of stating that he

The Thief in the Empty House

All Jean-François Revel's books are interesting and polemical, but his memoirs, which have just been published under the enigmatic title *The Thief in the Empty House*, are also good-humoured, an uninhibited confession of sins, passions, ambitions and frustrations, written in a light and sometimes hilarious tone by a Marseillais who found himself, due to the vagaries of life, having to give up the university career he had dreamed of in his youth and become an essayist and political journalist.

He seems saddened, as he looks back, by this change of career. However, as far as his readers are concerned, it was not a misfortune but rather a stroke of luck that, because of Sartre and a beautiful journalist whom he made pregnant when he was very young, he had to give up his academic plans and head to Mexico and then to Italy to teach French language and culture. Dozens of philosophy teachers of his generation languished in university lecture halls teaching a discipline that, with very few exceptions (one of which is the work of Raymond Aron, whom Revel describes in this memoir with affectionate perversity), has become so specialised that it now seems to have little to do with life. In his books and articles, written in newsrooms or at home, spurred on by history in the making, Revel has never stopped writing about philosophy, but, in the style of Diderot or Voltaire, he bases it on a current problem. His brave and lucid contributions to contemporary debates have shown – like Unamuno in Spain – that journalism can be highly creative, a genre that can combine intellectual originality with stylistic elegance.

In its depiction of key events and characters, the book shows us an intense and varied life, where important moments – the resistance to the Nazis during the Second World War, the vicissitudes of French journalism in the second half of the twentieth century – mix with rather more bizarre ones, like the joyful description that Revel gives of a famous guru, Gurdjieff, whose circle he frequented in his early years. Sketched with the broad brushstrokes of a deft caricaturist, the celebrated visionary, who dazzled a great number of gullible people and snobs in his Paris exile, appears in these pages as an irresistible drunken bloodsucker, draining the pockets and the souls of his followers. These followers included – however surprising this might seem – not just gullible people who could easily be duped, but also a number of intellectuals and well-read people who saw Gurdjieff's confusing verbiage as a doctrine that could lead them to rational knowledge and spiritual peace.

It is a devastating portrait, but, as with several other people described in the book, the severity of the criticism is softened by the good-humoured, understanding attitude of the narrator, whose benevolent smile rescues, at the last moment, characters who are about to be crushed under the weight of their own cunning, vileness, cynicism or stupidity. Some of the portraits of friends, teachers, enemies, or other people, are affectionate and unexpected, like his depiction of Louis Althusser, Revel's teacher at the École Normale, who appears as a much more human and attractive person than one might expect from the Talmudic and asphyxiating commentator of *Capital*, or of Raymond Aron who, despite occasional disputes and misunderstandings with the author when they were both star contributors to *L'Express*, is always treated with respect, even when Revel became exasperated at his inability to maintain a coherent position in conflicts that he often caused.

On other occasions, the portraits are ferocious and the humour cannot counterbalance the vitriol. Take the brief appearance of the French socialist minister during the Gulf War, Jean-Pierre Chevènement ('A provincial and devout Lenin, belonging to the category of idiots who look intelligent, that are more lethal and dangerous than intelligent people who look like idiots'), or the portrait of François Mitterrand himself, who Revel was very close to before Mitterrand's rise to power, and who vies with Jimmy Goldsmith for the title of the most unusual and deplorable person in the great parade of characters in this book.

Revel depicts Mitterrand as a man fatally uninterested in politics (and also in morality and in ideas), who resigned himself to politics because it was a prerequisite for the only thing that mattered to him: to get to power and keep hold of it. It is a memorable portrait, like an identikit picture of a certain type of successful politician: outwardly friendly, professionally charming, superficially cultured, relying on actions and phrases learned off by heart, a glacial mind and a capacity for lying bordering on genius, together with an uncommon ability to manipulate human beings, values, words, theories and programmes as the situation demanded. It is not just the leading figures of the left who are treated with jocular irreverence in the memoir. Many right-wing dignitaries, beginning with Valéry Giscard d'Estaing, also appear as models of demagogy and irresponsibility, capable of endangering democratic institutions or the future of their country out of petty vanity and a small-minded, short-term vision of politics.

The most exquisite (and also the most cruel) portrait of all, a small masterpiece within the book, is that of the Anglo-French Jimmy Goldsmith, the owner of *L'Express* at the time when Revel was the editor of the magazine, a time when, incidentally, the magazine achieved a quality that it did not have before and has not had since. Scott Fitzgerald thought that 'rich people were different', and the brilliant, handsome and successful Jimmy (who now keeps boredom at bay by squandering twenty million pounds, in the upcoming elections in Britain, on a Referendum Party that will defend British sovereignty against the colonial aspirations of Brussels and Chancellor Kohl) seems to prove him right. But it might be difficult in this case to share the admiration that the author of *The Great Gatsby* had for millionaires. A human being can have an exceptional talent for finance and be, at the same time, a pathetic megalomaniac, self-destructive and awkward in every other respect. The account that

Revel gives of the delirious political, social and newspaper projects that Goldsmith dreamed up and then forgot almost at the same moment, the intrigues that he stirred up against himself, in a constant sabotage of a company that, despite this, kept providing him with benefits and prestige, is hilarious, something out of a Balzac novel.

Of all the facets of Revel's life – he was a teacher, an art critic, a philosopher, an editor, a gourmet, a political analyst, a writer and a journalist – it was as a writer and a journalist that he found the greatest fulfilment and in which he made his most lasting contributions. Every journalist should read his account of the highs and lows of this vocation, to realise how passionate it can be and, also, how beneficial and harmful. Revel refers to some key moments in which French journalism has uncovered a truth hidden until that moment by 'the deceptive fog of conformity and complicity'. For example, when a gimlet-eyed journalist made an incredible find, among the rubbish piled up outside a bank during a dustmen's strike in Paris: evidence of a financial racket by the USSR in France to bribe the Communist Party.

Another important story was the clarification of the mysterious comings and goings of Georges Marchais, the secretary-general of the Communist Party during the Second World War (he was a voluntary worker in German factories). This second scoop did not, however, have the repercussions that might have been expected because, at that political moment, it was not just the left that was anxious to keep the revelation quiet. The right-wing press also kept it secret, because they were afraid that the presidential candidature of Marchais would be damaged by the revelation of the Nazi sympathies of the Communist leader in his youth, and that his potential votes would switch to Mitterrand, which would have damaged Giscard. In this way, rejected by the left and the right, the truth about Marchais's past was thus minimised and denied until the matter faded away, and Marchais could continue his political career without hindrance, right up to his comfortable retirement.

These memoirs show Revel on top form: ardent, troublesome and dynamic, passionate about ideas and pleasure, insatiably curious and condemned, because of his unhealthy intellectual integrity and his polemical stance, to live in perpetual conflict with almost everyone around him. The lucid way he detects the deceit and self-justification of his colleagues, the courageous manner in which he denounces the opportunism and cowardice of intellectuals who serve the powerful out of fanaticism or for personal gain, have made him a modern *maudit*, heir to the great tradition of French non-conformists, the tradition that caused revolutions and incited free spirits to question everything, from laws, systems, institutions, ethical and aesthetic principles, to style and cookery recipes. This tradition is in its death throes today, and, however much I scan the horizon, I cannot see who might continue it among the new batch of scribes. I fear, therefore, that it will disappear with Revel. But it will disappear with the finest honours.

London, April 1997

Culture and the New International Order

It might be a good moment, in the extraordinary times we now live in, in a world deeply affected by the advances of globalisation in every sphere of life, to reflect on the ways in which cultural life will be affected by the increasing interdependence between nations that has come about as a result of the internationalisation of communications, the economy, ideas and technology. There is a great deal of confusion around this issue and a number of prejudices that need to be addressed.

But we must first clarify what we mean by the word culture. For an anthropologist, this word, with its agricultural resonance, signifies quite simply the whole gamut of customs and beliefs that are most representative of a society, from the language which its inhabitants use to communicate, to the meals they eat and the sports that they play, including their customs, gods, devils and ghosts of every shape and hue. But this conception of culture is so vast that, by including so many things, it becomes rather imprecise. It is better to restrict the term and just refer to the spiritual dimension of human life in which knowledge and beliefs – ideas and myths – meld together, giving us a perspective which allows us to understand the world in a certain way, with a degree of confidence and safety, and to form a relationship, in a precise way, with things around us and with our fellow men and women.

As we go back further in time, we find that cultures share fewer and fewer things: they tend to be more separate and in conflict. That is why, in antiquity, in that archipelago of culturally self-engrossed and isolated islands, mistrust, hatred and warfare dominated relations between cultures. Trade had a civilising and pacifying influence over time, building bridges between warring cultures and opening up routes through which adventurers, explorers, wise people and artists (along with conquistadors and plunderers) would gradually make contact with each other and start to mix, so that, after a time, their shared values would gradually replace former differences.

This brings me to the situation today, which is both terrifying and wonderful. For we are now living in a world which, thanks to internationalisation, is ever more interdependent, a world in which a common outlook seems to be rapidly reducing and removing what before had seemed like strong and impregnable barriers between cultures.

Is this a positive thing or a tragedy for humanity? The debate on this issue is just beginning, and it is sure to become more widespread and heated in years to come as antagonism intensifies between those for and against so-called globalisation. It is a wide-ranging debate in which it is not easy to differentiate cultural matters from political and economic issues, because they are so inextricably linked. In some areas, like communications, the opening of borders has had an enormously beneficial effect, because now it is much more difficult than before – and soon it will be impossible – for governments to impose censorship in the way they did in the past, by keeping people in the dark and thus manipulating public opinion. The development of audiovisual media and new technologies means that today, with a minimum of effort, citizens of any country can access diverse and contrasting information, and that authoritarian regimes, which are anxious to turn information into propaganda, find it more and more difficult to stop the free circulation of independent news and opinions that are not subject to their control. This is a great advance in terms of freedom, and gives a great democratic impulse to societies that have not yet managed to shake off dictatorships.

This opening up of information is very important in cultural as well as political terms. The technological revolution in the field of communications also opens up enormous possibilities, without historical precedent, for the diffusion of ideas, literature, science and arts, that is, for the democratisation of culture, putting it within reach of large sectors of humanity who, until relatively recently, due to their isolation, marginalisation and poverty were culturally excluded.

It is true that the large media organisations do not always use the hypnotic power that they have over their vast audiences with sufficient creativity and rigour, and that the majority of the most popular programmes could not be called cultural. But let us not confuse the effect with the cause. If television and the Internet do not enrich our sensibilities, imagination and knowledge, choosing instead to pander to the most vulgar and tasteless common denominator, it is because the audiences that they are aimed at lack the basic spiritual and aesthetic refinement to spurn these offerings and demand instead more worthwhile and better-made programmes. In any event, the means are there, and it is up to us to make sure that the content improves and enhances us intellectually and as citizens, instead of dulling our minds, drowning us in what Flaubert called 'received ideas', in stereotypes and prejudices.

It is necessary to democratise culture, but that also has its risks, if that means that we make ideas banal in order to make them accessible to everyone. That is not democratising culture, but rather corrupting it and replacing it with a caricature. The democratisation of culture can only be understood as the creation of conditions that facilitate and promote access to culture for those who are prepared to make the necessary intellectual effort to enjoy and enhance their lives through culture. And democratisation must ensure that everyone should have this opportunity.

Let me offer a brief illustration. In the sixties, for almost seven years, I lived in France, earning my living as a journalist, first in the France-Presse Agency and later in French Radio-Television. One of the stories that I had to cover, and I always remember it because it was so innovatory and stimulating, was a series of public readings that a group of writers were giving in different locations which appeared at first sight to have little to do with literature: mining centres, factories, offices, sports clubs, army barracks. I don't remember what institution sponsored this initiative; but I do remember that it wanted to find out whether it was possible to present successfully the best of literature to relatively uninformed audiences. The writers did not read their own works, but rather the works of their favourite authors. And they were asked to make no concessions with regard the difficulty of the pieces. I went to two of these sessions and I have a vivid and splendid memory of what happened when a well-known critic and novelist – Michel Butor, if my memory serves – read some stories by Borges (a difficult and highbrow writer if ever there was one) in a factory. Helped by his very clear explanations, a clever selection of texts and the engaging way he read them, his audience was fascinated by the baroque stories of the author of *El Aleph*, and I am sure that they had a very good time. That initiative, to my knowledge, was a one-off, never repeated. But it showed me, at least, that good literature is, in addition to many other things, a source of incomparable pleasure; and that, however complex it might be, it can soon captivate large audiences. The same can be said of culture in general.

It should not be seen as strange that these finely wrought, unusual stories dreamed up on the other side of the world by an Argentine writer should excite for a few hours the imagination of those French workers (who were doubtless not used to reading literature). If literature is good, it knows no borders; or rather, it is one of best ways to bring down the barriers between people and allow them to communicate and feel part of a single community. Don Quixote began his adventures riding through La Mancha, but now he rides throughout the world and in almost all the languages of the earth, just as the tragedy of Romeo and Juliet brings a tear to the eyes of most of humanity, and the voices of Tolstoy, Dante, Homer and Molière are a heritage that everyone who has heard, read or reread their characters' adventures and misfortunes, and has embraced them, can claim for themselves. Many centuries before we heard the word globalisation, the great artistic and literary creations had already begun systematically to break down the borders that kept people apart, establishing a common denominator between cultures.

The worst disasters that humanity has suffered have always been the result of a lack of communication between countries or societies, which used confrontation and violence instead of dialogue. If you want to confront enemies with the utmost conviction and force, then it is essential to dehumanise and demonise them. This is an eminently cultural task: to replace an objective perception of reality with mirages that reflect our fears and hatred, replacing human beings with phantoms, depriving them first of their true nature and then of their lives themselves. Religion, ideologies and nationalism have traditionally supplied arguments and pretexts for dehumanising adversaries, a first stage that can lead to the genocides and holocausts that have stained world history with horror and blood.

Culture is the most effective antidote we have to this behaviour, allowing us to recognise the humanity of the *other*, of *others* above and beyond the differences that exist between the different ethnicities, creeds and languages that give the world its rich and stimulating diversity. It allows us to discover beneath the differences in clothes, customs, beliefs or geography an underlying community of interests between people. This should create a sense of community that would make wars and killings impossible. But we know that this is not the case, and that, instead, despite the prodigious development of knowledge and technology, in many parts of the globe religious or political antagonisms (or the two mixed together) continue to wreak havoc, as in the Middle East, while in other places, like the border between India and Pakistan, the old territorial disputes keep millions of people on tenterhooks, threatened with a nuclear apocalypse.

If it continues spreading to, and including, all the countries of the world in a web of exchanges and common interests and responsibilities, globalisation is likely to be the most effective method that humanity has to end armed conflict, begin disarmament and work towards peace in the world.

This ideal is possible as long as this process of integration that we call globalisation is not primarily economic, as a narrow definition of the process might have us believe. Of course, if it is confined to trade, to opening up world markets for all products, then the most pessimistic predictions about the consequences of globalisation could become a reality. Purely economic globalisation would be sterile and indeed impossible. Open and competitive markets are not those that are left to the whims of buyers and sellers, investors and consumers. They are clearly and fairly regulated, by efficient and honest courts, that make sure contracts are in place and sanction those who violate other people's rights. And the only political system that guarantees the existence of independent judges is democracy. For that reason, it is not a coincidence that the most strident opponents of globalisation are also opposed to democracy. These are the people who feel nostalgic for the vertical, totalitarian systems of the extreme right and the extreme left. For globalisation to be beneficial to the world, it is fundamental that, alongside markets, it should look to globalise political democracy.

There are some tenacious prejudices in the cultural sphere that are opposed to globalisation. The argument goes that, if globalisation becomes a reality, then all the cultures of the world will disappear, flattened by Anglo-Saxon culture which, in the hands of the superpower, the United States, will impose conformity on all the countries of the planet, in a new form of cultural colonialism.

I would like to explore in some detail this cultural argument against globalisation, which goes along these lines:

The disappearance of national frontiers and the establishment of a world connected by international markets will deal a death blow to regional and national cultures, to the traditions, customs, mythologies and modes of behaviour that determine the cultural identity of every community or country. Unable to resist the invasion of cultural products from developed countries – or rather from the superpower, the United States – which inevitably come in the wake of the big multinationals, US culture will end up taking over, making the entire world uniform, destroying the rich variety of cultures that are still thriving. In this way, all the other communities, not just those that are small and weak, will lose their identity – their soul – and become the colonised people of the twenty-first century, slavish followers, zombies or caricatures modelled by the cultural values of the new imperialism that will rule the world not just through its capital, technology, military power and scientific knowledge, but also by imposing on others its language, its ways of thinking, its beliefs, pastimes and dreams.

This nightmare or negative utopia of a world which, through globalisation, has lost its linguistic and cultural diversity, and become instead a uniform Americanised culture is not, as some people think, an idea developed just by political minorities of the extreme left who feel nostalgic for Marxism, Maoism and Third World Guevarism, a sort of persecution mania allied to a hatred and bitterness towards the American giant. It can also be found in developed countries, culturally highly developed countries, and is shared by people on the left, on the right and in the centre. Perhaps the most striking example is France, where governments of different political orientation periodically start up campaigns in defence of French 'cultural identity', that is supposedly threatened by globalisation. A great swath of intellectuals and politicians become concerned that the land that produced Montaigne, Descartes, Racine and Baudelaire and set the standards for fashion, philosophy, painting and cooking, and in all matters of the intellect, might find itself invaded by McDonald's, Pizza Hut, Kentucky Fried Chicken, rock and rap, Hollywood movies, blue jeans, sneakers and polo shirts. This fear has meant, for example, that France has massively subsidised its local film industry, and there have been numerous campaigns demanding a system of quotas limiting the screening of US films and guaranteeing that of a certain percentage of local films. That is also the reason why there have been strict municipal regulations (although, if you walk round Paris, they do not seem to be strictly observed) imposing heavy fines on advertising that denationalises the language of Molière by using Anglicisms. And let's not forget that José Bové, the farmer turned crusader against *malbouffe* (bad eating), who smashed up a McDonald's, has become something of a popular hero in France.

Although I think that the cultural argument against globalisation is not acceptable, one has to recognise that at its heart there is an unquestionable truth. The world that we are going to inhabit in the century that is just beginning will be much less picturesque, much less full of local colour than the century that we are leaving. Fiestas, clothing, ceremonies, rituals and beliefs that in the past offered a great folkloric and ethnological variety will start to disappear, or be confined to very small groups, while the bulk of society will give up these forms and take on others that are more appropriate to the times we are living in. This is a process that all the countries of the globe are going through, some more quickly, others more slowly. But this is not due to globalisation, but to modernisation, and is an effect, not a cause. We can, of course, regret that this is happening and feel nostalgia for the passing of forms of life from the past which, especially if seen from the comfortable perspective of the present, seem to us graceful, original and colourful. But I think that what we cannot do is avoid this happening. Not even countries like Cuba or North Korea, which are fearful that openness will destroy the totalitarian regimes that govern them, and thus close in on themselves and look to keep modernity at bay with sanctions and censorship, can halt this process, keep it from undermining their so-called 'cultural identity'. In theory, a country could perhaps preserve this identity were it to live, as happens with certain remote tribes in Africa or the Amazon, in total isolation, cutting off any form of exchange with other nations and being totally self-sufficient. A cultural identity preserved in this sway would take that society back to the times of prehistoric man.

If it is true that modernisation causes many forms of traditional life to disappear, it is also true that it opens up opportunities and offers, in broad terms, a great stride forward for humanity. This is why when people can choose freely, they choose modernisation, without hesitation, often against the wishes of their leaders or of traditional intellectuals.

The argument in favour of 'cultural identity' and against globalisation is based on a conception of culture that is resistant to change and which has no basis in history. What cultures have remained identical over time? We would need to find them among primitive magical-religious communities, beings living in caves, adoring thunder and wild beasts, beings that because of their primitive nature are more and more vulnerable to exploitation and extinction. All other cultures, above all those that have the right to be called modern, living cultures, have been evolving to such an extent that they are now

merely a remote reflection of what they were even two or three generations ago. This is precisely the case of countries like France, Spain
and Great Britain, where, in the last fifty years, the changes have
been so profound and spectacular that today a Proust, a García Lorca
or a Virginia Woolf – whose works of literature did so much to bring
about these changes – would scarcely recognise the societies in
which they were born.

The idea of 'cultural identity' is dangerous because, from a social
point of view, the term is conceptually weak, and from a political
point of view, it might jeopardise that most precious of all human
achievements, which is freedom. Of course, I am not denying that a
group of people that speak the same language, have been born and
live in the same area, confront the same problems and have the same
religion and the same customs, share common characteristics. But
this collective denominator cannot define what is specific to each
member of the group, the attributes and distinctive traits that differentiate them from others. The concept of *identity*, when it is not used
to define individuals, but rather to represent a group, is reductive
and dehumanising. It is a magical-religious sleight of hand that
makes abstract everything that is creative and original in men and
women, everything that has resisted inherited values or geography
or social pressure, in the name of individual freedom.

In fact the notion of *collective identity*, the breeding ground of
nationalism, is an ideological fiction. It is a concept that many ethno-
graphers and anthropologists argue cannot be applied to the most
archaic communities. For, however important shared customs and
beliefs are for the defence of the group, there is always a great mar-
gin for initiative and creation among its members, outside the group,
and individual differences are more important than collective features when we examine individuals on their own terms and not as
mere secondary to the collective. And one of the great advantages of
globalisation is that it greatly extends the possibilities that each citizen on this interconnected planet – the motherland of everyone – has
to construct their own cultural identity, in accordance with their own
preferences and inner motivation, and through their own voluntary
action. Because now they are no longer forced, as in the past, and still

in many places in the present, to comply with an identity that, like a straitjacket, obliges them to take on the language, the religion and the customs of the place where they were born. In this sense, globalisation should be welcomed because it greatly increases the scope of individual freedom.

Perhaps Latin America is the best example of how artificial and unreal, if not downright absurd, it is to try to establish *collective identities*. What would a Latin American cultural identity be? Could we identify a unique and coherent set of beliefs, customs, traditions and mythologies? Our history is full of intellectual polemics – some of which have been very fierce – that have sought to answer this question. Perhaps the most famous was the polemic in the 1920s between Hispanists and Indigenists that reverberated throughout the continent. For Hispanists such as José de la Riva Agüero, Víctor Andrés Belaunde and Francisco García Calderón, Latin America was born when, through Discovery and Conquest, it entered into a relationship with Europe, when, through the Spanish and Portuguese languages brought over by discoverers and conquistadors, and through the adoption of Christianity, it became part of Western civilisation. The Hispanists did not look down on pre-Hispanic cultures, but for them, these cultures were just a substratum – and not the most important substratum – of a historical and social reality that took on its final form and definition thanks to the revitalising influence of the West.

The Indigenists, by contrast, rejected, with moral indignation, any supposed benefits that the Europeans might have brought to America. For them, our identity had its roots and its soul in pre-Hispanic cultures and civilisations whose development and modernisation were brutally checked by violence and subject to iniquitous censorship, repression and marginalisation, not only throughout three centuries of colonisation, but also after Independence. And, according to the Indigenists, the authentic American expression (to borrow a phrase from Lezama Lima) could be found in all the cultural manifestations – from native languages to beliefs, rituals, arts and popular customs – that had resisted Western cultural oppression and survived to our times. A famous historian of this school, the Peruvian Luis E. Valcárcel, went so far as to say in one of his books – *Ruta colonial del Perú* (*The Colonial Route of Peru*) – that churches, convents and other colonial architectural monuments should be destroyed because they represented the 'Anti-Peru', an imposition, a negation of pristine American identity, that could only be based on Indian foundations. And one of the most original novelists of Latin America, José María Arguedas, narrated, in stories of great delicacy and vibrant moral protest, the discreet, heroic survival of Quechua culture in the Andean world despite the suffocating and distorting presence of the West.

Hispanism produced some excellent historical essays, as did Indigenism, as well as important fictional works, but, from today's perspective, both doctrines seem equally sectarian, reductive and false. Neither of them was able – caught up as they were in their ideological and slightly racist straitjackets – to capture the great diversity of Latin America. Who would dare to say, today, that only the Hispanic or only the indigenous can legitimately claim to represent Latin America?

However, attempts to define and isolate our 'cultural identity' continue to surface, with an intellectual and political stubbornness that would be better spent on worthier causes. Because to try to impose a cultural identity on a people is like imprisoning them and depriving them of their most precious freedom: the right to choose what, who and how they want to be. Latin America does not have one but many cultural identities, and none of them can claim to be more legitimate, more pure or more genuine than the others; they all make Latin America the plural land that it is, with its diverse languages, traditions, customs and ethnic filiations.

Of course Latin America is the pre-Hispanic world and the cultures that continue it to our day and which, in countries like Mexico, Guatemala and the Andean countries, have such an important bearing on society. But Latin America is also a great cluster of Portuguese- and Spanish-speakers, with a tradition of five hundred years, whose presence and actions have been decisive in shaping the continent. And is there not something of Africa in Latin America, which arrived on our shores along with the Europeans? Has not this

African presence indelibly marked our skin, our music, our way of being, our social landscape? When we explore the cultural, ethnic and social mix that is Latin America, we find that we are linked to almost all the regions and cultures of the world. And this, which prevents us from having a unique cultural identity – we have so many that we have none – is, contrary to what nationalists believe, our greatest wealth. It also gives us excellent credentials to feel fully-fledged citizens in the global world of today.

The fear of the Americanisation of the planet is based more on ideological paranoia than on reality. There is no doubt, of course, that, with globalisation, the dominance of the English language, which has come to be, like Latin in the Middle Ages, the general language of our time, will continue to grow, because it is essential for communications and for international transactions. Does that mean that English will develop to the detriment of the other important languages? Of course not. Probably the reverse will occur. The disappearance of borders and the prospect of an interdependent world has become an incentive for the new generation to try to learn and assimilate other cultures (which could now be theirs if they so desire) out of interest but also out of need, because to speak different languages and to be comfortable in different cultures is today a very important credential for professional success. Let me take the case of Spanish. Fifty years ago, we Spanish-speakers were still a community that was more or less closed in on itself, with very little resonance outside our traditional linguistic confines. Today, by contrast, this community is increasing in strength, spreading its influence across five continents. The fact that in the United States there are currently twenty-five to thirty million Spanish-speakers explains why, in the last US elections, both candidates, Governor Bush and Vice President Gore, conducted their presidential campaigns in Spanish as well as in English.

How many young people of both sexes across the globe have, thanks to the challenges of globalisation, started to learn Japanese, German, Mandarin, Cantonese, Arabic, Russian or French? Very many, of course, and this is a trend that, fortunately, can only increase in years to come. For that reason, the best defence for one's own languages and cultures is to promote them the length and breadth of the new world we live in, instead of trying naïvely to guard them against the threat of English. People who suggest this remedy, even though they talk a lot about culture, are usually an uncultured bunch trying to hide their true vocation: to the cause of nationalism. And there is nothing more anathema to culture than the parochial, exclusive and confused vision of cultural nationalists. The most admirable lessons that cultures teach us is that they do not need to be protected by bureaucrats or commissars, or confined behind bars, or isolated by customs houses in order to remain fresh and healthy. Cultures need to live in freedom, exposed constantly to other cultures, which enrich and renew them. In antiquity, Latin did not kill Greek; quite the contrary, the artistic originality and the intellectual depth of Hellenic culture pervaded Roman civilisation and through this civilisation, the poems of Homer and the philosophy of Plato and Aristotle reached the entire world. Globalisation will not make local cultures disappear; everything good about them will find a place to grow in this open world.

In a celebrated essay, 'Notes Towards the Definition of Culture', T. S. Eliot predicted that humanity in the future would witness a renaissance of local and regional cultures, and his prophecy seemed rather speculative at the time. However, globalisation will probably turn his prediction into a reality in the twenty-first century, and we should be pleased. A renaissance of small local cultures will restore the rich multiplicity of behaviour and expressions that – and this is something that is usually forgotten or people avoid remembering because of its moral implications – from the end of the eighteenth century and in particular in the nineteenth century, the nation state annihilated, sometimes in the literal rather than the metaphorical sense of the term, in order to create so-called *national cultural identities*. This was often achieved by force, by banning the teaching and publication of vernacular languages or the practice of religions or customs that were not seen as suitable for the Nation. Thus in most countries of the world, the nation state was formed by the forced imposition of a dominant culture over other weaker, minority cultures, which were stifled and then excised from official life. But, contrary to what those fearful of globalisation might think, it is not easy to erase cultures from the map, however small they might be, if they have a rich tradition behind them, and there is a group that adheres to their culture, albeit in secret. And we are today beginning to see that, as the nation state becomes less rigid, the forgotten, marginalised or silenced local cultures are beginning to re-emerge and show signs, on occasion, of quite vigorous life.

This is occurring everywhere in Europe. Perhaps we should point to the case of Spain and the dynamic growth of its regional cultures. During the forty years of the Franco dictatorship, they were stifled and had little opportunity to express themselves, condemned as they were to a semi-clandestine existence. But with democracy came the freedom to develop the rich diversity of Spanish culture, which has been extraordinarily successful, mainly in Catalonia, Galicia and the Basque regions, but in other areas as well. Of course, we must not confuse this regional cultural renaissance, which is positive and enriching, with the phenomenon of exclusive nationalism, which is a source of problems and a serious threat to the culture of freedom.

Globalisation presents many political, legal and administrative challenges. And if it is not accompanied by the global spread and strengthening of democracy – freedom and law – it could have damaging consequences, facilitating, for example, the internationalisation of terrorism and crime syndicates. But compared to the benefits and opportunities that it brings, above all for poor and backward countries which need to move quickly to reach decent living standards for their people, then we must look to face up to these challenges with enthusiasm and imagination. And with the conviction that never before, in the long history of civilisation, have we had so many intellectual, scientific and economic resources at our disposal to fight against the atavistic evils of hunger, war, prejudice and oppression.

Madrid, September 2002

Responses to 9/11

Just as after severe earthquakes the ground keeps shaking for many days, the responses to the terrorist attacks of 11 September 2001 in New York will be lengthy and will radically transform the public and private life of the twenty-first century. Although some of these outcomes will be unpredictable, in particular in the political and military spheres, in one specific area the effect will surely be positive. The terrorist groups and movements in five continents, and the parties and states that protect them, will find life much more difficult than before, because they will be pursued and hunted down in a systematic way by the democratic powers, which will show none of their previous indulgence. The United States and the European Union have realised how exposed they are to attacks similar to those that destroyed the Pentagon and the Twin Towers in Wall Street, and in future will coordinate their anti-terrorist activities, finally realising that among the fanatical practitioners of terror there is a basic solidarity, a common aim, above or beyond specific governments, to destroy the rule of law and liberty as forms of life.

That is the reason why ETA in Spain, the ELN in Colombia and Fidel Castro in Cuba, to give just Spanish and Spanish American examples, have rushed to condemn the attacks in Manhattan and distance themselves from Islamic fundamentalism. And, through their spokespersons, allies and figureheads, they are advancing the strange idea that not all terrorist activities are the same, that, in certain historical contexts, blowing apart peaceful citizens with car

256

bombs, putting bullets into the necks of political opponents, or using kidnapping and extortion to finance their activities, are justifiable operations. If the campaign that democratic countries are organising against those that commit terror can be transformed into an effective and systematic support for the democratisation of countries suffering dictatorship, then the world would make rapid progress, not just in terms of coexistence and basic human rights, but also in terms of security.

But, following the declaration by the White House that the United States will not look to overthrow the Afghan-Taliban government and replace it by another less intolerant and repressive government, but rather that it will concentrate exclusively on the capture of Osama Bin Laden and his right-hand men, we are faced with alarming uncertainty. It's clear that this declaration was made for diplomatic reasons, so as not to over-alarm the satraps of the Persian Gulf, like Saudi Arabia, that the United States relies on for logistical support, in whose despotic regimes the very idea of democracy strikes fear. But what is clear is that if the reprisals for 11 September are going to be confined just to the persecution of the Saudi terrorist and his accomplices, even if they are captured or killed, then very little gains will have been made in the fight against terror. See what happened during the Gulf War, when Kuwait was liberated but the authoritarian regime of Saddam Hussein was left intact. Saddam has not only enslaved the Iraqi people but also supports political violence against the West and harbours terrorists. If the internationalisation of human rights, the rule of law and freedom are not held up as goals, then the campaign against terror that is currently being waged will be mere show, devoid of any content.

To date, the main political beneficiaries of the tragedy in the United States are Vladimir Putin and Ariel Sharon. Acting with undeniable speed and skill, by coming out immediately in support of Washington and placing at its disposal the vast amount of experience acquired by Russia during the Afghan War, the Russian prime minister has put himself and his government centre stage in international affairs. He has gained an audience and sympathy that he did not have before, and he has used this, with the instinct of a bloodhound, to promote his view that there is a strong alliance between Islamic fundamentalism and terrorist groups like Al Qaeda and the Chechen independence movement. Whether this is true or false – and the truth doubtless lies between these two extremes – his argument is now much more widely accepted than in the past. It is possible that, in the immediate future, the West will stop putting pressure on Russia over violations of human rights in Chechnya, and, perhaps, even help the Russian government, this brand-new ally, in its fight against the Chechen independence movement, a movement that has been dealt a terrible blow by the destruction of the Twin Towers.

The same is true of the Palestinians, whom the Israeli government of Ariel Sharon is now presenting to democratic countries as fundamentalists and terrorists (the Minister of Defence has called Arafat the 'Palestine Osama Bin Laden'). This is a caricature that some weeks ago would have been roundly rejected, but now, by contrast, it is being given serious consideration and, in some sectors, is gaining approval. It is true that under pressure from Washington, Sharon lifted his ban on talks and has allowed the President of the Palestinian Authority and his own Foreign Minister, Simon Peres, to meet and make a vague declaration that seems to leave the door open for fresh negotiations. But let's not deceive ourselves. If before 11 September Sharon was a declared opponent of the Oslo agreement, now he is even more so. That is because he feels more secure in his extremist positions, convinced that the blood of the seven thousand people murdered in the United States by Islamic terrorism can also stain the Palestine cause and strengthen those in Israel, like him and his followers, who refuse to make the smallest concession in the interests of a solid peace with the Palestinians, and believe that drastic police and military action – including state terror, that is, selective assassination – will put down the Intifada and the aspirations of the subordinate population. I, and many other old friends and defenders of Israel, think that this is a monstrous attitude and also an illusion, because apart from condoning terrible injustice and crimes, it will just serve to detract further from the international image of Israel, depriving it of the moral legitimacy over its opponents that it could claim as a democratic state in a region where despotism abounds. But, in the short term, it is possible that through proverbial reasons of state, Sharon will get his way and the Western countries, starting with the United States, will be more tolerant and even supportive of the policy of intolerance and excess of this well-trusted 'ally' in the fight against fundamentalist terrorism. The explosion in Wall Street has finally buried the Oslo agreements and put back the Middle East peace process a very long way indeed.

But, perhaps, the greatest damage caused by the terrible attacks of 11 September, working like a virus, will be the erosion of the culture of freedom in the democratic countries themselves. I am writing this article in London where, in contrast to the normal sangfroid of the population, public opinion is now in a state of tension and alarm over security that could be termed, without exaggeration, paranoid. In newspapers, radio broadcasts and television programmes, the obsessive topic is where the next terrorist attacks will take place: if there will be an escalation and if the next act of Bin Laden or one of his kind will be to explode an atomic device that would destroy the city, or poison the water, the air or food with biological weapons. All these possibilities are presented and assessed by experts who, quite unperturbed, explain the mechanisms of these potential acts of collective homicide, and produce horrifying statistics on the number of estimated victims. In such a climate, can all the individual liberties that Great Britain is justifiably proud of survive? For a start, a poll in a local newspaper found that a majority of the people were in favour of introducing identity cards, to be carried night and day by all citizens, so as to facilitate the monitoring and control of suspects. This might seem an unimportant measure, which is already standard practice in many democratic countries. But let us not deceive ourselves.

For the same logic that forces citizens to carry identification with them can justify a telephone tap, house searches, preventive detention, anti-immigration policies and restrictions on press freedom. It might well be the case that, faced with the threat of mass annihilation that, since 11 September, now hangs like a sword of Damocles over the inhabitants of the richest and most powerful countries on the planet, the adherence to the great values of legality and individual freedom will be weakened, and take second place to the obsessive and perfectly legitimate desire for security. Who can deny that an open society is more vulnerable to the terrorist action of small fanatical groups than a police state, where all the movements and actions of its citizens are controlled by an absolute power? Of course, the United States and the European Union are not going to become totalitarian states because of the quite understandable insecurity and fear that has spread in the wake of 11 September. But there is no doubt that the need for security, that has become the number one priority, will erode the rights and prerogatives that democratic culture had won for ordinary men and women. The fanatical criminals who crashed the planes into the Twin Towers and the Pentagon were not mistaken: the world is now, thanks to them, less safe and less free.

London, Sunday 30 September 2001

and their solidarity in the face of the violence inflicted on a city that Manolo Valdés is a part of.

In the residence of the Spanish Ambassador to the UN, Inocencio Arias, I discover an oil painting that I have seen before, but which now has become another painting. On the canvas, the artist himself, with his back to us, is contemplating a New York of radiant skyscrapers, in which, in the foreground, the Twin Towers of Wall Street stand out. It is a very beautiful painting, with very vivid colours, which, in my memory, communicated a cheerful and playful image, full of joy and life. The 11 September changed that canvas; it imbued it with a sense of apocalyptic prophecy, so that now, although it is still beautiful, it is a picture without a trace of humour, a tragic work that evokes nostalgia, mute rage and sadness.

But I found the most dramatic homage to the victims of the most lethal terrorist attack in history not in New York, but in the Arts Institute in Chicago, where I went to see an extraordinary exhibition dedicated to the nine weeks that Vincent Van Gogh and Paul Gauguin lived together in Arles in 1888. This difficult period of coexistence, that caused traumas and deep wounds in both artists, also produced a flowering of master works which leave the viewer astonished, dumbstruck. In the Arts Institute there is also, in a secluded and shaded room, among imposing columns that seem funereal, a collection of large photographs in which the Twin Towers are depicted at different times of the day and night, in different seasons and climates. These images are a selection from a vast artistic undertaking, which lasted almost three years, and seems to have been born out of a mysterious premonition. The photographer, Joel Meyerowitz, whom I had occasion to meet, told me this with a certain anxiety, as if he had yet to comprehend fully the strange mixture of chance, coincidence and working on a hunch that induced him, without really knowing why, over these last three years, to photograph hundreds, thousands of times, from the window of his New York studio, the towers of the World Trade Center, those giants of steel, mortar and glass that exerted such a fascination over him. In his photos, the Twin Towers are one and many at the same time, as they float half blurred in the mist of dawn, illuminate the night with their thousands of fireflies, or burn like torches in the splendour of the midday sun. Ostentatious or furtive, explicit or half enveloped by shadows, these constructions that were captured by the enquiring lens of Joel Meyerowitz, and are now viewed from a point of absence, have acquired the nature of icons, symbols, totems, gravestones to a civilisation brutally faced with a threat of extinction. The danger comes not just from the bombs or the biological weapons that terrorist obscurantism can use to attack civilisation; it also comes from the panic and rage that might lead that civilisation to limit its most precious attribute, freedom, in the name of security. I have rarely seen a photographic exhibition as intense and provocative as the one that has turned the basement of the Arts Institute into a funeral chamber.

The terrorist act that, on 11 September, blew up the Twin Towers and killed almost five thousand office workers, employees, workers, firemen and policemen, was diabolically planned to cause not just a human tragedy and enormous material damage, but also a psychological effect that will, perhaps, be more difficult to overcome than the grief or the physical destruction: a sense of insecurity, instability and uncertainty that US society had not known before now. If a band of fanatics could bring down those towers that challenged the heavens, what even worse atrocities might they commit? Suddenly, as an effect of 11 September, the entertaining horrors of science fiction and blockbuster cinema have lost that sense of unreality that made them innocuous and enjoyable; they seem realist and prophetic. Now, the idea that a gang of demented fundamentalists, with ample economic resources, might explode a nuclear device in Fifth Avenue – or in Piccadilly Circus or the Champs-Elysées – or poison the air, the water or the food of a city, or infect it with killer bacteria, is no longer an entertaining amusement and has become a sinister reality of our time. From now on, that nightmare will haunt us.

I say 'us', because although I am not a New Yorker and do not live in New York, I have never felt a foreigner in Manhattan and, like many millions of beings from around the world who have spent time in this city of skyscrapers, or visited as tourists, I also felt, on 11 September, that this apocalyptic event had also inflicted personal damage on me, destroying and obliterating something that, it's difficult to explain, also belonged to me.

I have only once spent several months at a stretch in New York – teaching for a semester at Columbia University – but, since 1966, when I went for the first time, I have visited the city on innumerable occasions, usually for a few days. However, on each of these visits, I always felt that I was living much more intensely there for this handful of days, doing more things, getting more enthusiastic and tired than I could have done in any other city. I have always felt in New York that I was in the centre of the world, in modern Babylon, a sort of Borgesian aleph, containing all the languages, races, religions and cultures of the planet, a place that, like a giant heart, sends out to the furthest corners of the globe fashions, vices, values, trivia, ways of behaving, music and images that have been formed by the incredible mixture of people in the city. The feeling of being a tiny grain of sand in an *Arabian Nights* cosmopolis might be somewhat depressing; but, paradoxically, it is at the same time very energising, as Julio Cortázar once remarked about Paris: 'It is infinitely preferable to be nothing in a city that is everything than to be everything in a city that is nothing.' I never felt what he felt about the capital of France; but in New York, yes, every time.

New York belongs to nobody and everybody, from the Afghan taxi driver who can barely mutter a word of English, to the turbaned and long-bearded Sikh, to the Asians cooking up mysterious concoctions in China Town, to the Neapolitan who sings tarantellas to customers in a restaurant in Little Italy (but who was born in Manhattan and has never set foot in Italy). It belongs to the Puerto Ricans and the Dominicans who drown out the streets of the barrio with *plena* and salsa and *merengue* music, and to the Russians, Ukrainians, Kosovars, Andalucians, Greeks, Nigerians, Irish, Pakistanis, Ethiopians and citizens from dozens of countries, from the most exotic and even imaginary places, who, as soon as they set foot on this soil, through the integrating magic of the city, became New Yorkers.

Cosmopolitanism is diametrically opposed to fanaticism. A fanatic is a fanatic because he sees himself as the absolute master of a single truth, incompatible with any other, and for that reason he has the right to use any means to abolish differences, all the beliefs and convictions that do not coincide identically with his own. For that reason it would be impossible for fanatics of whatever shape or hue, with their obtuse tunnel-vision mentality, not to hate the mixed, plural diversity, that cannot be reduced to a single way of believing, enjoying, thinking and acting, of this Babelic, multiracial and multicultural city, this refraction on a small scale of the infinite variety of humanity. For those who dream of unifying, integrating and levelling the planet inside a straitjacket of a single dogma, a single god or a single religion, New York is without doubt the first enemy to be defeated.

But, for that same reason, all those of us the world over, who might disagree on some things, but who believe that accepting the diversity of beliefs, traditions and cultures within a system of pacific coexistence is the basic foundation of civilisation, have been affected by the blowing-up of the Twin Towers on 11 September. This assault came to remind us that the old obscurantist enemy is still there, obstinate, always trying, despite all its defeats, to obstruct in the name of a single inhuman truth, the advance of a humanity without dogmas, made up of relative truths, in permanent dialogue and interaction. The struggle against the ever renewing Hydra's heads will never end.

New York, November 2001

Iraq Diary

1. Savage Freedom

Iraq is the freest country in the world, but since freedom without order and without law is tantamount to chaos, it is also the most dangerous. There are no customs houses or officers, and the CPA, the Coalition Provisional Authority, presided over by Paul Bremer, has abolished until 31 December of this year all tariffs and duties on imports, so the borders of Iraq are like sieves through which every product imaginable, except arms, can enter the country without difficulty and at no cost. On the border with Jordan, an American officer on guard told me that this week an average of three thousand vehicles a day had entered Iraq, laden with goods of all kinds.

For that reason the two long highways, Karrada In and Karrada Out, that zigzag through Baghdad, are full of countless shops that have spilled out onto the street and turned the pavements into an exuberant bazaar, offering an enormous variety of industrial goods, food and clothing. It is also a paradise for pirate records, compact discs and videos. But what the inhabitants of Baghdad are buying most eagerly are satellite dishes, to pick up stations from all over the world, something that they could never do before, and which angers the conservative clerics who see television as an invasion of corrupt Western pornography. Iraqis can now surf the Internet freely, which was a crime under Saddam Hussein, and it is interesting to see in the Internet cafés, which have spread like mushrooms throughout Baghdad, the passion with which people in that city, especially the young, are embracing this new technology that links them to the world. But the commerce on the street is more akin to primitive barter than to modern buying and selling. Since there are no banks, cheques or credit cards, everything is paid for in cash, and, because of the freefall of the dinar (there were 1,500 dinars to a dollar the day I left), to make any purchase buyers must take along great bundles of notes – suitcases sometimes – which can be snatched from them at any moment by the current plague of ubiquitous Ali Babas. For, if there are no customs officials, there are also no policemen or judges or police stations where one can report a robbery or an assault. The Ministries are not working, nor are the public services, the post or the telephones, and there are no laws or regulations to control what a citizen can and cannot do. Everything is left to the intuition, the resourcefulness or the prudence of each individual. The result is an uncurbed freedom that leaves people feeling abandoned and terrified.

The only authority is represented by the tanks, the armoured personnel carriers, the trucks, the armed jeeps, and by the foot patrols of the US soldiers who are everywhere, crossing and re-crossing the streets, armed with rifles and machine guns, shaking the buildings with the power of their armoured vehicles, but, up close, looking as lost and terrified as the people of Baghdad. Since I arrived, attacks against them have been increasing systematically, with some thirty killed and about three hundred wounded. It is not surprising, therefore, that they seem apprehensive and finger their weapons nervously as they patrol these streets full of people with whom they cannot communicate. The heat is stifling, and the soldiers, laden with helmets, bulletproof vests and military paraphernalia, must suffer from it even worse than everyone else. The four times I tried to speak to them – many are very young – I got only the briefest of replies. They were all sweating profusely and their eyes were darting everywhere, like nervous grasshoppers. But my daughter Morgana had a more personal conversation with a soldier of Mexican origin, who, from up high in his tank, suddenly opened his heart to her: 'I can't stand it any more. I've been three months here and I can't bear it. Everyday I ask myself what the hell I am doing here. This morning they killed two of my friends. I don't know when I'll get back to my wife and son, damn it.'

There are lots of stories about the Americans who are patrolling

Baghdad, most of them doubtless exaggerated or apocryphal. For example, that in desperation at the mounting attacks, they burst into houses and ransack them under the pretext of looking for arms. I tried to confirm some of these charges and they were invariably unfounded. But the truth is that no one knows what to believe, about this or anything else. For the first time in its history, there is complete freedom of press in Iraq – anyone can bring out a newspaper or a magazine without needing permission – and there are more than fifty newspapers in Baghdad alone (where, since April, some seventy political parties have emerged, some comprising just one person), but the reports that they print are so contradictory and fantastical that everyone complains that they have no idea what is happening.

I went to the house of Kahtaw K. Al Ani, in the Sadea neighbourhood, because I'd been told that there had been a violent incident in a house next to his the previous night, with a number of deaths. In fact, it had happened five houses down. A patrol had kicked the door down. 'This is no good, sir!' And there was an Iraqi fatality. But did they find arms? He does not know and does not want to know. Mr Al Ani had lived three years in Reading and has good memories of England. He had worked in the Ministry of Agriculture and now, like all civil servants of the deposed regime, he had been sacked by the CPA. Isn't that most unfair? He and his fellow workers hated Saddam Hussein and the Ba'ath Party that they had been forced to join, and they were happy that the Americans were liberating them from dictatorship. But what sort of liberation is this that has left tens of thousands of families who felt that they were victims of the regime unemployed and facing poverty? 'This is no good, sir.' He is an elderly, solemn man, with closely cropped hair, who sweats profusely. His sons mop his sweat with paper napkins and he repeatedly apologises that, because of the lack of electricity, the fan is not working. Before, he had hated Saddam Hussein and the Ba'ath Party, but now he hates the Americans. When he says goodbye to me, he shows me his car: he does not take it onto the road because he does not want it stolen, and he is afraid to leave the house in case it is burgled and burned to the ground. 'This is no good, sir.'

Anti-Israeli feeling is deeply rooted in the Iraqi people, because they sympathise with the Palestinians, because under the dictatorship there was a remorseless propaganda offensive against Israel, and, also, doubtless, because in 1981 the Israelis blew up the Osirak nuclear station that was under construction with French technical aid. Since the liberation, you hear all kinds of rumours about an invasion of Jewish capital into Iraq, some of them wildly fanciful. As we passed the Hotel Ekal, on Wazig Avenue, two Iraqi friends pointed out the old, grey building that looked closed and assured me: 'The Jews from Israel have bought it. They are buying the whole city at rock bottom prices.' In the following days, I would hear, from different sources, that Israel had obtained from the CPA a monopoly control over future tourism in Iraq, a total fabrication, but my informants were convinced it was true. One morning when, after visiting the second-hand book market in Al Mutanabbi Road, I was having a coffee in the Merchants' Champion café, there was a bit of a commotion when customers noticed in an adjoining street, surrounded by spectacular bodyguards – black waistcoats, designer sunglasses, sub-machine guns – an elegant gentleman with a flowered tie and a multicoloured handkerchief in his jacket pocket (accessories that nobody sports in the heat of Baghdad). Everyone in the café muttered indignantly: 'That's the Israeli Ambassador.' In fact, this flamboyant individual was the Italian Ambassador. But fantasies generate realities, as novelists know very well: a few days after this episode, the Sunni imams in Mosul issued a fatwa, threatening with death any Iraqi found selling houses or land to Jews.

Three wars, twelve years of international embargo and thirty plus years of the Ba'ath Party satraps have turned Baghdad, which in the fifties was known as a very attractive place, into the ugliest city in the world. The strategic centres of power of Saddam Hussein, the Ministries and the state enterprises and many of the tyrant's residencies, have been gutted by American precision bombing. And everywhere there are the houses, buildings and installations that were looted and burned in the great criminal witches' sabbath that gripped the city after the American troops moved in, and which has still not yet run its course. The Ali Babas ransacked and stripped half the city bare. But who were these looters? To celebrate his re-election to the presidency with one hundred per cent of the vote on 15 October 2002, Saddam Hussein opened all the prisons in the country and released all the common criminals (while, at the same time, ordering the execution of most of the political prisoners). How many did he let out? I am given different figures, ranging from thirty thousand to one hundred thousand. This does not explain all of the excesses, but certainly a good number of them, Archbishop Fernando Filoni, the papal nuncio, assures me. (He is a specialist in the field of international disaster areas: he began his diplomatic career in Sri Lanka, when the Tamils began their killings, and he represented the Vatican in Tehran during the bombing raids of the war with Iraq, 'which did not let us sleep'.) 'The lack of experience of freedom is what causes these disasters. That is why the Holy Father, who knows a great deal, was opposed to this war. Because they were in such a hurry, the Americans were suddenly faced with something that they had not foreseen: generalised vandalism.'

It is also true that the accumulated hatred of the governing clique encouraged many of their victims to destroy the houses of people in power and all the buildings associated with the regime. But, why the factories? A seasoned industrialist, Nagi Al Jaf, who has businesses in the Iraqi capital and in the Kurdish city of Suleymaniya, tells me that the large Farida beer factory in Baghdad, a mixed company in which he has shares, was stripped by the Ali Babas. 'I can understand them stealing things that they can use or sell. But I can't see why they destroyed all the machines and then, as if that were not enough, they burned them.' How many industries in Baghdad were wrecked in this way? He is categorical. 'All of them.' I ask him not to exaggerate, to be objective. He takes a long look at the stars in the sky above Suleymaniya and repeats, 'All of them. There is not a single industrial plant in Baghdad that has not been completely destroyed.' What is the explanation then? Perhaps it is that a people cannot live in such abject terror and servility in the way the Iraqis were forced to live during the three decades of the dictatorship of the Ba'ath Party (a pro-Arab, nationalist, fascist and Stalinist party rolled into one, founded in 1942, in Damascus, by a Syrian Christian,

Michel Aflaq) and the twenty-four years of the presidency of Saddam Hussein, without reacting violently when they have an opportunity. So when, on 9 April, the Iraqis suddenly felt completely and absolutely free, there was an explosion of anarchy, dissolute behaviour and savagery which has destroyed Baghdad and left a bleeding wound in the hearts of every Baghdad citizen.

Since there is no public transport working, and there are no traffic police on street intersections, traffic in Baghdad is pandemonium. (Petrol is given away: it costs scarcely fifty cents to fill a tank). Drivers go wherever they please, so traffic accidents are very frequent and the jams are extraordinary. But at least in this area I noticed signs of the 'spontaneous institutions' that Hayek argues are more lasting and representative because they emerge naturally from civil society and are not imposed by the powers that be. When the jams become completely impossible, there are always volunteers armed with a stick and a whistle prepared to direct the traffic. And the drivers stuck in the jam obey their instructions, relieved that finally someone is giving them orders. This is also happening in neighbourhoods around the city: the local residents are forming groups to defend themselves against the thieves, or to take piles of rubbish to the end of the street and burn it. That is why when you walk around Baghdad, you have to pick your way through not only rubble, ruins, burned-out buildings and piles of vermin-ridden filth, but also the pestilential bonfires by which the inhabitants of Baghdad try to control the rubbish that threatens to swallow them up.

But perhaps the worst thing of all for the long-suffering inhabitants of the Iraqi capital is the lack of electricity and drinking water. There are continual power cuts which in some districts last for days on end. The neighbours are defenceless against the torrid temperatures that never drop below forty degrees in the shade and sometimes rise above fifty degrees. To be subjected to this burning heat, in total darkness and without running water, is torture. In the apartment of Spanish friends working for the Iberoamericana-Europa Foundation, that has brought five hundred tons of food and medicines and a drinking water plant to Iraq, where I was put up during my first week in Iraq, I experienced at first hand the hardships that the Iraqis had been suffering for three months. The light came on intermittently, but at times the cuts went on for so many hours that it was impossible to cook, wash or air the place and, to prevent us burning up in the oven temperatures of the bedrooms, my hosts took mattresses out into the garden, choosing the cockroaches over asphyxia. The demoralisation that all this produces is one of the obstacles that the Iraqis will have to overcome in order for their country, which is emerging from one of the most corrupt and brutal experiences of authoritarianism known to humanity, to leave behind that long night of despotism and violence that is their history and become a modern, prosperous and democratic nation.

Is this a possible, realistic idea, or an illusion, since we are talking about a society that lacks even the most minimal experience of freedom and that is also torn by many antagonisms and internal rivalries? Is it feasible to imagine Arabs, Kurds and Turkmen, Shia and Sunni Muslims and the internal currents that divide them, Chaldea, Asirian, Latin and Armenian Christians, tribal clans, primitive country dwellers and vast urban communities to coexist in an open and plural, tolerant and flexible system, a lay state with a solid consensus that would allow the twenty-five million inhabitants of Mesopotamia, where writing was born and which is a fundamental reference point for all the great religions and modern cultures, the cradle of the first great collection of the historical laws – the Hammurabi Code – finally to lead a worthy and free life, or is it a fantasy as delirious at that of the mythical ancestors of these people, who wanted to build a tower that would reach the sky and ended up frustrated and lost in the frightful confusion of Babel?

I have come to Iraq to try to find out if these questions have a convincing answer. Twelve days is very little time, but it is better than nothing.

25 June–6 July 2003

2. Baghdad People

Captain Nawfal Khzal Aied Abdala Al Dolame is a tall, slim, serious, elegant and tough-looking man. He studied in the Al Almiraya Military Academy, in the outskirts of Baghdad, and after graduating spent several years in the Ministry of Defence. But when things got difficult for the regime, he was assigned to a combat battalion and was stationed in Basra, coming up against the UK coalition forces. Then his battalion retreated to Baghdad and, once there, as happened in many other divisions of the Iraqi army, his commanding officers decided that it was useless to put up resistance to the Americans, and sent their officers and men back home. It was there that he learned that the captain of the Coalition Provisional Authority, headed by Ambassador Paul Bremer, had dismissed the almost half a million members of Saddam Hussein's armed forces, and that he was without a job. Since then, he has earned his living as a bodyguard, a profession which has become very popular, given the widespread anarchy in this country without a state, or services, or a police force, or any other authorities, that is prey to myriad Ali Babas.

Armed with a pistol (authorised by the CPA), and for the modest sum of one hundred dollars, he follows me everywhere like a shadow. As a bodyguard, he is charmingly useless. The only time his services were needed, in the Imam Ali mosque in the sacred – for the Shia – city of Najaf, when an enraged believer tried to attack my daughter Morgana who, with characteristic irresponsibility, was taking photos in the midst of the wailing masses, all that he managed to do was raise his hands to his face and deplore this demonstration of fanaticism and ignorance. It was other believers in the crowd that spared Morgana's face from the blow that was aimed at her. But I like this captain with his interminable name: Nawfal Khazal Aied Abdala Al Dolame. Without a flicker on his severe face, he comes up with lines like: 'I am a Muslim at night and a Christian during the day, so that I can have a cold beer'. I understand and approve of what he is saying: there is no sin that any normal personal would be unwilling to commit to placate to some degree this fifty-degrees-in-the-shade inferno that is the capital of Iraq.

The captain knows many stories about Uday, Saddam Hussein's son, who adds weight to the tradition by which the sons of the great satraps usually outdo their fathers in terms of abuses and crimes. The stories that I hear on a daily basis about the scions of the Iraqi dictator remind me, like a recurrent nightmare, of those that I heard in the Dominican Republic, about the sons of General Trujillo. But I suspect that Uday even beat the record of Ramfis and Radhamés Trujillo, for example by having the Health Minister of the regime, Dr Raja, who, like Saddam Hussein, was from Tikrit, eaten by a pack of wild dogs. One story that the captain knows very well concerns a very pretty young woman, a close family friend, who earned her living as a teacher and whose name he does not disclose to me, out of respect. Uday saw her in the street when she was on the way to the school. He ordered his bodyguards to kidnap her, and he took her to one of his palaces, where the young woman was at his mercy for almost two months. When he let her go, her family, in shame, moved with her to Mosul, where they are still living. The captain assures me that the figure of at least three hundred women kidnapped in this way by the criminal psychopath that was (and is, since he is still on the run) Uday Hussein, is completely realistic.

Despite not speaking Arabic, I understand everything that I hear around me thanks to my splendid translator, Dr Bassam Y. Rashid. He is a professor at the University of Baghdad and was for a time the director of the Spanish Department, that has more than eight hundred students. He obtained his doctorate from the University of Granada, with a critical edition of a treatise on astrology by Enrique de Villena, that took him seven years of erudite and happy study. That was where his son Ahmed was born, and his son still dreams of his childhood in Granada the way others dream of paradise. In the professor's modest house, young Ahmed has turned his small room into a kind of shrine, with photos of the King and Queen of Spain and places in Spain – he knows the history and geography of Spain by heart and he repeats facts about the country like a mantra – the way other kids of his age would have plastered their walls with film stars or the latest rock group. Professor Bassam Y. Rashid was mysteriously summoned one day by Saddam Hussein to be his interpreter during a visit by Comandante Hugo Chávez, the demagogue who rules Venezuela, and I am sure that he must have lots of juicy anecdotes about that assignment. But I don't ask him about it, because, knowing him, I know that he would maintain a strict professional silence and not open his mouth.

Professor Bassam is one of those decent people who are the moral backbone of a country, who might be frustrated and ruined by dictatorships, but who still manage to survive with their moral values intact all the vileness, fear, corruption and stupidity that tyrannies create, poisoning the very air that everyone breathes. In these twelve days that we have spent together, I have not heard him complain once about the infinite deprivations that he is forced to put up with, like almost all his compatriots: the complete lack of security, the uncertainty, the lack of light and water and the absence of any authorities, the terrifying mounting mounds of rubbish on all the roads and the pavements, the prevailing chaos, the economic shortages, the terrorist assaults that are multiplying daily, the attacks in the street. The only time I saw him sad was when he showed me the libraries and lecture halls of the University, where he has spent all his life, that had been ransacked and burned in the orgy of vandalism that gripped Baghdad following the fall of the regime of Saddam Hussein, and which literally destroyed, along with thousands of other institutions, homes and premises, the five universities in the Iraqi capital. But he is not defeatist. Freedom is always good, even though it comes at a high price, he says, and he has not lost hope that Iraq will one day be a free, modern, and democratic country, 'like Spain' (is the way he puts it). In his very modest house in the Al Magreb district, he and his wife greet me with the magnificence of the *Arabian Nights*, in the best tradition of Arab hospitality, though I fear that this means that they will go hungry later. If, by chance, circumstances take you one of these days to Baghdad, try to meet Dr Bassam Y. Rashid, because just talking to him for a few minutes will raise your spirits.

And, after that, take a stroll around the old centre of the city and go to the Clock Tower, on the banks of the Tigris. You won't be able to enjoy the gardens of the old building that was the seat of government in the times of the monarchy, where King Faisal I was crowned in 1922. All that has been destroyed by the Ali Babas and has disappeared into thin air. And the looters, not content with carrying off the windows, the doors, the beams, the ironwork and floor tiles of the ancient building, chipped and broke and gutted and smashed everything that they could not manage to carry away, so that, in there, you feel as if you are stepping through the ruins left by some devastating earthquake. No, go there, because, as happened to me, you may well bump into the likeable and affable Jamal N. Hussein, a small and formal man from Baghdad, in his forties, who works in the Library of the National Museum and who savours the English language as if it were sugar. He is effusive and will be delighted to tell you his story. He used to live there, on the top floor of a block next to the government building. When the looting began, he was out, and he ran back here, to protect his apartment. When he got back, out of breath, he found that the Ali Babas had taken all his belongings – his books, his clothes and his music – and were setting fire to his apartment. From these gardens he could see the smoke enveloping everything that had not been stolen.

But what is really interesting is not this seemingly banal event that hundreds of thousands, if not millions of Iraqis, have also suffered, but rather that, at this point in the story, the delicate Jamal N. Hussein will raise his voice a shade and, gesturing energetically, will let you know that he was not so concerned that the Ali Babas had taken his things and burned his house, he could get over that. What really plunges him into despair and anguish, and keeps him awake at night, and brings him here every day to these destroyed gardens, is his Fiat. And then, with a wave of his child's hand, Jamal N. Hussein will say to you: 'Come sir, come and meet her.' It was the apple of his eye, more important than a dog or a relative: it was like a lover or a personal deity. He cleaned it, took care of it and showed it to his friends with delight and admiration. And when you see the mortal remains of the Fiat, in a corner of that stripped garden, that heap of

276

twisted and burned metal, bathing in the inclement heat of the Iraq summer, you will see Jamal N. Hussein's greyish brown eyes mist over with sadness. You should leave at this point. Don't be uncouth and try to console him with one of those stupid banalities that you hear at funerals. Tiptoe away and leave the unhappy man to his memories.

If you are very depressed at what you have just seen, less than two hundred yards from there, in among the ruined buildings and the pestilential rubbish, in a run-down street that crosses the narrow Al Mutanabbi Road, where every Friday there is a colourful second-hand book fair, you will find a crammed, timeless little café, with a surprising name: The Merchants' Champion Café. Go there and I promise that it will cheer you up. Don't be put off by the male throng, elbow your way into the café and sit down in any space you can find. Order a tea, a coffee or a hookah and start talking to the person next to you. If you are lucky, you'll meet the lawyer, whose name I did not catch, with whom I shared a red-hot narrow bench, that burned my backside. He was a broad and jovial man, bathed in sweat, who chewed the mouthpiece of his hookah and blew out puffs of smoke smelling of tobacco mixed with apricot and apple, while he held forth. He told me that he was a lawyer, but that since, due to recent events, the country had no courts or judges or laws, and thus no clients, he found that, after a successful career in the courts, he had become a 'nobody', almost non-existent. 'Just think, the country that gave the world the first written laws in history – the Hammurabi Code – is now a country without even shyster lawyers.' His mocking smile flitted across the burning room, as if to say that, for someone like him, this did not matter a jot. For the time he was here, surrounded by poets, literary people and wastrels who are the locals at the Merchants' Champion Café, and with a slow burning hookah, he was a happy man, without any problems.

'Who do you think governs Baghdad?' he asks suddenly, gesticulating in the air and posing like a diva to attract everyone's attention. 'The Americans?' The lawyer pauses for a few seconds for effect before finally giving the eagerly awaited answer: 'No, *habibi*. The real rulers of Baghdad are the Ali Babas, the cockroaches, the bugs, the fleas.' A polite chuckle greeted his words. The other regulars must have heard his jokes many times over and did not find them very funny. I did. Cynical stoicism is like a breath of civilisation in these cases, an excellent way to fight despair.

25 June–6 July 2003

3. The Believers

Ayatollah Muhammad Bakr Al Hakim is sixty-three, and spent twenty-three years in exile in Iran. As well as being a leading authority on the Shia religion, he is a most important political figure since he is the president of the Supreme Council of the Iraq Islamic Revolution, which is the main body of the Shia Muslims in the country (that comprise some sixty per cent of the twenty-five million Iraqis). When he returned from exile, a huge crowd turned out to greet him. His solemn, bearded face is everywhere, on posters adorning walls and buses, in particular around the Shia mosques. He is considered to be the leader of the most radical sector of the Shia religion, and many accuse him of being close to the Iranian model, that is, a theocratic, fundamentalist government, controlled by the ayatollahs. But he categorically denies this: 'Iraq is not a photocopy of Iran or of anywhere else. Every country has its own distinctive characteristics. Our idea is that Iraq must establish a democratic government where all ethnic groups and religious minorities are represented, but which, at the same time, respects our identity and our history.'

He has very pale skin and blue eyes, and his presence – with his long grey beard, his black turban and grey robes – has a studied dignity. He receives me in the city of Najaf, a sacred site for Shias, for it is where Emir Ali, Muhammad's son-in-law, who was murdered in year 41 of the hegira and is considered to be the spiritual figure of the Shia, is buried. Imam Muhammad Bakr Al Hakim lives in spartan austerity, and the offices of his movement are also extremely simple. But the precautions that they take are very tight.

Clerics, bodyguards and assistants search us, take our shoes off

278

and confiscate our cameras and tape recorders (which they return to us once they have checked that there are no arms or explosives hidden in them). There is not a single female presence in the house, and Morgana has to comply strictly with the dress code by wearing the Muslim veil so that she can come in with me and take photographs. When I tell Ayatollah Al Hakim that she is my daughter, he replies curtly, without looking at her: 'I have six daughters.' I do not commit the impertinence of asking him how many wives have borne these six children. (The Shia, apart from having four legitimate wives authorised by the Koran, can add a fifth – the so-called 'pleasure marriage' – if they are travelling without female company, so that they do not have to suffer the privations of abstinence. This fifth wedding can last solely for the duration of the journey).

The day before receiving me, the ayatollah had declared – in this country where attacks are increasing every day – that it is a mistake to kill US soldiers, and that whatever objectives the Iraqis seek to achieve by assassination can be reached by peaceful means, through dialogue. I thought that he would repeat to me the same diplomatic declaration, but I was wrong. Speaking slowly, and gesturing gently to illustrate his words, he delivered a severe diatribe against the 'coalition forces'. He never speaks about the Americans or the British, just about the 'coalition', but we both know very well who he is talking about.

'The liberation was a mere pretext. The coalition troops have become occupation forces. Bush and Blair made many promises that they have been incapable of fulfilling. There is no security at all in the country, and our sovereignty has been snatched away from us. As a pretext for the war, they argued that Saddam Hussein had weapons of mass destruction, but they have not been able to find them. Nor have they been able to capture the former dictator and his followers, despite the fact that they are people who eat and move around and leave tracks. If they had let us act, we would have found them by now.'

He speaks without raising his voice and without looking at me, his blue eyes are staring into the distance, with the quiet determination of one who knows that he is in possession of the truth. His half-dozen assistants listen to him with wrapt attention, indifferent to the horrendous heat that has turned this small, bare room, with a large bunch of plastic flowers as its one adornment, into a frying pan. Ayatollah Al Hakim is a man who rarely smiles and who pontificates and proclaims rather than speaks, like the prophets and the gods on Olympus. Crouching behind him is a man who never takes his eyes off me, ready to leap on me if I make any suspicious movement. Being so close to Ayatollah Al Hakim makes me feel deeply uneasy. Although, like all agnostics, I recognise that I secretly envy believers, when these believers are as absolute and categorical as the Iraqi imam in front of me, it makes me shiver.

'The war has not ended,' Ayatollah Al Hakim continues. 'Discontent among the people is increasing every day, as are the acts of resistance against the occupying forces, which is very serious for the future of Iraq. There are different reasons for this resistance: promises made to us are not kept and our dignity is humiliated. I'm referring to the behaviour of the occupation forces. They kill innocent people and they are incapable of finding the real culprits for the crimes committed by the dictatorship. They steal quite brazenly from the private houses that they search, taking the family's money. They take advantage of the fact that since there are no banks, people have to keep their money in their houses. As well as stealing they offend our women, they touch them and that hurts and upsets our people. Here, in Najaf, we have already organised five demonstrations to protest against these abuses. It is true that surviving groups attached to Saddam Hussein and the Ba'ath Party also commit terrorist attacks and sabotage. But this, to a great extent, is the fault of the coalition troops, because, instead of hunting down the Ba'athists and the followers of Saddam, they disarm us, the popular forces. But that just increases the anger of the Iraqis against the occupiers.'

Indeed, adorning the earthen walls in the drab, run-down, poverty-stricken streets of Najaf, a two-hour drive to the south of Baghdad, where the dust from the surrounding desert swirls around, staining everything the colour of yellow ochre, alongside the death notices for the many people who are brought to this holy city to be buried, there are many anti-coalition inscriptions and graffiti praising the 'Soldiers of Islam' who are fighting against the infidels and Satan. But none of them mention the Americans by name; they all rail against 'foreign hegemony' as well as proclaiming 'Death to Saddam and the Ba'athists'.

The hostility towards the coalition troops, and the anti-American feeling, is very tangible among the crowd of believers heading towards the mosque in a great procession, the women dressed in severe *abayas*, tunics and black veils, that cover them from head to foot. Many of them, in addition, wear black woollen stockings and some even gloves, in temperatures of forty-five degrees in the shade. The mass of the faithful grows even denser around and inside the imposing mosque that contains the tomb of Emir Ali. My translator, Professor Bassam Y. Rashid, who is the director of the Department of Spanish at the University of Baghdad, is constantly explaining to all and sundry that we are not 'Americans', but we are stared at and gestured at in a hostile manner as we make our way to the mosque. The people are even more belligerent inside the mosque.

This is very different to what happened to me in the main Shia mosque in Baghdad, the mosque of the Khadim Brothers (the grandsons of Emir Ali), where I was greeted most cordially by the people who ran the place. They even joked that they had to make a good impression on foreigners to dispel the rumours put about by their enemies, that Shia are fundamentalist. This accusation is doubtless quite unjust. Along with the Kurds, the Shia were the ones that suffered the worst excesses of Saddam Hussein, who was a Sunni and surrounded himself with Muslims of the same religious tendency. There are doubtless many moderate Shia just as there are fundamentalist Sunnis. In broad terms the division between the two main currents of Islam is that the Shia religion is rooted in the more primitive sectors, the rural and marginal groups, while the Sunnis come in the main from the urban sectors, are better educated and better connected socially. The Shia have always been excluded from power, which has been a Sunni monopoly.

The worst poverty and neglect I have seen is here in Najaf and in the other sacred Shia city near by, Kerbala. Realising that the crowd was hostile to us – we are the only 'Westerners' in sight – the two people in charge of the Emir Ali mosque decide to put us in an office and then ask us to take our shoes off. There the man in charge of the mosque decides to give me a history lesson and tells me in great detail about the remains of Prince Ali. (The same thing happened to me yesterday, in Baghdad, in the mosque of the Khadim Brothers, when a holy man explained to me at length that, at the end of time, Christ would come to kiss the hand of El Madi and, from then on, Muslims and Christians would become brothers.) I listened patiently. After he was murdered in Kerfa, the remains of Muhammad's son-in-law were buried secretly by the faithful. They remained hidden for many years. Some time later, during the caliphate of Harun Al Rachid, the caliph noticed when he was out hunting crows that the dogs always kept a respectful distance from a certain mound. There they discovered the remains of the Emir. This beautiful mosque was then built to honour them.

While he is instructing me, I observe the mass spectacle of the believers. They come into this enormous rectangular patio with the coffins of the dead held aloft and they walk them around the crypt of the Emir. The great throng of men push and elbow each other, chanting, praying, praising Allah, some in a state of hysterical paroxysm. It is doubtless impressive but, for me, very depressing. Hands and lips reach out to touch and kiss the walls, the railings, the grooves and ridges of the doors, and some of the faithful sob at the top of their voices, prostrate, touching the ground with their forehead. Around the crypt, the group is all male. The women, dark shapes, remain behind, crowded together at the rear of the mosque, keeping a magic distance from the men, who are the only protagonists in this dramatic ceremony. My teacher explains that many of the faithful are pilgrims who have come here from far off – 'some from Bosnia' – and that they sleep on these sacred tiles.

'Isn't it the same in Lourdes or in Fatima?', a Spanish friend tries to console me that same evening in Baghdad when I tell him about how uneasy I felt after the visit to Najaf as we drank a warm, acid beer in the semi-darkness during the latest power cut. Is it the same? I don't think so. In these great centres of Catholic pilgrimage, there is a whole commercial apparatus involved, a major tourist exploitation of faith, which rather undermines this faith, but also makes it seem inoffensive. There is nothing of this here: here faith is pure, integral, disinterested, extreme, the only thing that many of these people, destitute and ravaged by poverty, have to hold on to as they scream and shout out their prayers, and this could easily be channelled into violence – a holy war or jihad – by a charismatic ayatollah like the one I am visiting in Najaf.

Taking the advice of friends in Baghdad, I asked Morgana and her friend Marta, from the Iberoamerican-European Foundation, not to try to enter the mosque of Prince Ali, and to wait for me instead in the main square at Najaf, and look around the colourful market. But I've never had the slightest authority over my daughter, so there they were, swathed in borrowed *abayas*, with their foreign faces visible to all, passing themselves off as Afghan Muslims! And Morgana, with that temerity that she's always shown ever since she made her cot shake with her furious tantrums, started taking photographs. An agitated believer went up to her and flung a blow at her face, which was deflected by the camera. The bodyguard accompanying her put his head in his hands, upset at this show of obscurantism. Marta was more fortunate: instead of being greeted with aggression, she received, in English, a marriage proposal, which she turned down.

We visited the other Shia holy city, Kerbala – more open and less claustrophobic than the cramped, poverty-stricken city of Najaf – which is the site of two immense and strikingly beautiful mosques, one of which is the burial place of Imam Hussein, the son of Prince Ali, who was killed in the Yazid invasion. But the hostility in the air was such that we decided to cut short our visit and leave, with great regret, that beautiful place with its golden cupolas, tiled walls and squares and marble floors. In that city as well, in the shady arcades of the market, and in the narrow streets with its houses that looked on the point of collapse, we are pressed on all sides by a crowd that looks on us with hostility and disgust. The attempts of the three Baghdad friends that were travelling with me to convince them that we were not Americans but Spanish Muslims on a religious pilgrimage, does not convince them. My friends tell me that we should hurry up and get out. The democratic virtues of tolerance and coexistence in diversity seem alien to these parts.

When I ask Ayatollah Al Hakim what he thinks about what is happening in neighbouring Iran, where we have recently seen an increase in demonstrations by young students demanding more freedom and democracy from the repressive conservative government, he wriggles out of the question: 'I do not have reliable information as to what is happening in Iran. We do not even know accurately what is happening in other provinces in Iraq. I do not dare take seriously what certain information media, in Qatar, the Emirates and Jordan, put out because they are just looking to incite violence and hate, so I prefer not to have an opinion on this matter.'

He doesn't reply very openly when I ask him if he would accept a secular government for Iraq: 'Would a secular government mean a government against religion?' he replies tersely. I tell him not, that such a government would not be in favour or against religion, it would be independent and neutral on religious issues, it would restrict itself to guaranteeing respect for all beliefs.

Imam Al Hakin can barely disguise his displeasure: 'Islam must be respected,' he says firmly. 'Like in Pakistan, Egypt or the Maghrib, which are Islamic countries. That is the type of state that Iraq will have.'

I have been given scarcely half an hour and my time is nearly up. One of the imam's assistants is indicating in a peremptory fashion that I should take my leave. I try to move the conversation on to a more personal level and ask him how he felt when he came back to Najaf, after an absence of more than two decades. The imam is a politician who never drops his guard and he gives me the official answer: 'I feel both happy and sad. Happy because I am among my own people and the tyrant has been overthrown, but saddened by the two million disappeared that we had in the years of Saddam Hussein, by the common graves where we find the remains of tortured and murdered brothers, and by the suffering and hardship that the Iraqi people are still suffering today.'

I left there convinced that Al Hakim would certainly like the future Iraq to be like Iran, but that he knows that the people of Iraq and, above all, the Americans would find it very difficult to agree to this, and that, as a pragmatic politician, he has given up for now this goal in favour of a more realistic and less theocratic formula: a coalition of religious, political and ethnic forces, in which the Shia, because of their overall majority, would still have majority representation. Despite his vociferous criticism of the occupying forces, I am quite sure that at this stage, at least, he would work with the Provisional Coalition Authority and Paul Bremer.

I discuss this issue with my Baghdad and Spanish friends in a restaurant full of the turbans and *abayas* of Kerbala, called The Pearl of Najaf, with the inevitable fried chicken with rice, pureed beans and gherkin salad with yoghurt. A menu that would shadow me throughout the twelve days of my stay in Iraq. Morgana and Marta have taken off their veils to eat, and our fellow diners look at them out of the corner of their eyes, with surprise.

I return to Baghdad, with a heavy heart, without being able to get out of my mind the image of these women buried their whole lives – in Najaf and Kerbala, you see young girls buried beneath these robes – in these mobile prisons that deny them any comfort in these suffocating temperatures, which prevent them from developing their bodies and their minds freely, a symbol of their subordinate position, their lack of independence and freedom. This is the Middle Ages, severe and harsh. And if this prevails over the other social and political forces in Iraq, the idea that this country can become a modern, functional democracy in a short period of time, is illusory.

25 June–6 July 2003

4. Looters and Books

If the visit to Najaf and Kerbala was a journey back to medieval Iraq, the morning that I spend in the National University of Baghdad shows me the most modern and progressive aspect of Iraqi society. Young men and women mingle in the courtyards, in the corridors and in the lecture halls with complete naturalness, and many young women walk around without any headgear, showing their arms, although most of them cover their hair with the Islamic veil. The only thing that still brings to mind the *Arabian Nights* in Baghdad are the eyes of the Baghdad women. It is graduation day and there is a festive, boisterous atmosphere. Entire subject year groups are being photographed under the trees, with bunches of flowers and with their professors in the middle. Young men are dancing to lively music that is being broadcast through loudspeakers, singing at the top of their voices, cheered on by the women. Morgana moves among the dancers, in her element, and she is very well received. The atmosphere is friendly, happy and trusting. (But, the following day, in this cafeteria, a US soldier who was talking to a group of students was killed with a bullet in the head by an individual who ran off.)

I am in the Languages Faculty, which has close to five thousand students, eight hundred of them in the Department of Spanish. They have good teachers, and I interrupt a couple of classes and have a lively discussion with students of both sexes, who are very keen to hear about Spain. By contrast, they know little about Latin America. The building is in a ruinous state because of the looting, but no one seems to be bothered since all the students are in excellent humour.

The lecturers have just been paid their salary for April, a delay of two months. The recent upheavals have meant that salaries have seen some extraordinary readjustments. People who were formerly paid the equivalent of five dollars a month (they were always badly paid, but after the Gulf War and the international embargo salaries reached rock bottom) have now received 250 dollars. However, the Rector has already announced to them that this will be cut back next month to 165 dollars. Nobody knows the reasons for these arbitrary rises and falls, or how long this fickle system, which reflects the chaotic economy of the country, will last. The only thing that is clear is that Iraqi university teachers find it very difficult to live on what they earn, which is why so many of them go to teach in Libya, Jordan or the Gulf Emirates, where the salaries are high.

It is a pleasure to talk to the head of the Languages Faculty, the stout, curly-haired and exuberant Dr Dia Nafi Hassan, a specialist in

Russian literature and language and an expert on Chekhov and Turgenev. His office is an oven, and is practically empty because everything in this university – in the five Baghdad universities – was looted and burned when the dictatorship fell on 9 April, so they do not have ventilators, desks, chairs, computers, filing cabinets or books. The walls are blackened, the windows and window-panes are broken, and there are no tiles on the floor of the corridors and stairs. Perhaps worst of all, they have no records of student enrolments, grades and files because they have all been burned. 'Like all institutions, the University of Baghdad has returned to a virginal state,' the Dean jokes. But this hurricane of barbarism which devastated the university, like the Huns of Tamerlane, 'the sons of hell', who devastated ancient Mesopotamia, indifferent to the civilisation that produced the artistic and intellectual marvels of Nineveh and Babylon, seems not to have made the slightest dent in the good humour and optimism of the colleagues and students of Dr Dia Nafi Hassan, who tells me excitedly that, as a forerunner of what would soon be happening throughout Iraq, the University of Baghdad had undertaken to implement a democratic system. There had been recent elections, and here, in the Faculty, he had been elected Dean with forty-two of the fifty-three votes cast. He is proud of the legitimacy of his mandate. His enthusiasm seems to be shared by the other members of staff present.

He hopes that what has happened here will soon happen throughout Iraq. That the Iraqis themselves will take control, without the supervision of 'foreigners' (for foreigners, read Americans). And that this would become a free and democratic country, like Western European countries – he mentions France, Spain and England – with a lay state, tolerant of all beliefs, including, of course, Islam, which is his religion. I ask him whether events in Iraq might be similar to Algeria in the early nineties when, in the first more or less free elections in Algeria's independent history, it looked as if the fundamentalists would win power, through democratic processes, and would then have ended up abolishing democracy and imposing a theocracy. The Dean disagrees with my analysis, waving his arms with absolute conviction. 'Here the fanatics will never win free elections,' he assures me. 'Here the great majority of us Muslims are civilised, open, democratically inclined people.'

I hope with all my heart that this will be the case. But it is quite clear that there are a good number of fanatics on the loose, because the university teachers tell me that some of the thieves who took part in the looting and vandalism that destroyed this site and burned the libraries – I visit the Russian and German libraries where everything has been reduced to ashes, not a single book escaping the flames – and the offices in the Faculty, also daubed fundamentalist slogans on the wall, cursing this house of evil and the infidel.

Who were these looters, who have created more wounds, bitterness and anger than the coalition bombings? I'm not exaggerating when I say that in the dozens of conversations and interviews that I've had over the past days, I have not heard a single Iraqi lamenting the fall of Saddam Hussein, who was clearly detested by the majority of the people that he enslaved. Indeed, most if not all seem to celebrate his fall from power. I have not even heard many complaints from the victims of the bombing. But what everyone is agreed on is their detestation of the dreadful looting that followed the fall of the dictator and has reduced Baghdad and, so it seems, a good number of other cities and towns in Iraq, to ruins, with gutted and burned houses and piles of rubble everywhere. And a very large number of citizens who were full of hope at the end of the dictatorship – the ones who toppled the statues of the dictator and who have defaced his image wherever they find it – have lost everything they had, their furniture, their memories, their housing, their clothes, the savings that they kept hidden in their houses out of fear that the banks would confiscate them. Everyone asks: 'Why did the Americans not get involved?' 'Why didn't they stop them?' It's a mystery that has yet to be resolved. There were hundreds, thousands of soldiers in the streets who from the outset could have dealt robustly with that maddened swarm of Ali Babas who, like a cloud of hungry locusts, laid waste to Baghdad and other Iraqi cities over several days, without any intervention from the Americans. Up to that time they had been greeted by many Iraqis as liberators but, after the looting, this friendly feeling turned into frustration and hostility.

One of the explanations for the vandalism is the large number of common criminals let out of prison in Iraq by order of Saddam Hussein. How many were there? Between thirty and a hundred thousand. The figures never tally and sometimes reach fantastic extremes, as always happens in countries without freedom of information in which people are informed by hunches or hearsay. However, a great deal of this havoc was caused by a bunch of criminals who were allowed free rein in this country without law and order that Saddam Hussein wished to bequeath to posterity. It was also caused by the agents, torturers and bureaucrats of the regime, who were anxious to destroy all traces of their misdeeds. But it was also inevitable that circumstances turned many mild citizens into Ali Babas. Finding themselves free and uncensored, in a world without any checks or laws, some gave vent to the unbridled, savage thirst for violence that we all carry within us. The environment caused some to show their frustration and protest in the most ferocious way, or to take the revenge that they had so long dreamed of, to settle accounts with their neighbours, colleagues, relatives, litigants or enemies. Fanatics saw that the time had come to punish the pornographers and the degenerates; the envious saw it as an opportunity to take revenge on the people they had envied; in general, a people humiliated, maltreated, terrorised and alienated by thirty-five years of authoritarianism wallowed in a bath of purifying brutality and licentiousness, as in the great Dionysian festivities that began as a song to happiness and ended in human sacrifice and mass suicides. All this is comprehensible, after all. But what is not comprehensible is that the forces that occupied Iraq and had prepared for this war to perfection, right down to the technological minutiae – to judge from the speed of the victory and the mathematical precision of the bombing – had not anticipated this, and had no plan to combat it.

I hear all this, in his florid Italian, from Archbishop Fernando Filoni, the apostolic nuncio of His Holiness, who has been in Baghdad for two years. He is small, astute, tough as nails, talkative and an expert on emergencies. In Sri Lanka and Tehran he had received excellent training for this hotbed of tensions that is Iraq. 'The Holy Father was against the war because he knew what would happen,' he tells me, with a sad expression on his face. 'It is very easy to win, but then it is incredibly difficult to administer the peace.' The nuncio's residence is a simple house, obsessively clean and tidy, an unusual haven of peace in this city.

The dictatorship literally destroyed a society that four decades earlier had reached a high level of culture, with hospitals and universities among the most modern in the Middle East, and world-ranking professionals. In the fifties, Baghdad's culture and art were the envy of its neighbours. The Ba'athists and Saddam Hussein ended all that. There was a haemorrhaging of doctors, engineers, economists, researchers, teachers and intellectuals to the four corners of the world. (While I'm listening to him, I remember that on my way to Iraq, during my stopover in Amman, a diplomat who had spent many years in Jordan told me: 'For this country, the tragedy in Iraq has been a blessing: the most important musicians, artists and intellectuals here are Iraqi immigrants.') Censorship, repression, fear, corruption and isolation had increasingly impoverished the country culturally until it reached the low point that it is at today. For that reason there was so much hope among ordinary people at the time of the liberation. Whatever people say, the Americans were initially greeted in a friendly manner. But with the looting and the complete insecurity that followed, this initial sympathy turned into dislike and hostility. 'You shouldn't see this as love for Saddam Hussein, but rather as a hatred of chaos, of how precarious life has become.'

Monsignor Filoni says that fear of robbery, assaults, kidnapping and rape has become a real psychosis. Many families have stopped taking their children to school; they hardly leave their houses and, since there is no police force, keep the weapons that the Americans have asked them to hand in to defend themselves against robbers. The nuncio does not seem very optimistic about the possibility of a modern democracy emerging in Iraq out of all this. There are many social tensions, a complete lack of political experience among the people, little evidence of democracy and too much anarchy for any democratic process to be implemented in a short space of time. In the long term perhaps. The very, very long term. His words repeat, almost literally, what I heard from my friend in Amman: 'The best that one can hope for in Iraq, realistically, is a controlled and relative democracy, like Jordan. Here there have just been elections and not a single woman was elected. But, according to the law, there will be six women in Parliament since there is a quota for women. The Islamists have only obtained seventeen-and-a-half percent of the vote, a triumph for the regime of King Abdallah. But, if it hadn't been for an intelligent ad hoc electoral law which prevents candidates getting on closed lists, the Islamist extremists would have gained a much higher percentage. Also, the tribal chiefs who decide the vote of the bulk of the electorate are more macho and intolerant than the Islamists themselves. For me, a system like this is the best that could happen in Iraq.'

When I tell Monsignor Filoni that Iraqi friends have assured me that the case of Tarek Aziz, a Catholic who was the Foreign Minister and accomplice of Saddam Hussein, was not exceptional, for there were many members of the Catholic communities who sympathised with the dictatorship, he shakes his head. Catholics in Iraq, he tells me, approximately one million of them, five per cent of the population, were divided into different branches – the Chaldeans, who still use Aramaic, the language of Christ, in their liturgy; Asirians, Armenians and Latin – felt protected in the early years of the regime because the Ba'ath party proclaimed itself a secular party and put in place a system that recognised all beliefs. But, after the Gulf War, this secularism disappeared. Saddam Hussein used Islam to gain support in Muslim states, and declared himself the standard bearer of the faith against the infidel enemies of Allah. There was strict religious censorship, the regime encouraged the use of the *hijab*, or Islamic veil, the situation of women suffered a grave setback, and on the radio and television readings from the Koran and broadcasts by clerics and theologians became compulsory; as a result, the Catholic communities became nervous. There were also some isolated acts of religious violence that spread terror. The nuncio tells me about the murder of a seventy-one-year-old nun, Sister Cecilia Mouchi Hanna. In August 2003 she was knifed to death by three young men who, it seems, were released when Saddam Hussein decided to empty the prisons. 'The Catholics, like every minority, are very interested in having a democratic system in Iraq that would guarantee freedom of religion. But this won't be achieved without some kind of firm authority.'

The first time Monsignor Filoni came to Iraq, there was not the freedom that there is today, but at least there was order and a degree of safety. At this time of the year, he remembers, in the torrid heat, people would take their mattresses onto the roof and sleep there, looking up at the stars. Have I seen the stars in the Baghdad sky? I confess that I have been so preoccupied with earthly matters that I have not done so. You really must do so straight away, he tells me; make use of these blackouts that leave the whole city in darkness. Up above, in that inky vault, the stars shine so brightly and so clear- ly that you have to think about God. Perhaps it was these starry nights back in ancient Mesopotamia that, at the dawn of life, caused men and women to start a dialogue with the divinity. 'Legend has it that Abraham was born here, in Ur, did you know that? Perhaps here, between the Tigris and the Euphrates, not just writing but also faith was born.'

25 June–6 July 2003

5. White Beans

Kais Olwei is a strong and handsome thirty-seven-year-old Iraqi, with a scar like a small snake on his forehead. He feels unwell every time he sees a plate of white beans on a table. This is because of what happened to him eighteen years ago, but he'll remember it until he dies and perhaps even after that.

He was nineteen then, and was arrested in one of those raids on students that Saddam Hussein's security forces carried out ritually. They took him to the Headquarters of the Security Services (the *Mukhabarat*) in Baghdad, and the following morning, before they had even begun to interrogate him, they started torturing him. That was also routine. They hung him up by the arms, like a carcass of

292

meat, and, soon after, while they questioned him, he received electric shocks through electrodes attached to his body. The chief of the three policemen who shared the narrow, dark cell with Kais administered the shocks by pressing a button. He received the shocks in short bursts, at regular intervals, firstly on the legs. Then the wires moved up his body until they reached the most sensitive parts: the anus, the penis and the testicles.

What Kais Olewi remembers of that morning – the first of many such mornings – are not what were doubtless his screams of pain or that slight smell of scorched flesh coming from his own body, but rather the fact that his torturers often forgot about him and became involved in personal conversations, about their families or trivial matters, while Kais Olewi, trussed and suspended in mid-air, reduced to a living wound, wanted to lose consciousness once and for all, but could not manage to do so. At midday they brought the three policemen their lunch: a bowl of steaming white beans. Kais still has a very strong memory of smelling that delicious waft of cooking while he heard the three men discussing which of the cooks at the Headquarters of the Security Services prepared this dish the best. From time to time, while he was still chewing, the head of the group would remember what he was supposed to be doing and turned his attention to the hanging man. Then, as if to assuage his professional conscience, he would press that button and Kais Olewi felt the shock to his brain. Since then he has not been able to smell or taste white bean stew without feeling faint.

Kais Olewi was condemned to life imprisonment, but was lucky since he only spent eight years in Abu Ghraib prison, from 1987 to 1995, before being released under an amnesty. Since the fall of Saddam Hussein, he is one of the Iraq ex-political prisoners working as a volunteer in the organisation that I'm visiting: the Association of Free Prisoners. It is housed in an enormous run-down mansion in Khadimiya, on an embankment along the river Tigris where the people of Baghdad, in quieter times, would stroll in the evenings while the setting sun turned the sky red.

What now turns this place red are the posters with photos of thousands of people who disappeared during the dictatorship. Some

293

images – of prisoners with their faces eaten away by acid – are almost impossible to look at. They were all found in the files that the *Mukhabarat* kept of their victims, many of which were unfortunately lost in the fires. But the Association of Free Prisoners, which began to operate immediately after the fall of the dictatorship, have collected from police stations and other organisations involved in the repression all the documentation that had not been destroyed. There is a crowd of people in the corridors, rooms and stairs, where the volunteers, working on improvised desks or on their knees, are filling in forms, establishing lists of names, collating data and trying to attend to the innumerable people – many of whom are women – who have come here to ask for help in finding their parents, sons and daughters, nieces and nephews, brothers and sisters, who one fateful day, x years ago, disappeared from their lives.

There are other Human Rights organisations doing similar work in Iraq, but this association is the largest. It has offices in the eighteen provinces of the country, except Ramadi, and it receives some – albeit little – support from international bodies and from the CPA run by Paul Bremer. Its main function now is to help relatives locate the disappeared and provide them with documentation which will allow them to present petitions to, and seek reparation from, the Iraqi government (when it exists). The Association also has a group of volunteer lawyers who counsel the families of the disappeared who come to the building. I speak to one of them, Ammar Basil, who tells me about some of the horrifying cases that he has become involved in, like the shooting of a newborn baby, the son of a couple of doctors who were opposed to Saddam Hussein. They were subjected to the terrible ordeal of being made to watch the infanticide before they themselves were executed.

The vice-president of the Association of Free Prisoners, Abdul Fattah Al Idrissi, assures me that, however exaggerated the figure might seem, the number of people killed or disappeared since the Ba'ath Party took power in a coup in 1963, which led to the irresistible rise of Saddam Hussein, is between five million and six-and-a-half million. That is, about twenty per cent of the population of Iraq. 'Not even Hitler had a record like that,' he says. Since I've become used to hearing fantastic figures from different Iraqis, I don't tell him that I find that figure improbable. But it doesn't matter: exaggerations are more expressive than the objective facts that will never be established. They show the desperate reaction of people who were powerless in the face of the extraordinary horror of the regime, which no one will ever be able to document precisely, only through vague approximations.

The repression affected all sectors, ethnic groups, social classes and religions, but it mainly affected Kurds and Shi'ites. Among those particularly targeted were intellectuals – teachers, writers, artists – whom Saddam Hussein, a thoroughly ignorant man despite his feeble attempts at studying Law in Cairo, where he was exiled, particularly mistrusted. The vice-president of the Association tells me that, based on a study of some fifteen hundred cases, it became clear that 'the regime had intended to do away with every cultured person in the country. Because the proportion of educated people, with degrees, among the murdered and disappeared is very high'. Villages, whole neighbourhoods, clans and families disappeared in extermination operations that frequently took place, with no apparent motive, at times when Saddam Hussein had complete control over a cowed population, in a country where terror held sway. It was, says Abdul Fattah Al Idrissi, as if the despot had a sudden attack of homicidal paranoia, and decided on a quick massacre as a preventative measure, stirred by some hunch or macabre nightmare. That is the only way one can understand the extraordinary number of victims, the entire families that are turning up in the common graves that have been discovered in the past months. On other occasions, the collective killings had a precise objective: for example, to make the oil region of Kirkuk completely Arab, forcibly uprooting the Kurdish settlements and replacing them with Sunni communities, or punishing the Shia majority for their 1991 rebellion. All the Ba'ath Party buildings in the provinces were used as torture centres, since the offices of the *Mukhabarat* did not have enough room. The most frequent tortures inflicted on prisoners were electric shocks, pulling out their eyes and nails, hanging them until their bones were dislocated, burning them with acid, and daubing their bodies with alcohol-soaked cotton and turning them into human torches. When, as happened very infrequently, the families were informed of the death of a person, they received a death certificate that invariably attributed the death to 'meningitis'.

The Association has a real find, an eyewitness to one of those extraordinary massacres, which took place in Tuz, a town to the north of Baghdad, on the way to Kirkuk. He was a bus driver, and he and his bus were requisitioned by the police. He thus became a passive observer of the whole operation. As he drove around different villages across the region, he saw the police loading up his bus with entire families, parents along with grandparents and children. With his human cargo he was directed by Ba'ath Party members, who were in charge of the operation, to a piece of open ground on the outskirts of Tuz. There were already thousands of people there, being taken off lorries trucks and buses like his by policemen and party activists. As soon as they were unloaded, they were immediately put to work digging a long ditch, in the form of a trench. The witness says that he arrived there at four in the afternoon and that the activity went on all night. When the ditch was deep enough, the police and Ba'ath Party activists put on gas marks and gave him one as well. He was paralysed by terror.

Bludgeoning and firing at the terrified throng, they forced them into the excavated ditch and threw toxic gas cylinders on top of them. By dawn, it was all over. The driver was warned to keep his mouth shut and then sent off by the assassins. The ditch has now been found. It is one of many that are appearing across Iraq, often with four or five thousand corpses in each. 'They were trenches rather than ditches,' Abdul Fattah Al Idrissi specifies. And also that, in certain cases, the victims did not have the fortune to be gassed, because the Ba'athists preferred to bury them alive.

These ditches that are being excavated attract thousands of people, who come to see whether, among the remains that are being uncovered, that bear witness to the horror of the recent past in Iraq, they might discover their disappeared family members. One of these couples, who, since April, have been searching the country for the bones of their son who disappeared twelve years ago, are two old people. The woman is very ill, and her daughter tells me that the only thing keeping them alive is the hope of finding the remains of their loved one. Her name is Mrs Al Sarrat, and I visit her in a small, precarious house built on pillars, also in the Al Kadimia neighbourhood. 'My life is thirty-five years of grief,' she declares, without crying, her Spartan face chiselled out of despair. She is a woman of indeterminate age, swamped by a black *abaya* that only allows her face to be shown, flanked by her two very young daughters, who are also veiled and remain motionless throughout the entire interview, like tragic statues. The room is very modest and hot, crammed with pictures, and there is a majestic view of the Tigris through the windows.

'We cannot breathe or pray because misfortunes kept befalling us, one after the other. He was one of the youngest boys in the family. He was a secondary-school student and signed a petition asking for money to bury a dead school friend. Someone sent that list, which was just a charitable gesture, to the security services. All the boys were arrested and sentenced to ten years in prison, as conspirators. Some of them died in prison.'

Another of Mrs Al Sarrat's brothers was a soldier. He was wounded three times in the eight-year war with Iran. 'A hero, no?' Well one day he was arrested, accused by someone of wanting to get out of the army, a crime that often meant a death sentence or otherwise a prison sentence and the added penalty of having an ear cut off. The family found out about this through rumours, since they never received any information in their frequent enquiries to official bodies. They never heard of him again.

Soon after this second misfortune, a third blow fell. Her father was arrested and disappeared into the night of the dictatorship. Three years later a stranger brought a note to the family. 'Go to Abu Ghraib prison', the prison on the outskirts of Baghdad, where the worst tortures and political murders took place. There was her father, and she was able to visit him for several minutes every few months. He was released six years later, as mysteriously as he had been arrested. He was never told why he was detained.

Finally there was a younger brother who disappeared when the

Shia uprising of 1991 was put down in an orgy of blood. He was a soldier during the war in Kuwait. The last time anyone saw him, he was still in the forces, in Najaf. He has not been heard of since then, and Mrs Al Sarrat's parents are searching for him in their painful pilgrimage to the common graves scattered throughout Iraq.

When I leave, rather dazed by my morning's immersion in suffering and barbarity, instead of saying goodbye to Mrs Al Sarrat with the usual right hand on the heart, I stretch out my hand. She looks at me, alarmed.

Just in case I hadn't had enough barbarity, this evening, in the Hotel Rimini, where I have come to take refuge, betraying the hospitality of my friends in the Ibero-American-European Foundation for a few miserable hours of air conditioning which might finally help me to sleep a bit, I have a conversation with a woman who works for the United Nations which has sunk me into depression and will probably bring me nightmares tonight. She tells me about an investigation by America's Watch, which has yet to be made public, but which she has read, into the rape and kidnapping of women in Baghdad since the anarchy began, on 9 April. This is a taboo subject because, in terms of traditional morality in Iraqi society, a raped woman is a disgrace that dishonours her entire family and, instead of receiving compassion and support, she is shunned and despised. She knows that her life has ended, that she will never be married and that in her own household she will be subject to exclusion and derision. To wash away this affront, it is often the case that her father or one of her brothers will kill her. The law has always been lenient towards these medieval 'honour-cleansing killings', and the perpetrators receive symbolic sentences of two or three months in gaol. Americas Watch has twenty-five testimonies from girls, young women and older women who were kidnapped and raped in Baghdad by criminals and who, for obvious reasons, do not want to report the abuse that they have suffered. Not only because right now there is no police force or functioning judiciary, but also, and above all, because even if these bodies were in place, the procedures and infinite humiliations that heroic women in the past suffered when they dared to report such crimes did not bring them justice. It just exposed them to the disdain and humiliation of public opinion, which increased the hostility of their families. For that reason, according to the Americas Watch report, the girls and women try desperately to hide what has happened to them; they are ashamed and sorry, as if it is they who were responsible for their misfortune.

Now I understand more clearly why, at the gates of the University of Baghdad that I visited yesterday, there were so many mothers waiting to take their daughters home, as if they were nursery-school children.

25 June–6 July 2003

6. *Othello* Back to Front

The dramatist, journalist, soldier, artilleryman, bon vivant and firm optimist Ahmad Hadi is tall, strong and engaging, and, with his exuberant anatomy, he seems very cooped up in the narrow rooms of the house where the newspaper *Azzaman* (*The Times*) has located its editorial offices. The paper was started up, in exile in London, by a famous opposition journalist, Saad Al Bazzaz, after he split with Saddam Hussein in 1991. The cause of the split was the despot's eldest son, the ineffable Uday, who controlled the Press Union, along with innumerable other responsibilities (including the Olympic Committee, the Football Association, the newspaper *Babel* and many other activities). With the fall of the regime, the newspaper now brings out four editions: in London, in the Arab Emirates, in Basra and here in Baghdad. It started printing in the capital on 27 April and already has a circulation of sixty thousand. *Azzaman* is considered to be the widest read and perhaps most influential newspaper. It is produced by forty-five journalists, fifteen of them women, who fit with great difficulty in this small house where we can scarcely breathe, because the electricity cuts frequently shut down the ventilators, leaving us sweating and stifling. Despite this, there is a great energy in the air, one might even say joy, and the editorial staff –

almost all young people - who are coming and going, or else toiling on the computers, are very friendly.

Bathed in sweat, the main editor of *Azzaman* is enthusiastic, and gives a cheerful account of his busy life. He had studied theatre, graduating from the Baghdad School of Dramatic Arts with a study and a stage adaptation of Molière's *Le Malade imaginaire*. He wanted to pursue a career as an actor and theatre director, but the regime decided otherwise and made him join the army, in the artillery division. He was kept in the army for eleven years, eight of which he spent in the mad war against Iran that Saddam Hussein instigated and which cost a million lives. Ahmad Hadi, who was by then an artillery captain, hung up his uniform and tried to return to his old love, the boards, when the Shia intifada against the dictatorship broke out, in which he became actively involved. Following the failure of the uprising, when the punishment killings were in full flow, he managed to escape across the border to Saudi Arabia. While he was in exile, as a reprisal for his rebellion, the regime burned down his two houses along with everything inside them. He tells me all this laughing out loud, as if the matter was funny or the victim of these misfortunes was his worst enemy.

Perhaps Ahmad Hadi is happy because, in his forties, he has finally managed to take up his theatrical vocation after so many frustrations. His work, *Obey the Devil*, which was performed four times in an open-air setting, amid the rubble in Baghdad, has been a monumental success and many Iraqis have told me about it, praising it to the skies. There were nine male actors and one female, who was also a dancer, and the actors appeared daubed with the ashes of the fires that every passer-by comes across in the streets of the city.

To hear the robust, sweating, gesticulating Ahmad Hadi explaining his work to me is, I am sure, almost as stimulating as seeing it myself. He describes it with great verve, lots of arm movements and loud guffaws, mopping the rivulets of sweat that soak his face and his shirt. The work is a recreation of Shakespeare's *Othello*, a work which, Hadi assures me, could have been written with the Iraq tragedy in mind, since it fits so perfectly. There are also other coincidences, real premonitions by the Elizabethan bard. *Othello*, read backwards, from right to left, as is the case in Arabic, produces in that language a sound very similar to 'Leota', which means, 'Obey him'. My translator, Professor Bassam Y. Rashid, who is a linguist, gets caught up in a philological discussion with him, and finally he admits that he's right: it does mean 'Obey him'. Ahmad Hadi added the word devil; although, he tells me, an infernal presence is implied in the idea that a society must 'obey' an irrational and destructive force. Life in the palace of the despot was indeed a world of jealousy, open hatred, rivalry, envy, crimes and betrayal. Iago's betrayal, he assures me, is symbolic of the treachery of Saddam Hussein's Head of General Staff, who, out of jealousy, handed over Baghdad to the American forces without letting the Iraqi soldiers fight. There is no doubt about it: his version of *Othello* represents what Iraq has lived through all these years, which is why the people of Baghdad identified so closely with the work.

This is the only time, in our conversation, that the optimistic Ahmad Hadi says something that could be construed as a veiled criticism of the coalition forces. In every other aspect, his view of the current situation in Iraq exudes confidence and appreciation. 'I am optimistic for one very simple reason: nothing could be worse than Saddam Hussein. After that atrocious experience, things can only get better for us'.

He believes that once the CPA puts in place the Iraq Governing Committee which, he is sure, will be made up of significant figures from across the political spectrum, then the confidence of the people will grow, order will be imposed, services will be re-established and the uncertainty and insecurity everyone feels today will start to disappear. The main desire of the Iraqi people, he is convinced, is to live in peace, without hatred and violence, and to build a modern, tolerant, secular, pluralist democracy, on Western lines. This is what *Azzaman* promotes and exemplifies in its pages, where different opinions are freely expressed. Even among the most politicised religious sectors, be they Sunni or Shia, it is the moderates, not the extremists, who – now – prevail, and they are prepared to make an effort to coexist so that the nightmare of the Ba'ath Party does not recur.

The people will never forget these thirty-five years. Significant sites of memory are the common graves which continue to appear throughout all the provinces of Iraq, full of the bodies of disappeared, tortured and executed people. The figures he gives me, with emphatic certainty, are even greater than those I was given by the Association of Freed Prisoners. They make me dizzy. I know that they are more a fiction than a reality, but even after cutting them down drastically, the total remains horrifying. Every time I hear from Iraqis accounts of the horrors of Saddam Hussein, I am reminded of the Dominican Republic and what I heard there about General Trujillo's exploits.

Ahmad Hadi states categorically that the figure of eight million victims of the Ba'ath tyranny is perfectly realistic, despite my look of incredulity. I tell him that it doesn't matter if he is exaggerating. I didn't come to Iraq to listen just to the truth but also to the fictions that the Iraqis believe, since the lies that a people invent very often express a very deep truth, and are as instructive a way of understanding a dictatorship as the objective truth. He insists that this mountain of eight million corpses is close to the historical truth. He adds that you can make calculations based on the numbers of bodies in common graves that have appeared since April: there are at least three in every province in Iraq, and in just one of them, in Babilonia, there were some 115,000 bodies. I tell him that this is the largest figure I have heard of in any city since the butchery perpetrated by the Nazis in the Holocaust. He insists on giving me more horror statistics: in the city of Shanafia, which has scarcely twenty thousand inhabitants, they have already counted almost eighty-five thousand human remains, victims of the homicidal rage of the Ba'athists and Saddam Hussein. After a past in which so many extraordinary horrors were committed, how could one not feel hopeful about the future, despite the blackouts, the lack of water, the anarchy and the insecurity? Ahmad Hadi wants exemplary sanctions to be imposed on Saddam and his sons (Uday and Qusay died in a fire fight with American troops on 22 July, after this statement was made) and henchmen, but he does not want them to be taken to an international tribunal. They must be judged here, in an Iraqi court, with Iraqi judges. That would be an example that would inure Iraq for ever against dictatorships.

I ask him whether one can say that today there is complete freedom in his country to write and publish. 'Absolute freedom, like never before in the history of Iraq.' And even in the economic sphere, those with jobs must recognise that their situation has improved (for those without jobs, the majority of the people, it is another matter, of course). For example, under Saddam Hussein, journalists earned some ten thousand dinars a month (the equivalent of five dollars). Now they earn the equivalent of two hundred dollars. Isn't that a big improvement? He tells me that, for example, with his first two-hundred-dollar pay cheque he rushed out to by a spare part for his fridge that had been broken for two years. His wife, who is a school teacher, spent her first salary after the liberation on a satellite dish, which means that she can now pick up television stations from around the world. And she is very happy!

Ahmad Hadi is from the south, from the region of the mystic Shia cities of Najaf and Kerbala. He invites me to his house – Iraqis always do this, when they scarcely know you, something that reminds me of Latin American hospitality – so that I can visit this beautiful part of the country. But he is not thinking about Shia mysticism or the sacred emanations of the place, but rather of more material things: 'Between Najaf and Kerbala they produce the best rice in the whole of the Middle East,' he effuses. 'Do come and I'll prepare you a treat that you won't forget for the rest of your life.' Guffaws well up from inside that enormous body every now and then, like one of those cries that warriors make to give themselves confidence before going into battle. 'Of course things are better in Iraq,' he exclaims. 'Before I had to drink that poisonous alcohol that they sell loose, and now I am drinking malt whisky.'

It is good to talk to someone like the journalist and playwright Ahmad Hadi, who is convinced that, even in this problematic, destroyed country of Iraq, life is worth living. I leave the newspaper and take a walk around the centre of Baghdad. I feel that I am walking in a world that has been conquered by the surrounding desert: the façades of the buildings, the squares, the trees, the public monuments and even the faces and the clothes of the people are all stained an earthen colour. Dry sand is floating in the air and gets into your mouth and nose. In the Al Ferdaws (Paradise) Square, where the titanic statue of Saddam Hussein had been that television viewers all over the world saw toppled the day the coalition forces entered the city, there is now an inscription in black paint, addressed to the Americans in idiosyncratic English: 'All done/Go home.'

In my rather intermittent readings during these past weeks, as I tried to get some sort of idea about the country that I was coming to, Al Rachid Street was always mentioned, for in the forties and fifties it had been the great commercial artery at the centre of Baghdad. With its luxurious shops and jewellery stores, this was the place that the most prosperous families of the Middle East dreamed about and came to on shopping expeditions. My heart sinks when I walk along it, skirting round the foul-smelling rubbish, the scraps that scrawny dogs are scavenging, and the rubble. It takes imagination to make out the former mansions of the rich and powerful, and the elegant shops of what was Baghdad half a century earlier in these crumbling, shaky, windowless, lopsided, looted and burned-out constructions, many of them about to collapse on top of the residents who sit on benches or on the floor under the portals and columns, impervious to the impending disaster, talking and sipping at their glass of hot tea balanced on a small plate.

One street off Al Rachid is Al Mutanabbi Street, and on Friday mornings there is always a second-hand book market. I've visited it twice, and each time I've felt happy and stimulated in among the motley crowd browsing, buying and selling, or asking questions about the books and magazines that are so old that the pages come apart in your hands when you leaf through them. It is a narrow, rubble-strewn, earthen street, but it has a warm and friendly atmosphere and does good business. There are a lot of readers in this city, that's clear. Some of them must be middle-class, but the majority are very poor, and of all ages. They eagerly thumb the old religious folio volumes, they look in astonishment at the magazines with semi-naked dancers on the cover and point at the headlines of old newspapers. There are large photos, of ayatollahs and imams who were

killed or exiled, and also of politicians and revolutionaries, communist leaflets, and many books of poetry. In one of the stalls I find the
memoirs of Pablo Neruda, *I Confess I Have Lived*, translated into Persian and published in Tehran.

I end the day in one of the few restaurants still open in Baghdad,
The White Palace, where I hope to get away from that wretched fried
chicken dish to which I have gained a completely unjustified aversion. The speciality of this place is *Cusi*, lamb seasoned with spices
and served with white rice. A real feast, I am assured. But I can't
accompany it with the appropriate glass of ice-cold beer because the
place does not serve alcoholic drinks. The friends I am eating with
are surprised: they drank beer here a few days ago. The explanation
is that religious fanatics have threatened to kill restaurant owners if
they do not enforce a non-alcohol rule. It doesn't matter, even with
water – as Ahmad Hadi might exclaim, licking his fingers – the *Cusi*
is really delicious.

5 June–6 July 2003

7. The Kurds

Travelling north out of Baghdad towards Iraqi Kurdistan, we move
into a different landscape, language and culture, and also, over the
days, the towns and cities look different. After four hours' drive by
car, through a flat, scorched desert, with Bedouin villages and
burned-out personnel carriers and scattered army lorries, there are
the mountains, which we begin to climb an hour later, in the middle
of the oilfields, up to the city of Kirkuk. Leaving that city and heading for Suleymaniya, the road gets steeper and the roadside is covered in green, in pine forests and slopes covered by cultivated areas
where a few weather-beaten labourers with timeless faces are working. No one would say that there had been a war in these parts.

Still less in Suleymaniya, an attractive city with broad, clean, tree-
lined streets, traffic control officers on street corners, women dressed
in Western styles, Internet cafés everywhere, McDonald's and a

forest of satellite dishes on the roofs of the houses. I knew that the war had scarcely touched the place, but I was not expecting to find a scene of such normality. I was also not expecting to find posters thanking President Bush for 'The liberation of Iraq' and greeting Paul Bremer, the proconsul, who had just been here to visit the members of one of the two Kurdish governments that have divided Iraqi Kurdistan. The government in Suleymaniya is run by Jala Talabani's Patriotic Union Party of Kurdistan; the other government, whose capital is Irbil to the north, is the domain of Masud Barzani's Democratic Party of Kurdistan. The fierce rivalry between the two parties, and the fratricidal violence – in the 1994 conflict between the two communities there were more than three thousand casualties – has merely increased the misfortunes of the Kurds, who represent twenty per cent of the Iraqi population (somewhat under four million). They were systematic victims of the Saddam Hussein dictatorship, which attacked them viciously, especially during the attempted rebellions of 1975, 1988 and 1991, when they sought greater autonomy and resisted the enforced 'arabisation' of Kurdish villages that the regime was implementing, massacring the native population and replacing it with Sunni Arabs. In 1988, entire Kurdish communities – including children, women and old people – disappeared, an extermination programme that culminated in the massacre at Halabja, in March of that year, in which more than four thousand Kurds were killed with chemical weapons.

But walking through the streets of Suleymaniya, one would say that all this belonged to the far-distant past. There are no American soldiers to be seen ('They are dressed in civilian clothing, in the cafés and restaurants, fraternising with the locals,' Shalaw Askari, Jalal Talabini's Minister of Information would later tell me), and the only soldiers visible are the local *peshmergas* (fighters) dressed in their baggy trousers, their baroque turbans that seem like something of a Rembrandt self-portrait, and the long lengths of printed fabrics that they roll around their bodies like belts.

Iraqi Kurdistan has made very good use of the twelve years of total autonomy imposed by the Allies in the aftermath of the first Gulf War, setting up a regional government and establishing an exclusion zone outside the authority of Saddam Hussein. As well as having a government of their own for the first time in their history, the Kurds have enjoyed considerable economic prosperity, as can be seen in the building work, the well-stocked food and general stores which have goods from across the world, and the throng of people in the cafés, refreshment stalls and restaurants throughout the city. However, there is not a single Kurd prepared to tell a stranger wandering around Suleymaniya that the community wants independence. They have all learned their lesson and repeat, like a slogan, that they want to remain part of a federal and democratic Iraqi government that would guarantee them the autonomy that has worked so well for them. They are very aware of the fears that the very idea of an independent Kurdistan raises in neighbouring Turkey, whose twelve million Kurds live in a state of constant tension with the central government.

All this is explained to me in perfect English – he studied in the United States and in Britain – by the young and dynamic Shalaw Askari, the Information Minister, who receives me instead of Jalal Talabini, with whom I had an appointment, but who had to travel unexpectedly to Moscow. In the past, the Patriotic Union of Kurdistan was Marxist and received aid from the USSR, but now it is procapitalist and an active supporter of the coalition. The *peshmergas* had worked closely with the coalition forces, which is why this region remained almost untouched by the invasion.

'For us, the Americans are our friends, the liberators of Iraq, and we are grateful to them for having overthrown the tyrant Saddam Hussein', Askari tells me. Now we are speaking quite openly, but a few minutes earlier, when I came into the room and found the Minister waiting for me surrounded by advisers and private businessmen that worked with him, I felt somewhat disconcerted. Why so many people? Because of a monumental error. Shalaw Askari and his entourage were expecting someone who could immediately invest considerable sums in the reconstruction and development of Jala Talabani's Kurdistan. They explained to me persuasively and in great detail that their most urgent need was for a four-hundred-bed hospital, for which the government already had the land and the building plans (which were at my disposal), and which would not cost more than forty million dollars, and an abbatoir for Suley- maniya, which would cost no more than fourteen million. It really upset me to have to tell them that it was not in my power to make these investments, because I didn't represent anyone, I was just a South American writer finding out what was happening in Iraq. The young minister blanched, swallowed and – what else could he do? – smiled. 'We Kurds have learned our lesson,' he tells me, 'which is why now, instead of remembering the martyrdom of our people under the dictatorship, or the unfortunate internal disputes that have done so much damage to our cause in the world, we want to work, collaborate and contribute to the establishment of a free and democratic Iraq where we can coexist in peace with the other com- munities. We have had this peaceful coexistence in Kurdistan for the past ten years. For example, aren't the Turks respected? Don't they have their own newspapers and their political organisations operat- ing in complete freedom? It is exactly the same for the Shi'ites, the Sunnis, the Christians and the other religions. There is a place and work for everyone. We are the forerunners of what Iraq should be in the future.'

When I ask him whether the Patriotic Union of Kurdistan will be part of the Governing Council that Paul Bremer is putting together, he assures me that this is the case: this was something that had been clarified during the recent visit of the head of the CPA. (And, indeed, a few days after this interview, when the new organisation formed to lead the country to a democratic and federal system is announced in Baghdad, both Jalal Talabini and his rival Massud Barzani figure prominently.)

'The key word for the pacification of Iraq is work', declares Minis- ter Askari. He is ardent, optimistic and very thin, and he talks with his hands as well, like an Italian. 'Islamist fanaticism, for example, would drastically reduce if the great number of unemployed could all start to work and earn a salary. When you have time on your hands, you can go to the mosque five times a day and become men- tally imprisoned by what is being preached there. If you work eight hours a day, plus travel to and from work and the time spent with family, then religion can no longer be your only concern in life. Other equally important things crop up. And certain cobwebs in the brain get blown away and more modern ideas come in'.

According to him, the violence unleashed against the coalition forces – assaults and ambushes kill one or two American soldiers on a daily basis – are not just the work of the remnants of the repressive forces and Republican Guard of Saddam Hussein. It also stems from foreign fighters sent by Al Qaeda, the terrorist organisation of Osama Bin Laden, and also terrorists from Iran, controlled by the most conservative clerical sectors of that neighbouring country. 'These people are very afraid of the establishment of democracy in Iraq. They also think that sooner or later the United States will come after them. And they have decided that the war should begin in Iraqi territory.' But, he is convinced, once the country has its institutions in place, the coalition and the Iraqi forces will soon defeat the terrorist resistance.

His ideal is transparent: an Iraq made up of professionals and engineers, incorporated into the world, emancipated from political and religious dogma, attracting capital from all parts to develop the enormous resources of the country, with coexistence guaranteed by freedom and the law, and with private enterprise as the motor for development. He points to the businessmen alongside him. They have begun to work, despite the precarious conditions and the difficulties involved in any financial operation given the uncertainty, the legal vacuum and the fact that there are no banks yet, or even a common currency for the whole of Iraq. Here in Kurdistan the dinars bearing Saddam Hussein's face do not circulate as in the rest of the country – they use an earlier minting. (Though the truth is that the economy is becoming swiftly dollarised). Can one do business and make investments amid such disorder? One of the businessmen, the exuberant and extremely friendly Nagi Al Jaf, smiles triumphantly: 'Tomorrow we are expecting a delegation of Swiss bankers we have almost convinced to open up a bank in Suleymaniya.' The Minister reminds me that capital is always attracted to places where there are viable returns on investment and stable and attractive conditions. 'Here we will have both things.'

Minister Askari becomes less loquacious when I ask him if it is true that both Jalil Talabani and Massud Barzani have promised Paul Bremer – who mainly came to talk about this issue with the two opponents – to integrate their two governments into one, so that the Kurds can have a single representative voice in the new Iraqi government. 'We are working together and the rough edges and the old disputes are gradually being smoothed over. The desire for union exists. It is just a question of time.' That is the only time in our long interview when I get the feeling that the friendly Minister is giving me the official line.

On the other hand, I am convinced that he entirely believes what he tells me about the Kurds' desire to reassure Turkey, to assuage the fear that the goal of Talabani and Barzani is an independent Kurdistan, something that the Turkish government has said quite categorically that it will not tolerate. 'On this point we are all in agreement: we will not fight for secession; we want to be part of an Iraq that represents our rights.' And he adds, 'Turkey made a big mistake, don't you think? They turned down the offer of forty million dollars from the US to allow the coalition forces through their territory to free Iraq. Really stupid, wouldn't you agree? And, as well as the money, to lose such a powerful friend. Well, that's their problem.'

When we left the meeting, Nagi Al Jaf, the businessman, takes me to a place that, he assures me, is 'paradise'. He is not exaggerating. Suleymaniya is ringed by mountains, and we go up one of them on a very modern road, through pine forests, the gentle slopes lush with vegetation, until we reach the summit, which is wide and offers a splendid view of the whole region. Down below, dotted with gardens and parks and trees, are the white houses of the city, just as the lights are beginning to come on. It's a large area, and at each end there are ochre-coloured rocks and wooded sections. At this altitude, the stifling heat disappears, cooled by a fresh breeze that smells of resin. All this side of the mountain is full of families or groups of friends, many of them young, who have installed themselves under the trees, cooking dinner on small braziers, while they talk, drink and sing. Along the road there are refreshment points, and a few isolated houses. And wherever you look everything is clean, beautiful and peaceful. I have to shake my head and tell myself that this is all superficial and misleading, that in fact I am in a country that only yesterday suffered the most atrocious injustice, and that a great number of these mild-mannered trippers who are settling down contentedly to observe the myriads of stars that are just beginning to appear – the most dazzling and the greatest number of stars that I have ever seen – will have many dead, tortured or wounded people to mourn, as a result of the savagery of the dictatorship or the fratricidal blindness of the Kurds themselves.

Everywhere that I visit the next morning, the market and the adjacent streets, and all the people I talk to, leave me with the same impression: that despite the tragedies of the past and the difficulties of the present, things here are heading in the right direction, and that the people are constructive and hopeful and have a firm resolve to put an end to the ignominious past.

But when I am about to leave, a casual conversation in the hotel over a cup of hot, steaming coffee with a young construction worker from Erbil, whose name I won't mention, undermines my optimism: 'Don't go away with such a positive idea of what is happening here,' he tells me in a low voice, after hearing how impressed I have been during my brief visit to Suleymaniya. 'Don't be naïve.' It's true that a lot of progress has been made, compared to the bloody past, but other problems remain. Iraqi Kurdistan is now divided between two parties which hate one another but have set up two monopoly governments. 'Can there be democracies with single parties? Only a democracy that is very relative and very corrupt. If you want to do any kind of business, here or in Erbil, you have to pay steep commissions to the Democratic Party of Kurdistan or the Patriotic Union of Kurdistan, and to the leaders themselves, many of whom have become very rich in recent years with these new powers. There are no real audit mechanisms of any sort that apply to the governments, either here or there.' Is he right or is he exaggerating? Is his criticism objective or an expression of some resentment or personal failure? I have no way of knowing, of course. But I get onto the jeep that will take me back to Baghdad with a sour taste in my mouth.

25 June–6 July 2003

8. The Viceroy

At the first light of dawn, about half past five in the morning, Ambassador Paul Bremer leaves the non-air-conditioned trailer where he spends the night and runs his daily three miles through the gardens of the old palace – which is a really a fortress – of Saddam Hussein. He showers, and for the next fifteen hours is submerged in his office, at the heart of that giant construction full of crystal chandeliers, marble tiles and golden domes that the Iraqi dictator built as a monument to his megalomania. Indeed, so that there would be no doubt about his intentions, Saddam Hussein crowned the enormous complex with four giant copper heads depicting himself as Nebuchadnezzar.

Bremer is sixty-two, but he looks a lot younger. He graduated from Yale and Harvard, he was an ambassador in the Netherlands and in Norway and a roving ambassador for President Reagan. He's an expert in crisis management and counter-terrorism, and had been working in the private sector for ten years when President Bush called him to offer him the most difficult job in the world: to shape the democratisation and reconstruction process in Iraq. He accepted because he has always believed in public service and because his father taught him that if one is lucky enough 'to be born in the best country in the world' ('Well, we believe that it is the best country in the world,' he qualifies), then one is morally obliged to do everything that the president asks. He also accepted because he is convinced that it is possible to turn post-Saddam Iraq into a functional democracy that will have an effect on surrounding countries and will lead to an essential transformation of the whole of the Middle East.

He speaks clearly and coherently and, at times, he departs from the banalities that are the stuff of any holder of a public office and says intelligent things. But, in his enthusiasm to describe Iraq's promising future to me, he forgets the laws of hospitality and doesn't offer even a glass of water to me or to my daughter Morgana. We are suffering from thirst and sunstroke because we had to go through a great deal before finally reaching this office (an hour late).

The interview was arranged for 11.15 and we arrived at the entrance at 10.30, alongside the great arch, amid the barbed wire and barriers of the guard post. We should have been met there by two officers of the Spanish Military Mission of the CPA. But Lieutenant Colonel Juan Delgado and Colonel Javier Sierra had parked their car in front of the arch, and we were waiting for them behind the arch. This mix-up placed my daughter and me in the hands of some soldiers who searched us, asked us for some incomprehensible passes and told us that they would never let us cross the barriers and get to Bremer's distant office. For about an hour, we went back and forth to different palace doors, each several hundred yards apart, that we had to cover on foot in the burning sun. When an officer finally agreed to call the information office of Ambassador Bremer, he could not reach anyone because all the staff had gone to the airport to greet the actor Arnold Schwarzenegger who was coming out to spend the 4 July with the US troops in Baghdad.

In the hottest morning of my life, when we were already half an hour late for the interview, Morgana decided, boldly and inopportunely, to teach the US army a lesson in good manners and started to shout at the platoon sergeant that she would not put up with abuse, with people raising their voices, or with this complete lack of cooperation from uncouth army men, to the extent that I thought that, apart from not seeing Bremer, it was quite likely that my bones would soon be resting in one of the dungeons of the despot's palace. At that moment, providentially, a lieutenant appeared in his slippers, who saw reason. He understood the whole thing and asked us to follow him. That is how we reached the antechamber of the ambassador. Fifteen minutes later a friendly colonel appeared, one of the proconsul's deputies, who asked us if we were here for the interview that Ambassador Bremer was to give to a Nobel Prize winner. Had the splendid Miguel Moro Aguilar, the head of the Spanish Embassy who had arranged the interview for me, invented this credential so that Bremer could not say no? When I explained to the disappointed colonel that there was no Nobel Prize winner around, and that the interview was to be with a mere novelist from Peru, he muttered in a rather demoralised attempt at humour: 'If you tell the ambassador about all this confusion, he'll fire me.'

An hour after the appointed time, here we are with the man whom the terrorists – who have already killed twenty-seven US soldiers since 9 April, and wounded a further 177 – tried to kill yesterday at the National Museum, an attack that, of course, the security forces had detected and dealt with in time. He tells me that he spent his honeymoon in Peru in 1965 and that, thanks to a rail strike, he and his wife were lucky enough to visit Machu Picchu on their own, without the normal hordes of tourists.

What is going to happen now in Iraq? In the short term, an Iraqi Council of Government is to be set up, made up of twenty-five people, representatives of all the political, religious and ethnic tendencies, that will have executive powers, nominate ministers and appoint commissions of engineers and experts to get the public institutions back working. The Council will have a role in preparing the Budget, establishing a market economy and privatising the public sector. Ambassador Bremer says that the market economy and political democracy will turn this country, that Saddam Hussein ruined with his frenetic arms expenditure and his state socialism, into a prosperous nation. 'If Lee Kwan Yoo managed to do it in Singapore, a country with no resources other than its people, imagine what Iraq can achieve with its vast riches. And I'm not just thinking of oil, but also of the land, which in the central region is even more fertile than the French Midi.'

A couple of weeks after my visit, the Council of Government was established, its twenty-five members reflecting a proportional representation of the political and social make-up of the country: thirteen Shiites, five Kurds, five Sunnis, one Turkmen and a Christian. Among them, three women and a communist. In Bremer's first statements, this Council was just to act as an 'assessor', that is, to have a decorative function, but it seems that due to the insistence of Sergio Vieira de Mello, the UN special envoy, the ambassador agreed to give it executive powers. When I ask him about this, he replies: 'I work very well with Vieira de Mello.'

According to his plan, this Council of Government will see the beginning of many different initiatives, with increasing popular participation in all areas, which will help foster democracy in a practical way. At the same time, an assembly or constituent commission, made up of respected and capable people, will establish a Constitution, 'guaranteeing freedom, legality and the rights of women', that the Iraqi people will need to ratify through a plebiscite. Then Iraq will celebrate the first free elections in its history, and he, along with his six hundred staff in this palace and the 140,000 US soldiers, will leave.

Bremer is emphatic that this will happen and that the terrorists that are ambushing and killing US soldiers on a daily basis will not weaken the resolve of the United States to carry this democratising process through to the end. Will US public opinion continue to support this, despite the very high economic cost and the cost in human lives? Without the slightest doubt. He receives bi-party delegations here on a daily basis, and despite the public disputes over the elections which have increased recently in the US, Democrats and Republicans agree that this must be carried out successfully, whatever the cost.

Who are the terrorists? Various groups that operate in a dispersed manner, without any central control. Common criminals that Saddam Hussein released from prison. Remnants of the dictator's armed forces, officers of the Republican Guard, Saddam's *fedayin*, torturers and other members of the political police (the *Mukhabarat*) who, for obvious reasons, are anxious that chaos should spread. International militants from Al Qaeda coming in from abroad as well as fighters sent by the most fanatical sectors of the Iran government that fears, with good reason, a free and democratic Iraq on its borders. These forces will be defeated, methodically and with determination, through the collaboration of the Iraqi people themselves, once the police and the local militias, who are already being trained by the coalition forces, begin to operate. The capture or death of Saddam Hussein (there is a twenty-five-million-dollar reward out for him) will free many Iraqis from the terror they still feel at the possibility that one day the tyrant will return to power and seek vengeance for having had his statues toppled.

I have heard it said many times, by Iraqis and foreigners, that Paul

Bremer is not in his element here, that Iraq, the Arab world, the Middle East, are exotic topics for him. That is not my impression. Quite the reverse – he seems very much at ease in the murky waters of the differences, enmities and affinities between the innumerable Iraqi factions, communities, ethnic groups and religions – the Shi'ites and Sunnis, the Arabs, Kurds, Turks, Armenians, Christians, etc. – and makes subtle observations about the difficulties in making this disparate mosaic of interests coexist. 'It will be difficult, but it will happen, it will happen,' he repeats on several occasions. For him the determining factor will be not so much the institutions that are set up and the electoral commissions, but rather the everyday things, the discovery that Iraqis are making of what freedom means in this country which, despite the insecurity, the lack of water and electricity and the rubbish, has, since 9 April, been open to some fifty newspapers and has seen the establishment of seventy political parties. 'All of this might appear somewhat anarchic. But what is happening is a real seismic shock, the direct and daily experience of freedom, of civic participation, at all levels of social life. Once they have understood what this means, the Iraqis will never again have it all snatched away from them. In many towns and neighbourhoods, real municipal bodies are already functioning through consensus, the residents are participating in, and funding, these initiatives with a freedom of action that this country has never known before.'

When I tell him that I have not heard a single Iraqi lament the fall of Saddam Hussein or even the bombings that brought an end to his regime, but that, by contrast, everyone that I have spoken to is upset, humiliated and offended at the passivity of the US forces in the face of the looting, robbery and arson that has destroyed Baghdad and ruined hundreds of thousands of its citizens, he reminds me that this happened 'when I wasn't here, when I was leading a quiet life in the private sphere'. But it is true: 'Not to have stopped the looting was the biggest mistake that we made, and it is going to cost us billions of dollars to repair this damage.' The United States will be unstinting in providing resources to reconstruct services and restore the infrastructure, so that the country can take off and be at the forefront of political and economic modernisation in the Middle East. He speaks with the conviction of a missionary, and I am sure that he believes what he is telling me.

Can this dream become a reality? Only, I think, if the United States or the United Nations take on the very high cost, in human losses, and in the outlay of considerable resources, of a long occupation. It is an illusion to think that the acts of sabotage, attacks and ambushes by different groups of the resistance, in a country where Ambassador Bremer estimates that there are about five million weapons in the hands of the civilian population, will be quickly crushed, even after the death or capture of Saddam Hussein. What is most likely is that for a long period of time, they will increase, the victims will multiply and the damage and sabotage to the infrastructure will be great, so that economic recovery and creation of employment, a pressing issue for seventy per cent of the population who are unemployed, will go slowly or will come to a halt. Furthermore, the adoption of democracy will not be a rapid process or one without difficulties in a country where the religious question presents complex problems for any real freedom and equality between the sexes. I'm not just talking about fanatical extremists, who are doubtless a minority. Even among ordinary and progressive Muslims and also the Christians in Iraq, when it comes to talking about women's issues, freedom of expression or the secular state, I have heard such strong prejudice and resistance that it will take a great deal of time and patience to overcome it. The animosity and the friction between the different religious, political and ethnic communities is currently very raw and perhaps inflamed now that they can be expressed openly and not be suffocated by a repressive authority. So it will also be difficult to establish a common consensus on which to build a democracy in this mosaic that is Iraq.

But nothing is impossible, of course. Especially if, as Bremer argues, the Iraqi people are beginning to use this freedom that they have never known, and can get used to it, in a climate in which basic order is guaranteed. Today this order can only come from the coalition forces, or – and this would be a better option – from an international peace force sponsored by the United Nations.

As I'm leaving Ambassador Bremer's office, Lieutenant Colonel

Juan Delgado and colonel Javier Sierra turn up. They breathe a sigh of relief. They have spent the entire morning looking for us in the labyrinth of enclosures, barriers, control points and patrols in the former domains of Saddam Hussein.

'We are alive,' we reassure them, 'but we're dying of thirst. Give us any cold drink, please, even one of those sweet Coca-Colas'.

The following morning, during the long journey through the desert from Baghdad to Amman, from where I'll fly back to Europe, I ask myself yet again – I have done so every day in Iraq – if I was right or wrong to oppose the war that the United States decided uni-laterally, without the support of the United Nations, to overthrow Saddam Hussein. The truth is that the two reasons offered by Bush and Blair to justify armed intervention – the existence of weapons of mass destruction and the link between the Iraqi government and the Al Qaeda terrorists – have not been proven and, at this moment, seem more improbable. Formally, then, the reasons I had to oppose the war were valid.

But what if the argument to intervene had been, clearly and explicitly, to put an end to an execrable and genocidal tyranny which had caused innumerable deaths and kept a whole nation in obscu-rantism and barbarity, and to restore their sovereignty? Three months ago, I'm not so sure, but now, with what I have seen and heard in this short stay, I would have supported the intervention, without hesitation. Without the intervention, Saddam Hussein might have fallen, but from a coup organised within his own clique, which would have prolonged the tyranny indefinitely, with other despots taking his place. And the fate of the overwhelming majority of Iraqis would remain the same for an indefinite time, a life of shame and backwardness. That isn't a pessimistic view – just look around the whole of the Middle East – but a strictly realistic one. All the suffering that the armed intervention has inflicted on the Iraqi people is small compared to the horror they suffered under Saddam Hussein. Now, for the first time in its long history, they have the chance to break the vicious circle of dictatorship after dictatorship that they have lived under and – like Germany and Japan after the war – begin a new phase, embracing the culture of freedom, the only thing that can ward off any resurrection of the past. For this to become a reality depends not just on the Iraqis, although theirs, of course, is the main responsibility. It depends above all now on the cooperation and the material and political support of the democratic countries of the entire world, beginning with the European Union.

25 June–6 July 2003

A Story about Rats

When President Fujimori fled Peru and the dictatorship that he headed for ten years collapsed like a deck of cards, the new people in charge, who had been elected by Congress to ensure a clean electoral process, found that the Government Palace had been completely stripped by its former occupants (they had taken away even the ashtrays and the sheets) and had been horribly decorated with *huachafo* touches (*huachafería* is the Peruvian variant of vulgar taste).

They also found that the former House of Pizarro was a rats' nest. The company hired to cleanse the palace of rats captured and counted before burning them – they assured me that these were round figures – some 6,200 rodents which had been lodging in the basements, the nooks, the shelves and the recesses of the building that for four-and-a-half centuries has been an emblem of the history of Peru.

I see these palace rats bequeathed by the dictatorship to a democracy that is now rising from the ashes, in the midst of great difficulties, as an allegory for what is happening in Peru. In many respects the changes are great and exciting. The country has recovered its liberty, its freedom of speech, and criticism is now wide-ranging and often quite fierce, parties and political leaders debate and contest positions on all sides, and the fight against the corruption of the infamous decade has not stopped. Quite the reverse – for the first time in the history of Peru we find a considerable number of military men, businessmen, media owners, traffickers of influence and privilege, behind bars for robbery and other crimes committed under the protection of the authoritarian regime, and the Judiciary, which is being purged, is going about its business quite independently and firmly. It is the case that a good number of those accused of fraud, corruption and violations have fled, within the country or abroad, before the law could catch up with them. But, even so, for once it seems that there will be no impunity – no cleaning of the slate and starting again – for a large number of people who, over ten years, committed serious crimes against human rights and democracy, and pillaged the state, amassing vast fortunes.

This encouraging outlook is somewhat overshadowed by the deep economic crisis which has impoverished the country, caused very high unemployment and a fall in the standard of living, and has hit, with particular brutality, the most disadvantaged sectors. For that reason, social demands are very high, which doubtless caused President Toledo to make exaggerated promises in his electoral campaign which can never be fulfilled. All this has caused a state of unrest and social conflict, which makes agreement difficult.

To a large extent the economic crisis is a direct consequence of the systematic and widespread plunder that the gang headed by Fujimori and Montesinos perpetrated over ten years, by use of force and coercion. To give you an idea: of the almost ten billion dollars that came into the state's coffers over this period as a result of privatisations, which were usually only carried through to transfer public monopolies over to private monopolies or to benefit groups that were complicit with, or acted as straw men for, the regime's inner circle, not a single cent remains. Taking off certain concrete debt repayments and payments to cover the fiscal deficit, it is the case that most of this enormous sum mysteriously disappeared without trace. That is, it became lost in the labyrinth of fiscal havens and secret bank accounts of the Fujimori mafia who have been evicted from power but have left the country in a comatose economic state.

The economic power of this Fujimori mafia is almost intact because very little money has been recuperated or frozen in the foreign bank accounts of the numerous guilty parties. And the recent experience of countries that have liberated themselves from kleptomaniac dictatorial regimes and tried to recoup what has been stolen shows us that, unfortunately, we should not hold out too much hope of getting back the money stolen by the henchmen (and some hench-women) of the dictatorship.

How was it possible that a regime of this nature, controlled by shameless, undisguised villains who not only committed innumer-able abuses every day, but also were recorded by Vladimiro Mon-tesinos in hundreds and perhaps thousands of videos, which document, day after day, the extraordinary scope of the corruption, could be, throughout most of these ten years of dishonour, a *popular* regime? Because, to the shame of Peruvians, it was popular, right up to the last two years, perhaps less, of its insolent existence. The reply to this question is: thanks to the intelligent and unscrupulous manipulation of the media, especially the television channels acces-sible to all viewers, that the dictatorship placed at its service, by buy-ing off the owners.

The way in which Montesinos, the handy evil genius of the dicta-torship's intelligence service, proceeded was both subtle and brutal. He blackmailed some media organisations through the tax office. In return for silence, servility and complicity, he could withdraw the sword of Damocles of heavy taxation that could threaten the sur-vival of a company. Those who did not comply had to pay their debts, which increased at the whim of the regime; in other cases, the operation was cruder and more direct: the media owners sold for hard cash their editorials, their headlines and their news stories. They introduced lies, spread rumours or kept silent about certain issues in order to bolster the regime's campaign of propaganda, and they vilified and discredited critics of the regime in invective cam-paigns that Montesinos thought up, administered and orchestrated. This demagogic orchestration of public opinion through the main media outlets was the main factor in the popularity of a regime that lived off and in lies.

When the journalists of Channel 2 – Latin Frequency – rebelled against these methods and began to tell the truth – they revealed the millions that Montesinos was putting into his accounts and spoke of some of the murders by the dictatorship's death squads – the regime took away the owner, Baruch Ivcher's Peruvian nationality and handed his channel over to minority shareholders (now in prison) that he had bribed. From that point on, Channel 2 was also, like the rest, a mouthpiece for the regime's disgusting political actions.

The owners of the two most powerful channels in the country – 4 and 5 – were bought with dollar bills, many millions of them. And naturally, they were also filmed by Montesinos, appearing in scenes that make one nauseous, counting their pyramids of dollars and, in revoltingly coarse tones, begging the lord and master of the strong-arm regime for even more millions in return for their work as media acolytes. These characters have now fled the country: Crousillat to Miami and Schutz to Argentina. But, even though it beggars belief, they remain the owners and controllers of the channels that they rented out to the dictatorship to manipulate public opinion, broadcasting disinformation and lies, spreading calumnies, defending electoral fraud and violation of the Constitution and, of course, keeping out the opposition, to such a degree that in the last fraudulent elections, they did not even broadcast the advertisements paid for by the candidates opposing Fujimori. To keep up appearances, the fugitives have transferred their shares to family members who act as fronts.

In my opinion, to leave these channels in the hands of people who committed, through them, the worst crime that can be committed against a society – destroying democracy and supporting a dictatorship – would be a mortal danger for the democracy that is now beginning to surface in Peru, surrounded by lurking threats, after an abject decade. It would be the same as leaving in the hands of its owners a laboratory licensed to produce medicines that instead manufactured narcotics, or leaving a gun in the hands of someone who has just committed a murder. The criminal weapon that these fugitives used were the licences that they sold to the dictatorship and which they are now using through intermediaries gradually to undermine democracy. In an act of real provocation, not just to democracy but to common decency, one of these channels is looking to relaunch a 'news' programme fronted by one of the worst media henchmen of the dictatorship, Nicolás Lúcar, whose methods I bear testimony to, because at the time of the government coup, he prepared an ambush for me that I naïvely fell into. He offered me his programme to give my opinion of what was happening in Peru and, when the interview was to be broadcast, cut off my microphone; while I was moving my mouth without any sound coming out, he proceeded to spew out Fujimori propaganda and slogans. His return to the screen is a symbol of the shameless way in which the Fujimori mafia has started out on a new campaign to frustrate the democratisation process in Peru.

These licences must be withdrawn, not by force but by rigorously following legal procedures to ensure freedom of expression and criticism that these people helped to violate and now seek to debase in order to obstruct the democratic transition. Naturally the process must look to transfer these licences to other private enterprises through a transparent procedure, closely monitored internationally, so that neither the government nor the state of Peru can benefit directly or indirectly from this transfer, or get their hands on these companies, because, were that to happen, the cure would be as harmful as the illness. But there are many different ways of guaranteeing this transfer within civil society, without government intervention, through the involvement of organisations of proven independence – international communications associations and prestigious international auditors – to clear this obstacle that obstructs the complex process of re-establishing law and liberty in Peru. This democracy will never become a reality while, as in the Palace of Government before the purging of the rats, the vermin that the dictatorship adopted remain in their caves and hiding places preparing new attacks on freedom, in the name of freedom!

Lima, December 2001

The Captain in His Labyrinth

There are echoes of the elegant and baroque paradoxes we find in Borges's stories in the current plight of Captain Vladimiro Montesinos, who is buried alive in one of the cells for high-risk terrorists that he himself designed, in the Callao Naval base, for Abimael Guzmán – Comrade Gonzalo of the Shining Path group – and Victor Polay from the MTRA (Túpac Amaru Revolutionary Movement), the leaders of the two organisations that immersed Peru in violence in the eighties. The ironic and humorous note to this, also very Borgesian, is not just that Fujimori's right-hand man declared that he was on hunger strike, in protest against the dreadful conditions in the prison, but that – lying and greedy to the last – he cheated during his strike, eating chocolates that he had hidden in his trousers.

Montesinos belongs to an ancient lineage – of discreet and violent criminals who are like the shadows of the tyrants they both serve and profit by in their secret dealings. They use terror and commit major state crimes as well as numerous robberies, following the orders of, and in close complicity with, their masters, who see them as both absolutely essential but also, and with good reason, very suspicious. Dictatorships suppurate such people, the way infections suppurate pus, and almost all of them, such as Stalin's Beria, Perón's Sorcerer López Rega, Pérez Jiménez's Pedro Estrada, and Trujillo's Colonel Abbés García usually die – as millionaires in Paris or in mysterious, violent deaths – without opening their mouths, taking with them to hell the precise details of their misdeeds.

This is the big difference between this universal history of authoritarian infamy and the now famous Vladimiro Montesinos. Unlike
others of his kind, who remained silent about their crimes, he is
going to talk. He has already started talking, like a parrot, trying to
show that no one is a villain in a society where everyone is a villain
and where villainy is the only political and moral norm that is universally respected. To prove the point he says that he has some thirty thousand videos that document the ethical depravity and the civic
filth of his compatriots, something which, if it is true, would make
him not the high-profile criminal that the press writes about, but
rather a hard-working Peruvian who, through skill and Machiavel-
lian stratagems, created the conditions whereby an immense number of his compatriots could act on a deep-seated propensity: to sell
out to a dictatorship and fill their pockets in the shortest time possible.

It is improbable that this apocalyptic line of defence will be successful; it is almost certain that – if the stars of this extraordinary
video collection do not arrange for him to die of a heart attack or by
suicide beforehand – the Law will decide that this singular character
will spend, like Abimael Guzmán and Víctor Polay, men as cruel and
completely lacking in scruples as him, most of the rest of his remaining life behind bars. Nothing would be more just, of course:
although the long list of tyrannies that Peru has suffered has created
a good number of rogues, torturers and despoilers of the public
purse, none of them had ever before wielded so much power or done
so much damage as this obscure captain who was thrown out of the
army for selling military secrets to the CIA, this lawyer and front-
man for drug-runners, a man who gave a 'legal' veneer to the abuses to the legal system perpetrated by Fujimori, his right-hand man in
the coup that destroyed Peruvian democracy in 1992, a gun-runner
for the Colombian guerrilla groups, a representative of the big drugs
cartels, to which he offered the services of the army and the use of
Peruvian territory in the Amazon, the head and organiser of the state
terrorist commando groups that, between 1990 and 2000, tortured,
assassinated and caused thousands of people to disappear who were
suspected of being subversives, a blackmailer, a thief and a system-

atic manipulator of the Judiciary and the media which, with very few exceptions, he bought, bribed or intimidated until they gave their unconditional support to the abuses and violations committed by the dictatorship.

A mathematician has taken the trouble to calculate how many hours of tape would be on these thirty thousand videos – at an average of two hours a video – and has concluded that the ten years of the Fujimori regime would not be long enough for a production on such a scale unless, in addition to his office in the Intelligence Service, which Montesinos turned into a secret film studio after Fujimori took power in 1990 and appointed Montesinos to his coveted post, there were several other camouflaged studios where the SIM also secretly filmed other operations of pillage and political intrigue by the regime. We cannot discount this theory, of course. But it is likely that the figure is exaggerated, the desperate boasting of an official in a tight corner wanting to scare his likely prosecutors. However, even if only ten per cent of these videos exist and, as happened with Fujimori when he broke into Montesinos's house, took the videos that incriminated him and escaped with them to Japan, many other members of the Fujimori mafia have managed to steal or destroy the videos that they star in, what is left – there are some fifteen hundred tapes in the hands of the Judiciary – is a precious, rare document, unprecedented in history, that reveals in a direct and vivid fashion the organisation and the extent - the extraordinary extent – of corruption in an authoritarian regime. For this alone, future historians will always be grateful to Vladimiro Montesinos.

There has been a great deal of speculation about what prompted him from the outset to film these scenes which both implicated legally and politically the military, professionals, judges, businessmen, bankers, journalists, and government and opposition local officials and parliamentarians, but also incriminated himself with a document that, with a sudden change of government, as happened in Peru, would be seen as a form of hara-kiri. The accepted view is that he filmed his accomplices so that he could blackmail them and bring them into line should the need arise. There is no doubt that to have, for example, Fujimori's ministers captured on film by the hidden cameras, receiving every month thirty-thousand-dollar supplements to their salary, would turn these poor mercenary devils into loyal servants of the head of the SIM when it came to signing specific decrees. And it is not surprising that the newspaper editors or heads of television channels that received thousands or millions of dollars – that they had to count, note by note, patiently, observed by the hidden camera – would then become tame supporters of government policy and implacable opponents of anyone daring to criticise its policy.

But when you see these videos, or read the transcriptions of the conversations, you realise that they are more than just a form of coercion. They offer a particular, utterly contemptuous, view of humankind; a constant reiteration of how cheap and grimy and abject people can be when they move into a sphere where the dictator holds sway and can tempt them. They were important public figures in the country, who enjoyed great prestige and a high profile because of their office, their influence, their money, their stripes, their surnames or because of services rendered in the past. There is an entire philosophy underpinning this long sequence of images where a single scene is repeated time and again, with minimal variation, with different people and voices: some evasive and hypocritical preliminaries, to justify the imminent transaction with flatulent arguments, and then, in a few words, the essential: How much? That much! Right away and in cash.

In the ten years of the Fujimori dictatorship – perhaps the most sinister and divisive that we have ever suffered and without any doubt the most corrupt – Montesinos's office was visited not only by mediocre opportunists and the usual suspect politicos who, like vermin in putrid waters, always prosper during strong-arm regimes. There were also people who appeared respectable, with seemingly decent political or professional credentials, and a considerable number of successful businessmen – including one of the richest men in Peru – who, because of their influence, power and wealth, one would have thought of as incapable of getting involved in such ignominious dealings. Some of this human filth that went to Montesinos's office to sell themselves and sell the best thing that Peru had – a democratic system re-established with difficulty in 1980 after twelve years of military dictatorship – for fistfuls or suitcases full of dollars, for tax breaks for their companies, to win a hearing, or gain a tender, a ministry or a parliamentary job – were people known to me and whose support of the dictatorship I thought was 'pure', a production of the sad conviction that seems so widespread among the wrongly named Peruvian ruling class: that a country like ours needs a strong hand in order to progress because the Peruvian people are not yet ready for democracy.

I trust that the government of Alejandro Toledo, which is coming to office after clean elections that nobody has disputed, can show to the world that this belief is as false as the falsifiers that brought the political process into disrepute. It is clear that the new government is not able to resolve the immense problems facing the Peruvian people, which the dictatorship aggravated while adding a raft of new problems. But it can and must establish the foundations for any future resolution of these problems by preventing, once and for all, the possibility of a further collapse of the constitutional order. For that reason it must pursue the moral policy that it has initiated so firmly, giving judges all the support they need to judge and sentence criminals and thieves, starting at the top. It is a unique opportunity. The putrefaction of the Fujimori regime had spread to such an extent that when it collapsed, all the institutions collapsed with it. This means that now all the institutions – the Armed Forces, the Judiciary, the Administration – can be reformed root and branch. And the videos that, unintentionally, Montesinos has bequeathed so opportunely to democracy must be used to cleanse and reform this democracy and its leaders in the most limpid way.

Marbella, 18 July 2001

The Pinochet Affair

The ruling of the British magistrate Roland Bartle is another step towards the extradition of General Pinochet to Spain to be tried for crimes committed against human rights during the seventeen years of the dictatorship he presided over. This is a historical judgement that extends well beyond the particular case of Chile, and should be greeted with jubilation by all those millions of people across the world who have been persecuted, ill-treated or silenced for their ideas, and by all those who are not content for the culture and practice of democracy to be the prerogative of a mere handful of countries, while the barbarity of despotism and autocracy holds sway over seventy-five per cent of the planet.

People who, without being in favour of dictatorial regimes, question the right of Spain and the United Kingdom to extradite the ex-dictator, put forward a series of arguments that, for me, do not stand up to close scrutiny. The most common of these arguments is pragmatic: the international pursuit of Pinochet is endangering the Chilean transition to democracy and might destabilise the present government, aggravate and inflame the political debate, and even provoke a new coup. This doom scenario is not borne out by the facts. Quite the reverse: the reality is that, although it is very virulent, the dispute between those for and against Pinochet being tried outside Chile is being spearheaded by radical minorities, while most of Chilean society follows it at a distance and with increasing indifference. The national debate about the forthcoming elections is much more intense, and in this debate – something that the international media tend to leave out – the Pinochet affair is no longer a central issue, in what seems like a tactical (and very sensible) agreement between the main candidates, Lagos (centre left) and Lavín (centre right).

There is no serious argument to support the gloomy prediction that the Pinochet affair will destroy Chilean democracy. The opposite is true, as the *New York Times* has recently shown in a report on the state of justice in the country. The prosecution of Pinochet in Spain has seen a revival of legal initiatives in Chile against the crimes and abuses committed during the dictatorship, and in the last twelve months twenty-six officers accused of these crimes have been imprisoned after court cases. This is a very clear demonstration that Chilean judges have a greater willingness and freedom to act on this issue now that the obstacle to the normal development of justice – the presence of the ex-dictator, who, as a senator elected for life to one of the ruling bodies of the Chilean state, cannot be impeached – has been removed. Instead of weakening democracy, international action against Pinochet is helping to complete and accelerate the democratisation process that is already firmly rooted in Chile.

Another objection to the prosecution of Pinochet by Judge Baltazar Garzón is based on nationalism: the violation of national sovereignty implied in judging the ex-dictator outside his own country. This is an extraordinarily anachronistic argument which ignores the current historical moment of globalisation, the systematic erosion of borders and of the nineteenth-century concept of the nation state. The economy has led the great modern onslaught against this narrow and exclusive view of sovereignty, which is incompatible with the interdependence that the development of science, technology, information, commerce and culture has established between all the societies of the world at the end of the twentieth century. Why should justice be excluded from this general process of internationalisation of contemporary life? In fact, it is not excluded. No one objects if common criminals, drug-runners or smugglers are prosecuted and sentenced outside their 'countries'; quite the reverse – it is normal for governments to seek the joint action of other countries against their criminals (for example, with regard to terrorism). Why should crimes and abuses against human rights be a separate case? Are these crimes less serious from an ethical or legal point of view?

The importance of the Pinochet affair is, precisely, that it sets a precedent to end the impunity that a great many little tyrants and satraps have enjoyed. For up until now, after perpetrating their misdeeds, robbing the public purse and amassing large fortunes, they have been able to retire and enjoy a magnificent old age, free of any sanction. Now everyone from Baby Doc to General Cedras, from Idi Amin to Menghistu, from Fidel Castro to Saddam Hussein, and so many others of the same ilk know that they will not be able to live peacefully, that wherever they go and wherever they are, the law can reach them and demand that they answer for their crimes. The deterrent effect that this might have on potential coup plotters should not be underestimated.

There are people who argue that instead of dissuading future dictators, the legal pursuit of Pinochet will encourage those who have usurped power to remain entrenched, and not commit the ex-dictator's error of giving up office, that had made him invulnerable to sanctions. People that think this must have an image of dictators as archangels, for they believe that they retire from power because one day they will become good or democratic, and that we must encourage them towards this moral and political conversion by guaranteeing them impunity in advance. The truth is that never in history has a dictator stopped being a dictator by choice, through a sudden spiritual, ideological or ethical transformation. All of them would like to stay in power for ever (this is true of many democratic governments too, of course), and if they do not manage to do so it is simply because they cannot, because a particular situation at a specific moment forces them, irresistibly, to leave. Fidel Castro, Colonel Gaddafi, Saddam Hussein and their kind will not cut short by a single moment their stay in power if the legal prosecution of Pinochet is stopped.

Another reason given against the Pinochet prosecution is the different criteria that some media and some intellectuals and politicians use to judge dictatorships: why do the satraps of the left not deserve

332

the same condemnation as the satraps of the right? Has Pinochet been more cruel and bloodthirsty to his opponents during his seventeen years as dictator than Fidel Castro during his forty years of tyranny? Anyone reasonably well informed knows that, although they are ideologically different, both men are responsible for unspeakable abuses against very basic human rights, which should mean that they would receive the same condemnation and sanctions from the international democratic community. However, as we know, while not one democratic government defended Pinochet, only a tiny number of democratic governments dare to call Fidel Castro what he really is: a little satrap with bloodstained hands. And in a few days, twenty or so Spanish American presidents and prime ministers are going to travel down to Havana, in a grotesque political coven, to embrace this repugnant character and to legitimate him, signing with him once again, without their hands trembling or their faces falling with shame, a declaration in favour of freedom and legality as the necessary framework for the development of the Spanish American community.

Of course, this double standard in morality (this 'moral hemiplegia' in the words of Jean-François Revel) when it comes to dealing with dictators of the right or of the left is outrageous, in particular when it comes from the mouths or the pens of cynical people who call themselves democratic or, even more ridiculous, progressive. However, to turn this sense of outrage into a reason for exonerating Pinochet of any guilt since (for now) one cannot punish him and Fidel Castro in the same way, would give carte blanche to the excesses of fascist dictators since communist dictators are often less vulnerable than them to international sanction. It would be like saying that that since we have no absolute and universal system of justice, then humanity should abandon any form of justice, however relative and partial. This is a fundamentalist and Manichean attitude that is at variance with social reality, where it is simply not possible to aspire to perfection and the absolute in any sphere. In the penal system it is always preferable that a murderer be judged and sentenced even though many others escape punishment for their crimes. The same is true for crimes against human rights. The 'Pinochet affair' is encouraging from a moral, legal and political point of view because it opens the door, in future, for other dictators – whatever their politics – to be investigated and punished for their crimes, and also because, in this particular case, concrete victims of torture, murder, imprisonment and robbery are receiving lawful, if belated, redress. This is good news for all victims of persecution and abuse the world over, a sign that, finally, a new era is beginning in the history of humanity in which the great political criminals can be taken to court to answer for their crimes, without being able to hide behind 'national sovereignty' or amnesties that they instituted when they were in power, and go off into retirement with a clear conscience and their pockets stuffed with money. The fact that it is a right-wing and not a left-wing dictator who is the first in what will be in the future – and this depends on all of us, not just on Judge Baltazar Garzón – a long list of satraps to be punished is an incidental detail that should not in any way affect the transcendent importance of the Pinochet affair from a legal point of view. It depends on genuine democrats, on the true lovers of liberty and law throughout the world, to ensure that what has happened with Pinochet is not the exception but rather the rule, not a mere victory for the 'left' but a first effective legal act aimed at bringing about a drastic reduction in political murders and torture across the world, irrespective of who commits them and on whatever religious or political pretext. To some extent, by putting Pinochet in the dock, the Spanish and British judges have summoned to appear in court with him an entire harmful and immemorial dynasty.

Madrid, October 1999

Chilean Yawns

Anyone like me, who has been following closely the elections in Chile, where Michelle Bachelet, the centre-left candidate, defeated the centre-right candidate, must have felt both envy and considerable surprise. Was Chile a Latin American country? For the truth is that this election campaign seemed like one of those boring civic contests, where, say, the Swiss or the Swedes change or re-elect their government after a certain number of years, rather than a Third World election where countries going to the ballot box are staking their political model, their social organisation and often even their very survival.

In a typical Third World election, everything seems to be in question and goes back to square one, from the very nature of the institutions to the political economy and the relations between government and society. The election result can turn everything around, which means that countries can suddenly go backwards, losing overnight what they have gained over the years, or else carry on indefinitely along the wrong path. That's why it is normal in underdeveloped countries to be continually jumping, usually jumping backwards rather than forwards, or simply jumping on the spot.

Although it is not a First World country – it is still some way from being so – Chile is not an underdeveloped country. In the last quarter of a century it has progressed systematically, consolidating democracy, opening up its economy and strengthening its civil society in a way that has no equal in Latin America. It has reduced the level of those living in poverty to 18% (the average in Latin America is 45%), a rate of progress comparable to Ireland or Spain, and its middle class has grown consistently, so that now it is, in comparative terms, the largest in Latin America. One million Chileans have escaped poverty in the last ten years. This is due to the extraordinary stability of Chilean society, which can attract all the foreign investment it wants, and can equally sign free-trade agreements with half the world (with the United States, the European Union and South Korea, and now it is negotiating agreements with India, China and Japan).

All this has come out very clearly in these elections. In the debate between Michelle Bachelet and Sebastián Piñera, which took place a few days before the end of the second round, you would have had to have been psychic or a diviner to discover on which points the candidates from the left and the right disagreed openly. Despite their respective attempts to distance themselves from each other, the truth is that their differences are not important. Piñera, for example, wants to put more police on the street than Bachelet.

When an open society reaches these levels of consensus, it is a long way down the road of civilisation. This is a word that finds little favour with intellectuals who are infatuated with barbarism – and it is true that, seen from a distance and from somewhere safe, barbarism seems much more amusing and exciting than civilisation, that smacks of tedium and routine – but it is the most effective framework for defeating hunger, unemployment, ignorance, human rights abuses and corruption. And it is the only environment that guarantees its citizens freedom of expression.

President Lagos left power with a 75% approval rate, a really extraordinary figure in a democracy: only dictators, who can massage the figures, would seem to have that level of popularity. In the case of Ricardo Lagos it is absolutely deserved. He has been a socialist who, like Felipe González or Tony Blair, knew how to take advantage of the lessons of history and promote, without any sense of inferiority, a modern political economy which was liberal, open to the world, supported private initiatives and, during his government, led to significant growth.

He is also an intelligent politician, a man of ideas, a careful speaker, not charismatic, a leader who deserves the highest praise of all: that he left his country much better off than when he found it. During his administration, the anti-democratic traces of the Pinochet dictatorship were confronted and dealt with. And the ex-dictator himself, during these years, thanks to the tenacious and patient work of several judges, has appeared before the world stripped of the mask of the honest autocrat that his supporters had fashioned for him. Nobody would now dare to say that Pinochet was 'the only dictator who did not steal'. He did steal, large amounts, which is why he and his family and his close associates are now being tried or investigated for suspect transactions to the value of more than thirty-five million dollars.

In these elections the Chilean right, thanks to Sebastián Piñera, has managed to purge a great deal if not all of its original sin: its links with the dictator. Piñera campaigned against the dictator in the referendum, and no one that knows him could doubt his democratic convictions. Many people thought that his major economic holdings would get in the way of his political leadership. But that was not the case, and the energy and intelligence with which he conducted his campaign would seem to have guaranteed him a solid future as the leader of the Chilean right.

The victory of Michelle Bachelet, among other things, showed the Chilean people willing to make moral redress to all those people who were abused, tortured, exiled or silenced during the years of the dictatorship. And it is a giant step forward towards equality between men and women in a country where machismo seemed unmovable. (It was the last country in Latin America to allow divorce.) But it is not just the rights of women that will be boosted by this new president. Secularisation, that fundamental prerequisite for democratic progress, will also be encouraged. The Catholic Church has had a much stronger influence in Chile than in the rest of Latin America. Despite all these promising signs, Chile cannot rest on its laurels if it wants to continue to progress. One of its greatest problems is that it does not have energy resources to meet the increasing demands of its expanding industry and industrial infrastructure. For this reason it is essential that Chile looks to repair relations with its neighbours, especially with Bolivia. The dispute with Bolivia goes back to the War of the Pacific in 1879, when Bolivia lost its access to the sea. One of the great challenges facing Michelle Bachelet's government is to solve once and for all this dispute with Bolivia and also its maritime disagreements with Peru, so that active collaboration between these three countries can bring tangible benefits to all: the energy that Chile needs and that Bolivia has in abundance, the opening up of the prosperous Chilean market to Bolivian and Peruvian goods, and the investment and technology that Chile could bring to its neighbours, which they need for their own development. Such collaboration would also mean that they could put a stop to, and begin to reduce, the arms build-up in the region, which has had such disastrous consequences in the past and which currently creates suspicion and mistrust, a fertile breeding ground for xenophobic nationalism. Chile spends more on arms than any other country in South America, and under Lagos alone it spent two-and-a-half billion dollars on military equipment.

Compared with its neighbours, Chile is today a very boring country. By contrast, we Peruvians, Bolivians, Argentines and Ecuadorians live dangerously and never get bored. That is why we get what we get. Not like the Chileans, who now have to get their kicks through literature or the movies or sport rather than in politics.

Lima, January 2006

338

The Odyssey of Flora Tristán

The nineteenth century was not just the century of the novel and of nationalism: it was also the century of utopias. The fault lay with the French Revolution of 1789: the upheavals and social transformations brought about by the Revolution convinced both its supporters and its opponents, not just in France but throughout the entire world, that history could be fashioned like a sculpture, until it reached the perfection of a work of art. There was one condition: a plan or a theoretical model should be outlined in advance, that could then be neatly imposed on reality. This idea can be traced back a long way, at least to classical Greece. In the Renaissance, it appeared in such important works as Sir Thomas More's *Utopia*, which established a genre that continues to this day. But it was in the nineteenth century that the idea was at its most powerful and seductive, generating daring intellectual projects and inflaming the imagination and idealism (and sometimes the madness) of so many thinkers, revolutionaries or ordinary citizens. It was the conviction that, with the right ideas, carried through selflessly and courageously, one could create paradise on earth and establish a society without contradictions or injustice, where men and women could live in peace and order, sharing the benefits of the three principles of 1789 in a harmonious blend: liberty, equality and fraternity.

The whole of the nineteenth century is full of utopias and utopian thinkers. Alongside groups committed to violent action, like those formed by the disciples of François-Noël Babeuf (1746–97), we find remarkable thinkers like Saint-Simon (1760–1825) and Charles Fourier (1772–1837), daring businessmen like the Scot Robert Owen, men of action and adventurers, among whom the Russian anarchist Mikhail Bakunin (1814–76) stands out, flamboyant dreamers like Etienne Cabet (1788–1856) or delirious examples of the genre like Jules-Simon Ganneau (1806–51), the messianic founder of *Evadisme*. The most important of all the nineteenth-century utopian thinkers, in historical terms, was, without doubt, Karl Marx, whose 'scientific' utopia would incorporate much of this earlier thought and end up overriding it.

Flora Tristán (1803–44) belongs to this lineage of great nonconformists, radical opponents of the society that they were born into, believing fanatically that it was possible to reform society root and branch, eradicate injustice and suffering and establish human happiness. She was a bold and romantic campaigner for justice who, first in her difficult life, plagued by adversity, then in her writings and finally in the passionate militancy of the last two years of her life, offered an example of rebelliousness, daring, idealism, naïvety, truculence and adventurousness which fully justifies the praise she received from the father of Surrealism, André Breton: *'Il n'est peut-être pas de destinée féminine qui, au firmament de l'esprit, laisse un sillage aussi long et aussi lumineux'*. ('There is perhaps no feminine destiny that, in the firmament of the spirit, has left such a long and luminous trace.') The word 'feminine' is key here. Not just because in the vast panoply of nineteenth-century social utopian thinkers, Flora Tristán is the only woman, but also, fundamentally, because her desire to reconstruct society in its entirety stemmed from her indignation at the discrimination and servitude that women of her time suffered and which she herself experienced more than most.

Two traumatic experiences and a trip to Peru were the decisive events in the life of Flora Tristán, who was born in Paris on 7 April 1803 and christened with the long, grandiose name of Flora Celestina Teresa Enriqueta Tristán Mocoso: her birth and her marriage. Her father, a Peruvian, Don Mariano Tristán y Mocoso, belonged to a very prosperous and powerful family and served in the armies of the King of Spain. Her mother, Anne-Pierre Laisnay, a Frenchwoman, had fled the Revolution and taken refuge in Bilbao. It was there that they met and apparently were joined – there is no proof of this – in a religious marriage conducted by a French priest, another exile, which had no legal status. For that reason, Flora was born as an illegitimate child, a shameful condition which, from the cradle, condemned her to life as a 'pariah', a term that she would later use insolently in the title of the most famous of her books, *Peregrinaciones de una paria* (*Peregrinations of a Pariah*, 1837). When her father died in June 1807, when the child was not yet five, mother and daughter, since they lacked any legal status, were evicted from the elegant property they lived in, in Vaugirard, and all Don Mariano's possessions reverted to the family in Peru. After a few years, as their situation declined, we find Flora and her mother living in a poor neighbourhood in Paris – around the Place Maubert – and the young girl beginning to work mixing colours in the print shop of the painter and printer André Chazal, who fell in love with her. Their wedding, on 3 February 1821, was, for Flora, a catastrophe that would affect her life even more dramatically than her illegitimacy.

This was because, from the outset, she felt that this marriage made her a mere appendix of her husband, a child-breeder – she had three children in four years – someone completely deprived of her own life and freedom. It was from this time that Flora became convinced that matrimony was an intolerable institution, a commercial transaction in which a woman was sold to a man, thus becoming to all intents and purposes his slave, for life, because divorce had been abolished with the Restoration. And, at the same time, she began instinctively to reject motherhood and to develop a deep distrust of sex, which she saw as part of women's servitude, of their humiliating subjugation to men.

When she was twenty-two, Flora committed the boldest act of her life, which would definitively mark out her destiny as a pariah and a rebel: she left her home, taking her children with her, which not only brought her into great disrepute because of the prevailing moral sanctions of the time, but was also an illegal act for which she could have been imprisoned if André Chazal had reported her. From this time on, between 1825 and 1830, we enter an unclear period in her life about which we know very little, and the little that we do know comes from her and has probably been doctored to hide the depressing truth. What is clear is that in these years she was living on the run, in hiding, in very difficult circumstances – her mother did not approve of what she was doing and from that time their relationship appears to have ended – living with the constant fear that André Chazal, or the authorities, would catch up with her. Two of her three children would die in the following years; the only survivor was Aline Marie (the future mother of Paul Gauguin), who spent most of her childhood in the country, being looked after by different women while her mother hid and earned a living in whatever way she could. Later she would say that she was employed as a travelling companion (it is very likely that she was a mere servant) for an English family whom she accompanied throughout Europe, making her first trip to England. None of this is certain, and anything could have been possible in these years. What is absolutely certain is that they must have been very hard for Flora and must have shaped her strong character, her limitless courage, her bravery and her conviction that the world was badly made, unjust, brutal and discriminatory, and that the main victims of the prevailing injustice were women.

Flora's trip to Peru – where she was to live for a year – was, according to her, quite accidental, something out of a romantic novel. At an inn in Paris she had run into Zacharie Chabrié, a ship's captain who often travelled between France and Peru. In Arequipa he had met the wealthy and powerful Tristán family, whose head was Don Pío Tristán y Mocoso, the younger brother of Don Mariano, Flora's father. It was Chabrié, she said, who convinced her to write to her uncle. She did so in a heartfelt, imploring letter, referring to the hardship and difficulties that she and her mother had endured since the death of her father, due to her parents' irregular marriage, and asking for assistance and even for recognition. Months later Don Pío replied with an astute letter in which, alongside the expressions of affection for his recently appeared little niece, and protesting his love for his brother Mariano, he firmly states that he will not legally recognise a woman who, by her own admission, had been born in an illegal union. But he sent her some money of his own and some other money from her grandmother, who was still alive.

After three years of matrimonial disputes with Chazal and repeated attempts to escape, in April 1833 Flora finally embarked, in Bordeaux, on the boat that would take her to Peru. Her captain was none other than Zacharie Chabrié. The six-month crossing, in the company of sixteen men – she was the only woman – had a Homeric element to it. Flora stayed in Arequipa for eight months and in Lima for two months before returning to France in the middle of 1834. This is the transitional moment in her life, which separates the rebellious, confused young woman who fled her husband and dreamed of a stroke of fortune – to be recognised as the daughter of Don Mariano by her Peruvian family and thus suddenly acquire legitimacy and fortune – from the social militant, the writer and the revolutionary who would resolutely direct her life to fighting, with her pen and her words, for social justice, for the emancipation of women.

In Arequipa, her uncle Don Pío dashed her hopes of being recognised as a legitimate daughter and thus claiming her birthright. But this frustration was to some extent alleviated by the good life that she had in the family house, surrounded by servants and slaves, spoiled and flattered by the Tristán tribe, and sought after and courted by Arequipa's 'good society', which was turned upside down by the arrival of this young and beautiful Parisian with her large eyes, her long dark hair and very fair skin. She had hidden from everyone, beginning with Don Pío, that she was married and the mother of three children. There is no doubt that suitors must have swarmed around her like flies. Flora doubtless enjoyed all this comfort and security, this first taste of the good life. But she also observed and noted down, with fascination, the life and customs of this country that was so different to her own, which was just beginning its life as an independent republic, although the institutions, prejudices and conventions of the colonial period remained almost intact. In her memoir, she would paint a splendid portrait of that feudal, violent society, with its tremendous economic contrasts and its great racial, social and religious divisions, its convents and religious practices verging on idolatry, and its political turmoil, where caudillos fought for power in wars which, as she herself witnessed on the plains at Cangallo, were often bloody and grotesque. This book, which the citizens of Arequipa and Lima would burn in their indignation at the cruel way they were depicted, is one of the most fascinating testimonies that exists, amid all the chaos, pomp, colour, violence and frenzy, of life in Latin America after independence.

But it was not just racism, savagery and privilege that predominated in her father's country. To her great surprise, there were also some rare customs that Flora had never witnessed before in Paris, precisely in an area that was very important to her: the world of women. Society women, for a start, enjoyed considerable freedom: they smoked, bet, rode on horseback when they liked and, in Lima, women with faces half-covered by a veil – the most sensual garb that Flora had ever seen – went out alone to flirt with men, had autonomy and were treated with a considerable lack of prejudice, even from a Parisian standpoint. Even the nuns in the cloistered convents that Flora managed to slip into enjoyed great freedom of behaviour and committed certain excesses that were not at all in keeping with their nun's vocation or with the image of the humiliated, downtrodden woman, the mere appendage of father, husband or head of family that Flora carried in her head. Of course, Peruvian women were not free in the same way as men, nothing like it. But in some cases they could compete with men, as equals, in their own spheres. In wars, for example, the women known as *rabonas* accompanied the soldiers, cooked and washed for them and nursed their wounds, fought alongside them and had the responsibility of attacking villages to get food for the troops. Without their knowing it, these women had, in fact, a life of their own, and destroyed the myth of the helpless, weak woman, useless in a man's domain. The figure that, for Flora, personified this emancipated, active woman, invading the areas traditionally considered to be exclusively male, was Doña Francisca Zubiaga de Gamarra, the wife of Marshal Gamarra, an Independence hero and President of the Republic, whose figure paled alongside the dominant personality of his wife. Doña Pancha, or La Mariscala as the people called her, had taken over running the

Prefecture of Cuzco when her husband was out of the country, and she had put down conspiracies through her guile and courage. Dressed as a soldier, and on horseback, she had been involved in all the civil wars, fighting shoulder to shoulder with Gamarra, and had even led the troops that had beaten the Bolivians in the battle of Paria. When Agustín Gamarra was president, the word on the street was that she had been the power behind the throne, taking the main initiatives and causing some wonderful scandals, like whipping, in an official ceremony, a soldier who had boasted of being her lover. The impression that La Mariscala made on Flora, whom she met briefly when she was about to be exiled, was enormous, and there is no doubt that she helped Flora to realise that it was possible for women to rebel against their marginal status, and that she herself should work to change society. These are the decisions that Flora brought back from Peru when she returned to Paris at the beginning of 1835 and threw herself enthusiastically into a new life, very different from her earlier one.

The Flora Tristán of the years following her return to Paris is no longer the fugitive rebel of before. She is a resolute woman, sure of herself, full of energy, looking to become better informed and educated – she had had an elementary schooling, as her grammatical errors reveal – and to make her way in intellectual circles, where she could do battle in the name of women and justice. While she was writing *Peregrinations of a Pariah*, she made contact with the Saint-Simon groups, the Fourierists (she knew Fourier himself, and would always speak of him with respect) and other groups that to a large extent opposed the status quo, she interviewed the Scottish reformer Robert Owen, and began to contribute to important publications like the *Revue de Paris*, *L'Artiste* and *Le Voleur*. She wrote a pamphlet arguing that a society should be established to help women arriving in Paris for the first time, she signed petitions for the abolition of the death penalty and she sent a petition to parliament to re-establish divorce. At the same time, these years witnessed her own legal and personal battle against André Chazal, who even kidnapped her children on three occasions. In one of these kidnap attempts, the youngest child, Aline, accused him of trying to rape her, which led to a famous trial and a social scandal. This incident had such an impact because Flora was now very well known. The publication of *Peregrinations of a Pariah* in 1837 was a great success, and she was a regular visitor to salons and rubbed shoulders with eminent intellectuals, artists and politicians. Unable to put up with the supreme humiliation of seeing his wife triumph in this way, with a book that laid bare her married life in horrifying detail, André Chazal tried to murder her, in the street, firing at her at point-blank range. He only wounded her, and the bullet remained lodged in her chest, a cold companion on her travels for the six remaining years of her life. At least on these travels she would no longer be haunted by the nightmare vision of André Chazal, who was condemned to twenty years in gaol for his crime.

Flora Tristán could have settled into the celebrity status that she had achieved and spent the rest of her life consolidating it, writing and moving in the intellectual and artistic circles in Paris that had opened their doors to her. She might have become a distinguished salon socialist, like George Sand, who always looked down on this upstart. But despite not having any formal education due to the privations of her early life, and also despite her sometimes explosive nature, she possessed a deep moral integrity which very soon made her realise that the justice and the social change that she so ardently desired would never be won from the refined and exclusive circles of writers, academics, artists, snobs and frivolous people for whom, in most cases, revolutionary ideas and proposals for social reform were mere bourgeois salon games, empty rhetoric.

While recovering from the attempt on her life, she wrote *Méphis* (1838), a novel full of good social intentions and forgettable from a literary point of view. But the following year she came up with a bold project that showed just how far her thinking had become radicalised, more openly anti-capitalist and anti-bourgeois: to write a book about poverty and exploitation in London, the hidden face of the great economic transformation that had turned Victorian England into the first modern industrial nation. She travelled to London and stayed for four months, visiting all the places that the tourists never saw, some of which she could only enter disguised as a man:

workshops and brothels, slum neighbourhoods, factories and insane asylums, prisons and thieves' kitchens, union associations and schools in poor neighbourhoods run by the parishes. Also, perhaps by way of contrast, she visited the Houses of Parliament, the races at Ascot and one of the most aristocratic clubs. The resulting book, *Promenades dans Londres* (1840) is a fierce and merciless – sometimes excessive – attack on the capitalist system and the bourgeoisie whom Flora holds responsible for the appalling poverty, the wicked exploitation of workers and children and the condition of women – forced into prostitution to survive or to work for miserable wages, much lower than the modest wages earned by men. Unlike the success of her memoirs of her journey to Peru, this book, dedicated to the 'working classes', was received in France with sepulchral silence by the *bien-pensant* press and received just a few reviews in working-class publications. That is not surprising: Flora was taking on serious issues and attracting powerful enemies.

The journey to the London she loathed also changed her when she returned to France. Because in the capital of England, Flora did not just see young children working fourteen hour days in factories, or serving prison sentences alongside hardened criminals, or adolescent girls in luxury brothels being forced by powerful men to drink contaminated alcohol so that they could watch the girls vomit and fall down drunk. She also saw major demonstrations of the Chartist movement, the way they collected signatures on the street, how they were organised, by district, city and workplace, and she also attended, with characteristic daring, a clandestine meeting of the leaders, in a Fleet Street pub. Due to this experience she conceived the idea, that no one has yet attributed to her, and which some six years later Karl Marx would proclaim to the world in the *Communist Manifesto*: that only a great international union of workers from all over the world would have the necessary power to end the current system and usher in a new era of justice and equality on earth. In London Flora became convinced that women would be unable to shake off their yoke alone: that, to achieve this aim, they would have to join forces with the workers, the other victims of society, that invincible army of the future that she had glimpsed in the orderly marches of

347

thousands of people organised by Chartists in the streets of London.

Flora Tristán's personal utopia is expressed succinctly in *L'Union Ouvrière* (1843) – a small book that, because she could not find a publisher willing to take the risk, she published herself, by subscription, calling on all her friends and acquaintances in Paris – in her correspondence and in the *Diary* that she wrote during her journey around France, that would only be published many years after her death, in 1973. The objectives are clear and magnificent: '*Donnez à tous et à toutes le droit au travail (possibilité de manger), le droit à l'instruction (possibilité de vivre par l'esprit), le droit au pain (possibilité de vivre complètement indépendant) et l'humanité aujourd'hui si vile, si repoussante, si hypocritement vicieuse, se transformera de suite et deviendra noble, fière, indépendante, libre, et belle, et heureuse*' ('Give everyone, men and women, the right to work (the possibility of eating), the right to education (the possibility of living for the spirit), the right to bread (the possibility of living completely independently), and humanity, which is today so vile, so repulsive, so hypocritically dissolute will be transformed and will become noble, proud, independent, free, beautiful and happy').*

This revolution must be peaceful, inspired by love of humanity and filled with a Christian spirit which (as Saint-Simon also argued) would get back to the values of early Christianity – generosity and support for the poor – that the Catholic Church later betrayed and corrupted by aligning itself with the rich. Even God is reformed by Flora Tristán: God becomes Gods in the plural (*Dieux*), but would still be a single entity, because the divine being 'is father, mother and embryo: active, passive and the seed of an unclear future'. The revolution would not be nationalist; it would cross borders and be internationalist. (In her first pamphlet Flora proclaimed: 'Our country must be the universe.') The body that would effect this social transformation would be the army of secular, peaceful workers, the 'Workers' Union', in which men and women would participate on an entirely equal footing. Through persuasion, social pressure and working through legal institutions, it would completely transform society. This union would need to be strong economically in order to

* *Le Tour de France II*, Maspero, Paris 1980, p. 192

undertake urgent social reforms straight away. Every worker would contribute two francs a year and, because there are eight million workers in France, that would be a capital of sixteen million with which one could immediately open schools for the sons and daughters of the workers, who would receive a free and common education. The Union, in line with the British Chartists, would demand that the National Assembly elect a Defender of the People – paid for by the Assembly – to promote revolutionary measures within that body: the re-establishment of divorce, the abolition of the death penalty and, the main measure, the right to work, through which the state commits to guaranteeing employment and a wage to all citizens without exception. Similar to the phalanges or 'phalanasteries' proposed by Charles Fourier, the Union would create Workers' Palaces, complex bodies offering many different services, where the workers and their families would receive medical attention and education, where they could retire and live a secure and protected old age, where every victim would be given help, advice and information and where those who spend long hours of the day working with their hands could enjoy culture and educate their spirit.

Even though some of these aspirations might today have been met by Social Security, we should not lose sight of the fact that these proposals were very daring, almost fantastic, in the context of the mid-nineteenth century, as can be seen from the criticisms and the reservations of the workers themselves to Flora's ideas, which they regarded as most unrealistic. But she was convinced that there were no obstacles that will-power, energy and action could not overcome, because she was both – and this was an unusual mixture – a romantic dreamer, capable of being caught up in fantasies completely disconnected from reality, and a formidable activist, with a contagious power of persuasion and a passion that led her to confront every difficulty. From the time that she conceived of the Workers' Union in 1843, until her death, some two years later, Flora Tristán was a real volcanic spirit, incessantly active and versatile: instead of artists and writers, her flat in the Rue du Bac was now full of workers and leaders of friendly societies and unions, and when she went out, it was to appear in workshops or to publish in proletarian publications, attending interminable meetings and sometimes getting caught up in heated discussions with those that objected to her ideas. It could not have been easy for a woman, with little experience of this work and unfamiliar with the political climate, to cope with these proletarian venues, which were not used to the involvement of women in activities which had until then been the domain of the men. And yet she threw herself into the task. For even though she saw that among the workers there were also many bourgeois prejudices and discriminatory attitudes towards women (which were also shared on occasion by the women workers themselves, some of whom insulted her, thinking that she was looking to seduce their husbands), she was not intimidated and she did not soften her message or her approach, that mystic, redemptive energy that fuelled her Union crusade.

That was why, in April 1844, she began her propaganda tour around the central and southern regions of France, which was to be just the beginning of a journey throughout other parts of the country and then through the whole of Europe. Weakened by illness and with a bullet lodged in her chest, she had to deal with innumerable obstacles on her journey, including the hostility of the authorities that searched her hotel room, confiscated her belongings and banned her meetings. She held out for a mere eight months, until her death in Bordeaux, on 14 November 1844. But in the course of her journey, she became ever more impressive and her actions became increasingly moving as she took her social message not just to the workers but also to the leading members of the establishment – bishops, businessmen, newspaper owners – convinced that her ideas for social justice would also win over the exploiters. Her tragic death, at forty-one years of age, brought to an end a richly varied life, admirable in its dedication – albeit marked by the nineteenth-century dream of utopia – which represents an important stage in the struggle for women's rights and for a society free of all forms of discrimination, exploitation and injustice.

There is no better introduction to the life and work of this extraordinary woman than *Flora Tristán. La Paria et son rêve*, a very thorough edition of her correspondence edited by Stéphane Michaud, Professor of Comparative Literature at the Sorbonne, President of the Society of Romantic and Nineteenth-Century Studies and the author of a recent important book on Lou Andreas-Salomé, which combines erudition with a clear and elegant style. Professor Michaud is probably the leading expert on the life and work of Flora Tristán, having tracked it for many years with the obstinacy of a bloodhound and the tenderness of a lover. Her studies on Tristán and the symposia she has organised on her intellectual and political achievements have been decisive in rescuing Flora Tristán from the unjustified critical neglect she had suffered, despite isolated work like the admirable book Jules Puech wrote on her in 1925.

This new edition of her correspondence, expanded and enriched by notes and commentaries, contains new letters alongside the ones we already know, and also many letters from her correspondents, as well as mapping the social and political context of Flora's life. The volume as a whole offers an excellent overview of her times: the hopes, polemics and personal disputes that were bound up in the first attempts in France to organise workers politically, the distance that often existed between reality and the ambitious messianic plans of the utopians, and the psychology of the main character herself, who is extremely frank in her letters and in the comments that she wrote in the margins of the correspondence that she received.

There are still major gaps in her biography, but these letters offer an absorbing portrait of her life following her return to France from Peru, especially the final two years. The letters are disarmingly fresh and sincere – luckily she did not write for posterity – revealing all her contradictions and weaknesses. She was a realist and a dreamer, generous and irascible, naïve and pugnacious, truculent and romantic, bold and never discouraged.

This book is the best homage that Flora Tristán could be offered in this the second centenary of her birth.

Marbella, July 2002

Copyright Acknowledgements

Literature

Culture and Politics